Handbook of Child and Adolescent Treatment Manuals

Handbook of Child and Adolescent Treatment Manuals

Edited by

Craig Winston LeCroy

LEXINGTON BOOKS
An Imprint of Macmillan, Inc.
NEW YORK

Maxwell Macmillan Canada
TORONTO

Maxwell Macmillan International
NEW YORK OXFORD SINGAPORE SYDNEY

Library of Congress Cataloging-in-Publication Data

Handbook of child and adolescent treatment manuals / edited by Craig
    LeCroy.
        p.   cm.
    ISBN 0-02-918485-1
    1. Child psychotherapy—Handbooks, manuals, etc. 2. Adolescent
psychotherapy—Handbooks, manuals, etc.   I. LeCroy, Craig W.
RJ504.H356 1994
618.92'8914—dc20   93-40136
                                                                   CIP

Lexington Books
An Imprint of Macmillan, Inc.
866 Third Avenue, New York, N. Y. 10022

Maxwell Macmillan Canada, Inc.
1200 Eglinton Avenue East
Suite 200
Don Mills, Ontario M3C 3N1

Macmillan, Inc. is part of the Maxwell Communication
Group of Companies.

Printed in the United States of America

printing number
        3 4 5 6 7 8 9 10

Contents

Preface

The primary purpose of the *Handbook* is to provide practitioners, researchers, and students with up-to-date descriptions and procedures used in practice with children and adolescents. The best way to do this is to make available treatment manuals that spell out the step-by-step procedures that can be used with various client problems. In my experience and that of others with whom I have spoken, what is most often requested from experts in various fields is a treatment manual.

The *Handbook* seeks to bring together these various manuals and make them available to practitioners and students interested in an assortment of clinical work with children and adolescents. Although there are numerous books that describe state-of-the-art treatment for childhood disorders (for example, Morris & Kratochwill, *The Practice of Child Therapy;* Bornstein & Kazdin, *Handbook of Clinical Behavior Therapy with Children;* Johnson et al., *Approaches to Child Treatment;* Barkley & Mash, *Treatment of Childhood Disorders*), I am not aware of any book that has as its focus specific treatment manuals. What is abundant are books, chapters, and articles that discuss various therapeutic models or review conceptual and methodological issues; what is missing are detailed procedural descriptions of treatment approaches that can be used with various childhood behavior problems.

The *Handbook* attempts to survey the broad and emerging areas of treatment with children and adolescents. It is intended to be comprehensive and consistent with new developments in the treatment of child and adolescent problems. The contents are intended to represent some of the major clinical disorders and social problems facing children and adolescents. Some of the treatment manuals reflect major approaches to treatment and are not necessarily tied to specific clinical disorders or social problems.

Although treatment manuals were selected to reflect the major areas of treatment when working with children and adolescents, some omissions are evident. The *Handbook* does not include such problems as childhood schizophrenia, pervasive developmental disorders, mental retardation, or speech and language disorders. These clinical problems are simply too complex to be addressed in the context of a treatment manual. In addition, while these are major clinical disorders, they do not represent the more frequent problems confronting the typical child and adolescent practitioner. With regard to social problems, there are also omissions. For example, I have not included a treatment manual directed toward victims of child abuse. Although such a manual would be desirable, I have not been able to locate anyone who could provide the kind of specificity needed for a treatment manual in this area. The experts in this field simply have not refined their procedures and gathered enough empirical data to produce a treatment manual at this time.

As the authors of the treatment manuals in this book can attest, it takes a lot of field testing, research, and refinement to produce a treatment manual. For many areas in which practitioners would like to see a treatment manual, I have been unable to produce it. In most cases this is because the treatment approaches were not refined enough to provide the kind of step-by-step procedures that are required in treatment manuals. However, the manuals that are offered in this *Handbook* represent an important first step in providing practitioners with procedural details for carrying out specific treatments.

In a general sense, the *Handbook* should also provide practitioners with excellent models of how to design a complete and comprehensive treatment manual. Many practitioners must develop new treatments for purposes of remediation or prevention. Unfortunately, there is very little information on how to design interventions. Examining the treatment manuals in the *Handbook* will provide a framework for others who are interested in developing procedural guidelines.

The *Handbook of Child and Adolescent Treatment Manuals* begins with a chapter on rational emotive therapy (RET) with children, written by Jean Linscott and Raymond DiGiuseppe. These authors have assembled the essence of RET with children. Their treatment manual does an excellent job of showing the practitioner how to implement RET concepts with children. The authors use a case example and demonstrate session by session the process of changing irrational thoughts to rational thoughts.

Joseph M. Strayhorn, Jr., describes a treatment model he has been working on for several years, psychological competence-based therapy for young children and their parents. He describes children's difficulties as deficits on a "skills axis" (he describes 62 skills or competencies) and their remediation resulting from the use of different methods of influence, on a "method axis" (there are nine different methods). In a very detailed manner he outlines how the practitioner can work effectively with young children. His approach combines traditional behavioral methods of change with more creative approaches such as dramatic play and story reading. He presents a very comprehensive skills-based approach.

Next Arthur L. Robin, Marquita Bedway, and Marcia Gilroy present their problem-solving communication training manual. Recognizing that problem solving and communication are skills essential for young people as they move into adolescence, these authors have developed clear guidelines for improving parent–adolescent relationships. This manual is helpful for both prevention and remediation of family difficulties. These authors describe in crisp detail how to teach families problem-solving and communication skills and also how to use these skills for intense conflict situations. Similar to the work of Arthur L. Robin and his associates in the past, this treatment manual is detailed and easy to follow and implement.

Craig Winston LeCroy describes the procedural aspects of conducting social skills training. Social skills training is being used increasingly as a treatment method in working with children and adolescents, and this manual presents a structured training approach. The treatment manual is organized according to social skills training units: for example, making requests, expressing feelings, and making responsible decisions. The process for teaching each skill is explicitly described, enabling the practitioner to learn it easily. The treatment format is described from a group perspective but could be adapted for individual use.

Eva L. Feindler and Jennifer Guttman have developed a treatment manual for anger control training. Child and adolescent practitioners work with many children and adolescents who have difficulty controlling their anger. These authors present a group approach to anger control training. This complex treatment manual includes such treatment procedures as deep breaths, recognizing antecedents and triggers, assertion techniques, reminders, thinking ahead, self-evaluation, and problem solving. This 10-session treatment manual should be very useful to practitioners in outpatient mental health clinics, schools, and residential treatment centers.

Mindy Hohman and Gary Buchik have worked extensively with adolescent chemical dependency. Their work led them to develop a treatment manual for relapse prevention with young people. Their treatment manual is a session by session description of how to teach relapse prevention. For example, the authors have sessions on understanding relapse and the use of a relapse map, making sober friends, dealing with parents, cue exposure and trigger identification, and coping with loss. This treatment manual describes all the essential procedures needed to develop and implement an adolescent relapse prevention program.

Brian A. Glaser and Arthur M. Horne have tackled a very difficult project, designing a treatment manual for children with conduct disorders. Treating common but complex child behavior disorder occupies a great deal of time for the typical child and adolescent practitioner. These authors have whittled away at the many complex issues associated with this disorder to describe the essential parts of treatment with these children. They describe how to use traditional behavior modification and they also present new ideas and methods for working with conduct-disordered children.

Lillie Weiss, Sharlene Wolchik, and Melanie Katzman offer a manual for the treatment of bulimia and binge eating in adolescents. This is an area that many practitioners have to address, but where few have experience. Any practitioner who works with adolescent girls will find the procedures in this manual helpful. This seven-week program covers such topics as eating and coping; self-esteem, perfectionism, and depression; cultural expectations of thinness for women; and enhancing body image. This research-based program offers clear guidelines for practitioners working with the eating disorders of young people.

Neil Kalter and Shelly Schreier have developed what they refer to as "developmental facilitation groups" for children of divorce. Practitioners will be pleased to see this manual as part of the *Handbook*. Too many children in today's society must cope with the difficult process of their parents' divorce. In response to this problem, Kalter has suggested a "developmental vulnerability model" that is based on the stress and coping paradigm. This model views parental divorce as a significant process that involves subsequent life changes that may unfold over or persist for many years. This treatment manual helps children cope more adaptively with their feelings and concerns about the divorce process. Particularly helpful for the practitioner is the authors' description and examples of universalizing statements to help children with their adaptive coping. This manual presents many unique and creative means for helping children with the coping process. For example, the authors discuss construction of a group story about an imaginary family that is "headed for a divorce," the use of a divorce court scenario, and design of a group newspaper for termination and summary.

Kevin D. Stark, Linda Raffaelle, and Anne Reysa address an important concern for child and adolescent practitioners, child depression. This very detailed program includes guidelines for 27 sessions with children and 11 sessions with families. The children's sessions are described within a group format. Each session identifies the objectives to be achieved and then describes the exercises used to achieve each objective. Borrowing important ideas about depression from the adult literature, these authors translate them into appropriate methods for children. For example, children are taught about the mood-behavior-thought relationship and how to self-monitor pleasant events. The authors recognize that working only with the children may not be enough, and therefore also describe a family therapy component.

In summary, the contents of the *Handbook* represent a comprehensive effort to address specific child and adolescent behavior problems, social problems, and major conceptual approaches to treatment. I believe the *Handbook* includes enough information about the major behavior and social problems seen by professionals, that it can be used by child practitioners as a reference volume. Those who work in the various settings that provide treatment and services to children and adolescents should find the *Handbook* invaluable in their efforts to design treatments.

I would like to acknowledge, first and foremost, those who contributed to this book. The authors who agreed to contribute a treatment manual have made this book possible. I sincerely appreciate their contributions. This book became a successful project because of the initial efforts of Margaret Zusky at Lexington, who supported the idea for this book, and because of Marilyn Ramirez who assisted in the reviewing and editing of the final manuscript. Also, I would like to acknowledge the support and encouragement I have received from Kerry Milligan.

Craig Winston LeCroy
River Toad Ranch
Tucson, AZ

1
Introduction

Craig Winston LeCroy

It is becoming increasingly clear that there are a large number of children and adolescents who are in need of mental health services and that these children do not receive the care and treatment they need. This lack of progress is due to many factors, including inadequate conceptualization of children's problems, inappropriate assessment and diagnosis, ineffective treatments, and failure to consider the interactions between intraindividual difficulties and environmental circumstances. It is estimated that over 12 percent of American children, more than 7.5 million, are in need of mental health services (National Institute of Mental Health [NIMH], 1990). At the most, one-third of the children who need services will receive them (Office of Technology Assessment, 1986).

The consequences of receiving no treatment at all, inappropriate assessment, or ineffective treatment are all very costly for the children themselves and for our society. Children with mental health problems often grow up to become adults with mental health problems. Many of these adults lack the skills to work consistently or to live independently. The absence of treatment or the results of an ineffective treatment can lead to a lifetime of problems and misery. Our children will face serious consequences—drug abuse, homelessness, suicide, criminal behavior—if they cannot receive the care and treatment they need.

Although what I have just written outlines a depressing scenario, dramatic advances have occurred in understanding and responding to the momentous issues in children's mental health. Indeed, a foundation of knowledge about the biopsychosocial factors that can help facilitate children's mental health is emerging. Meaningful strides are being made in the prevention of mental disorders, the discovery of effective treatments, and the coordination of multiple services.

Treatment Considerations

Practitioners face complex choices when selecting a treatment approach to use with children and adolescents. Kazdin (1988) has identified over 230

1

specific treatment approaches. Immediately confronting the practitioner are difficult questions such as which treatments produce the intended effects; where should the treatment be directed, to the child or to significant others; and how long must the treatment last to be effective? Although we are just beginning to discover the answers to these questions, we do know that child-oriented interventions can be very effective.

Meta-analysis, a statistical procedure for combining the results of independent research studies to compute an effect size, is being increasingly used to evaluate questions of treatment effectiveness. Two relevant meta-analyses (Casey & Berman, 1985; Weisz, Weiss, Alicke, & Klotz, 1987) were conducted on over 175 child therapy outcome studies and found effect sizes of .71 and .79. These results mean that the average outcome of child therapy is 71 percent and 79 percent better than that of untreated control children. Clearly, child-oriented treatment approaches can be effective.

Although these overall findings are encouraging, Saxe, Cross, and Silverman (1988, p. 803) remind us that "most treatment modalities have not been systematically evaluated, and the research does not indicate, for the most part, which treatments are most beneficial for which problems and children." Furthermore, it is unclear as to what problems are amenable to treatment or whether they should receive treatment (Kazdin, 1988). A related issue in evaluating treatment is the extent to which treatment interventions are specified or operationalized. In order to carry out successful research on treatment methods, there must be a high degree of specification. Furthermore, there are practical issues that demand specification of treatment methods.

Treatment Specification

In order to successfully evaluate and implement effective treatments, we must achieve greater specification of our methods. We have large amounts of literature about how professionals think about treatment interventions but much less literature regarding what professionals do as a part of their treatment interventions. One way to have a direct impact on clinical practice is to provide practitioners with more clear specification of treatment procedures. Understandably a difficult task, however, clear specification of treatment procedures is essential in order to make advances in clinical practice. Practitioners and researchers both have an investment in clearly understanding how to perform a clinical intervention. Practitioners need specification to provide clear structure, guidelines for supervision, and information about reliable administration of treatment methods. Researchers need clear specification in order to evaluate the impact and outcome of treatment procedures.

Thomas (1984) asks the relevant question: What makes for good interventions? He devised four general categories in response to this question:

objective capability, procedural adequacy, ethical suitability, and usability. *Objective capability* is the ability of the intervention to accomplish what it was intended to achieve. This is accomplished through the effectiveness of the intervention—producing desired outcomes and efficiency—implemented without too much effort or time. *Procedural adequacy* refers to whether the intervention can be considered a practical guide to action. Procedural adequacy requires an intervention procedure that is valid, complete, specific, correct, and behavior guiding. For the intervention to be valid, it must be based on valid sources of information. Interventions also need to be complete, which means that outside practitioners can learn how to replicate the procedure by reading the description of the procedure. The intervention needs to be specific, that is, it must provide the needed details about the procedure. Correctness refers to directing the behavior of the practitioner in an appropriate manner. For example, the practitioner may follow the specific procedure but implement it at an inappropriate time. Last, behavior guiding means that the treatment procedures should contain the necessary instructions for producing the intended practitioner behaviors.

All interventions should be *ethically suitable* by protecting the rights of the clients with whom the treatment procedure is being used. Ethics should always be kept in mind when designing intervention procedures. Thomas's notion of *usability* refers to the likelihood that the intervention itself will be used by the practitioners for whom it was intended. Many characteristics can influence usability, for example, whether it is relevant, simple, flexible, and inexpensive.

The treatment manuals in this book are good examples of how to design interventions for practitioners. In most cases they meet the criteria identified by Thomas for being a "good intervention." Most of these treatment manuals have been extensively field-tested. Many of the treatment manuals were developed for the purpose of empirically evaluating the treatment methods.

Treatment procedures are the raison d'être of the practitioner. Yet rarely do you find a detailed specification of treatment procedures. The purpose of this book is to be one small part of the emerging advances taking place in children's mental health by providing detailed treatment manuals to help enhance the intervention procedures offered by practitioners.

References

Casey, R. J., & Berman, J. S. (1985). The outcome of psychotherapy with children. *Psychological Bulletin, 98,* 388–400.

Kazdin, A. E. (1988). *Child psychotherapy: Developing and identifying effective treatments.* New York: Pergamon Press.

National Institute of Mental Health. (1990). *Research on children and adolescents with mental, behavioral and developmental disorders.* Rockville, MD: National Institute of Mental Health.

Office of Technology Assessment, U.S. Congress. (1986). *Children's mental health: Problems and services.* Washington, DC: U.S. Government Printing Office.

Saxe, L., Cross, T., & Silverman, N. (1988) Children's mental health: The gap between what we know and what we do. *American Psychologist, 43,* 800–807.

Thomas, E. J. (1984). *Designing interventions for the helping professions.* Beverly Hills, CA: Sage.

Weisz, J. R., Weiss, B., Alicke, M. D., & Klotz, M. L. (1987). Effectiveness for psychotherapy with children and adolescents: A meta-analysis for clinicians. *Journal of Consulting and Clinical Psychology, 55,* 542–549.

2
Rational Emotive Therapy with Children

Jean Linscott
Raymond DiGiuseppe

Introduction

Rational emotive therapy (RET) has become one of the most popular forms of individual psychotherapy and counseling (Heesacker, Heppner, & Rogers, 1982; Smith, 1982). RET has been applied to the treatment of emotional disorders in adults (Ellis, 1973; Walen, DiGiuseppe, & Dryden, 1992), families (Huber & Baruth, 1989), children (Bernard, 1990; Bernard & Joyce, 1984; DiGiuseppe, 1989; DiGiuseppe & Bernard, 1990; Ellis & Bernard, 1983), to marital dysfunction (Ellis, Sichel, Yeager, DiMattia, & DiGiuseppe, 1989), and to addictions (Ellis, McInerney, DiGiuseppe, & Yeager, 1988). Numerous clinical works have appeared on RET, but only a few provide the specificity needed to be used as a treatment manual (Walen, DiGiuseppe, & Dryden, 1992; Dryden & DiGiuseppe, 1990). Several manuals exist for teaching RET to schoolchildren as part of a preventive mental health curriculum (Gerald & Eyman, 1981; Knaus, 1974; Vernon, 1989a, 1989b). However, no specific treatment manuals for clinical interventions with emotionally disturbed children exist.

While RET was one of the first forms of cognitive behavioral therapy (CBT) (Ellis, 1989), and is similar in many ways to general cognitive behavioral therapy, some therapists fail to make the distinction between RET and general CBT (Haaga & Davison, 1991). There are significant differences between RET and other forms of CBT that have important implications for treatment (DiGiuseppe & Bernard, 1990; Ellis, 1980). The main difference between RET and most cognitive behavior therapies is the target of the intervention. First, RET makes a distinction between practical problems, such as not attaining one's goals, failure at tasks, or being rejected by others, and emotional problems (see DiGiuseppe & Bernard, 1990; Walen, DiGiuseppe, & Dryden, 1992). A person's emotional problems may be separate from, or related to, his or her practical problems. RET targets emotional problems

5

first; behavioral change strategies are a secondary goal. There are two reasons for this position. Disturbed emotions interfere with the execution of strategies to achieve goals, efforts to learn new skills to achieve goals, and problem solving to ascertain which strategies could achieve goals. Also, despite mastery of skills for goal achievement, clients (such as those with learning disabilities) may be unable to change their aversive activating events. Children who only learn cognitive strategies that help them change events that thwart their goals will have no coping strategies to face those events they cannot change. Second, RET distinguishes between inferences or automatic thoughts and irrational beliefs (DiGiuseppe, 1986). RET postulates that changing irrational beliefs provides a more elegant, generalizable solution for dealing with emotional problems than changing inferences or automatic thoughts.

Hajzler and Bernard (1990) reviewed 46 studies that used RET with school-aged children. These studies compared rational emotive education (REE—a version of RET used as a preventive mental health curriculum) with no treatment controls across different populations of school-aged children including "normals"; learning disabled; high-risk adolescents; children with interpersonal, speech, or test anxiety; and children with other clinical problems. REE studies showed, as expected, the most change on measures of irrationality. Ninety-two percent of studies that employed such measures showed decreases. Second were changes on dependent measures of behavior: 64 percent of the studies showed benefits of REE over the control conditions.

One would suspect that the teaching of emotional responsibility, the notion that emotions can be changed by changing one's thinking, would lead to changes in locus of control. In studies that included locus of control measures, 64 percent showed increased internality. Adjustment and personality measures showed positive changes in 63 and 57 percent of studies, respectively. Changes in anxiety occurred in 50 percent of the studies. The above studies suggest that REE has its greatest effect in changing measures of irrationality and global measures of adjustment and personality, and less effect in promoting changes in anxiety. While REE has some research support, few studies have been conducted on the use of RET with clinical populations of youth. We hope this treatment manual serves to facilitate this process.

This manual assumes that the reader is familiar with the basic theory and practice of rational emotive therapy. For an in-depth discussion of the theory and practice of RET, the reader is referred to the following references: Bernard and DiGiuseppe (1989), Walen, DiGiuseppe, and Dryden (1992), and Ellis and Dryden (1987).

To provide greater readability, the pronouns chosen in this manual's dialogues consistently refer to the client as "he" and the therapist as "she" in place of specifying "he or she" each time there is a reference to the gender-neutral terms "client" or "therapist." A male client was chosen to maintain consistency with the selected vignette of a case treated by the first author.

General Information

This manual is intended for use with children aged 8 to 12. Although we will use an individual case example, the treatment can be adapted for group therapy. The treatment setting can be the therapist's office, a school, or almost anywhere. The treatment outlined here consists of 17 sessions, each 45 to 60 minutes in length.

Framework for Each Session

Each session will include the following elements:

1. Meet with parents and child to discuss week's progress
2. Set session agenda with child
3. Review homework from past session
4. Set goals for current session
5. Introduce tasks to achieve current session goals
6. Explain rational for changing beliefs to modify emotions and behaviors
7. Generate alternate beliefs
8. Give child new homework assignment
9. Review homework assignment with parents.

It will be essential to include in each session frequent reference to the goals of emotional change. If the therapist fails to accomplish each session's activities, we recommend that the therapist spend additional sessions with the child and/or parents until goals are sufficiently met. Open, honest communication by the therapist, therapist self-disclosure and modeling (especially with internalized disorders), and direct confrontation of the child about the parents' concerns and vice versa are additional factors that will be critical to establishing a therapeutic alliance (DiGiuseppe, 1989). [*Note:* If parents are not available to participate in sessions, as happens in a school setting, the therapist might consider including the child's teacher in the treatment plan when possible. But one may also opt to work with the child alone.]

Case Example

Brett is a 10-year-old boy in the fifth grade. He lives with his mother, father, and two older brothers. Brett's school difficulties started in kindergarten. He had trouble learning the alphabet and writing letters. His parents reported that he progressed more slowly than his brothers. In later grades Brett had difficulty learning to read and spell. Each school year Brett received poor grades in reading, spelling, and language arts. A psychological evaluation in the fourth grade diagnosed Brett with a verbal-based learning disability. He began attending the school's resource room three times a week for help with verbal and language skills. Each year teachers reported to Brett's parents that he often failed to attempt class assignments. When he did attempt them, he became frustrated and stopped before finishing. Brett's parents reported similar responses with homework. Presently, Brett cries when he receives papers with poor grades or with many corrections. Brett frequently tells his parents that he hates school, that his teachers are stupid, and that the children in his class are mean to him. Brett's teacher says that the children tease him for crying. As a result, Brett isolates himself from his peers in the classroom and in his neighborhood. The teacher reported that Brett is so withdrawn and sad lately that she cannot engage him in the day's lesson. He puts his head on the desk and cries the more she encourages him to begin his work. Brett was referred to therapy by his resource room teacher. His parents support the goal of treatment for Brett.

In order to demonstrate the application of RET with children, Brett will be used as a case example throughout the manual. Childhood depression will be used as the treatment focus in this manual in order to present RET concepts with greater clarity and specificity. The concepts in this RET treatment manual can be used with a variety of child emotional and behavioral problems.

Assessment

Sessions 1 and 2 focus on assessment and formation of a working alliance between the child, the parents, and the therapist

Session 1: Session with Child and Parents

Goals. The goals of the first session are (1) to describe the problem from the parents' perspectives; (2) to describe the problem from the child's perspective; (3) to describe the problem to the parents and the child from the therapist's perspective; (4) to formulate preliminary treatment goals; (5) to explain the tasks of therapy (roles, procedures used to achieve therapy goals, and so on) to the parents and the child; and (6) to obtain diagnostic information by using standardized tests (child and parent reports).

Tasks. First, the therapist interviews the parents, and the child's teacher if possible, according to the guidelines contained in the "Structured Interview for Diagnostic Assessment of Children" (Hynd, 1991). Children who meet the DSM-III and DSM-III-R criteria for depression or dysthymia according to interview criterion will be suitable for this treatment plan.

Second, the therapist has the child complete the Reynolds Child Depression Scale (Reynolds, 1991), meanwhile, the therapist administers the structured interview to the parents. Parents are then asked to complete the Child Behavior Checklist (Achenbach & Edelbrook, 1988).

Third, the therapist meets with the parents and child together. The therapist asks the parents the following questions:

What problems bring them to therapy?
What is the history of the symptoms?
Why have they come to therapy *now?*
What have they done previously to try to solve the problem?
What has worked, and what hasn't worked?
What do they hope to accomplish/change by coming to therapy?

Then the therapist asks for the child's opinion of his parents' statements.

Why did his parents bring him to therapy?
What does he think his problem is/the family's problems are (if any)?
What has the child himself done to try to solve the problem?
What has worked, and what has not worked?
What would he like to accomplish or change in himself or in the family?

Then the therapist should question both the parents and the child (allow for separate responses), asking:

What did you think we would do in therapy before you came today?
How do you feel about coming here?

The therapist should give an open, honest explanation of what a therapist (psychologist, social worker, psychiatrist, counselor) does, what kind of people she sees, and how she can help the family. This sample dialogue, taken from DiGiuseppe and Bernard (1983, p. 54), illustrates an appropriate explanation:

Therapist: "Brett, I'm a psychologist. Do you know what that is?"
Brett: "Oh! No. Well a kind of doctor for crazy people?"
Therapist: "Well, that's not totally true. Psychologists are doctors who study how people learn things. Psychologists help people learn things they haven't been able to learn. For example, some children have trouble learning to read. Psychologists help them learn to read better. Other children are sad or scared. They haven't learned not to be un-

happy or afraid. Psychologists help them learn not to feel that way. We help children with other problems, too, like bed-wetting, making friends, and lots of things they don't know how to do. Do you understand that?"

Brett: "Yes."

Fourth, the therapist assesses the frequency, intensity, and duration of symptoms related to the presenting problem(s).

Fifth, the therapist asks the parents and the child to set priorities, and to choose the one problem they would most like to change.

Sixth, the therapist assesses the practical and/or emotional problems presented and chooses an emotional problem (for example, depression) or an emotional problem about a practical problem (for example, depression about having a learning disability) to focus on. The therapist then asks the parents and the child separately for a specific example of when the problem occurred recently. What was the circumstance surrounding the problem? What did they do? How did they feel? What did they think (or tell themselves about the circumstance)?

Seventh, the therapist assesses for secondary disturbance in the parents and the child (whose disturbance may arise from the presenting emotional problem):

Is the parent/child upset, depressed, angry about the child's emotional problem?

How does the parent/child react when the disturbed emotion occurs?

How does the child feel about being depressed, or feeling sad, stupid, lonely and crying frequently? Does he feel worse when he thinks about his problem?

What does everyone think about themselves as a family for having the problem?

Eighth, the therapist assesses for endogenous depression markers: family history, change in appetite, sleep patterns, anhedonia, and the like. She keeps referral to a psychiatrist open as an option. Ongoing assessment of the problem will help to determine the advisability of a recommendation for a trial of medication.

Ninth, the therapist gives a preliminary explanation to the parents and the child concerning how the therapist conceptualizes the problem. The therapist's explanation should include mention of how the beliefs, feelings, and behavioral reactions of the parents and the child combine to contribute to the child's depression. The therapist provides parents with the first step of what they can do to begin working on the problem (see Homework Assignment, Task 13, below).

Tenth, the therapist begins negotiating an agreement on treatment goals between the parents, the child, and the therapist. She chooses goals that are in the best interest of all parties (not necessarily the parents' originally stated goals). She shows how the goals she has chosen are in each party's best interest, even if these goals are not anyone's preferred goal. She emphasizes that the assessment process is ongoing: while working on the first chosen goal other problems may arise that will need to be addressed.

Eleventh, the therapist explains the details of the treatment plan. She explains what will occur in therapy sessions. She explains what the child's role, the parents' role, and therapist's role will be. She explains that the goals of therapy will be accomplished by targeting change in the child's/parents' thoughts to achieve change in their feelings/behaviors (ABC framework), and by having the child and his parents practice things that may be hard for them. The therapist points out that active participation in therapy sessions, completing homework assignments, and doing school work with the guidance of the therapist will lead to change. The therapist cannot work alone to change all these things. The session length is discussed. The therapist contracts with the family for the number of sessions. She asks parents to come back for the next session without their child and explains the rational for this meeting to the child.

Twelfth, the therapist explains to the child and his parents issues of confidentiality. When they meet together, there will often be information that arises that would be beneficial to share with the other party if both child and parents were not present when the topic was discussed. The therapist asks the child or parents in advance what information to share or not to share, and explains why in some instances in the latter case the therapist may believe it is best to share this information. If the child or parent does not agree, the information will not be shared. The therapist tells parents and child that if the child shows evidence of being dangerous to self or others, the therapist will immediately contact his family to ensure safety.

Thirteenth, the therapist discusses the homework assignment. She tells the parents to begin charting the times during the week when the presenting problem occurs. Parents are to take notes on what was happening prior to the problem's occurrence (antecedents); the child's behaviors, and how they, or others, reacted to the child's behaviors (consequences).

Session 2: Session with Parents Alone

Goals. The goals of Session 2 are (1) to continue developing a working alliance with the parents (agreement on goals); (2) to further assess the parents' role in the child's presenting problem; (3) to provide the parents with cognitive and behavioral strategies to employ concerning their child's problem; (4) to clarify therapy session structure; and (5) to stress the importance of an ongoing assessment process.

Tasks. First, the therapist continues clarifying for the parents the treatment strategy of targeting emotional problem solving to help the child feel happier, and to help solve the child's practical problems that result from the emotional problems. The therapist stresses the idea that they will begin by working on a specific problem, and then address other problems as progress in one area is made, or as other difficulties arise.

Second, the therapist assesses the parents' disciplinary strategies, which may be serving to reinforce the child's difficulties. The therapist explains how to use a behavioral reward system contingent on the child's performance of desired behaviors. The therapist points out that the reward system serves to motivate the child to continue working on changing emotions, thoughts, and behaviors.

Third, the therapist assesses and attempts to modify the parents' irrational beliefs that may prevent them from effectively implementing the behavior modification plan. (See DiGiuseppe [1988] and DiGiuseppe & Bernard, [1990] for a thorough description of parent involvement in child treatment plans.)

Fourth, the therapist explains subsequent therapy session structure to the parents as outlined below. Emphasizes the importance of the parents discussing any ongoing concerns that may arise during the treatment process.

Session Structure and Rational. For the first 5 to 10 minutes of each therapy session, the therapist meets with the parents and the child together. The therapist asks the parents and child for specific times during the week when (1) he felt depressed about school or peers; (2) times he avoided doing school-related activities (in class or at home); (3) information communicated from the school that week concerning the child's mood; and (4) any other information the parent or child thinks the therapist should know. Often children cannot remember specific events that have occurred over the past week. By asking for the parents' observations, the therapist can receive specific examples of problems to be discussed in session. In addition, the parents receive the assurance that they are informed about, and involved in, their child's treatment.

The therapist then meets with the child alone for the next 30 to 35 minutes to teach concepts, to relate the concepts to events that have occurred in the child's life during the week, or to review previously learned concepts using concrete examples brought in by the parents or child.

During the final five minutes of the session the parents, the child, and the therapist meet together again. The therapist offers a homework assignment for the week to the family and negotiates their agreement to follow it. Part of each session's homework assignments will include the child's reviewing with the parent the concepts learned in therapy. The therapist encourages the parents to teach the rational beliefs, coping statements, and emotional problem-solving techniques the child learns in session. The parents are instructed to watch for any instances when they could encourage the child to use the new thinking skills or model them for him. Parents are also encouraged to ask questions about the concepts taught in previous sessions at the beginning of the next therapy session to ensure a common approach between parent and therapist.

The therapist's encouragement of parent involvement during and between sessions fosters the parents' understanding of therapy tasks. The therapist enlists the parents as the child's learning partners. This can provide feedback and reinforcement for the child in between the sessions as the child practices the thinking skills learned in sessions. A sense of hope, efficacy, and collaboration with the therapist (as opposed to feeling resentful of the "know- it-all" therapist) will also be fostered by parental involvement in and between sessions.

Teaching the ABC's of RET

Sessions 3 through 6 are designed to teach the basic principles of rational emotive therapy.

Session 3: Identifying Different Emotions

Goals. The goals of Session 3 are to (1) increase the child's vocabulary of emotions; (2) to help the therapist and the child to identify occasions and circumstances associated with different emotions; (3) to discuss the differences in intensity associated with each emotion (strong to weak); (4) to teach the child how to distinguish between disturbed and nondisturbed (helpful and hurtful) emotions by how he acts, how others react to him, and how he feels inside when experiencing a particular emotion; and (5) to set the goal to experience the nondisturbed emotion when faced with specific problems.

Tasks. First, the therapist asks the child to define the word *emotion*. If the child does not know the word's meaning, provide the child with a definition and offer specific examples of emotions.

Second, the therapist asks the child to help her think of and list as many "emotion" words as possible. The therapist should list these emotions on a blackboard or a large piece of paper. The following is a suggested Emotion List:

Emotion List (from Bernard & Joyce, 1984)

happy	joyful	sorry
sad	glad	ashamed
afraid	embarrassed	disappointed

excited	funny	frustrated
upset	lonely	confused
cheerful	mad	guilty
annoyed	nervous	OK
angry	curious	relaxed
worried	silly	envious
loving	worthless	jealous

Third, the therapist takes turns with the child selecting approximately 10 emotions from the list. The therapist begins by choosing an emotion and then briefly describing a time when she felt this way. The child then picks an emotion, describes a time when he felt it, and so on. The therapist should be sure to include the emotions embarrassed, confused, frustrated, and worthless among her choices to serve as references in future sessions.

Fourth, the therapist introduces the "Feeling Thermometer" (graphic design by Cartwright [1977]) and incorporates goals 3, 4, and 5. The Feeling Thermometer is pictured in Figure 2–1. The following dialogue illustrates how to introduce and use the Feeling Thermometer:

Therapist: "This is a Feeling Thermometer. It's kind of like a thermometer you see outside, but different. An outdoor thermometer shows how hot

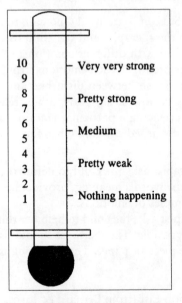

Figure 2–1. The Feeling Thermometer

Graphic design by Cartwright, 1977.

or cold it is outside, a Feeling Thermometer shows how much or how little of an emotion you have inside you—such as how happy or mad you feel.

Let's try to put some emotion words we just talked about onto the Feeling Thermometer. Remember, Brett, when you said you felt sad when you got an "F" on your spelling test? If we were going to measure your sadness about getting that "F" with this thermometer, how high would the red part go? What number do you think it would reach? The number 1 means you hardly felt sad at all. The number 5 means you felt medium sad. And the number 10 means you felt very, very sad. What number do you think it was?"

Brett: "Umm . . . maybe a 9."

(The therapist begins explaining differences in emotional intensity to the child.)

Therapist: "So that means when you got the "F," you were feeling very, very sad. Another word for very, very sad is 'depressed.' Did you ever feel sad another time?"

Brett: "Yeah, like the time when I missed 'The Cosby Show' last week because we had to come here."

Therapist: "OK, how sad did you feel then? Show me on the thermometer."

Brett: "Well, like a three, just kind of sad."

Therapist: "So you felt much less sad when you missed 'The Cosby Show' than when you failed your spelling test. Another word for less sad is 'disappointed.'"

Brett: "Yeah, I felt disappointed."

(The therapist continues to distinguish emotional intensities, and begins to distinguish between helpful and hurtful emotions.)

Therapist: "So Brett, when you failed the spelling test, and you felt depressed, what did you do?"

Brett: "I put my head on my desk."

Therapist: "And then what?"

Brett: "Then the teacher asked me what was wrong, and I started to cry."

Therapist: "Did you cry just a little, or a lot."

Brett: "I guess a lot."

Therapist: "How long did you cry?"

Brett: "I don't know, like 'til the end of spelling, and I couldn't stop crying so the teacher sent me down to talk to the school therapist person."

Therapist: "What did the other children do in the class when you were crying for so long?"

Brett: "They all started laughing at me, and John called me a baby."

Therapist: "That wasn't very polite of him. Did all the children call you names?"

Brett: "Sally didn't. She always comes up to me and keeps saying "What's wrong, what's wrong Brett?' And I hate it, cause I can't stop, and I can't say what's wrong cause I keep crying every time I try."

Therapist: "How did your body feel when you felt depressed? Did your stomach hurt, or did you feel hot?"

Brett: "My face gets really hot, and I just feel really bad, like I'm gonna get sick, and I just can't stop crying no matter what people say."

Therapist: "That sounds pretty hard for you when you're feeling depressed. It sure *isn't helping you* (HURTFUL INTENSITY OF EMOTION) when you feel depressed. But Brett, how about the time when you felt just a little sad, or disappointed— the time last week when you missed 'The Cosby Show.' What did you do?"

Brett: "I said 'Oh mom, it's not fair.' And I went to my room."

Therapist: "Then what did you do when you were feeling just a little sad?"

Brett: "Then I laid on my bed for a little while and then started playing my Nintendo game."

Therapist: "How long did you lie on your bed before you started playing your Nintendo game?"

Brett: "Just like five minutes."

Therapist: "Were you so sad that you wanted to cry?"

Brett: "No."

Therapist: "How did you feel inside when you were lying on your bed? Did you feel sick or hot?"

Brett: "No. Not really."

Therapist: "Did anyone at home tease you about being disappointed?"

Brett: "Sometimes my brother Rob does, but not this time. Mom came in and asked what was wrong, and I told her I missed 'Cosby' cause I had to come here. She said next week my brother would tape the show. And I could watch it when I got home."

Therapist: "So you felt disappointed, and you could tell your mother what was wrong."

Brett: "Yeah, cause it wasn't really a big deal."

Therapist: "Oh, *so you told yourself* it wasn't a big deal missing 'The Cosby Show,' and then you just felt disappointed instead of depressed."

(First introduction to the concept that thoughts, not just events, lead to feelings. It is best to teach this concept by using something the child says that indicates events are evaluated differently.)

Brett: "Yeah, right."

Therapist: "When you felt just disappointed, you told your mother what was wrong. When she knew what was wrong, she tried to help you feel better. She decided that your brother could tape the show for you next week. So it's *more helpful* to feel disappointed than depressed, right?"

Brett: "What do you mean?"

Therapist: "I mean when you feel just a little sad, or disappointed, you don't cry so much that you can't stop. Kids don't tease you as much. Also, you can still tell someone why you're sad and maybe they can help you. When you're depressed what happens?"

Brett: "I cry so hard, and feel sick, and I can't talk."

Therapist: "Right. And that sure *doesn't help* when you feel that way does it?"

Brett: "No."

Therapist: "Well Brett, if you don't do well on a test again, wouldn't it be fine to feel just a little sad (a three) instead of depressed (a nine)? Wouldn't that help you?" (Point to the Feeling Thermometer)

Brett: "Yeah, I guess so."

Therapist: "How come?"

Brett: "Cause when I get depressed I feel sick, and I can't stop crying, and people make fun of me."

Therapist: "When you feel just disappointed, you might feel a little bad inside, but you wouldn't feel sick. You probably wouldn't feel like you wanted to cry."

Brett: "Right. And then the kids wouldn't tease me maybe."

Therapist: "If you felt just a little sad, you could still listen to the teacher instead of working so hard to stop crying and worrying about the children teasing you. It might be easier to learn those hard spelling words if you could listen to the teacher, right?"

Brett: "Yeah."

(Therapist sets goal of decreasing disturbed emotion with child.)

Therapist: "So Brett, what we're going to try to work on together is to help you feel less sad when disappointing things happen like getting a bad grade on your spelling test. *Helping you not to feel depressed when bad things happen will be our goal.* That way you'll feel better, the children might pick on you less, and spelling might get a little easier for you."

Brett: "Do you think so? Can't I just quit school?"

Therapist: "No, I know you really don't like school. If we work on helping you not feel depressed in school, you might even start liking school a little."

Brett: "I guess. My mom and dad make me go anyway. I already asked them if I could quit."

Therapist: "I know school is hard for you, but all children still have to go to school. But wouldn't you like to have more fun in school even though the work is hard?"

Brett: "Yeah. I guess so."

Therapist: "So that's what you and I will work on together. Helping you not feel depressed, so school can be more fun for you, and so that your school work might get easier for you too. Sound OK?"

Brett: "Yup."

If time remains, the therapist can ask the child to depict other emotions on the Feeling Thermometer, and ask which number would represent the more helpful feeling to have in certain situations. The therapist should stress feeling more and less of an emotion, and how it helps or does not help the child to feel the emotional extremes.

The fifth task of Session 3 is homework. The therapist calls in the parents and discusses the homework assignment. The child will explain to parents what he learned about different types of emotions, the Feeling Thermometer, helpful and hurtful emotions, and the goal of not feeling depressed.

Session 4: Thoughts Lead to Emotions

Goals. The goals of Session 4 are (1) to teach the child that thoughts (B's) cause emotions (C's), not just circumstances (A's); (2) to teach the child that incorrect thoughts (IB's) lead to hurtful emotions, and that correct thoughts (RB's) lead to helpful emotions; (3) to repeat the concept that B's can be changed to produce emotions that are helpful; and (4) to provide a rational for changing emotions—if the child is feeling less disturbed, he will be better able to do school work, or accomplish other goals such as getting along with friends.

Tasks. First, the therapist asks the parents or child for a specific occasion during the past week when the child felt depressed, this incident will be used later in session.

Second, the therapist employs the "What Was Charlie Brown Thinking?" exercise. The therapist introduces a brief story about Charlie Brown from the Peanuts gang. This story will be fit into a happening-thought-feeling-behavior (HTFB) framework. The following sample dialogue demonstrates this exercise.

Therapist: "Brett, do you know who Charlie Brown is?"

Brett: "Yeah, he and Snoopy are on TV sometimes."

Therapist: "I want you to help me to try to figure out why Charlie Brown feels so sad and depressed so often."

(Therapist writes "Happening," "Thought," "Feeling," and "Behavior" categories on the blackboard, and gives child chalk to help write.)

Therapist: "Now let's think of a time when Charlie Brown felt depressed. Remember the time Charlie was in the spelling contest and lost?"

Brett: "No, I didn't see that one."

Therapist: "Oh, I'll tell you. Charlie Brown studied very hard, for weeks, so he could do well in the contest to prove to the other children that he wasn't a blockhead. He studied harder and longer than any of his friends. He missed the first word and finished in a tie for last place. The only person who did as bad as Charlie was Peppermint Patty who didn't spell one word right. The children laughed at both Charlie and Peppermint Patty when they missed their words. After the contest, Lucy said to them, "You see Charlie Brown, you really are a blockhead! I bet your dog knows how to spell better than you. And Patty, you did as bad as Charlie Brown! HA! HA! HA!' Charlie Brown felt so *depressed* afterward that he hung his head down and walked home from school all alone instead of going to play baseball with the rest of the children. He went to his room and didn't talk to anyone for the rest of the day. He didn't do any of his homework. Peppermint Patty felt different. She felt *frustrated* that she still hadn't done well in spelling, but she didn't feel as depressed as Charlie Brown. So she went to play baseball with the gang after school anyway. She even hit a triple. Let's figure out why Charlie Brown felt so depressed, all right Brett?"

(Therapist puts Peppermint Patty's name and "last place" under H category, has Brett put Charlie's name and "last place" under H category. Next, adds emotions to the F category: "frustrated" for Patty, and "depressed" for Charlie. Next behaviors are added under B category: Patty "goes to practice and hits a triple," Charlie "goes home alone, stays in room, doesn't talk all day.")

Therapist: "OK, now comes the key to solving the question of why Charlie felt so depressed. The same thing happened to Charlie and Patty. They both got last place, and the children laughed at them. Patty just felt frustrated but Charlie felt depressed. What do you think Patty did to feel just frustrated instead of depressed like Charlie?"

Brett: "Something she was thinking."

Therapist: "Right. What do you think Patty told herself after she got last place?"

Brett: "Probably something like 'It's no big deal, it's just a spelling contest.'"

Therapist: "And something like, 'I don't like it when the kids laugh at me, but it doesn't make me a total blockhead. Just means I'm not great at spelling.' What you and I just said were Patty's *helpful thoughts*. What do you think Charlie told himself about coming in last place to feel so depressed?"

Brett: "Probably that he was totally stupid, and the kids were right that he was a blockhead, and that he always messes up."

Therapist: "Right, the thoughts Charlie had were *not helpful*. So you see when Patty thought that (repeats T for Patty from board) she just felt frustrated. She was still able to go and have fun. When Charlie thought (has Brett repeat Charlie's thoughts from board) he felt depressed—so depressed that he shut himself alone in his room all day. He didn't talk to anyone, and missed having fun at ball practice.

It was really what Charlie told himself, or what he was thinking about—getting last place in the spelling contest—that made him feel depressed.

So Brett, what do you think Charlie could think instead to not feel depressed? How can Charlie *change his thinking to feel better?*"

Brett: "Maybe something like it stinks that I lost the contest, but it's not such a big deal, and maybe I'll do better next time."

Therapist: "And how about 'Even if the children call me a blockhead, that doesn't make me one. I may not be good in spelling, but I'm good at other things.' " If Charlie told himself these new thoughts, do you think he would feel depressed?"

Brett: "No, probably not. Maybe just pretty disappointed."

Therapist: "I think you're right Brett. If he felt just disappointed about the spelling test, do you think he still could have had fun with his friends after school and done his homework that night too?"

Brett: "Yeah, if it wasn't too hard."

Therapist: "That is true, but if he only felt disappointed about getting last place, and the homework was hard that night, he could still ask his dad for some help."

Brett: "Yeah, but if he felt depressed he probably wouldn't talk to his parents, or ask for help."

Therapist: "That's right. So what could be the goal for Charlie Brown the next time he does poorly in a spelling contest? Or maybe the next time he loses a baseball game? To feel depressed or just frustrated and disappointed?"

Brett: "To feel disappointed."

To start the third task for this session, the therapist takes an example of a time when Brett felt depressed that week from his parents' report at the beginning of the session. She then goes through a similar exercise with HTFB categories. This exercise ends with a thought change to produce the less disturbed emotional goal, and an explanation of the benefits and consequences of Brett feeling the helpful and hurtful emotion. The therapist spends additional time eliciting as many *hurtful/self-defeating thoughts* (irrational beliefs or automatic inferences) as possible from the child concerning the same activating incident. The therapist and the child then try to suggest more *helpful thoughts* (rational beliefs) to substitute for the hurtful thoughts.

The fourth task is homework. The therapist asks the child to explain the HTFB model to his parents, using either Charlie Brown's or his own example. The therapist tells the child to anticipate a time he might feel depressed this week. The child is asked to write down what he thinks when feeling depressed.

Session 5: Identifying Sensible/Helpful (Rational) versus Not Sensible/Not Helpful (Irrational) Thoughts

Goals. The goals for Session 5 are (1) to identify the difference between helpful and sensible (RB's) and hurtful and unsensible thoughts (IB's); (2) to practice identifying the nonhelpful thoughts (IB's) associated with disturbed emotions/behavior; (3) to replace the IB's reviewed with more helpful RB's; and (4) to connect the RB's with more desirable emotional and behavioral consequences.

Tasks. The first task of this session is to define the difference between helpful (rational) thoughts and hurtful (irrational) thoughts by asking the child if he knows the difference between the two types of thoughts, and providing the following definitions (Bernard & Joyce, 1984, p. 224; adapted from Knaus, 1974):

Helpful thought (rational): A sensible and logical idea that seems true.

Hurtful thought (irrational): An unreasonable or absurd idea that seems false.

The therapist's second task is to provide the child with examples of rational and irrational thoughts. The therapist also explains to the child why each thought is classified as such. The following sample dialogue illustrates this procedure.

Therapist: "An example of a helpful thought is something like 'I wish I could do better at spelling.' An example of a hurtful thought would be something like 'I'm really bad at spelling, and that means I'm totally stupid.' The first thought is helpful! If you think that you would like to do better in spelling when you get a bad grade on a test, you will want to work harder and try to improve next time. The second thought is hurtful! If you think you're totally stupid when you get a bad grade on a spelling test, you will feel depressed and probably will give up trying to do better."

For the third task, the therapist provides a list of rational versus irrational beliefs and asks the child to help classify the thoughts into helpful versus hurtful thoughts. The therapist should encourage the child to give reasons why each thought is either helpful or hurtful. The therapist should emphasize the B-C connection (that is, when one *thinks* this way, one *feels* better or worse). Sample thoughts for the child to evaluate include:

1. I can't stand school, it's too hard for me. (IB)
2. School is difficult for me, so I'll have to work hard to learn. (RB)
3. I never do anything right, I'm totally stupid, and that makes me bad. (IB)
4. If I am bad at doing some things I'm still an OK person. (RB)
5. Everyone in my class hates me and I'm worthless. (IB)
6. If some kids in my class tease me I'm still an OK person. (RB)
7. It's awful if I fail a test, I'll never do well. (IB)
8. It's not good to fail tests, but it just means I'll have to try hard to learn the work for next time. (RB)

Questions for the child to consider in evaluating thoughts (Waters, 1982) include:

1. Where is the proof that the thought is really true?
2. Where is the proof that this makes me worthless, or less worthwhile?
3. Is it true that I can't stand it?
4. Is it really too hard for me to even try?
5. Why do other people absolutely have to act the way I want?
6. Do I always have to get my way just because I want it?
7. Does it help me to think this way? Does it hurt me to think this way?

For the fourth task the therapist introduces the difference between the terms "fact," "opinion," and "evaluation." She defines each term with the child. A *fact* is something that we know is true, for example, that some birds fly or people have two eyes. An *opinion* is someone's idea about something that may be different from someone else's idea. It may be yes or it may be no, for example, your hair is too short or dogs are better pets than cats. An *evaluation* is how much you like something, a measure of better or worse, for example, school is a terrible, boring place or chocolate is absolutely delicious. The therapist explains to the child that some children believe that just because they think something, that makes it true, or a *fact*. The therapist provides examples of thoughts that are really *opinions* and/or *evaluations* instead of facts. The following dialogue illustrates teaching these important concepts.

Therapist: "Brett, if I thought that chocolate was delicious, would that make it true?

Brett: "Yeah, I really like chocolate."

Therapist: "Well, so do I. But I've asked other children if they think chocolate is delicious and some of them say no, they don't like it very much. You and I think it's delicious, but others don't. So who's right, we or they?"

Brett: "I guess no one."

Therapist: "Right, neither. So, is it true that chocolate is delicious just because we think so?"

Brett: "No. I guess that means it's not a fact."

Therapist: "Right. Our thought that chocolate is delicious could be an opinion. Or it could be an evaluation if we said that we liked it a lot."

Brett: "Yeah. I get it."

Therapist: "So Brett, if your classmate said that you were a stupid dummy, is that a fact?"

Brett: "No. It's their opinion." (See follow-up dialogue in Session 12.)

The fifth task for this session is homework. The therapist asks the child to explain the session content to his parents. He is also assigned to conduct a "thought survey" at home by asking his brothers for two facts, two opinions, and two evaluations. Then with his parents he is to examine the survey to see if any opinions or evaluations are mixed up with facts.

Session 6: Learning to Dispute/Challenge Your Thoughts

Goals. The goals of Session 6 are (1) to define "challenging one's thoughts"; (2) to teach the child questions to ask to challenge his thoughts (empirical, heuristic, philosophical; inelegant and elegant); (3) to identify clues to thinking in a disturbing, hurtful manner; and (4) to teach that if a thought does not stand the challenge, it should be changed to a more helpful thought.

Tasks. The therapist's first task in this session is to define the term "thought challenge." A thought challenge means questions that we ask to determine whether a thought is true, whether it makes sense, or whether it helps or hurts us. A thought challenge determines whether a thought is helpful or hurtful, and whether we should keep thinking that way or not.

Second, the therapist identifies forms that questions in the thought challenge will take, including:

Where is the proof that . . . ?

Is it true that . . . ?

Does it help me to think that . . . ?

Does it hurt me to think that . . . ?

Does it make sense that because I want . . . ?

I absolutely must have . . . ?

How do I feel when I think . . . ?

How do I act when I think . . . ?

Just because . . . is true about me, does that mean that I'm an all-bad person?

As the third task, the therapist provides clues to the child that signal an unreasonable or hurtful thought. Clue words include: awful, horrible, terrible, worthless, stupid, should, must, have to, need, got to, never, always, completely, all, none at all.

Fourth, the therapist takes a sample thought discussed in a previous session concerning the child's performance at school, or elicits a thought about a recent upsetting occurrence during the past week. RET advocates disputing the child's core irrational beliefs before disputing the child's inferences (DiGiuseppe & Bernard, 1990; Walen, DiGiuseppe, & Dryden, 1992). This strategy obtains a more "elegant" philosophical change (Ellis, 1989), and protects against the possibility that the child's inferences may be true, or become true in the future. For example, RET suggests challenging the child's core belief that he is "a worthless kid if he flunks spelling tests" before challenging the child's inference that he will "never do well in spelling." With learning disabled children, the child is often correct in assuming that spelling will never come easy to him, and that he may never do as well as other children do in spelling. There are certain beliefs, such as a child's belief that it is terrible to have no friends, that may be more successfully disputed at the inference level ("Is it really true that *nobody* likes you?") as opposed to at the more elegant or philosophical level ("What would it mean about you if nobody liked you?"). See DiGiuseppe (1989) for further discussion of this point.

To elicit the core irrational beliefs, the therapist uses the strategy of inference chaining (see Walen, DiGiuseppe, & Dryden, 1992, or DiGiuseppe, 1991, for discussion of inference chaining). The therapist hypothesizes that the child's inferences are true, and then asks the child to elaborate further using incomplete sentences as prompts such as: "and if (inference) is true, you feel (emotion) *because* . . . ? (child responds with new inference); (new inference) would happen, *and that would mean* . . . ? (child responds with new inference); and if (new inference) is true, you'd feel (emotion) because what would that mean *about you* (or other person) . . . ? (child responds).

In the fifth task the therapist and the child put the thought to the "thought challenge." The following sample dialogue illustrates this exercise.

Therapist: "OK Brett, let's see if we can make this thought challenge work for you. Last night when you were crying in your room instead of doing homework, how did you feel?

Brett: "Really sad."

Therapist: "How sad on the feeling thermometer, 1 to 10?"

Brett: "Like a 10."

Therapist: "OK. We call that depression. What were you depressed about?"

Brett: "Cause the homework was hard, and I kept making mistakes. My mom kept telling me to go back and try again."

Therapist: "So you felt depressed about the homework being hard because . . . ?"

Brett: "Because I couldn't do it."

Therapist: "And if you couldn't do it, then what could happen?"

Brett: "Then I wouldn't understand it, and I'd do bad on the test."

Therapist: "And if you did bad on the test what would that mean?"

Brett: "That mom and dad would be disappointed, and the kids would make fun of me."

Therapist: "So if your parents were disappointed and the kids made fun of you, what would that mean about you?"

Brett: "It would mean that I was a bad kid who can't learn anything."

(Child has identified both a core irrational belief and an additional inference in this statement.)

Therapist: "Aha! I think we've found the thought to challenge. You think that if you do bad on a test then that proves you're a bad kid who can't learn anything—right?"

Brett: "Right."

Therapist: "But let's challenge that thought.

(The therapist decides to break the thought into two parts, disputing the bad grade = bad kid thought first, the never learn anything thought second.)
Here's the first question. Where is the proof that you are completely, 100 percent bad just because you did poorly on this one spelling test?"

Brett: "But I've flunked lots of tests, and not just spelling."

Therapist: "OK, what other ones?"

Brett: "I don't know . . . like English tests and stuff."

Therapist: "All right, where is the proof that just because you have failed several spelling and English tests you are 100 percent bad?"

Brett: "My brother says so, and so do the kids in school."

Therapist: "But just because your brother and the kids at school say you're bad, does that make you bad?"

Brett: "No."

Therapist: "What about all the other things you do well Brett, like skating, and helping your father with the yard work. If you do poorly on spelling tests does that mean that you do poorly at skating and helping your dad too?"

Brett: "No, I can still do them good, better than lots of the kids on the block."

Therapist: "Right, but if it were true that you were completely bad because you failed your spelling test, it would mean that you would be bad in *everything* you did, spelling, English, skating, helping dad, *everything*, and worthless to everyone."

Brett: "That's not true."

Therapist: "I know it, so it doesn't seem like your thought is holding up to our thought challenge so far."

Throughout this exercise the therapist continues to challenge thoughts socratically, using disputes outlined in Task 2, and substituting each irrational thought and inference into the dispute formats. It is best to spend as much time as possible on disputing, challenging the thought in as many ways as possible. Continue until the child appears convinced that his thought is false, and it would be better to change that thought.

A possible fifth task is to employ alternative strategies to elicit the child's irrational beliefs, depending on the child's verbal and reasoning abilities. The therapist should attempt to elicit the child's beliefs with an open-ended question such as "And what were you telling yourself when you felt sad?" or "What were you thinking in your head when you felt sad?" If the child does not respond to this question, the therapist could employ the socratic format outlined above. The therapist repeats the happening (A) or inference (B). Then she restates the emotion, and asks an open-ended question such as "And if you failed your test (A) you would feel sad (C) *because* . . . ?." Or, "You would feel depressed (C) if you never did well in spelling (B), *because* that would mean that you were . . . ?" Children with less well developed verbal abilities may require assistance in labeling their beliefs. The therapist can provide such children with a list of possible irrational beliefs and ask the child to identify which belief he might be thinking. For example, the therapist might say, "When you felt sad about failing the spelling test, do you think you were telling yourself something like 'I'm a stupid loser!' or 'My parents won't love me because I failed?'" Allow the child to respond yes/no.

In the sixth task the therapist and child together generate a rational alternative thought to replace the irrational thought. The following sample dialogue illustrates this process.

Therapist: "OK Brett, now we agree that your thought that 'If you failed your spelling test, and then maybe your parents would be disappointed, and kids would tease you, that would mean you were stupid and will never learn anything' (Therapist writes this thought out on paper or on the blackboard) is not a sensible thought. In fact it's a hurtful thought. So now we need to come up with a more helpful thought to replace that old thought. You can use the new thought to keep from feeling depressed and giving up when you do poorly on tests in school. Have any ideas?"

Brett: "Maybe I could think that just because I messed up this time doesn't mean that I'll mess up next time."

Therapist: "Great, and what could you change in that thought about never learning anything?"

Brett: "Maybe that I could learn some things if I keep trying."

Therapist: "OK and let's add to that one. Even if you do poorly on your spelling and English test lots of times, it just means that those things are difficult for you to do. You'll just have to keep working harder than the other kids to learn those subjects."

Brett: "Right."

Therapist: "And Brett, what does it mean about you if you fail spelling and English tests lots of times, kids laugh, and your parents are disappointed? Does that make you completely bad?

Brett: "No, it just means I don't do as good in spelling and English as other kids sometimes, but I still do other things good, and I'm still a good kid."

Therapist: "That's right. So Brett, if you thought these new helpful thoughts, instead of your old hurtful thoughts, how do you think you'd feel if you failed another spelling test?"

Brett: "I guess not so bad, maybe just a little bad, like disappointed."

Therapist: "Right, because most everyone would feel disappointed if they failed at something they wanted to do well at, like a spelling test. But now Brett, if you felt just disappointed, instead of depressed, do you think you'd give up trying to do better?"

Brett: "No, I don't think so."

Therapist: "So let's test out the new thoughts to find out. If any time this week you do something wrong, or if you fail a test, I want you to try using these new thoughts. See how you feel after you use them, OK?"

Brett: "OK, I'll try them."

The therapist writes down the rational thoughts on an index card. The child can carry the card with him to school, or keep it in front of him when doing his homework. The therapist should encourage the child to practice using the new thoughts as often as possible.

For task seven, role play to practice disputing and changing irrational beliefs. The therapist should ask the child to imagine that he has a spelling test next week. The teacher gives him back the test with an "F" grade. The therapist says the child's irrational beliefs aloud, and the child rehearses challenging these beliefs aloud. The child replaces the old beliefs with new ones aloud. Repeat the imagery, with the therapist repeating the irrational beliefs aloud, and the child challenging and changing the beliefs silently to himself.

Task eight is homework. Have the child practice the disputing/changing beliefs role play with his parents concerning a specific incident that occurred this week.

Modifying Specific IB's

Sessions 7 through 12 focus on modifying specific irrational and hurtful thoughts.

Session 7: Self-Rating

Goals. The goals of Session 7 are (1) to teach the child the concept that he is a complex person made up of strengths and weaknesses, like everyone else in the world; (2) to identify some of the child's and the therapist's strengths and weaknesses; (3) to teach the concept that the child's weaknesses do not make him all bad, nor do his strengths make him all good; (4) to explain the emotional consequences of focusing on weaknesses and thinking he is an all-bad person; and (5) to explain that weaknesses can sometimes be improved (Things we do wrong sometimes call for consequences and punishments. This, however, does not make the person an all-bad person for having weaknesses or doing things wrong).

Tasks. First, drawing on the Complex Me = Self-Concept Circle (Bernard & Joyce, 1984, p. 414; adapted from Knaus, 1974), the therapist introduces the concept that all people are complex people: everyone has a mix of good points and bad points. The therapist draws a circle in the center of the page with six spokes extending outward from the center circle. She connects a circle to each of the six spokes, and places plus (+) or minus (−) signs in alternate circles. She asks the child to place his name in the center circle. She then asks the child to think of his good points, things he does well, or things he likes about himself. The child writes these in the plus circles. The therapist next asks the child to write his bad points, or things he does not like about himself, in the minus circles. If the child has difficulty naming positive or negative characteristics, the therapist should assist the child. The therapist should help the child to focus on strengths or weaknesses that are relevant to the presenting problem.

The second task is adding/subtracting strengths and weaknesses. The therapist asks the child to pretend to remove one of his strengths ("Suppose you weren't good at running anymore because you hurt your leg.") Then she asks the child if removing this strength makes him a worthless person. She points out that removing one strength does not take away his other strengths. The therapist next asks the child if taking away one of his strengths would make him a "less good person" than someone who still had that strength. She explains to the child that taking away the strength would only mean that he wasn't as good as someone else in doing that one thing. That would not mean he was a bad, or a less good person. The therapist then does a similar exercise with one of the child's weak points. She asks the child if having this weakness (for example, has a hard time learning some subjects in school) makes him a less good person than a child who does not have this weakness. She teaches the child that his weaknesses are in specific areas. She argues that having those particular weaknesses does not change one's worth as a person, or make one less good a person than anyone else. The therapist asks the child to imagine being able to add strengths or take away weaknesses from the self wheel. She has the child tell her whether he would now be a better person. She stresses the concept that strengths do not make the child all good, nor do weaknesses make the child all bad.

To start the third task, the therapist asks the child to state how he would feel (C) if he thought he was a completely bad or worthless person because he had one weakness (B). The therapist then links the disturbed emotion to the overgeneralizing, irrational thought that the child *is only* what he does, or does not do (for example, the therapist asks, "If you play baseball well, does that make you only a good baseball player?" or "If you don't write well, does that make you only a bad writer?" Then the child would respond, "No, it only means you're a person who does some things well (like play baseball) and some things not so well (like writing). Everybody does some things well and some things not so well.")

For the fourth task, the therapist begins by asking the child if having weaknesses means that he is an entirely bad person, and does that mean that he should be able to do bad things without being corrected or punished? She teaches the concept that some things we do are harmful to ourselves or to other people. She points out that others will sometimes punish us, or provide consequences for the bad things we do. Punishment sometimes helps us learn not to do harmful things, and to correct our mistakes. The therapist should stress the idea that even if the child is punished or corrected, it never makes him an all-bad person. For example, Brett may get a poor report card. His parents might ask him to come home right after school to do his homework, instead of going to baseball practice, until his grades improve. Should Brett go home and say to himself that he is not an all-bad person for doing poorly on his report card? Answer: Yes. Does that mean that he doesn't have to try harder to do better next time? Answer: No. The therapist explains to the child that it is best to try to improve the things that he does poorly, and try not to do things that would hurt other people. However, he is never an all-bad person for having those weaknesses, or for behaving poorly.

The fifth task is called "Voting on Others: Who's More Worthwhile?" The therapist gives the child a list of scenarios involving children who have varied combinations of strengths and weaknesses. The therapist varies the number of strengths/weaknesses outlined. For one child the therapist might list five strengths and one weakness, and for another five weaknesses and only one strength. For example: Mary is good at a, b, c, d, and e, and bad at f; Rachel is bad at a, b, c, d, and e, and good at f. Asks the child to vote who is a better person, and to select among the choices "Mary," "Rachel," or "Neither one, just the same." After the child votes, the therapist explains that neither child is a better person, both are equally good, they just have some things that they do well or poorly. She explains that although Rachel has fewer strengths, there are probably many different things that Rachel does well that we don't know about, or did not think about. The therapist relates this vignette to the child's experience: how he might rate himself as less good than another child when he is thinking only about his weaknesses and forgetting his strengths.

The sixth task is homework. Ask the child to write down the strengths and weaknesses of one of his heroes. If his hero thought he was no good because of the weaknesses, how would he feel, what would he do?

Session 8: Expressing Feelings

Goals. The goals of Session 8 are to (1) understand the nature of emotions and the different ways children express them; (2) to assess and challenge any IB's associated with showing one's emotions; (3) to evaluate the benefits/consequences of not expressing emotions; (4) to distinguish between situations when it would be best to hold in your emotions versus those in which you should let others know your emotions; and (5) to help the child to list more and less helpful ways of communicating his emotions.

Tasks. First, the therapist explains that everyone (children and adults) experiences emotions. People show them differently (by keeping quiet, by talking about their emotions, by doing things to keep their mind off their emotions, and so on).

Second, the therapist explains that all people have unpleasant emotions (anger, sadness, embarrassment, fear, and the like). Our thoughts decide just how unpleasant we allow ourselves to feel. The therapist uses an example from a previous session to demonstrate how an unreasonable thought (IB) can influence the intensity of our emotions.

Third, the therapist evaluates with the child's input different styles of expressing emotions. The therapist asks which style is more helpful/less helpful to the person's goal of feeling better, and changing things that lead to upsetting emotions.

Fourth, the therapist discusses irrational beliefs that underlie the child's hesitancy to express emotions. These irrational beliefs might include:

"If I cry that means I'm a wimp."

"It's not so bad, so I shouldn't feel (emotion) about it."

"If I show that I'm angry (or other emotion), my friends (parents) won't like me anymore."

"If I let myself feel (emotion), I won't be able to stand it."

In the fifth task the therapist describes the "Emotion Pot" to the child. She might say something like this:

"What happens when someone turns on the stove [happening], puts a full pot of soup on the stove, and leaves the lid off? The soup will bubble and cook without overflowing [appropriate emotional response to the happening]. But when you put the lid on the pot [belief that you must hide your feelings] without turning down the stove [changing the happenings], or taking out some soup that's already in the pot [emotional problem solving], the soup will boil over [too intense an emotional response]."

After presenting this story, the therapist then explains it:

"Some children hold their emotions inside when bad things happen to them. They don't talk about their emotions. A boy like you might think he has to put a lid on his Emotion Pot. For a little while he might feel better because he didn't let himself think about how he's feeling sad [or some other emotion], and why he's feeling that way. If he doesn't do anything to help himself feel better, like telling someone such as his parents how he's feeling, his parents might not be able to change the things that he's upset about. But what can happen if he leaves the lid on too long? He stuffs too many feelings away into the feeling pot in his head. His head becomes too full, and there's not enough room left. The emotions can start bubbling out so that he might start feeling depressed [or some other emotion]. He has kept so many emotions inside, instead of working on his depression each time it happens, that the emotions have become jumbled up with all the others. It's really hard for him to figure out just why he is feeling depressed. He doesn't know which happening and thought has caused the depressed emotions because there are so many of them bunched up together. So it becomes much harder for him to feel better."

For the sixth task, the therapist asks the child to describe emotional and behavioral consequences, and problem solving difficulties that may occur when he does not express his emotions for a long time.

In the seventh task the therapist asks the child to think of a time when it might be desirable not to express emotions. For example, you are feeling very angry with your friend for breaking your skateboard. Would it be a good idea to tell him that you hate him and he is wearing the ugliest sneakers you ever saw? Why or why not?

For the eighth task, the therapist and the child outline alternative ways to deal with the anger at his friend for the imaginary incident introduced in task seven:

1. Challenging your thoughts to help you feel less angry, and maybe just very disappointed.
2. Telling your friend calmly why you feel disappointed (because he broke your skateboard, and not because he has ugly sneakers).
3. Problem solving. Trying to talk to your friend, or your parents about how you might be able to fix the skateboard, or get money to buy a new one.

The ninth task is homework. Assign an Emotions Diary. The child is to write in a notebook each day one emotion he experienced. He must also write down the HTFB associated with each emotion. He is to bring in the diary to discuss it at the next session.

Session 9: Making Mistakes

Goals. The goals for Session 9 are (1) to teach the concept that everyone makes mistakes; (2) to teach the concept that a person is not equal to his performance; (3) to teach the concept that people can learn from their mistakes; (4) to demonstrate how the child's worrying about making a mistake may make it more likely that he will make a mistake; and (5) to teach coping statements to use after having made a mistake.

Tasks. For the first task the therapist discusses the idea that everyone (child, siblings, friends, therapist, parents) makes mistakes. She asks the child if he can think of any mistakes his parents have made or that the therapist has made.

In the second task the therapist discusses the concept that making a mistake is only one part of the person, or only one thing the person does. The therapist reinforces the concept learned in the "Complex Me" demonstration (see Session 7). She points out that making a mistake or failing does not remove the boy's strengths (his good qualities) and does not make him a worse person than a child who didn't make the same mistake.

For the third task, the therapist shows the child that mistakes are opportunities to try to learn and to improve himself, especially when he feels ashamed of himself for making mistakes. She asks the child if he knows any famous people who made many mistakes. Then she suggests people who have made mistakes. For example: Babe Ruth struck out 1331 times, the Wright Brothers' airplane crashed many times before it finally flew, Beethoven's corrections appear all over his manuscripts. Ask the child if he thinks these famous people gave up after they made mistakes. What did they do when they made a mistake? They all tried to learn something from their mistakes so they could do better next time.

In task four the therapist teaches the B-C connection in which unreasonable thoughts about making a mistake lead to anxiety or fear that may make another mistake more likely to occur. She asks the child to go to the blackboard and spell a very difficult work ("rhythm" or "synonym"). As the child is trying to spell the word, the therapist says rapidly and in a loud voice many irrational beliefs about making a mistake such as:

"I can't ever make a mistake."
"If I make a mistake it will be horrible."
"My therapist will think I'm an idiot if I make a mistake."
"If I make a mistake, that means I'm stupid."

The therapist keeps repeating the irrational beliefs aloud until the child finishes his attempt at spelling the word. She then asks the child how he felt when the therapist was saying the unhelpful thoughts aloud: worried, anxious, tense, scared? When he felt worried, was he able to think hard about how to spell the word, or was he just thinking about not making a mistake?

For task five the therapist works with the child to come up with rational coping statements about making mistakes such as:

"Everyone makes mistakes sometimes."

"If I make a mistake, too bad. Maybe I can learn from it."

"Even if other people think I'm stupid for making a mistake, it doesn't make me stupid."

"If I make a mistake it just means that I'm not perfect, just like everybody else."

For the sixth task the therapist asks the child to recall his "very worst mistake." She has the child go through an HTFB diagram concerning the mistake incident, including thought challenge, and replacing irrational thought with rational coping statement.

For the seventh task, homework, the child is to ask his mother, father, and teacher to tell about two mistakes they have made.

Session 10: Asking for Help When You Need It

Goals. The goals for Session 10 are to (1) convey the consequences of not asking for help; (2) to help the child identify irrational thoughts that may impede his asking for help; (3) to teach the child behavioral skills involved in asking for help; and (4) to role play asking for help with schoolwork at home (using rational disputes and coping statements).

Tasks. In the first task the therapist helps the child to identify the emotional and behavioral consequences and response costs involved when the child does not ask for help. Consequences may include: frustration about not knowing what to do; anger when he continues to make the same mistakes since he does not understand the task; giving up a task too early because he thinks he can't do it; getting a poor grade on the test because he didn't understand the material, and so on.

For the second task, the therapist asks the child for thoughts he might be telling himself when he doesn't wish to ask for help. The therapist uses the methods for assessing child's irrational beliefs described in Session 6 ("Learning to Challenge One's Thoughts"). The child and therapist devise rational thoughts to replace the irrational thoughts.

In the third task the therapist asks the child for a good way to ask for help if he needs it. She asks the child to demonstrate. The therapist teaches the child the skills of keeping direct eye contact, asking in a pleasant voice that can be heard, and using polite phrases such as "Please" and "Thank you" as needed. The therapist teaches the concept that some times are easier than others for people to help you. The child and therapist then think about good and bad times for the child to ask for help from his parents or teacher.

The fourth task is a role play in which the child is doing his homework and needs to ask for help. The child says rational thoughts about asking for help aloud, then asks the therapist (who is role playing the child's parent) for help. Next, repeat the situation, but now have the child say rational thoughts silently to himself, and then ask for help.

The fifth task is homework: tell the child to ask his parents and teacher for help at least once this week using the cognitive and behavioral skills practiced in this session.

Session 11: Building Frustration Tolerance

Goals. The goals of Session 11 are to (1) help the child learn the difference between tasks that are easy, difficult, very difficult, and impossible; (2) to help the child learn that since some tasks are more difficult for him, he will need to practice more and longer than other children; (3) to help the child learn that persisting on learning difficult tasks, although mistakes and frustrations occur, may make them less difficult to do in the future; (4) to help the child learn that if he does not try, he may never improve; and (5) to help the child identify thoughts that lead to his frustration and giving up at tasks before he has tried.

Tasks. In the first task the therapist asks the child to give examples of school-related and play-related tasks that are easy, hard, very hard, and impossible to do. She asks the child if a task is very difficult for him, and he has never done it before, does that make the task impossible?

For the second task the therapist explains to the child that because some school-related tasks are very difficult for him, he may require working longer and harder than the other children to learn them. She asks the child if having to work harder makes him an all-bad person?

For the third task the therapist asks the child to describe a time when he felt very upset with his parents for asking him to do something that he thought was too hard. The therapist may need to ask the parents to provide a sample situation.

During the fourth task the therapist and the child identify irrational beliefs associated with depression, such as:

"I can't stand it when my parents ask me to do this stupid homework!"
"They should know I can't do this, they shouldn't keep asking me!"
"It's too hard!"
"I'll never be able to do this!"

The therapist and the child connect the emotion and behavior with the above thoughts (for example, the child gets upset, throws his books on the floor, yells at his parents, and gives up trying to get the lesson right).

During the fifth task the therapist and the child generate rational alternative beliefs such as:

"I don't like it when they ask me to do my homework, but I can stand it."

"I sure won't die of doing my homework."

"I wish my parents would stop asking me to do this. But they're trying to help me. They don't have to stop just because I want them to."

"It's hard, but it's not impossible or they wouldn't ask me to do it."

"It might take me awhile to learn this, but if I keep trying and ask questions, I'll probably get it."

The therapist asks the child, How will it help him if he thinks these new helpful thoughts? The child should respond that it may make the task easier with practice, or that he will have a better chance of improving than if he just gives up.

For the sixth task the therapist and the child do additional HTFB diagrams around tasks that the child thought were too hard, so that he either gave up trying, or didn't try at all.

For the seventh task, homework, the child is asked to make a list of the difficult things he has been able to do successfully in the past. Also, he must think of something hard that he has to do next week. He is to rate how hard he thinks it will be on a scale from 1 to 10 (10 being the most difficult). He is to do the task, and then rate how hard it really was after he did it.

Session 12: Handling Peers' Criticism

Goals. The goals for Session 12 are (1) to teach the concept that if some people reject you or do not want to be your friends, it does not prove that you are all bad, less good, or that no one will ever like you; (2) to teach the concept that other's opinions and comments are not necessarily facts; (3) to teach the concept that even if people's criticisms are true, it is only one aspect of the child, and does not make him an all-bad or less-good person; (4) to emphasize that other people's insults/criticisms will not make the child upset unless the child lets them (the B's lead to the C's); and (5) to teach rational coping statements to help the child deal with criticisms more effectively.

Tasks. In the first task the therapist assesses the child's HTFB of a recent episode in which a classmate in school rejected him. For example, the peer said, or acted like, he did not like the child, or did not want to be his friend.

For the second task the therapist presents a paradigm to the child about one of the child's favorite kinds of food that has many varieties, for example, candy or ice cream. She shows the child that if he does not like a particular variety of the favorite food, it doesn't make that variety bad, it just means it's not the child's preference. She discusses the peer incident. The therapist stresses the concept that if the peer does not choose, or prefer to be, friends with the child, it does not make the child bad or less good. The following sample dialogue illustrates how to effectively employ the paradigm.

Therapist: "Brett, you told me before that you really liked ice cream, right?"
Brett: "Yeah, I love it!"
Therapist: "So what's your favorite flavor of ice cream?"
Brett: "Mint chip—Yummm!"
Therapist: "And what's your least favorite flavor of ice cream?"
Brett: "Sherbert—Yuck."
Therapist: "Do you know anybody that likes sherbert?"
Brett: "Yeah, my mom, she always gets it. And my friend Ryan will eat it too."

Therapist: "So, Brett, if you went to the ice cream shop and asked for one scoop of mint chip, would that mean anything about the sherbert?"

Brett: "I guess that I don't like it."

Therapist: "I know, but just because you don't like sherbert, does that mean there's anything wrong with the sherbert?"

Brett: "No, it just doesn't taste good to me."

Therapist: "Right, but your mom still likes it, right?"

Brett: "Right."

Therapist: "And Ryan still likes it, right?"

Brett: "Right."

Therapist: "So that must mean that there's nothing wrong with the sherbert, it's just that you don't like it. OK now, Brett, suppose that kid in school, (name), says that he doesn't like you, and doesn't want to play with you. What does that mean about you?"

Brett: "It means he doesn't like me."

Therapist: "It could mean that. And does that mean you're a bad person because he doesn't like you?"

Brett: "I guess not, just like the sherbert, right?"

Therapist: "Right. And does that mean that no one else likes you because (name) doesn't like you?"

Brett: "No, cause Ryan still likes me, and my parents too."

Therapist: "That's right. Not everyone will like you all the time, but that doesn't mean that no one likes you at all."

In the third task the therapist assesses the child's HTFB of a recent episode in which a classmate made fun of him or called him a name. She teaches the concept that calling someone a name does not make the child the thing he is called. She asks the child to respond to a series of questions (Bernard & Joyce, 1984):

If I call you an alligator, does that make you an alligator?
Do you turn into one?
If I call you a martian, does that make you a martian?
If I call you a geek, does that make you a geek?
If I call you stupid, does that make you stupid?

For the fourth task, the therapist asks the child about a situation when children were teasing him about something that was or is true (for example, the child received a bad report card or the child has to go to the resource room). What does that mean about the child? Is he bad and worthless, or less good a child than the others? No, it just means that he's not perfect, just like the children who are teasing him.

For the fifth task, the therapist asks the child if it was *only* his classmates rejecting or teasing him that made him feel so depressed, angry, and the like?

The therapist helps the child produce the response that it was his own thoughts about what the children said that made him feel very upset.

For the sixth task, the therapist helps the child generate coping statements to build "tease tolerance" (Vernon, 1989a, 1989b). These statements could include (adapted from Bernard & Joyce, 1984):

> "Sticks and stones can break my bones, but words can never hurt me."
> "So what if they called me (name). I won't worry about it."
> "I know I'm not only a. . . . "
> "I don't like being called names, but it's not terrible."
> "Names can only hurt me if I let them."

The therapist asks the child how he would feel if he said these thoughts in his head the next time someone teased him.

The seventh task is homework. Have parents help the child build his tease tolerance. Have parents tease the child, while the child responds aloud with rational coping statements. Repeat the scenario with the child saying coping statements silently to himself. Practice this exercise several times that week. Later have the child try his new skills with a peer in school, or with a sibling.

Review and Closure

Sessions 13 through 16 will consist of review of the concepts presented in previous sessions, using specific problems brought in by the parents and child to the therapist. At this point the therapist decides which concepts may need further work: cognitive skills, identifying irrational beliefs, challenging irrational beliefs, emotive skills, expressing feelings in an assertive (versus passive or aggressive) manner, behavioral skills, knowledge of behavioral alternatives, or practicing newly learned skills. The therapist should spend additional time on topics as needed. She should evaluate symptom change, change in parent–child system functioning, and the child's and the parents' ability to use thoughts to modify emotions and behaviors. Is it the circumstances that have changed (for example, a new classroom with a different teacher), or has the child's/parents' ability to cope with the circumstances changed? Review with parents and the child the concepts with which they request additional help.

Session 17: Review of Previous Concepts Learned,
Recontracting, or Termination

Goals. The goals of Session 17 are (1) to help the child review what he learned in sessions; (2) to help the parents review what they learned in sessions; (3) to comment on, and add to, any missing points in the child's and the parents' reviews; (4) to stress and praise the family's accomplishments in therapy, and to describe weaknesses or areas in which the family may still need improvement; (5) to recommend termination; or (6) to call for recontracting for work on additional goals.

Tasks. The therapist stresses the ongoing process of working on thoughts, feelings, and behaviors after termination of therapy. The therapist recommends a family practitioner model of treatment—if the family runs into future problems, they are encouraged to return for refresher sessions.

References

Achenbach, T., & Edelbrook, C. (1988). *Manual for the child behavior checklist.* Burlington, VT: University Psychiatry Press.

Bernard, M. (1990). Rational-emotive therapy with children and adolescents: Treatment strategies. *School Psychology Review, 19,* 294–303.

Bernard, M., & DiGiuseppe, R. (Eds.) (1989). *Inside rational emotive therapy. A critical appraisal of the theory and therapy of Albert Ellis.* Orlando, FL: Academic Press.

Bernard, M., & Joyce, M. (1984). *Rational-emotive therapy with children and adolescents: Theory, treatment strategies, and preventive methods.* New York: Wiley.

Cartwright, R. (1977). *The feeling thermometer.* Unpublished graphic design, Melbourne, Australia.

DiGiuseppe, R. (1986). A cognitive behavioral approach to the treatment of conduct disordered children and adolescents. In N. Epstein, S. Schlesinger, & W. Dryden (Eds.), *Cognitive behavioral therapy with families* (pp. 183–214). New York: Brunner/Mazel.

DiGiuseppe, R. (1988). Cognitive-behavior therapy with families of conduct-disordered children. In N. Epstein, S. Schebinger, & W. Dryden (Eds.), *Cognitive-behavior therapy with families* (pp. 184–223). New York: Bruner/Mazel.

DiGiuseppe, R. (1989). Cognitive therapy with children. In A. Freeman, K. Simon, L. Beutler, & H. Arkowitz (Eds.), *Comprehensive handbook of cognitive therapy* (pp. 515–534). New York: Plenum.

DiGiuseppe, R. (1991). A rational emotive model of assessment. In M. Bernard (Ed.), *Using RET effectively* (pp. 151–172). New York: Plenum.

DiGiuseppe, R., & Bernard, M. (1983). Principles of assessment and methods of treatment with children: Special considerations. In A. Ellis & M. Bernard (Eds.), *Rational-emotive approaches to the problems of childhood* (pp. 45–88). New York: Plenum Press.

DiGiuseppe, R., & Bernard, M. E. (1990). The application of rational-emotive theory and therapy to school-aged children. *School Psychology Review, 19,* 268–286.

Dryden, W., & DiGiuseppe, R. (1990). *A primer on rational emotive therapy.* Champaign, IL: Research Press.

Ellis, A. (1973). *Humanistic psychotherapy: The rational-emotive approach.* New York: McGraw-Hill.

Ellis, A. (1980). Rational-emotive and cognitive behavior therapy: Similarities and differences. *Cognitive Therapy and Research, 4,* 325–350.

Ellis, A. (1989). The history of cognitive therapies. In A. Freeman, K. Simon, L. Beutler, & H. Arkowitz (Eds.), *Comprehensive handbook of cognitive therapy.* New York: Plenum Press.

Ellis, A., & Bernard, M. E. (Eds.) (1983). *Rational-emotive approaches to the problems of childhood.* New York: Plenum.

Ellis, A., & Dryden, W. (1987). *The practice of RET.* New York: Springer.

Ellis, A., McInerney, J., DiGiuseppe, R., & Yeager, R. (1988). *Rational emotive therapy with alcoholics and substance abusers.* New York: Pergamon Press.

Ellis, A., Sichel, J., Yeager, R., DiMattia, D., & DiGiuseppe, R. (1989). *Rational emotive couples' therapy.* New York: Pergamon Press.

Gerald, M., & Eyman, W. (1981). *Thinking straight and talking sense: An emotional education program.* New York: Institute for Rational Living.

Haaga, D., & Davison, G. (1991). Disappearing differences do not always reflect healthy integration: An analysis of cognitive therapy and rational emotive therapy. *Journal of Psychotherapy Integration, 1*(4), 287–304.

Hajzler, D., & Bernard, M. (1990). *A review of rational-emotive education outcome studies.* Manuscript submitted for publication.

Heesacker, M., Heppner, P. P., & Rogers, M. E. (1982). Classics and emerging classics in psychology. *Journal of Counseling Psychology, 29,* 400–405.

Huber, C., & Baruth, L. (1989). *Rational-emotive family therapy: A systems perspective.* New York: Springer.

Hynd, G. (1991). Structured interview for diagnostic assessment of children. Personal communication.

Knaus, W. J. (1974). *Rational-emotive education: A manual for elementary school teachers.* New York: Institute for Rational Living.

Reynolds, W. (1991). *Reynolds Child Depression Scale Manual.* Odessa, FL: Professional Resources.

Smith, D. (1982). Trends in counseling and psychotherapy. *American Psychologist, 37,* 802–809.

Vernon, A. (1989a). *Thinking, feeling, behaving: An emotional education curriculum for children grades 1–6.* Champaign, IL: Research Press.

Vernon, A. (1989b). *Thinking, feeling, behaving: An emotional education curriculum for adolescents grades 7–12.* Champaign, IL: Research Press.

Walen, S., DiGiuseppe, R., & Dryden, W. (1992). *A practitioner's guide to rational-emotive therapy* (2d ed.). New York: Oxford University Press.

Walen, S., DiGiuseppe, R., & Wessler, R. (1980). *A practitioner's guide to rational-emotive therapy.* New York: Oxford University Press.

Waters, V. (1982). Therapies for children: Rational-emotive therapy. In C. R. Reynolds & T. B. Gutkin (Eds.), *Handbook of school psychology* (pp. 570–579). New York: Wiley.

3
Psychological Competence-Based Therapy for Young Children and Their Parents

Joseph M. Strayhorn, Jr.

Introduction and Overview

1 Scope of This Manual

1.1 *Age range of children:* The techniques described here were refined primarily with children under 8 years old. However, with some modifications the techniques are applicable to most preadolescents; the general principles are applicable to all ages.

1.2 The scope does not include techniques of biological treatment (for example, stimulant medication) or techniques of situational intervention (for example, custody determination, foster placement, school consultation). The scope does include all problems that can be helped to some degree by learning how to handle situations better. This set of problems does include those whose first cause was biologic or situational, for which new learning can override some of the consequences of the primary etiology. For example, the child with drug-responsive attention problems can still often benefit from influences toward learning greater skills of sustaining attention; a child who has been abused can benefit from learning skills of trusting and depending.

The most applicable population for this method is the vast number of children with disruptive behavior, poor relations with people, sadness, fear, or poor academic performance, whose problems can be helped by their learning new ways of handling situations.

2 Preparation of Therapist

2.1 The therapist requires knowledge of the skills axis, the methods axis, and the overall strategy of the approach, as follows.

41

2.1.1 Mental health and happiness and productivity, to the extent that they are not attributable to biological and situational factors, are attributable to the possession of a set of skills: the ability to trust, to enjoy being kind to others, to feel good about accomplishments, to tolerate frustration, to sustain attention to tasks, to tolerate rejection, to be assertive, and others. The "skills axis" (see appendix 3.1) is a list of 62 of these competences.

2.1.2 People promote the growth of skills in others in several ways. For example, they persuade or promote insight, leading the other to adopt the attainment of the skill as a goal; they arrange a series of small hierarchical steps the learner can progress along on the way to the goal; through their attribution of traits to the learner, they promote a self-image conducive to learning the skill; they model positive examples of the skill; they provide opportunities for practice of the skills; they provide reinforcement for the positive examples the learner performs, or punishment for the negative examples; they give direct instruction and explanation about how to carry out the skills; they provide the stimulus conditions most likely to elicit them; they monitor the ongoing progress of the learner. The "methods influence axis" consists of these nine methods of influence (see appendix 3.2.)

2.1.3 There is a set of parenting skills, highly related to the psychological skills axis, but more specific to the job of being a parent to a young child. These include use of tones of voice of enthusiasm and approval, dramatic play, story reading, empathic listening, avoidance of unnecessary commands, use of time out, use of reprimands, and others. See appendix 3.3, or follow the outline of this manual.

2.1.4 The diagnostic and treatment tasks of the competence-oriented therapist are (1) to identify the most important skills for the child to develop, (2) to identify the most important skills for the parent to develop, (3) to identify and enact the most effective methods of influence for promotion of those skills in both child and parent, and (4) to promote the most cost-effective logistic arrangements in which those influences can be delivered in the quantity necessary to overcome habits acquired in the past. Conclusions about these should constantly be refined as new information accumulates.

2.2 The therapist's interpersonal skills are very important. The therapist benefits from skills in empathy and reflective listening, the art of persuasion and salesmanship, the use of humor, and playfulness. Another important area for both therapist's and families' mental health is the therapist's ability to let families continue to own their problems while trying to help them with them, that is, the ability to take great pleasure in the growth of people while tolerating the factors beyond the therapist's control that sometimes preclude such growth.

2.3 The therapist also needs facility in assessing, instructing, and modeling each of the psychological skills and parenting skills. This is a very tall order.

3   The Mastery Learning Paradigm versus the Fixed Curriculum Paradigm

The trouble with a session-by-session curriculum is that people come into treatment with far different initial levels of skills, and far different speeds of learning.

Ideally, the therapist uses the mastery learning paradigm, as follows: the task is to (1) assess the present state of skill development of the child with respect to psychological skills, and of the parent with respect to parenting skills; (2) to teach those skills most in need of improvement; (3) to reassess the new state of skill development; and (4) to continue the assess-teach-assess cycle until "criterion level" has been reached for the important skills, or until the limit of effort the family is willing to expend has been met.

In work with groups of parents, or even with individual parents, it is not always possible for the therapist to individualize education to this extent. It is often more efficient to teach all the skills: to use what Strayhorn (1988) has called the "multiskill" rather than the "prescriptive" approach. However, it is still possible to teach parents to use the mastery learning paradigm with themselves: to assess their own level of skill in each area taught, and to continue to read, observe models, practice, and self-monitor until the desired level of skill has been obtained.

4   Types of Sessions Held

4.1 *Information-gathering sessions, with the parents alone;* the first session is usually of this nature.

4.2 *Sessions containing child-directed activity and/or adult-directed activity between therapist and child, with parent watching;* these sorts of sessions have several purposes: (1) for the therapist to get information from and about the child, (2) for the therapist to directly promote skill development in the child, and (3) for the therapist to model interaction skills and specific techniques for the parent.

4.3 *Sessions between therapist and parent, with the child not present;* their purpose is for the therapist to instruct the parent, role-play skills, or get further information from the parent without the child present. The child will benefit by not hearing the negative examples of his own behavior that the parent recounts. The parent will be more comfortable renouncing a position of dogmatic adherence to certain parenting practices if the child is not present.

4.4 *Sessions between therapist and child, with the parent watching videotapes or doing computer-assisted parent instruction, in a separate room;* the therapist may videotape the interaction.

4.5 *Visits during which the parent watches videotapes or uses the com-*

puter program in the waiting room, without having any contact with the therapist; these sessions needn't be scheduled with the therapist, but can be informally arranged with the secretary.

4.6 *Sessions with groups of parents, in which videotapes are shown, instruction is given, interaction techniques are modeled and practiced by role playing, and responses to hypothetical and real vignettes are discussed;* this can be an extremely cost-effective way of doing good. Sometimes the performance anxiety that would preclude role playing in individual work can be reduced by development of group norms.

4.7 *Sessions with groups of children;* stories, songs, dramatic play, and celebration of positive examples of skills may be used in this context. A separate manual exists for these techniques.

4.8 *Sessions between parent and child, with therapist watching or videotaping;* these are the most anxiety-provoking sessions for the parent, and the most difficult for therapists to get themselves to do, but are almost essential to the mastery learning paradigm. Without these the therapist is dependent upon informal observation of the parent and the child together during transition times or in the waiting room, and on the accuracy of the parent's report, to see how parent behavior toward the child is changing. Immediate feedback may be given to the parent via written notes the therapist makes during the session.

4.9 *Sessions with therapist and parent watching a previously made videotape of parent–child interaction or therapist–child interaction, interspersed with discussion of the interaction.*

4.10 *Brief meetings with child and parent;* these are held at the beginning of all sessions the child attends, in which the therapist reviews the entries in the "Positive Behavior Diary" and models how to respond to them (see below).

4.11 *"Don't" sessions;* sessions with the child in the therapist's office, with the parent sitting idly in the waiting room. This type represents a waste of resources, tends to perpetuate the idea that the therapist will fix the child, and is usually the product of the exhaustion or the laziness of the therapist or the parent or both.

5 Philosophy of Work with Child Alone versus with Parent

The child's mental health is influenced in one direction or another, by every person he interacts with, and every minute of interaction. The people the child considers most important are the most influential, all other things equal, and the people whom the child spends more time with are more influential, other things equal. Corollary: it is better to make the parent's relationship with the child a little better than to make the therapist's relationship with the child a lot better. Empirical experience: Our group did two years of intervention, one with children with or without parents, the other teaching parents to do the good things we had done with the children the year previously. The second intervention was much more effective.

Research

6 Research Support of Treatment Method

The most direct research trial of this treatment method took place as reported by Strayhorn and Weidman (1989, 1991). The research design included random assignment to experimental versus control groups; and pre-intervention, postintervention, and one-year follow-up behavior ratings by teachers and parents. Follow-up ratings by teachers were blind. Blind ratings were also made, using videos, of the quality of parent–child interaction at preintervention and postintervention.

Findings included improved child behavior as rated by parents at postintervention, and as rated by teachers at follow-up. Hyperactivity-attention problems were most sensitive to the intervention, according to both sets of raters. Improvement in parent–child interaction on videos was significantly correlated with improvement to postintervention as rated by parents and improvement to follow-up as rated by teachers.

The intervention has been refined since that time, in hopes of increased efficacy.

Training Procedures

7 Assessment of Skills on Priority List for Child

7.1 *Semi Structured Interview of Parent:* "Semi structured" means to listen to the parent talk, be an empathic listener—but when the parent tells a *particular concrete vignette* that illustrates the child's problem behavior, point out to the parent that you want to hear more of those.

> "That's exactly the sort of vignette I'm interested in hearing more of. Can you think of others?"
>
> "Make a mental movie for me: of what he said or did, what you said and did next, what he said or did in response, and so forth."
>
> "Help me to see and hear in my mind exactly what went on."

After hearing a set of problem vignettes, ask about vignettes illustrating positive behavior, illustrating a strength that the child has. *Note:* How easily does the parent come up with these? These are the vignettes the future therapy will be constantly searching for, not just to monitor progress, but to promote it.

7.2 *Inference from Vignettes So Gathered:* The therapist thinks about each vignette: "What skill would have allowed the child to handle this situation better?" The therapist thinks about the set of problem vignettes: "What four or five skills, if improved, would help this child the most?" The therapist refers to the skills axis as a guide in deciding upon the four or five top priority skills. We call this decision the "skills axis diagnosis." The therapist thinks about the set of positive vignettes: "What skills is the child presently strongest in?" The diagnosis of "skill sufficiencies" occurs alongside conclusions about "skill deficiencies."

7.3 The therapist can draw on an array of other assessment tools.

7.3.1 The therapist can interview the teacher, the other parent, or other significant people in the child's life, in the same way, as necessary.

7.3.2 The therapist can require completion and scoring of the Psychological Skills Inventory (Strayhorn, Weidman, & Majumder, 1990) regarding the child's skills—by parents, teachers, significant others, and for children over 8 or so, by the child. In this the respondent rates 22 of the child's psychological skills on a five-point scale from "almost no skill" to "exceptional skill in this." (See list of ancillary materials in appendix 3.4.)

7.3.3 The therapist can observe the parent and child together and makes inferences from the vignettes directly observed. The therapist may make use of the Child Behavior in Play with the Parent Scale. (See list of ancillary materials in appendix 3.4.)

7.3.4 The therapist can interact directly with the child and makes inference from the vignettes directly observed.

8 Assessment of Highest Priority Skills for Parent

8.1 The therapist makes inferences from the same interview(s) mentioned above. During the interview with the parent the therapist frequently asks, "And what was your response to that," when the parent describes something the child did. The therapist also asks more direct questions to the parent about parenting practices.

8.2 The parent fills out the Parent Practices Scale (Strayhorn & Weidman, 1988), a questionnaire that asks parents how frequently they carry out certain desirable and undesirable examples with respect to the skill areas covered here.

8.3 The therapist watches the parent and child interact for a time (15 minutes recommended minimum) and makes inferences from the directly observed vignettes. The therapist may make use of the Parent Behavior in Play with the Child Scale (see the list of ancillary materials included in appendix 3.4).

8.4 The therapist notes the child's behavior in the therapist's direct interaction with the child, and makes inferences by noting the similarity or difference in the child's behavior with the parent and with the therapist.

8.5 *Caveat:* Inferences about the skills of parent and child, and about the child's behavior with any individual, are only as valid as the sample size of observations. Thus conclusions are more tentative at first, and gradually gain strength as the number of observations increases. However, it is not necessary to come to an absolutely firm conclusion about what the highest priority skills are before beginning to teach the skills. It is better to begin teaching skills, even if they are low priority, than to prolong assessment to the point of wasting time. Working on low priority skills at least sets up the learning framework that can be used with higher priority skills.

9 Teaching Parents the Theory of the Skills

The therapist teaches theory by using the methods of influence matrix, briefly, as follows:

> "We don't want to think just in terms of reducing negative behavior. We want to increase the skills that are the opposites of those negative behaviors. For example, the opposite of tantrums may be the skill of frustration tolerance. The opposite of aggression may be the skill of taking pleasure in making people feel good. The opposite of inattentiveness may be the skill of sustaining attention to words and ideas. Both you and the child will experience it as much more fun to teach or learn a skill than to stamp out a negative behavior, since there are some very fun ways of teaching children skills, and I intend to teach them to you. But the main idea is that there are certain skills that are very useful, or necessary, for productivity, happiness, and psychological health, and there are certain methods that one person can use to help another person develop those skills. We want to pick the skills that are most important for your child to learn, and use the methods that will most help him learn them. We'll constantly revise our choices as we get more information. . . . "

10 Dealing with the Parent Who Wants the Therapist to "Fix" the Child While the Parent Waits

If the parent has this attitude, the therapist undertakes as a first priority a gentle strategy of explaining why, although this strategy has been tried, it usually doesn't work as well as teaching the parent to provide positive influences.

10.1 The therapist emphasizes that the parent is, and should be, a much more important person to the child than the therapist, and points out that the parent spends much more time with the child than the therapist can. The therapist explains the concept that the child is being influenced all the time, especially by important people, and to settle for an hour a week of influence in the therapist's office as the only influence the therapy uses would be to give the family a watered-down and rather weak therapy.

10.2 The therapist avoids making the parent feel bad about "causing" the child's misbehaviors or fears or unhappiness. Many times no one knows, or is able to find out, why and how a child got into some unfortunate habits. "Temperament" is sometimes an explanation of sorts. Many times the philosophy is that the degree of parenting skill that would suffice with most children will, for whatever reason, not suffice with this child, and for this reason we need to teach the parent to become more of an expert in dealing with children than most parents ever become. At other times, the parents have done clearly harmful things; even in these circumstances, the best use of energy is in new learning, not in negative emotion about the past.

11 Teaching the Parent a Reinforcement Program for *Child's Highest Priority Skills*

11.1 The therapist helps the parent to recognize the positive examples when they occur. The therapist constructs or retrieves a written list of concrete examples of skills for the parent to post and frequently refer to, and uses this list in role playing or fantasy practice exercises described below. See appendix 3.5 for sample list of concrete examples of skills.

11.2 The therapist teaches the parent the principle that attention, approval, and excitement are the best reinforcers for the child's positive examples of skills. Tangible reinforcers tend to wear off, and also tend to promote haggling behavior in the child. Having the child formally "earn" outings with the parent passes up an opportunity for the parent to model freely giving, and sometimes leads the child to devalue or reject time with the parent to avoid feeling controlled. However, the parent's attention, given in a natural, informal way, remains a potent reinforcer over the long run. This is not surprising when one considers that over the course of evolution young children have been able to survive without almost all tangible objects, but not without adult attention.

11.3 The therapist teaches the parent to use immediate attention, excitement, and approval in response to positive examples of the high priority skills. *Exercise:* The parent and therapist look at the list of concrete positive examples they have constructed. The therapist models how to respond when the child has done a positive example. The parent practices responding in a similar way to the same or other examples. The responses do not have to be "praise," but can be descriptions or classifications of the child's behavior, spoken in a positive tone. Thus not only, "I like it when you share your toys!," but also, "Hey, Tommy wanted to play with the plane, and you let him use it! That was a kind act!"

11.3.1 *Tones of Approval Exercise:* Therapist first explains that for young children, the tones of voice are much more important than the semantic content of statements to the child. The therapist demonstrates that the child would probably rather hear the nearly meaningless phrase, "Hey, wow, what do you know" spoken in a tone of large approval, than to hear "You just did something extremely wonderful" spoken in a monotone. Then the therapist and parent practice with phrases like "Look at that," "There goes another one," or "Look what you did!" First the therapist says phrases with either a neutral tone (monotone,) with small approval, or with large approval, and the parent discriminates which tone was used. Then the parent practices saying all the phrases with tones of neutrality, small approval, and large approval. For many parents the problem is attaining the enthusiasm of tones of large approval. If necessary the therapist models a tone of large approval and asks the parent to mimic it. This exercise is much more comfortable for parents when done in groups, when tones of large approval can be practiced in choruses and chants instead of (or in addition to) putting one person on the spot.

11.3.2 *Differential Use of Excitement Exercise:* This exercise might also be called "Stop yelling about the bad behavior and start yelling about the good." The therapist explains that for many children, arousing excitement of any sort in the parent is reinforcing for the child. If this is the case, anger and exasperation that lead to loud, fast, high-pitched tones can be rewarding when they are meant to be punishing. In the exercise, the therapist gives the parents a list of both reprimands and approving statements. The therapist models, and the parents practice, reading the approving statements with higher volume, pitch, and tempo, and the reprimands with lower volume, pitch, and tempo.

11.4 Teach parents to "talk behind the child's back" in child's earshot about the positive examples the parents see. For example, when one parent tells another about a positive example, in the child's presence, the child is often greatly reinforced.

11.5 *The Positive Behavior Diary:* The parent gets a notebook and records, in brief paragraphs, the positive things the child has done, with dates. Any time the child wants the diary read to him, the parent enthusiastically obliges. The parent is asked to bring the positive behavior diary to the therapist each session. The therapist can (1) verbally chat about the examples, (2) put on a modeling play about one or more of the examples (see section on putting on modeling plays), or (3) make an illustrated modeling story from one or more of the examples (see section on making real-life modeling stories).

11.5.1 Teach parents to be concrete and specific. Thus "Thursday, May 20: He was good all afternoon and was helpful to me" is an entry that is better than nothing, but too abstract to elicit a clear image in anyone's mind. A more concrete example is "Friday, May 21. At the beginning of supper when we sat down at the table he smiled and said to me, 'Wow, you made all this! Thanks for getting this together for us!'"

11.5.2 Teach parents to look for positive examples of all the skills on the high priority list for the child, including the more subtle interaction skills. Most parents can recognize the child's helping with a household chore as a positive example of helping, but some become overly focussed on this sort of example and miss the others.

11.6 *The "Nightly Review":* The parent sits down with the child at bedtime and reviews the positive examples of the day, verbally. "I want to think back on some of the things I liked that happened today. When we were in such a hurry to drive to pick up your brother, and you got right into the car with your seat belt on and were even waiting for me, I thought, 'Wow, she's helping the cause! That's teamwork!'" The task of achieving concreteness of examples is important for the nightly review as well as the positive behavior diary.

11.6.1 *Variation:* Act out positive examples with toy people rather than recounting them purely verbally. The child's positive example is a "modeling play," put on as are the modeling plays I have written.

11.6.2 *Variation:* Making a "real-life modeling story" from the vignette. See section 17 on making real-life modeling stories. The adult writes down the vignette, one or two lines per page, for one to four pages, and the adult and child illustrate them and staple them together down the side. Then the story becomes a "modeling story" to be read to the child whenever the child wants, just as the stories I have written.

11.6.3 *Variation:* Child spontaneously remembers more positive examples of his own behavior, and tells them to the parent. *Variation:* Child remembers positive examples of parent's behavior, tells them to the parent.

11.6.4 *"Don't" Variations:* Don't do the nightly review by sitting down and grilling the child, for example, "OK, tell me what good things you've done." The parent should take on the task of remembering. If the child remembers, the child should do this either spontaneously or with one gentle invitation to the child to recall additional examples. Don't recall the negative examples with the child. Save conversation about them for another occasion, or forget them. The parent is to include in the nightly review only those vignettes that the parent would like to be repeated. This is sometimes hard. Finally, don't lie to the child that he had a great day when he didn't. The parent can say, "This was a very hard day. But in any day some things we do are better than others, and the thing you did that I liked best today was. . . ."

11.7 The therapist models for the parent how to do all of the above, in the therapist's sessions with the child.

11.7.1 The therapist models for parent by posting on the wall a written list of the desirable concrete behaviors that are examples of the skills, the therapist will be watching for; the therapist reads over the list very quickly in the parent's presence.

11.7.2. During session of dramatic play, story reading, conversation, and so on, with the child, the therapist watches carefully for positive examples of skills. The therapist responds immediately with attention, excitement, and approval. If the parent is watching the session, the parent gets the model of how to use immediate attention, excitement, and approval.

11.7.3 During the session the therapist takes a piece of paper or a spiral notebook and writes down positive examples, modeling for the parent how to use the Positive Behavior Diary.

11.7.4 If the parent was out of the room watching videotapes or doing the computer exercises during the therapist's session, the therapist models for the parent how to "talk behind the child's back" to the parent about the positive examples.

11.7.5 The therapist does a "session review" with the child, in the parent's presence, using any or all of the variations noted above, modeling for the parent how to do the nightly review.

11.7.6 In looking for positive examples, the therapist includes the positive examples the child's fantasy characters have done, as well as the examples the child has done in real life; a clear distinction must be made in recounting the examples.

12 Teaching Parents to Discontinue Unnecessary Commands

12.1 *Instruction:* The therapist sells the parent on the value of discontinuing unnecessary commands. Lobitz and Johnson's 1975 study giving evidence of the connection between unnecessary commands and misbehavior is useful to recount to parents. In this study the experimenters asked parents to make their children's behavior worse; the parents successfully did so. The parents did so by issuing a large number of stern commands.

12.2 *Discrimination Exercise:* Which commands are absolutely necessary, which are not? The therapist reads to the parent from a list of vignettes in which parents give commands to children; together they decide which are necessary and which aren't. (See *Training Exercises for Parents of Young Children,* in ancillary materials list in appendix 3.4.)

12.3 *Home Monitoring Exercise:* The therapist asks the parent to spend time at home with child, for an hour or two, and to keep track of each command by writing it down. The parent is to reflect later upon: (1) How did doing the exercise affect the rate of commands? (2) Which commands were necessary, which not? (3) If doing the exercise itself cut down the unnecessary commands, was there an effect on the child's behavior?

12.4 *Exercise for a Parent–Child Session in the Therapist's Office:* "What I'd like for you to do is to spend some time talking and playing and reading with your child, while I watch. I'll keep track of every command or request that you give to the child during this time. Afterward, we'll think about which were necessary and which were not, whether doing the exercise in itself cut down the unnecessary commands, and if it did, what the effect was on the child's behavior."

If the parent feels a command was necessary, and the therapist feels that it was unnecessary, the therapist usually does not just say, "That command was unnecessary." The therapist says, "What do you think would have happened if you had not given that command?" The therapist gets the parent's prediction, and then says, "We can't know for sure. My prediction is that _____ would have happened. Next time, you might try not giving that command, and seeing what happens, as an experiment."

13 Teaching Parents to Use "Stimulus Control" with Respect to the Child's Play Environment

Early childhood educators give great emphasis to the nature of the physical surroundings, the environment, that children spend time in. Parenting courses have underemphasized this element.

13.1 Instruct parent about the simple underlying principles of arranging children's environments.

13.1.1 It is natural, right, and normal for a child to want to explore whatever objects are within his reach, especially those he has not explored before.

13.1.2 Providing a child with something he *wants* to explore, *is safe* for him to explore, and *can learn something* from exploring, will save *hundreds* of commands that the child not explore something else.

Put another way, You can quit telling a child to "come back" and to "stay out of that" and to "put that down" so often if you can provide the child something fun and good to play with.

13.1.3 If at all possible, have all those things that are too valuable, or not safe, for the child to explore, out of the child's view and reach where they will not tempt the child.

13.1.4 It is extremely useful to have some high shelves or cabinets so that you can put things out of a child's reach when you want him to pay attention to something else. To put it another way, if you want the child to focus on one thing, you need to put the other temptations out of reach, and ideally out of sight.

13.1.5 Children do thrive on novelty. Supplying novel things for children to fiddle with and absorb their attention is an endeavor less expensive than either psychotherapists or divorce lawyers.

13.1.6 The toys that hold young children's interest the longest tend to be those where the child learns not just to explore the toy, but where the child uses the toy as a vehicle for his own imagination. For example, with sets of toy people and houses and cars, when the child learns to have the people interact in pretend play, the child is now playing not just with the toys, but with his own fantasies.

13.1.7 There are two ways of manipulating the stimulus situations for interaction with children. In the first, the plan is that the adult and child will interact one on one, and the stimulus scene is meant to encourage a focus on one activity at a time. In this case, the ideal setting is to have various units of materials on shelves or on top of file cabinets, out of reach, where the adult can fetch one set, use it with the child, put it away, and then use the second set. In the second case, the plan is that the child will occupy himself without adult one on one attention; the adult is nearby but accomplishing other tasks. In this case, the ideal setting is a number of "areas" with objects conducive to constructive activity, similar to those in preschools.

13.2 Help parents consider arranging nooks and crannies of the home so that the following "areas" are part of the total set of stimulus temptations for the child. In the latter case they compete more successfully with knocking over vases, climbing up bookshelves, bouncing off couch backs, pulling dogs' tails, and provoking siblings.

13.2.1 A block area. I suggest blocks made of sponge, not wood.

13.2.2 A dramatic play area, with toy people, houses, and the like. This can be combined with the block area.

13.2.3 An art area, with child-size table and chairs, lots of blank paper, and crayons or colored pens.

13.2.4 A listening area, with a tape recorder, with headphones to avoid disturbing others, with carefully selected audiotapes and audiotape-book combinations. The audiotapes should contain both stories and songs.

13.2.5 A videotape viewing area, if expenses allow it, with a machine without access to television, with carefully selected videotapes.

13.2.6 A large motor area, preferably fenced in or otherwise secure, with tricycles, jump ropes, things to climb on, a ball to kick and run after, and the like.

13.2.7 If expenses allow, a computer area with carefully selected educational software.

13.2.8 Conspicuous by its absence from this list is a television allowing free access to commercial channels.

14 Teach Parents Not to Inadvertently Reinforce Negative Behavior

14.1 Adult attention and "giving in" are reinforcing to almost all young children; adult excitement is reinforcing to most of them. Parents must strive not to reinforce negative behaviors with attention, excitement, or "giving in."

14.2 *Exercise for Parents:* The parent examines examples of vignettes where someone reinforced undesirable behavior by giving in to the child or increasing the child's power in response to negative behavior. Are there any real-life examples like these examples?

14.3 *Mantra for Parents:* I will not respond to the child's unpleasant behavior by giving him what he wants.

15 Using "Differential Attention" as a Positive Influence on the Child

15.1 *Definition of "Differential Attention"*: The adult pays a good deal more attention to one sort of behavior than to another, and thus influences the child to do more of the type that is attended to. The direction of this influence can be desirable or undesirable.

15.2 Using differential attention will require skill in the art of ignoring negative behavior.

15.2.1 When to ignore negative behavior: When the behavior is not harmful or dangerous enough to require intervention, when there is a possibility that adult attention would reinforce it, or as a first-line response to see what will happen, with the possibility of reprimands or punishment or other responses always available for the future. "Ignore it and maybe it will go away" often works.

15.2.2 But the decision is not so simple as just whether to ignore or not to ignore. The parent can choose to respond to behaviors, with varying degrees of attentiveness. *Example:* The parent and child are in a store, and the child stops and picks up an object off the shelf, which must be put back. Parental response 1: "Put that back. You can't just take things from shelves like that. It goes right back there, put it up now. No, not there, over there." Parental response 2: Parent takes the object and puts it back, saying "This has to go back . . . Would you like to help me carry these things to the check-out counter? It's time for us to take them up to the folks and pay for them, and then go out the door."

15.2.3 *How to Ignore Negative Behavior:* Standing silent, glaring at the child, is not ignoring. Getting interested in something else is more fun and more productive.

15.3 *Exercise:* For a list of hypothetical situations wherein differential attention is working in the wrong direction, try to construct a plan whereby it can work in the right direction. Here are a few samples:

Situation 1, Bedtime Problems: The child is having trouble getting to sleep. On nights when the child can't sleep, and comes and asks for the parents, the parent sits in the child's room and rubs the child's back, or sings to the child, or lies next to the child until the child can get to sleep. On nights when the child can get to sleep, the adult says a quick good night and goes about his or her business.

Situation 2, Dressing Problems: The child is having big troubles with getting dressed in the morning. The child gets dressed just before leaving for school, after eating breakfast and chatting with his or her parent for a while. On mornings when the child gets dressed quickly, off he goes to school. On mornings when the child dawdles and refuses to get dressed, the parent spends a lot of time prodding and pleading and arguing with the child to get dressed before the child goes to school.

Situation 3, Arguing: A child is an unpleasant arguer. If someone says that black is black, the child will argue that it is white. When the child is argumentative, the adult will spend lots of time trying to show the child that the child is mistaken, and they will talk back and forth, sometimes with much excitement. When the child is not argumentative, they tend to have much less conversation, and much less animated conversation.

Situation 4, Sibling Hostility: The brother and the sister fight with each other. When they start yelling at each other, the parent will come from the other room and say, "Hey, what's going on here?" and try to intervene. When they are playing quietly together, the parent will leave them alone and take care of his or her own business.

Sample new plans to harness differential attention in a positive way:

Situation 1, New Plan for Bedtime Problems: The parents work out a routine of doing the nightly review and reading stories each night before bed. Then once it is "Good night and lights out," if the child gets out of bed the only attention the child gets is to be directed or led back to the bedroom and the bed. If the child does not get out of bed after "Good night and lights out," the parents hold a celebration in the morning for the child, and talks a lot about the child's accomplishment.

Situation 2, New Plan for Dressing Problems: The parent invites the child to get dressed first thing in the morning after washing, before breakfast and before chatting with the parent. There will be neither breakfast, much chatting, or television until the child is dressed. If the child starts getting dressed, the parent stays and chats with the child in a pleasant way, perhaps "tracking and describing" the dressing part of the time. If the child refuses to get dressed, the parent sets a timer and tells the child that if he isn't dressed by the time the timer goes off, the child will quickly be physically dressed by the parent. While the timer is running the parent ignores the child. If the child isn't dressed when the timer goes off, the parent physically dresses the child without saying much.

Situation 3, New Plan for Arguing: When the child argues in an unpleasant way about things like what somebody did or what makes night and day, the parent does not respond, or perhaps empathizes with the child's interest in the subject. If the child has anything close to a pleasant discussion or conversation with the adult, without arguing, the adult responds in a very animated way. If the child argues about something the child is asked to do, the adult refuses to argue, but either physically guides the child to comply or imposes a consequence for noncompliance, doing either with a minimum of interchange between adult and child. If the child complies, the adult is very animatedly grateful.

Situation 4, New Plan for Sibling Hostility: When the two children are playing nicely with each other, the parent goes over and sits down with them and watches, and makes an occasional comment without being too intrusive or interrupting the activity. When they start getting angry at each other, the adult leaves the scene and takes care of some business. If they actually hit one another, the adult uses a "time out" with very little talk about the incident. The parent talks about the nice things they did for each other in the nightly review.

16 Prepare the Parent to Learn "Mutually Gratifying Activities" with the Child

Story reading, doing modeling plays, doing modeling songs, doing nondirective play and conversation, doing dramatic play are all forms of mutually gratifying activities.

16.1 Some parents will need an explanation as to why mutually gratifying activities are important. "I didn't come here to learn to entertain the child and myself; I came to get him to listen better."

16.1.1 The theory is that reciprocity is a very important principle in all human relations: you tend to get what you give. The more the adult can do things with the child that are fun for both of them, the more the child will tend to do things with the adult that are fun for both of them. Noncompliance, hostility, defiance, aggression, and other "externalizing" behaviors on the part of the child are by definition those that are not mutually gratifying. Cooperation, kindness, and positive affect become habitual when mutually gratifying activities are frequently done.

16.1.2 Stories, plays, songs, exploratory play, conversation, and dramatic play are "versatile vehicles" whereby any of the psychological skills the child needs to learn can be modeled and practiced in fantasy. Thus when each of these media is used by parent and child, there are abundant mechanisms whereby positive models may be sent to the child in a way that is pleasant to the child.

17 The Therapist Teaches the Parent to Use Modeling Stories to Present Positive Models to the Child

17.1 Explain to parents the power of modeling, the data to the effect that modeling through fiction can influence behavior, just as can modeling in real life. A crucial event is the child's storing the adaptive pattern in the child's memory bank.

17.2 Teach guidelines for making story reading fun with a young child.

17.2.1 Pick a time when the child is ready—when there are not other distractions in the environment, when the child is interested, preferably when the child asks the adult to read. If all else fails, use the following tactic at bedtime: "Would you rather have the lights out now, or would you rather hear some more stories?"

17.2.2 Pick a story that is short enough so that the child's attention span will not be exceeded.

17.2.3 Read with enthusiasm and drama in the tone of voice, perhaps using different voices for different characters.

17.2.4 Give the child frequent eye contact while reading.

17.2.5 If the child wants to chat during the story, welcome this digression; don't punish it.

17.2.6 If the child's attention wanders away from the adult, the adult should stop reading and wait, starting back with enthusiasm if the child returns, thus using differential attention to reinforce the child's continuing interest in the story. If the child continues not to be interested, terminate the reading for the time being. Maybe get interested in whatever the child is interested in. The parent does not define success as being able to get the child to pay attention any time the parent wants the child to pay attention, but rather that the story-reading is a mutually gratifying activity when it does occur. If this is true then it will tend to occur more and more often.

17.2.7 Allow the child to cuddle with the adult or sit in the adult's lap if it is appropriate for the nature of the relationship (for example, if the adult is the parent).

17.2.8 Use a tone of approval to signal the end of the story, by saying, for example, "And that's the end of the story!" This reinforces the child's paying attention until the end.

17.3 Use role playing to practice the above principles, particularly in group sessions with parents. *Procedure:* Practice using none of these principles, practice using all of them. The reader and the person being read to get to experience first hand what the difference feels like.

17.4 *Definition of "Modeling Stories":* For young children, the protagonist models thought, feeling, or behavior constituting a psychological skill useful for the child; nobody, including any antagonist, models a negative example that is by any stretch of the imagination attractive or imitation-inspiring; for the youngest children, no characters model any negative examples at all. The protagonist may or may not be rewarded by the external environment for the skillful pattern; the protagonist usually rewards himself or herself internally. I have written some 150 illustrated stories and some 200 nonillustrated stories meant to model psychological skills. (See list of ancillary materials in appendix 3.4.)

17.5 *Selection of Modeling Stories for a Given Child:* Take into account the child's vocabulary level, and attention span. Intersperse stories modeling high priority skills with stories modeling other skills. If only high priority skills are modeled, the child may feel threatened. In general, however, children like stories that are clearly meant to model positive behavior, and the didactic nature of them does not put them off in the slightest.

17.6 Send modeling stories home with the parent and the child (give, lend, or sell) and encourage regular and repetitive reading to the child.

17.7 Teach parent to encourage (by attribution and reinforcement) without pushing the child, the child's pretending to read the story to the adult, and retelling the story while looking at the pictures. This promotes "fantasy practice" of the positive pattern as well as modeling.

17.8 The therapist may send home with the child a videotape of the modeling stories, as an adjunctive exposure to them. (See ancillary materials available in appendix 3.4.)

17.9 *Acting Out the Modeling Stories:* The adult and the child, or two or more children, first read and listen to the whole story. Then they start over, and pick who will be which characters. They read a page, then act it out; read another page, then act it out.

This technique is especially useful with groups of children, where the story may be projected on a screen with an overhead projector. Children volunteer for the various parts in the story, and act it out as the adult reads the captions and displays the pictures.

17.10 The therapist teaches the parent to use "real-life modeling stories" with the child. Therapist models the technique with the child, and encourages parent to do the same. The technique is as follows:

17.10.1 The adult gets in mind a vignette of a psychologically skillful pattern the child enacted. This can be by: (1) directly observing it from the child, (2) listening to the child tell about the vignette, or (3) listening to another adult (parent, teacher) tell about the vignette.

17.10.2 The parent may be tempted to choose a vignette in which the protagonist does a negative behavior and gets negative consequences. This temptation should be avoided; the rule is that all the actions portrayed in modeling stories are imitation-worthy.

17.10.3 The adult writes down captions, usually in one to four pages, with one or two lines of writing on each page, that tell the story of the positive example.

17.10.4 If the child has a long enough attention span and likes to draw, the child can illustrate each page; to the extent that these are not true, the adult can help achieve quicker gratification by drawing illustrations himself or herself. The resemblance of the drawing, by child or adult, to the real-life thing can be almost nonexistent and the illustration will still serve its purpose.

17.10.5 If there is access to a photocopier, the product can be photocopied, and one copy kept in archives by the therapist and one copy taken home by the child. Whether or not this is done, the story is stapled with about three staples down the left side so that it will open like a book, and then is read like any other modeling story.

17.10.6 The therapist monitors the extent to which the parent and child use this technique at home by asking to see any real-life modeling stories they illustrate.

18   The Converse of the Positive Use of Modeling Stories

Eliminate as much as possible from the child's diet of models those presenting violence, hostility, sarcasm, and other "psychologically unskillful" patterns.

18.1 The first task is for the therapist to familiarize herself with the literature on the effects of media violence, so as not to be misled by the discredited catharsis hypothesis and other theories contradicting the basic finding that people imitate what they see (See Comstock & Paik, 1991; Centerwall, 1989; Liebert, Sprafkin, & Davidson, 1982).

18.2 The second task is that the therapist communicate this research data to the parent, or both parents if there are two, going into the details of studies according to the interest level and educational level of the parent. The parents then make their own decision as to what they want to do about violent entertainment in the home. The following suggestions are for parents who do decide to effect a major reduction in violent entertainment.

18.3 The parents must raise their consciousness about the degree of violence in entertainment. A useful exercise is counting the violent acts in even G-rated Disney classics, and pondering the consequences of injury and death if those acts were carried out in real life. A slapstick blow on the head could result in concussion and permanent seizure disorder. The Motion Picture Association of America's rating system is *not* a sufficient guide to the extent of violence in entertainment. The PG-rated *Indiana Jones and the Temple of Doom* contains a sequence of a person having his heart ripped out before he is lowered screaming into a flaming pit. Idolizing violent sports heroes, such as boxers, violent hockey players, and violent football players also falls into category of revering violent entertainment figures; consciousness-raising about these pursuits entails changing the value system of a vast segment of the population.

18.4 The parents immediately reduce or cut out their own use of violent entertainment. This is a major sacrifice for some parents, and if they are able to do it, the therapist should recognize them as exceptional.

18.5 For a child who has problems with physical aggression, and is in the habit of watching shows or videos modeling violence, the parent sits down with the child and explains that violence is sometimes a problem in the family, and it's probably the biggest problem in the world. The family has recently become aware that entertainment violence tends to promote violence. Therefore, the violent shows and videos are being permanently removed.

18.6 The parent is careful, however, not to present the boycott of violent entertainment as the withdrawal of a good thing that should be a privilege and a pleasure for everyone. The parent takes some time to explain that violence is a big problem in our society, that violent entertainment promotes this problem, and that the family is trying to boycott violent entertainment out of a spirit of not wanting to "vote" for the continuation of a major cause of such a bad problem. In other words, the parent attempts to convert the child to a social activist stance rather than to attribute to the child a high vulnerability to violent behavior.

18.7 In order to decrease the child's sense of loss, the parents make available nonviolent videos that are interesting for the child. One example is a tape of modeling stories, plays, and songs (see appendix 3.4).

18.8 Ways to reduce access to television: use a combination video player and television, without the television antenna plugged in. Some televisions have programmable access to various channels. Low-tech solution: put strapping tape over the channel changer.

19 Therapist Teaches Parent to use "Modeling Plays" with the Child

19.1 *Definition of a "Modeling Play":* Like a modeling story in plot. Instead of being read to the child and illustrated on paper, the adult acts it out for the child and illustrates it with the movement of toy people and other props.

19.2 Therapist explains to the parent the rationale for this technique. Like modeling stories, the plays get the positive examples into the child's memory bank. They model via a medium that the child can use for fantasy practice of the positive patterns, through dramatic play. The modeling plays can be constructed quickly and easily, although they require more initiative and energy for the adult to put on than the stories.

19.3 *Suitable Toy People:* Playmobil, Fisher-Price, Lego, Duplo, others. Playmobil has a complete black family.

19.4 *How the Plays are Put On:* Adult reads the play, gets the plot in mind, gets the characters and ad libs the lines while moving the characters according to the action of the drama. Adult does not read the play to the child, or refer to the script while putting on the play for the child.

19.5 Guidelines for how to put on a modeling play in a way that a child will like are similar to the guidelines for modeling stories: choose a good time, choose a short enough play, keep the pace fast, use enthusiasm in the voice(s), give the child in the audience eye contact, use a tone of approval to announce the end.

19.6 Similar guidelines should be used for the choice of skills to model. Model the skills the child needs to work on the most, but intersperse them among examples of other skills including some that are strengths for the child.

19.7 As with the modeling stories, if the child wants to reciprocate for the adult by putting on a similar play for the adult, this is to be greatly reinforced by the adult's enthusiastic response.

19.8 The therapist shows the parent how to create "real-life modeling plays."

19.8.1 The adult gets the positive example in mind from chatting with the child, another adult, or observing the example directly. Any entry in the Positive Example Diary is already a plot for a modeling play.

19.8.2 The play can be put on at the time of the nightly review, or at any other time. It is useful to put on plays of positive examples done previously, not just on the day of the play, so that the child realizes that the positive examples are remembered for a long period of time.

19.8.3 One technique is to intersperse real-life modeling plays among prewritten ones, to surprise the child with an incident from his own life.

19.8.4 Another technique is useful for groups of children: Watch their behavior in free play, reconvene the group, put on real-life modeling plays, and then have children guess who was the protagonist in real life.

19.9 For skills that the child particularly needs, for which there is not a good prewritten modeling play, the therapist may write modeling plays. The therapist can decide, for any individual child, how much to make the protagonist's life circumstances resemble the child's.

20 The Therapist Uses "Modeling Songs" and Dances with the Child and Teaches the Parent to Do the Same

20.1 *Definition of a "Modeling Song"*: One whose lyrics model a pattern of thoughts, feelings, or behaviors constituting a positive example of a psychological skill. Some have been written by Joe Strayhorn; many others exist "out there," interspersed among not-so-positive models.

20.2 *Goals of the Song-and-Dance Activities*: (1) to allow the lyrics of the modeling songs to be stored in the child's memory bank, with a positive emotional association; (2) to promote fantasy rehearsals, through the songs, of the adaptive patterns the songs depict; and (3) to have mutually gratifying activities for the adult and child.

20.3 The therapist may engage in any or all of the following activities with the modeling songs, and teach the parent to do the same:

20.3.1 *Songs as Background Music*: The adult simply puts on a tape of the modeling songs to play in the background while the adult and the child are doing something else, so as to get the melodies of the songs into the child's memory.

20.3.2 *The Dance and Freeze Activity:* This is like musical chairs, only without the competition. I have done it with as few as 1 and as many as 25 children at once. The adult plays the modeling songs on a tape recorder held in his hand. When the music plays, all dance around vigorously. When the adult presses the pause button and the music stops, all sit or lie down on the floor and become perfectly still and quiet before the music starts up again.

The goals of this activity are to get the modeling songs into the memories of the children, to practice voluntarily regulating the level of activity and arousal (getting "revved up" and "revved down" at will, a subunit of the skill of relaxation), and having fun together.

20.3.3 *Putting on a Song and Dancing as a Celebration:* When something good happens, including when someone reports a positive example on the part of the child, the adult responds by putting on a tape of the modeling songs and dancing around, to the amazement of the child. Or, the adult invites the child to dance around also.

20.3.4 *Singing the Songs with the Child or Children:* The adult may wish to play the audiotape as accompaniment, or accompany with an instrument, or have no accompaniment at all. Singing a song or two is a great way to start out a group gathering, including a group of two or three. This can be done with or without free-style dancing to the songs.

20.3.5 *Letting the Child Strum:* If the adult plays a guitar or autoharp, the adult fingers the chords, while letting the child strum a constant rhythm; this is then used to accompany the singing of the songs. The child has the experience of playing a musical instrument.

20.3.6 *Talking with the Child About How the Lyrics of the Songs Apply When the Child Has Done a Positive Model:* In order to make the connection between the song lyrics and real life more apparent, the adult may sing the lyrics to the applicable song, or say to the child, "You did something just like the song talks about . . . " For example, the child exhibits an example of frustration tolerance, and the adult refers to the words of "I Can Take It."

21 The Therapist Teaches the Parents the Techniques of Nondirective, Responsive Interaction

Nondirective, responsive interaction allows "child-directed activity": tracking and describing; telling about one's own experience; empathic reflections; follow-up questions; prompt, wait, and hurry; and ping-pong interactions.

21.1 Some adults need to be enlightened as to the reason for using techniques that allow the child to "follow his own lead." Why do these? This can be the topic of a conversation between the therapist and the parent. Reasons are as follows:

21.1.1 There seems to be a "hard-wired" need for children to interact in some way with an adult. If the major interaction patterns in the adult's repertoire are directives, the child in order to bring those out will tend to do those behaviors that elicit directives, for example, provocations and unpleasant behaviors. On the other hand, if the adult's interactive repertoire contains lots of ways to comment upon the normal play of the child and the normal ranging of thoughts and ideas of the child, there will not be such a need of the child to provoke the adult.

21.1.2 The child tends to give back to the adult the types of interactions the adult gives to the child. If the interactions the adult gives tend to say to the child, "That's interesting, what you are doing," and "Here's a thought I have about the thought you just told me," and "If I understand you right, here's what you're thinking and feeling," then the adult will get these back from the child. These are inherently more pleasant and more conducive to positive interaction than more directive interactions.

21.1.3 Other children tend to like children who can talk with them without bossing them around. Thus the nondirective techniques tend to model for children how to be more popular with peers.

21.1.4 The nondirective techniques help the parent to understand fully where the child is coming from, what is going on in the mind of the child. They promote the child's communicating with the adult. They give the adult the knowledge with which to know how to relate to the child. They keep the adult from sending solutions to problems before the adult really understands the problem.

21.1.5 It is usually pleasurable for people to have someone attend to them in a nondirective way. It is gratifying for most people to experience someone else's pure interest, without being bossed in any way. For this reason, many adults will pay therapists to listen to them, even if their problems are not being solved. If the child and adult can learn nondirective interaction with one another, they add to their repertoire another "mutually gratifying activity." Mutually gratifying activities are essential to positive relationships.

21.2 Teach the skill of "tracking and describing."

21.2.1 *Definition of "Tracking and Describing:"* The adult observes the child's activity (tracks) and puts the observed actions into words (describes) with a tone of interest.

21.2.2 *Examples of Tracking and Describing:* "There go the blocks on top of each other. They're making a house. Mr. Farmer is going into the house. Looks like you're going to bed, Mr. Farmer. Here comes the tractor, into the house. Hey, Mr. Farmer, you're through with your nap, and up for a tractor ride, huh? There you go. Wow, the tractor is going up to a very high place."

21.2.3 *An Exercise to Teach Tracking and Describing:* The therapist sits with back turned to the parent and child, and just listens without watching, while the child plays with toys. The parent's tracking and describing should enable the therapist to know what is going on.

21.2.4 Combine the concept of tracking and describing with that of differential attention. *Exercise:* Watch and participate in a child's play, and selectively track and describe, with a tone of approval, the more positive elements of the play, and be silent immediately after the less positive elements. (More positive elements can be examples of the skills of using imagination, sustaining attention, being kind, experiencing glee, tolerating frustration, and many others.)

21.3 Teach the skill of "telling about one's own experience."

21.3.1 *Definition of "Telling About One's Own Experience":* The adult talks to the child, telling about his own thoughts, feelings, acts, especially present reactions to present events, and also past experiences. The adult avoids appealing to the child for support, but selects the more upbeat portion of the adult's experience to tell about.

21.3.2 *Examples of Telling About One's Own Experience:* "Before you came in, I was just looking at those people out the window. I think they're trying to carry that piano onto a truck. I moved a piano one time. They're really heavy. But we put it onto something with wheels so that we could roll it. It was called a dolly. That made it a whole lot easier to move."

"I got the chance to do something nice to someone this morning. Someone was walking around outside looking for a certain place, and they asked me how to get there. I took out my pencil and this little notebook I carry, and drew them a map that told them how to get there. I think it helped them!"

21.3.3 *Reason for Telling About One's Own Experience:* Many adults, when they want to hear about a child's experience, do so by grilling the child with questions. This usually makes a reticent child only more reticent. Rather than commanding a child to talk about himself, in telling about one's own experience the adult *models* how to tell about oneself. When the channels are open for both people to tell about themselves, a very important avenue for a mutually gratifying activity has been achieved. Plus, the adult gets a window on what the child is thinking and feeling; this assists in all decisions about what to do with the child.

21.3.4 *Method of Teaching Parent:* After talking about the above with the parent, the therapist and parent think of parts of their own experience that would and would not be appropriate to tell the child about. Then, when the therapist is in a session with the child, he tells about his own experience in the parent's presence. The effects on the ensuing conversation are noted. In future sessions, the parent is encouraged to tell the child about his or her own experience.

21.4 Teach the skill of using empathic reflections. Empathic reflections have also been called paraphrases, active listening, and checking out.

21.4.1 *Definition of "Empathic Reflections":* The adult listens to the child's words and attends to the child's expressions and gestures, and states back to the child what the adult perceives the child to be thinking and feeling. The reflection can sometimes be a question, and sometimes a statement.

The adult restates what the child means, not just what the child says. For example, a reflection of "You're a pig!" would not be "You think that I'm a pig," but "It sounds like you're angry at me," or "It sounds like you're wanting to hurt my feelings," or "I was messy eating that last bite of food, and you caught me on it, didn't you?"

21.4.2 *Examples of Empathic Reflections:*

Child: "Guess what, just a while ago I did some math problems with the other tutor, and I got them really easily."

Adult: "Wow, I'll bet you're proud about that!"

Child: "They're easy, they're no problem for me any more."

Adult: "You've got them knocked, huh?"

Child: "Yeah, but it's strange, the other day at school I got a bunch of them to do and just didn't do any of them. I hate doing them in school. My teacher thinks I can't do them."

Adult: "That's interesting to hear. You could do them in school, just like you do them here, but you hate doing them at school?"

Child: "Yeah. I don't know why. Maybe because I'm so mad at her for yelling at me all the time."

Adult: "So for that reason it just doesn't feel good to do math problems when she asks you to, huh?"

Child: "I feel like whatever she wants me to do, I'll just do something else. But I guess it really hurts me rather than hurting her."

Adult: "It seems to cause you more problems than it causes for your teacher?"

Child: "Yeah, because then I just get yelled at more."

21.4.3 *Reasons for Using Empathic Reflections:* It is pleasurable for a person to know that he or she has been understood by another person, and empathic reflections, perhaps more than any other communication, confirm such understanding. They provide an error-trapping method: any misunderstandings on the part of the adult give the child a chance to say, "No, that's not what I meant," and to clarify. After the adult does an empathic reflection, the child is free to say whatever he wants next, so that the child feels a freedom in conversation, a feeling of not being directed; when the child is able to choose his own direction, he has more opportunity to home in on what he most wants to talk about. In order to do empathic reflections the listener must concentrate on what the other person is communicating, rather than thinking up the next point he is going to make, as people often do in conversation. Finally, doing empathic reflections keeps people from using premature advice, criticism, commands, and other communications that often provoke defensiveness or stop communication.

21.4.4 *Method of Teaching Empathic Reflections:* After reviewing the above with the parent, the parent listens to an audiotape illustrating empathic reflections. The parent is encouraged to read the first third of Thomas Gordon's *Parent Effectiveness Training.* Then the parent is asked to do an exercise with the therapist in which the therapist uses a written dialogue in which one person speaks and the other consistently uses empathic reflections. The therapist reads the speaker's utterance; the parent fashions an empathic reflection to it; the therapist then reads the reflection from the dialogue, and the next utterance of the speaker. They continue like this until the parent's reflections are as good as those modeled in the written dialogues. The therapist models use of empathic reflections with the child. Finally, the parent uses empathic reflections with the child, while the therapist observes.

21.5 Teach the skill of using follow-up questions.

21.5.1 *Definition of "Follow-Up Questions":* Questions to the child that are on the same topic as the child just spoke about. They do not take the child away from the present focus of his attention, but prompt a more complete discussion of the present focus of attention.

21.5.2 *Examples of Follow-Up Questions:*

Child: "The teacher just seems to yell at me all the time."
Adult: "What does she yell at you for?"
Child: "Mainly getting out of my seat. But you'd get out too, if you had the same guy sitting in back of you as I do."
Adult: "Why, what does he do?"
Child: "He just bothers me. Whenever he can get away with it he does a friz job on me."
Adult: "What's a friz job."
Child: "That's what we call it when someone takes their knuckles and rubs them across the top of someone's head. It is supposed to be funny, but it can hurt."

21.5.3 *Reasons for Using Follow-Up Questions:* They communicate to the child that the adult is interested in what the child just said. They help a child flesh out his reports on topics, so that the adult can understand the full picture. As contrasted to silence in response to the child's utterance, or as contrasted to a new-topic question, they prompt a sustaining of attention to a single topic.

21.5.4 *Method of Teaching Follow-Up Questions:* Follow-up questions, as contrasted with empathic reflections, are already in the repertoires of most people. If they are not in the parent's repertoire, then the same process of modeling and practice can be used as was used with reflections.

21.6 Teach the skill of "prompt, wait, and hurry."

21.6.1 *Definition of "Prompt, Wait, and Hurry":* This refers, more than anything else, to the rhythm of the adult's interaction with the child. We are looking for a rhythm which most reinforces the child's initiating interactions with the adult. For this reason we want a rhythm that emphasizes *responsiveness* to what the child does, rather than *bossiness* in ordering the child to do or say things or to answer questions.

The "prompt" is placing the child in a situation where the child is tempted to say something to the adult or otherwise initiate an appropriate interaction. The "wait" is for the adult patiently to spend time near the child until the child does say something. When the child does say something to the adult, or have a pretend character say something, or look to the adult for approval, or otherwise make a bid for the adult's response, then comes the "hurry": the adult very quickly and enthusiastically responds to the child, in a way that hopefully reinforces the child's interacting, and prompts a further interaction.

21.6.2 *Example of "Prompt, Wait, and Hurry":* In dramatic play, the adult puts a wadded-up piece of paper or a little ball somewhere and has one of the toy characters say, "Humh, where did that ball go? I saw it somewhere just a little while ago." Then there is silence for about 10 seconds. If there is no response, the adult may continue the drama with another character coming onto the scene and offering to help look. Again there is silence as they look, and the adult sits motionless for a few seconds. If at any point the child has a character find the ball, the adult has a character quickly say, "Hey, you found it for us! Thank you! How did you know where it was?" If the child does not respond, the adult may have a character find the ball and respond in the same way, and then issue another prompt.

A more mundane example: the adult sits silently with the child while the child plays with a toy; when the child asks a question or makes a remark, the adult enthusiastically responds.

21.6.3 *Reason for Using "Prompt, Wait, and Hurry":* At one point we emphasized this skill primarily as a way of helping reticent and shy children to "come out," and indeed it is extremely helpful for that purpose. However, it is perhaps just as useful for the hyperactive, attention-seeking child. The child's hunger for adult interaction is gratified quickly in response to the child's appropriate bids for attention; there is less necessity for the child to resort to more disruptive means of getting an adult's interest.

21.6.4 *Method of Teaching "Prompt, Wait, and Hurry":* Parent reads about this technique; sees examples on videotape; sees examples in the therapist's interaction with the child; practices in interaction with the child with the therapist observing.

21.7 Teach the meaning of the concept of ping-pong interaction.

21.7.1 *Definition of "Ping-Pong Interaction":* This is the result that an observer sees when many of the above techniques are used. One person "serves" a new direction for the focus (and sometimes the server is the adult, sometimes the child). The other "returns" it by responding to the same topic, and the other "returns" again by responding to the other person's response. The two people are obviously hearing each other and responding to each other.

21.7.2 *Rationale for this Activity:* The game of child-directed activity is characterized more by ping-pong interaction, whereas the game of adult-directed activity is more akin to baseball. In adult-directed activity, such as when an adult administers a test to the child, the adult pitches each ball, and the child either hits it, misses, or "lets it go." At the close of therapy, we want both child and parent to be good at both games. But the game of child-directed activity is easier for the child, and is lower on the developmental hierarchy. Thus if a child is not good at either child-directed or adult-directed activity, it will be easier to first help the child to become expert at child-directed activity before beating heads against walls trying to get the child to be good at adult-directed activity. There is a child-initiated component to even such activities as the child's taking a test from an adult; these tend to provide the gratification to the child that enables the child to continue acceding to adult requests in the adult-initiated parts.

22 Teach the Parent to Do Dramatic Play with the Child

22.1 *Definition of "Dramatic Play":* The adult and the child or children use toy people or animals, usually with other toy props, and have the characters interact in a spontaneously created drama.

22.2 *Rationale for This Activity:* It can be tremendous fun for the child; it can be a play activity that the child never tires of. It can be a mutually gratifying activity for child and adult. It provides an opportunity for the adult to present positive models of psychological skills, including thought, feeling, and behavior, in a more unobtrusive and informal way than does the presentation of modeling plays for the child. It enables the child to practice positive examples, and to be reinforced (by the adult via the adult's characters) for positive examples. It stimulates the child's imagination and creativity. It provides practice in an activity appropriate for children to do with other children: if they can do it well their popularity with other children is enhanced. It enables the content of the practice opportunities to be determined by the content the child has on his mind.

22.3 *How to Make It Fun:* Many adults aren't naturally good players. Here are some problems in their dramatic play with children, and the solutions to them.

22.3.1 *Problem:* Speaking from the persona of the adult to the child, rather than from the persona of the character to another character. *Effect:* The child can't get into the fantasy as much, because he has a real-life person who keeps talking to him. *Solution:* If you are doing dramatic play, and expect the child to, you need to play the part of someone else other than yourself. Have almost all your utterances be from the point of view of one of the toy people, speaking to another toy person. *Example:* Not "Hey Johnny, why is the farmer putting the pig in the barn?" *but* "Hey, Mr. Farmer, why are you putting the pig in the barn?"

22.3.2 *Problem:* Being too passive, counting on the child to initiate all the plots, rather than initiating some yourself. *Effect:* Some children need to be shown how to spin interesting plots, and they don't get nearly as creative until they've seen you get creative. *Solution:* If you are familiar with the plots in the set of modeling plays, spin out one of them, or make up a new one, when there is a lull in the action.

22.3.3 *Problem:* Being too directive or active, overpowering the child with your own plots or telling the child's characters what to do too much. *Effect:* The child doesn't enjoy the play as much, may want to quit, or sits and watches without getting a word in edgewise. *Solution:* Be active not too much, not too little, but just right. Just right is defined as that which is maximally conducive to a ping-pong interaction. If the adult tends to be too active, the antidote is to have the adult's characters "track and describe" more and be silent more.

22.3.4 *Problem:* Speaking with an even, calm, understanding, therapistlike tone of voice throughout the dramatic play. *Effect:* The play isn't as much fun if the adult's characters don't get excited about anything. *Solution:* Have your characters show excitement over positive anticipation, show intense involvement in solving a problem that comes up, show intense pleasure when a problem gets solved.

22.3.5 *Problem:* Not being able to think up plots, or not being able to think of plots other than violent ones, for example, the persecutor pursues the victim, and a rescuer disables the persecutor. (This is the plot of nearly every one of our "action and adventure" violent films.) *Effect:* If the adult can't think up any plots, the play isn't as fun for the adult. If the adult can only think up the violent persecutor-victim-rescuer plot, the child learns that violence is useful and a good answer to problems. *Solution:* The adult should keep in mind a bunch of basic nonviolent plot structures. Here is a useful list of nonviolent plots:

Lost and found: Something, or someone, valuable is lost; the resolution comes when the person is found.

Danger from nature and protection: There is a tornado, a flood, a rainstorm, cold weather, and the resolution comes when protection is provided.

Useful task to do and help in doing it: For example, someone helps someone move a bed, plow a field, plant a garden, or feed animals.

Broken and fixed: A tool isn't working, and the resolution comes in getting it to work.

Enigma and explanation: There is a mysterious sound, or mysterious object, or knock at the door with no person, or anything else without an obvious explanation. The resolution comes when the explanation is revealed.

Conflict of interests and talking it out: Two people each have wants that either conflict or don't obviously mesh; the resolution comes when they figure out what to do.

Unique ability gets taught to another: Someone can do something wondrous or magical which inspires desire to learn in the apprentice; the resolution comes when the apprentice learns how to do it from the master.

Challenge with success or failure: People wonder whether a character will be able to come through with a positive example of a psychological skill. The person either proves himself or doesn't.

Desire to perform and approval of the crowd: Someone decides to put on a show of some sort, and the resolution comes when the people watching the show either enjoy it, or don't.

Danger of accident and its prevention: Something harmful is about to happen, and the resolution happens when someone recognizes the danger and prevents it, or fails to prevent it.

Hurt or sick and doctored: Someone gets hurt in an accident or gets sick; the resolution comes when the doctoring efforts succeed or fail.

Decision, choice, and result: A character has to decide what to do, and makes a choice, not knowing what the result will be; the resolution comes when we find out whether the result is what the decider thought it would be.

22.4 *How to Make It Useful:* If the above aspects of dramatic play are carried out by the adult in order to make it fun for the child, the play is almost sure to be useful. Why? The child and the adult are carrying out a ping-pong interaction, practicing socializing, and doing a mutually gratifying activity, and the child is getting models of positive emotional responses and models of a happy medium between passivity and bossiness. But more can be added, as follows:

22.4.1 *Problem:* The plots of the dramatic play have nothing to do with the high priority psychological skills of the child. *Effect:* the dramatic play is not as productive in presenting the most important positive models. *Solution:* The adult keeps in mind what the highest priority skills of the child are, and takes any opportunity to model an example of one of them, or to set up a situation where the child can enact a positive example.

22.4.2 *Problem:* The adult doesn't know what to do when the child's plots get violent. The adult either reinforces this by having the characters get excited and reciprocate, or the adult gets out of the persona of a character and disapproves of the child's choice. *Effect:* The first response reinforces violent dramatic play; the second punishes dramatic play in general. *Solution:* Several options, one of which is as follows: Wait quietly until the violent episode is over, so as not to reinforce it. Then have a character that is a friend of the victim be very concerned about the victim, sad that he was hurt, nurturing to the victim if he is still alive, supportive of the relatives if he is dead. Model the friends of the victims grieving and problem solving in an adaptive way.

22.5 *Method of Teaching the Art of Dramatic Play to a Parent or Other Adult:* Use the general mastery learning paradigm: monitor, teach, monitor, and repeat the cycle until criterion level of skill has been reached. The "teach" portion of the cycle can consist of: showing the parent videotape models, showing the parent live models with his or her own child, going over reading, getting verbal instruction, or doing role-playing exercises.

22.5.1 It's useful to monitor by observing the parent in dramatic play with the child. For some parents, performance anxiety will interfere with this activity. It may be helpful for the first session of monitoring of parent–child interaction to occur before the parent is aware of how many "fine points" of interaction skills exist. It may also be helpful if the parent does not get direct criticism of obviously undeveloped skills. Rather, some teaching follows each monitored session, with the instructor choosing what to emphasize based on the skills most in need of improvement.

22.5.2 It's useful to use the rating scale for behavior of parents in play with the child, more explicitly as the parent starts to come within reach of criterion level.

22.5.3 *Use of Videotape:* If the parent is videotaped before training, and then videotaped again after some progress has taken place in training, it can be quite gratifying for the parent to watch the two videotapes and observe the difference in the child's behavior. The result often motivates parents to acquire even more skill to move further.

23 *Use Attribution in an Honest and Effective Way as a Method of Influence on the Child*

23.1 *Definition of "Attribution":* The general principle is that people tend to be influenced by the expectations others have of them, by the traits (latent or revealed) that others attribute to them. They tend to follow the scripts that people define for their emerging personalities.

23.2 *Examples.* A negative example: "You are such a bad boy. You are going to wind up in prison, just like your no-good uncle." Positive examples: "That was a thoughtful question. You're getting to be more and more of a philosopher, the older you get." "What do you know, he likes broccoli! He's getting to like what older people like, more and more, isn't he?"

23.3 *Three Occasions for Using Attribution:* In response to negative behaviors, in response to positive behavior, and out of the blue.

23.3.1 *How to Use Attribution in Response to Negative Behavior:* For example, the child acts very withdrawn at a gathering of other children. Rather than saying, in the child's presence, "He's very shy," the adult says, "He hasn't learned yet how to make a lot of new friends in a situation like this. But when he does, I bet he will really have a lot of fun doing it." This linguistic format (1) names the positive pattern, not the negative adjective; (2) creates the image of learning it in the future; and (3) predicts a happy consequence of such learning. A second example: the child hits and kicks other children to get his way. The adult says to the child, "You haven't learned very well yet how to solve problems with other children by talking gently with them. When you learn that, the other children will like being with you a lot more."

23.3.2 *How to Use Attribution in Response to Positive Behavior:* For example, the child asks for something, is told no, and accepts this with cheerfulness. For the adult to say, "Wow, I like what you just did. When I told you no, you took it and stayed cheerful," is to use attention and approval, but not attribution. If the adult goes on to say, "I think this is an example of how you are getting better and better at putting up with frustration, the bigger you get," attribution is being used as well. Or if the child's lack of progress to date makes this statement a lie, "It sure will please me if this is an example of how you are going to get better and better at putting up with frustration, as you get to be a bigger boy."

23.3.3 *How to Use Attribution Out of the Blue:* The adult says, "I wonder what you will be like when you are five years older? I wonder if you will be the type who will be nice to the younger kids when someone wants to pick on them?" or "I wonder if you will be the type who really enjoys being with people, and has lots of friends?"

24 Teach Parents to Use Reprimands Appropriately for Undesirable Behaviors

24.1 *Guidelines for Reprimands:* Don't yell at the child, don't even raise your voice. Get the child alone, and speak to the child in privacy. Speak seriously. Give information as to why the behavior is undesirable, in terms of what harm it does: "When you did *x*, it made this bad effect, for this reason. For that reason it's important that you do this instead." Be silent a little bit, to let your words sink in.

24.2 Eliminating unnecessary reprimands is as important as eliminating unnecessary commands, and is taught in very similar ways.

24.3 Teach the child how to respond to reprimands from adults by using modeling plays. The desired response is a thoughtful one, acknowledging the harm if the child agrees, apologizing, and stating an intention not to repeat the action. This is a subskill of responding to criticism.

25 Use "Time Out" for Physical Aggression

25.1 *Definition of "Time Out":* After the act of physical aggression, the child is immediately made to stay in a place where there is no interaction between the child and anyone else, either visually or verbally, for a short period of time, perhaps two to five minutes. In order for time out to be effective, this place usually must be a room where the child is by himself. Before the procedure is begun, it is thoroughly explained to the child, and the course of events is acted out with toy people. The child gets a chance to see how long two to four minutes is. All the explanation about why hitting is bad takes place in instruction sessions during times of calm, not immediately after the hitting takes place. There are only a few words spoken and only a few seconds elapse between the hitting and the Time Out; the words are spoken with disappointment but not excitement: "You hit, so it's Time Out." There is a kitchen timer placed outside the room and set for the time; the child can come out when the bell rings. During the time the child is in Time Out, there is no interaction of any sort with the child. After the child comes out the parent does not fuss at the child, but starts all over with a clean slate. Time Out is used in exactly the same way, like clockwork, each time the child is physically aggressive, with no warnings. The child is not given a choice as to whether to go to Time Out or to stay in Time Out. The parents don't use Time Out for behaviors other than physical aggression or destruction of property, so as not to dilute its effectiveness.

25.2 *Teaching Time Out to Parents:* Parents watch a videotape on Time Out, read a handout, get a verbal explanation and demonstration from the therapist, and do the computer-assisted parent instruction module on time out. For those parents who have already tried Time Out and who feel that it does not work, it is emphasized that when most, but not all, of the guidelines are followed, Time Out frequently does not work; when all the guidelines are followed, it almost always works. In subsequent sessions the therapist specifically checks to see if each of the guidelines for Time Out was followed, and whether the frequency of physical aggression is falling rapidly, as it should when such a program is enacted.

25.3 *Why Time Out Is Not at the Beginning of the Curriculum:* Sometimes Time Out does not work, even when all the guidelines are being followed, if the adult is provoking the child's aggressiveness by yelling at the child, issuing too many unnecessary commands, or using differential attention so as to reinforce hostility. Also, it is much easier to eliminate negative behaviors if there are abundant positive patterns of interaction, for example, mutually gratifying activities, in the repertoire of the parent and child.

26 For Small Children, Use Physical Guidance for Noncompliance

26.1 *Definition of "Physical Guidance"*: Moving the child's body to enforce a command. For example, the parent says, "It's time for us to go now. Please come with me." The child ignores this. The parent gently takes the child by the hand and leads the child out the door.

26.2 *Rationale for Use of Physical Guidance*: Many times adults spend far too much time arguing with children, giving repeated verbal directives, and thereby giving children too much practice in ignoring adult request. Physical guidance shortens the agony for both adult and child. On the other hand, it is usually not pleasant for the child. If the child develops the expectation that the command will be enforced by physical guidance if he does not respond to the words, the child will often choose to comply rather than be subjected to the physical guidance.

27 Teach the Game of Adult-Directed Activity

27.1 *Basic Notion*: Education of the child, in both psychological and academic skills, best occurs through a mixture of child-directed and adult-directed activities. The former is easier for the child and often more conducive to creativity in the child; skill in doing child-directed activities may be very important for the child's peer relations. The latter, adult-directed activity, makes learning much more efficient at times, is absolutely logistically necessary at times, and the child's skill in doing it is very important for success in most schools. The ideal situation is one in which both adult and child are comfortable with both sorts of activities, and can do both joyously; neither totally dominates their repertoire.

27.2 The basic rhythm of adult-directed activity is like baseball rather than like ping-pong. The adult pitches a challenge to the child; the child either responds successfully to it, responds unsuccessfully to it, or does not respond to it. Ideally, the adult's response reinforces the child's attempt to respond, or his successful response, and then the adult issues the next challenge.

27.3 *Making Adult-Directed Activity Fun*: There is nothing inherently unpleasant about adult-directed activity for the child! Children can greatly enjoy taking IQ tests or achievement tests; these are prime examples of adult-directed activity. Children can greatly look forward to tutoring sessions containing a great deal of adult-directed activity. If adult-directed activity is not fun for the child, here are some problems that might be responsible, and solutions.

27.3.1 *Problem*: The challenges the adult is issuing are too hard or too easy for the child, rather than being at the "just right" level of challenge. *Effect*: The child is either frustrated or bored. *Solution*: The adult must have in mind a hierarchy of challenges, including some easier and some harder than the current one. The adult must be sensitive to the verbal and nonverbal signs of boredom or frustration in the child, as well as to the signs from the child's responses to the challenges, and move up or down the hierarchy of difficulty accordingly. Alternatively, the items are moved into the easy range, but some other aspect of the presentation (that is, they are presented in the context of interesting or well-illustrated stories) keeps the child's interest high.

27.3.2 *Problem:* The child has been asked to sit still too long. *Effect:* The child gets restless, more restless, and finally will do almost anything to get to move. *Solution:* Build in lots of physical, "gross motor" activities into the schedule, so as to alternate with the periods of having to stay still. This seems obvious, but it is overlooked by countless educational institutions regularly.

27.3.3 *Problem:* The child has been asked to do adult-directed activity too long. *Effect:* The child gets rebellious, or sinks into passivity. *Solution:* Use the "sandwich" technique, in which there is an alternation of the adult's choice of action with the child's choice. The child-directed activity reinforces the adult-directed activity, and there is not a need for the child to use avoidance maneuvers to get out of adult directed activity.

27.3.4 *Problem:* The young child has nothing to manipulate. *Effect:* Since young children are explorers, and are very concrete, their interest is best held when there is something for them to touch, look at from various angles, and fiddle with, or at least something to observe that changes often. When adults try to engage them for too long in a purely verbal activity, they often lose interest and get "off task" onto something more interesting to them. *Solution:* Try to devise activities that give the child something interesting to manipulate or something interesting and changing to observe.

27.3.5 *Problem:* The adult's response to the child's attempt to meet the challenge is too "blah": the tone of voice is monotone, the facial expression is too unchanging, the adult is obviously not excited. *Effect:* the child is not reinforced, and loses interest in the activity. *Solution:* The adult must cognitively reorganize so that the adult feels true joy and excitement when the child either attempts, or especially succeeds at, a challenge. The adult communicates the excitement by tone of voice, facial expression, and words, very quickly after the child's response.

27.3.6 *Problem:* The activity is prolonged past the child's attention span. *Effect:* The child gets off task. *Solution:* End it sooner, and gradually stretch out the attention span over time.

27.3.7 *Problem:* The adult is too rigid in prohibiting all child-initiated activity. For example, while reading a story to a child, the adult refuses to entertain the child's comments on the story. *Effect:* The child doesn't enjoy the activity. *Solution:* The adult permits a reasonable degree of child-directed activity, even within an adult-directed activity.

27.4 *The Development of Adult-Directed Activities:* The child's taking pleasure in adult-directed activity may take place in infancy, when the parent tries to get the child to imitate a facial expression or movement or vocalization, and exhibits pleasure when the infant does so. In toddlerhood, activities such as "What does the dog say?"—"Woof Woof!"—"Right!" are a classic example of adult-directed activity. Throughout early childhood logistic activities such as "Now it's time to go to bed," "Now it's time to brush your teeth," "Now it's time to get dressed and leave the house," represent adult-directed activity. Reading to the child represents a combination of adult- and child-directed activity. If the adult encourages the child to tell the story back, and if the child does so, or if the adult asks the child questions about what happened in the story, and the child answers them, those are classic adult-directed components. If the adult teaches the child a song and gets the child to sing along, this is adult-directed activity; if the child later initiates the singing and the adult sings along or listens attentively or they both dance, this is child-directed activity.

The child's early experiences of pleasure in activities like these set the groundwork for schooling. Most schools use a very high fraction of adult-directed activity.

27.5 *Teaching Adults—Including Parents—to Teach Academic Skills to Children, in Individual Tutoring:* The young child can learn to enjoy academic subjects, and can make academic progress, much more readily in a one-on-one experience than in a large group. Associating pleasure and confidence with the learning process is too important a task to be left up to schools if the parent is capable of doing it, or if there is another adult capable of doing it. Many games and tasks that promote academic learning can be mutually gratifying activities for children and adults. The tasks below are just a few of such activities, which are fully covered in another manual.

27.5.1 *The Basic Concepts Illustrations:* For preschool children, one of the most important academic foundations is the knowledge of the meaning of basic concepts such as top, closest, over, beginning, and so forth. The book *Basic Concepts Illustrations,* written by the author, is meant to give children exposure to several examples of the concepts, followed by a task asking the child to pick which of a set of pictures illustrates the concept; most of the vignettes are also meant to model prosocial actions as well. This book is read to the child and the child responds when the questions come.

27.5.2 *The Letter Stories:* These are a subset of the modeling stories, in which the characters are letters, with arms and legs. They come together and say their phonetic sounds in order to communicate words to people, which have the effect of helping people out. (The usual plot contains danger of accident and prevention.) If the child can learn to retell these stories, the child will have learned a great deal about phonics.

27.5.3 *The Math Stories:* These are another subset of the modeling stories, in which the characters use mathematics to help themselves or someone else solve a practical life problem.

27.5.4 *The Blending Game:* The adult takes words apart into their component sounds, and sees if the child can put them back together to guess what the word is. "I'm thinking of something in this room, and I want to see if you can guess what it is. It's the rrrr—uh—guh. Can you guess? (If that's too hard, the easier task is:) It's the rrrr—ug. Now can you guess?" An interesting variation is to do the blending game within a story. *Adult:* "While we're reading this story, I'll take some of the words apart, and see if you can put them back together. Once there was a boy named Jerry, who was playing outside at a puh-ar-kuk." *Child:* "Park!" *Adult:* "Right! And then Jerry . . ."

27.5.5 *The Which Picture Game: Adult:* "Do you know what this picture is?" *Child:* "An umbrella." *Adult:* "Right! Do you know what this is?" *Child:* "A boat." *Adult:* "Right! Now between umbrella and boat, which one do you think begins with uuuh?" *Child:* "Umbrella!" *Adult:* "You got it!" (If the child says "boat," the adult says, "If boat began with uuh, it would be an uuuuhoat. The right answer is umbrella." The same game can be done with ending sounds as well as beginning sounds.

27.5.6 *The Which Sound Game: Adult:* "Do you know what this picture is?" *Child:* "A lamb." *Adult:* "Right! Let's see if you can hear what sound the word lamb starts with. Is it ill, or is it tuh?" *Child:* "Ill." *Adult:* "That's it!"

28 Teach Family Members to Incorporate Ethical Readings and Affirmations, and Discussion of Ethical Dilemmas and Decisions, into a Pattern of Family Rituals

28.1 *Rationale for These Procedures:* Children do not become ethical people simply by being rewarded for positive acts and punished for antisocial acts. Rather, there is the need to teach a belief system, a philosophy, about what is right and wrong to do. The child learns moral reasoning, learns to be devoted to a set of values. The parents' modeling of these values is crucial, but the words that articulate these values are of great help also. If these can be stored in the child's memory bank, the child will be much better off.

28.2 *Ethical Readings and Affirmations:* For young children, the illustrated modeling stories are designed to illustrate prosocial acts and to constitute an introduction to ethics. For school-aged children, the unillustrated modeling stories provide more of the specific vignettes.

The religious family will probably want to include readings from their own religion such as devotions for children and readings from sacred texts.

I recommend the formation of a "family value statement," in which the family members write down what values are most important to them, for example, honesty, kindness, productivity, and joyousness, and also write down briefly what these words mean. The family value statement can be read, with an attitude of some importance and reverence, on regularly occurring special occasions.

A short version of the statement may be spoken by the family unit more frequently, for example, before meals, before bedtime, upon arising.

28.3 *Discussion of Ethical Dilemmas:* The family gathers in a group, and a hypothetical (or real) situation is posed in which the protagonist has to decide what to do. Family members give their ideas, not just about what the person should do, but why—what principle should guide this decision? In the process of this discussion it is useful if one person takes the "facilitator" role, and does not contribute to the content, but instead directs the process of the discussion, asking questions of various participants, for example, by asking for clarification, introducing the question, introducing new shades on the question: "Suppose this aspect were different. Would your decision remain the same?"

For preschool children, some illustrated stories are available from the author which pose dilemmas in which the protagonist has to choose between a more prosocial option and a more self-seeking one.

29 Teach Parents Specific Responses to Some Specific Child Problems

29.1 *Basic Strategy:* Give parents a handout written to cover the particular problem, go over the directions verbally, answer questions, make plans, and plan to monitor the enactment of the plan and the results it achieved in the following session. During the following session hear exactly what was done, and what the results were. Use corrective feedback if the parent did not enact the program in a way that would predict success.

Some examples of these specific problem-oriented programs follow, with a brief condensation of the instructions.

29.2 *Tantrums:* Follow the procedures listed above to promote the skills of frustration-tolerance. This entails much positive reinforcement and modeling of examples of *not* tantruming, and being cheerful in trigger situations that previously would have elicited screaming. For the tantrums themselves, explain beforehand to the child that the parent will ignore the child while the tantrum is going on. A useful adjunct to this is the parent's putting in ear plugs. When the screaming has ceased for at least 30 seconds, the parent interacts with the child as though the tantrum had never taken place. If the child hits or is otherwise physically aggressive, the child gets a 2-minute Time Out, which is ended when the time is up, whether or not the child is still screaming. If the child hits again, there is another 2-minute Time Out. All these procedures are followed without screaming back at the child, and with slow movements and no excitement, in as close as possible to the same way each time.

29.3 *Child's Refusal to Sleep in His/Her Own Room, with Many Requests for Parental Attention after Bedtime:* Set up a bedtime ritual including modeling stories and nightly review that begins early enough for pleasant and nonrushed interaction. Have a set bedtime that is consistently kept. Have the conditions under which the child falls asleep duplicate those which the child will encounter during a waking in the middle of the night. Explore for realistic fears and deal with them if necessary. Use modeling stories to teach child how to deal with scary fantasy characters by encountering them in fantasy and converting them to allies. Plan for celebrations to take place in the morning when the child has been able to stay in his bed all night. One celebration reinforcing to many children is a "parade," in which family members march around, sing songs, toot on kazoos, and the like. Model for the child with toy people the following procedure, explain it verbally, then carry it out. A piece of paper is posted. Each time the child gets out of bed, the parent makes a talley mark on the piece of paper, then without any excitement and with a minimum of conversation and eye contact, takes the child by the hand and leads him back to his own bed, and walks immediately back to the parent's own bed. Even if the child gets out again, immediately, the same procedure is repeated in exactly the same way, without exasperation and without emotion. The first night there may be dozens of marks on the talley sheet. However, there is celebration of the fact that on the last occasion, the child actually went to sleep in his own bed, without the parent present. After three or four nights the number of tally marks has usually dropped precipitously, and after a week or two the child is usually not getting out of bed. With children for whom the achievement of healthy dependency is a major milestone, for example, some abused children adopted into new homes, and with other circumstances as well, this procedure may be modified.

29.4 *Encopresis:* Teach parents the role of constipation in most cases of encopresis. Assess and treat constipation, with mineral oil or enemas if necessary. Alter fiber intake to prevent future constipation. Eliminate the use of hostility to try to control the symptom. Eliminate all punishment for soiling. Teach the child to help clean up after the soiling, or help the parent clean up, depending upon the child's age. Teach parent and child that the parameter to be followed is not so much the number of soilings (which can be decreased, temporarily, by a return of constipation), but the number of times the child places feces in the toilet. Each of these events is shown to the parent and joyously celebrated by parent and child. Arrange with school personnel, and anyone else, that the child can go to the rest room immediately whenever he has an urge.

29.5 *Refusal to Eat Enough:* First, have the child examined by a pediatrician. Monitor height and weight; in many cases where parents are struggling greatly with the child over eating, the child is not even underweight for age or height. Teach the parents the nature of the vicious cycle in which refusal to eat leads to parental fear, which leads to nagging the child to eat, which leads to rebellious refusal of the child to eat, and so forth. To break the cycle, stop nagging the child to eat, and in fact stop even using the word *eat* for a while. Use stimulus situation control by having nutritious foods that the child likes readily available for the child, with the child given free access to them in the home. Discuss nutrition with the parent; make sure the parent realizes that children need calories and that a certain amount of high-fat and high-sugar food is good for them. Have mealtimes in which the child is reinforced with attention and approval, not for eating, but for sitting at the table with the adults, with food in front of the child. When the child eats, the adult does not praise the child for eating, but reinforces the child by becoming even more upbeat in the discussion of whatever topic is being discussed. The adults' major initial goal is to make mealtime pleasant and to stop struggling over food. If the child does not eat at the table, the parents refuse to struggle with the child, and if the child wishes to leave the table, that too is permitted. The child's supper is put in the refrigerator, and if the child wants to eat it later on, the child is permitted to do so. If the child is eating too high a fraction of junk food, the parents simply reduce the access to junk food by putting it somewhere the child can't reach it, or not having it in the house. But if weight gain is desired, junk food may be just what the doctor ordered.

29.6 *Shyness and Withdrawal:* If the child is being pressured to interact with other children, take the pressure off. Let the child experience enough loneliness so that the shyness is experienced by the child as something the child wants to reduce, rather than as something that adults are pressuring the child to reduce. Model for the child, with toy people and in real life, the skills of social initiations. Most people think of teaching the child to say, "Do you want to play with me?" This is not usually the best way for a child to start playing with another, because it risks the possibility of rejection. Rather, if the child joins another child or group of children who are doing something, watches for a while, then begins to "track and describe" their actions, and join in the play, the child does not incur nearly so great a risk of rejection, and the other children experience the interaction as much more natural. Teach the child and the parents the art of joint dramatic play, as described above. Give the child lots of practice in social conversation, and ping-pong interaction, as described above, using prompt-wait-hurry to encourage interaction. In dramatic play model skills of tolerating rejection and tolerating criticism and reducing performance anxiety, to help the child develop a thicker skin. The parents may provide practice opportunities by frequently assisting the child to invite another child to the child's residence to play. Sometimes shy children do much better with children slightly younger than themselves. If adult attention is a potent reinforcer for the child, the adult uses differential attention by watching and joining in at times when the child is interacting, and by not rescuing the child each time the child withdraws.

30 Teach Parents Psychological Skills

All of the above put demands upon the maturity and patience and energy of the parents or other adults who are dealing with the children. What if the parent has trouble doing the activity or procedure with the child, despite adequate modeling, instruction, opportunity for practice, and so forth? It is very often the case that a skill deficiency in the adult will block effective execution of the parenting skills. For example, the parent who is too depressed will have a very hard time using the tones of approval and excitement in response to the child's positive acts. The parent who is too disorganized will have a hard time with remembering to use the Positive Behavior Diary, or to do the nightly review, or to have the modeling stories or toy people accessible, or perhaps even to get to appointments with the therapist. Below are some other psychological skills that can become, profitably, the main focus of treatment with the parents, leaving the child out of the action altogether for a time at least. There are separate manuals for each of these.

The therapist makes a judgment call as to when to incorporate skill training for parents into the course of the therapy, and when to recommend that the parent receive individual treatment not linked to the treatment of the child. One advantage of the latter arrangement is that the child isn't so affected by transference problems that develop between the parent and the therapist dealing with the parent's problems. Also the importance of the therapist to the family doesn't get so large as to promote such problems. An advantage of the former arrangement is that the therapist gets alerted to those psychological skill deficiencies in the parent that are most highly related to problems with the child or children. Also the parent is more likely to get to one place for therapy than two places.

Some parents may need to be taught additional skills. These skills are listed below, for more detail see Strayhorn (1988).

30.1 Organization skills

30.2 Cognitive restructuring of undesirable events and of desirable events. (Learning not to awfulize, get down on oneself, or blame others for undesirable events, but to problem solve and learn from experiences; learning to internally celebrate positive events. These skills are very useful for depressed parents.)

30.3 Individual problem-solving and decision-making skills

30.4 Joint problem-solving and decision-making skills—family negotiation strategies. Useful for couples or families in conflict.

30.5 Anger control skills

30.6 Assertion and limit-setting skills

30.7 Skills of building a social support system for parents.

31 Process of Interaction between Therapist and Parent

31.1 Obviously, with such a large amount of informational content to be conveyed, a certain amount of time can be spent with therapist lecturing and parent listening. However, this does not "close the feedback loop."

31.2 "Closing the feedback loop" means that the parent forms a goal of getting better at any of the skills mentioned, tries to practice positive examples of those skills, and either reports or demonstrates such attempts to the therapist, who then says some combination of "Congratulations" or "Let's consider a different way." In a different feedback loop, the parent forms a goal of getting better at a skill, tries to practice positive examples, notes the response of the child, and is rewarded or not rewarded by the pattern of the child's response.

31.3 Part of the function of the therapist is to help the parent choose personal goals for skill improvement, as well as goals for improvement of the child's skills. Sometimes the therapist can play a very directive role: "I think the top priority strategy to try at this point is to stop yelling about the negative behavior of the child and start yelling, with a positive tone, about the positive behavior, for the reasons we talked about. Are you willing to experiment with this for a while?" At other times the therapist simply presents a menu: "We've gone over lots of things that people have found helpful with their children. Which of them would you like to put on your priority list at this point?"

31.4 Once the goal is formed, a good part of the therapist's function is to remind the parent of it, and to monitor it informally: "How is your progress coming in the very difficult task of not yelling about the negative, and getting more excited about the positive?" "So what I'm hearing is that if 0 was where you started out, and 10 is where you'd like to get to, you're already at about 4 now, after only working at it for two weeks?"

31.5 The therapist also supports the parent through periods of nonprogress, while exhorting the value of persistence: "This is a habit where you practiced the way you don't want to do it for at least 5 years and got models of it for another 15 years; we should give you at least a month to change it! But since change is proportional to the rate of rehearsals, let's think about how to get that rate as high as possible."

31.6 The therapist has in the repertoire several ways of promoting practice, so as to accord with the parent's level of performance anxiety versus love of performance. For the "ham," role playing is made to order, as is direct work with the child with the therapist watching, and "fantasy rehearsal out loud," where the parent closes his or her eyes and speaks a first-person present-tense narrative of an imaginary sequence of doing the positive example. For the parent with more performance anxiety, it is usually comfortable for the therapist to explain the art of fantasy practice, that is, silently imagining oneself performing the positive pattern, as vividly as possible. The therapist permits the parent some moments of silence to perform the fantasy practice, and then in discussion afterward the parent describes the content of the fantasy practice. Too much of psychotherapy has consisted in endless recounting of details of real-life experience, and not enough in rehearsal of what experience is desired to become. "Some speak of things that are and ask why; I dream of things that never were and ask why not" can be a watchword to guide therapy into the practice of new patterns than the rehashing of the old.

31.7 Another important part of the therapist's function is to listen to the parent's report and focus on concrete positive examples of what the parent did, and to celebrate such examples, not just by relying on professional authority and saying something like "You did it right," but by querying about the child's positive response and celebrating that with the parent. Much of therapy should be celebration, with joy, laughter, cheers. The competence-based approach is meant to maximize joyousness, to help the parent and the child start as soon as possible feeling good about whatever bits of progress start first. Too much of psychotherapy has been needlessly painful.

31.8 In ideal circumstances, both the parent and the child, before termination, not only will have gained skills, but will have internalized the general competence-building strategy of defining a skill area, gathering information about what really works the best, setting goals for skill acquisition, getting maximum exposure to positive models, practicing positive examples, and celebrating and feeling good about each positive example. This can be an explicit goal that parent and therapist talk about, as well as the implicit process for both parent and child.

Appendix 3.1. Psychological Skills Axis

Group 1: Closeness, Trusting, Relationship Building

1. Deciding whom to trust and ally with, and trusting
2. Accepting help, depending
3. Enjoying sustained attachment
4. Self-disclosing
5. Being kind
6. Nurturing oneself with one's cognitions
7. Communicating positive feelings

8. Initiating social contacts
9. Social conversation
10. Listening empathically

Group 2: Handling Separation and Independence

11. Independent decision making
12. Tolerating separation from close others
13. Handling rejection
14. Tolerating disapproval
15. Tolerating aloneness

Group 3: Handling Joint Decisions and Interpersonal Conflict

16. Choosing interpersonal stances in conflict situations
17. Generating creative options for conflict resolution
18. Choosing reasonable solutions for conflicts
19. Negotiation skills
20. Assertion skills
21. Conciliation skills
22. Reinforcing the best portion of another's behavior
23. Tolerating a wide range of others' behavior
24. Forgiveness skills

Group 4: Dealing with Frustration and Unfavorable Events

25. Frustration tolerance
26. Handling one's own mistakes and failures
27. Tolerating someone else getting what one wants
28. Being fearless when appropriate
29. Feeling fear when appropriate
30. Feeling guilt when appropriate
31. Tolerating painful feelings
32. Tolerating impulses or fantasies that can't be enacted

Group 5: Celebrating Good Things, Feeling Pleasure

33. Enjoying approval from others
34. Taking pleasure in making accomplishments
35. Taking pleasure in doing acts of kindness
36. Taking pleasure from discovery and curiosity satisfaction
37. Feeling gratitude toward others

38. Celebrating good fortune
39. Enjoying physical affection
40. Attachment of erotic feelings to desirable stimuli

Group 6: Working for Delayed Gratification

41. Delaying gratification
42. Complying with reasonable authority
43. Sustaining attention to tasks
44. Maintaining healthy habits
45. Being honest, even when it is difficult to do so
46. Developing competences in work, school, or recreation
47. Money-saving skills

Group 7: Relaxing and Playing

48. Letting the mind drift, letting the body relax
49. Being gleeful and childlike
50. Enjoying and producing humor

Group 8: Cognitive Processing through Words, Symbols, and Images

51. Verbal fluency
52. Recognizing and verbalizing one's own feelings
53. Seeing things from others' points of view—empathy
54. Assessing the degree of control one has over an event
55. Systematic and rational decision making
56. Thinking before acting
57. Organization skills: time, money, object management
58. Accurately perceiving one's own skills
59. Perceiving other people without distortions
60. Using imagination and fantasy

Group 9: An Adaptive Sense of Direction and Purpose

61. Aiming toward making things better
62. Assigning meaning and purpose to activity

Appendix 3.2. Methods of Influence Axis

1. Objective-formation, or goal setting
2. Hierarchy (arranging learning steps in sequence of difficulty

3. Attribution (of certain traits or potentials to a person)
4. Modeling (through fiction or real life)
5. Providing practice opportunities
6. Reinforcement and punishment
7. Instruction
8. Stimulus control
9. Monitoring progress

(A mnemonic for the methods axis is OH AM PRISM.)

Appendix 3.3. Parenting Skills

1. Orienting oneself to the mastery learning paradigm
2. Deciding upon the highest priority skills of the child
3. Recognizing positive examples of the highest priority skills of the child
4. Using immediate attention and approval with positive behaviors of the child
5. Using tones of voice in a way that conveys approval
6. Using differential excitement
7. Telling about positive examples to a third person in the child's earshot
8. Using the Positive Behavior Diary
9. Doing the nightly review
10. Eliminating unnecessary commands
11. Using stimulus control in the child's environment
12. Avoiding reinforcing negative behavior by attention, excitement, or giving in
13. Using differential attention
14. Selecting modeling stories
15. Reading modeling stories in a way that the child enjoys
16. Using "real-life modeling stories" with the child
17. Reducing the violent models in the child's entertainment diet
18. Putting on prewritten modeling plays for the child
19. Using "real-life modeling plays" with the child
20. Selecting modeling songs
21. Carrying out fun activities with modeling songs
22. Nondirective conversation and interaction skills:
    22.1. Tracking and describing
    22.2. Telling about one's own experience
    22.3. Using empathic reflections
    22.4. Using follow-up questions
    22.5. The rhythm of prompt, wait, and hurry
    22.6. The rhythm of ping-pong interaction
23. Doing spontaneous, jointly created dramatic play with the child
24. Using attribution with the child
25. Eliminating unnecessary reprimands

26. Giving reprimands appropriately
27. Using "time out"
28. Using physical guidance for noncompliance
29. Doing adult-directed activities with the child
    29.1. Finding the correct level of challenge to the child
    29.2. Choosing the correct amount of time to ask the child to sit still
    29.3. Choosing the correct amount of time to stay engaged in any one activity, and in adult-directed activity in general
    29.4. Responding with enthusiasm to children's responses in adult-directed activity
    29.5. Facility in specific tutoring activities
30. Using ethical readings and affirmations in the home
31. Discussion of ethical dilemmas in the home
32. Specific skills in dealing with tantrums, refusal to sleep alone, encopresis, picky eating, shyness and withdrawal, or whatever the child's specific problem is
33. Psychological skills of the parent, able to be addressed in competence-oriented parent training
    33.1. Organization skills
    33.2. Cognitive restructuring of undesirable and desirable events
    33.3. One-person problem-solving and decision-making skills
    33.4. Joint problem-solving and decision-making skills
    33.5. Anger control skills
    33.6. Assertion and limit-setting skills
    33.7. Skills of building a social support system
    33.8. Certain other psychological skills on the psychological skills axis

Appendix 3.4. List of Ancillary Materials

Measures Available from the Author:

Psychological Skills Inventory (adult report rating of child's psychological skills)

Parent Practices Scale (self report of frequency with which parent does desirable and undesirable practices)

Parent Behavior in Play with Child Scale (rated by an observer who has watched parent and child play together)

Child Behavior in Play with Parent Scale (rated by an observer who has watched parent and child play together)

Modeling and Instructional Devices Available from the Author:

Illustrated modeling stories, including letter stories, math stories, prosocial dilemma stories

Unillustrated modeling stories

Modeling plays

Manual: *Training Exercises for Parents of Young Children*

Manual: *Training Exercises for Teachers of Young Children*

Manual: *Activities for Psychological Skill Training in Classrooms*

The Classification of Skills Exercise, a set of exercises to teach the psychological skill concepts to children

Cassette tape and words of modeling songs

Videotape, *Building Psychological Skills in Preschoolers through Stories and Dramatic Play*

CAPI: *Computer Assisted Parent Instruction* program

Video of modeling songs, stories, and plays

Materials by Others:

The Parents and Children Series, by Carolyn Webster-Stratton. On parenting young children. Distributed by Castalia Publishing Company, P.O. Box 1587, Eugene, Oregon, 97440, 503–343–4433.

Videocassette, *Time Out!,* by Gerald Patterson. Also distributed by Castalia.

Videocassette, *Parents and Children: A Positive Approach to Child Management,* distributed by Research Press, Box 3177 Dept. K, Champaign, IL 61821–9988.

Games for Reading, Games for Math, by Peggy Kaye, Pantheon Books, a division of Random House, 301–848–1900. Fun games, with adult-directed and child-directed components, for learning academic skills.

Teaching All Children to Read and the *Teaching All Children to Read Kit,* by Michael and Lise Wallach, University of Chicago Press, 11030 South Langley, Chicago, IL 60628, 312–702–7748 or 800–621–2736.

Modeling stories by Richard Gardner. Richard Gardner, M.D., has published *Dr. Gardner's Modern Fairy Tales, Dr. Gardner's Fairy Tales for Today's Children,* and other sets of modeling stories. They are available from Creative Therapeutics, 155 County Road, Cresskill, NJ, 07626.

Appendix 3.5: Positive Examples of Skills

Doing Kind Things: Saying "Thanks for the supper" to his parent; picking up something her mother drops and giving it to her; saying "Good morning" in a cheerful tone to a family member; speaking gently to his pet and petting him nicely; saying "That's OK" in a gentle manner when a parent forgets to do something she wanted him to do; saying "That's interesting" when his sister mentions some of her thoughts; saying "Don't worry about it" in a gentle way when her brother seems to feel bad about a mistake he made in a game; giving his brother a piece of his dessert; saying "What have you been up to?" and listening nicely to her sister when she tells her about her day; offering to help a parent carry something; saying "You're welcome" in a gentle way when someone says "Thank you"; sharing a toy with another child; patting another child on the back, affectionately; offering to push someone in the swing; offering to take turns, and letting someone else take the first turn; going up to another child and socializing in a nice way; smiling at someone . . .

Obeying: Saying "OK" without arguing when he's told it's bedtime; keeping her voice low when her mother asks her to because she is trying to read; playing inside on a rainy day for an hour and following the "no throwing the football inside" rule; leaving something alone that her parent asks her not to touch; playing gently with his friend after his mother tells them to stop wrestling; coming when her mother says "Come with me"; getting dressed without problems when asked to do so; brushing teeth when asked to do so; following the rule of staying at the table during a meal; turning the television off, or not turning it back on once it is turned off, as requested.

Putting Up with Not Getting His or Her Way: Saying "OK" in a nice way when he asks for some candy and is told he can't have any; keeping cheerful when the rain spoils her plans to play outside with her friend; handling it without yelling when his brother breaks one of the things he owns; looking calmly for something she can't find, without losing her temper; not yelling when he has to stop watching a television show to come to supper or to go out somewhere with his parent; being cool when her little brother grabs something out of her hand—getting it back, if she wants, but not yelling or hitting; being cheerful when he doesn't get a present that he has asked for; being cheerful when she has to come inside . . .

Paying Attention: Listening while someone reads to him, for a little longer than before; having a chat with one of her parents without having to run off to get into something else; playing with the same toys for a reasonably long time; paying attention to a play that someone puts on for him with toy people; telling a story, and staying on the topic for a reasonable time; working at a task longer than before.

Practicing Using Language: Listening while someone reads him a story, having a chat with someone; asking a good question about something she is curious about; telling about things he has seen and done; talking back and forth with someone; using a longer sentence than before; using some new words.

Putting Up with Not Getting Attention: Playing by himself when his parents pay attention to a sibling; paying attention to something else when a parent is on the phone; letting her parents talk to each other for a while without interrupting; watching what some peers are doing with each other, without butting in immediately; letting a sibling play with something, and get the parent's attention, without taking that thing away; drawing a parent's attention to a sibling in a favorable way; letting a parent read or write or lie down and rest without interrupting; being able to handle it if some peers do not want her participating with them in an activity.

Handling One's Own Mistakes and Failures: In a game, failing to make a goal or win a point without getting too upset; losing a game without getting discouraged; failing to do something he tries, and then working harder rather than giving up; being corrected for something, and then making an effort to do better; remembering a previous time she made a mistake, and saying "This time I won't (or will) do X, because I learned from the last time"; talking out loud to himself when he has made a mistake or failure, and saying "What can I do about this? I could do this, or that . . . "

Social Initiations: Watching some peers do whatever they're doing before joining in with them; paying attention to what peers are paying attention to rather than drawing attention to himself; starting to socialize in any way that does not irritate the peer; saying "Hi" to a peer she knows; introducing himself to a peer he doesn't know; asking if some peers would like another participant in an activity; finding someone who is lonely, and talking or playing with that person; offering to share something she has with a peer, as a way of getting interaction started; asking a question about something a peer is doing, as a way of getting interaction started.

Letting the Other Do What the Other Wants: In playing, letting the other play with a toy without taking it away from him or her; responding to the other's suggestion of "Let's do this" by saying "OK!"; responding to the other's question of "May I do this?" by saying "Sure!"; responding to the other's looking over her shoulder at something she is doing by tolerating it, rather than asking the other to go away; responding to a little brother or sister's tapping lightly on his knee by tolerating it rather than bossing the little sibling to quit doing it; in dramatic play, letting the other person direct the course of the plot for a while; in dramatic play, when the other person says something like "Pretend this is a lake" or "Pretend that this is a goat," going along with the suggestion; letting a brother or sister show off without telling him or her not to be such a show-off; letting a friend play with something that she is not particularly interested in playing with, without telling the friend to put it down and play with something else.

Doing Brave but Wise Things: Trying an activity he's never tried before; getting to know people she's never met before; venturing the answer to a question raised in a group, when he's not very sure of the answer; doing something in the dark; doing something that is not dangerous that she was inhibited about doing at some point in the past.

Having a Good Sense of Humor: Saying something funny; appreciating it and laughing when someone else says something funny; doing an imitation of something or someone that is funny but not derisive; imagining a silly situation and having fun with it; surprising someone with a trick that is not harmful.

References

Centerwall, B.S. (1989). Exposure to television as a cause of violence. In G. Comstock (Ed.), *Public communication and behavior*, (Vol. 2, pp. 1–58). New York: Academic Press.

Comstock, G., & Paik, H. (1991). *Television and the American child*. San Diego: Academic Press.

Liebert, R. M., Sprafkin, J. N., & Davidson, E. S. (1982). *The early window: Effects of television on children and youth*, (2d ed.) New York: Pergamon Press.

Lobitz, W. C., & Johnson, S. M. (1975). Parental manipulation of the behavior of normal and deviant children. *Child Development, 46*, 719–726.

Strayhorn, J. M. (1988). *The competent child: An approach to psychotherapy and preventive mental health*. New York: Guilford Press.

Strayhorn, J. M., & Weidman, C. S. (1988). A Parent Practices Scale, and its relation to parent and child mental health. *Journal of the American Academy of Child and Adolescent Psychiatry, 27*, 613–618.

Strayhorn, J. M., & Weidman, C. S. (1989). Reduction of attention deficit and internalizing symptoms in preschoolers through parent–child interaction training. *Journal of the American Academy of Child and Adolescent Psychiatry, 28*, 888–896.

Strayhorn, J. M., Weidman, C. S., & Majumder, A. (1990). Psychometric characteristics of a psychological skills inventory as applied to preschool children. *Journal of Psychoeducational Assessment, 8*, 467–477.

Strayhorn, J. M., & Weidman, C. S. (1991). Follow-up after parent–child interaction training. *Journal of the American Academy of Child and Adolescent Psychiatry, 30*, 138–143.

4
Problem-Solving Communication Training

Arthur L. Robin
Marquita Bedway
Marcia Gilroy

Introduction and Theory

The goal of this manual is to provide the clinician or advanced student with the information and skills necessary to intervene effectively to resolve parent–adolescent conflicts. The 12-session family-focused intervention program outlined here is based upon a behavioral family systems model of parent–adolescent conflict, which conceptualizes arguments about specific issues as exaggerations of the normal developmental processes of adolescent individuation (Robin & Foster, 1989).

Prior to the adolescence of their children, families evolve homeostatic patterns of interactions within which parents and children exercise mutual control over each other's behaviors. Adolescence severely disrupts such systems of checks and balances, as the biological/emotional/cognitive changes of the young teenager become associated with individuation. Developmental psychologists have carefully tracked the normal increase in family conflict that occurs during the junior high school years, and demonstrated that in most families this increased perturbation subsides by middle adolescence (Montemayor, Adams, & Gullotta, 1990).

A behavioral family systems model postulates three primary factors that determine whether the normal conflict associated with early adolescent individuation subsides or escalates to clinically significant proportions: (1) deficits in problem-solving communication skills; (2) distorted thinking about family life; and (3) family structure problems. The model postulates that these factors are additive: the more difficulties a family has in these areas, the more conflict they will experience during the adolescent years. Accumulating evidence supports portions of this model, although much more research needs to be conducted (Robin & Foster, 1989).

Skill Deficits

"Problem-solving skills" refers to the family's repertoire of cognitions and behaviors for negotiating mutually acceptable solutions to problems: sensing the presence of a problem, clearly defining the problem, brainstorming alternative solutions, evaluating the alternatives, reaching a mutually acceptable decision, planning the implementation of the solution, and verifying the outcome. "Communication skills" refers to the family's repertoire of sender and receiver skills for interpersonal interchanges, and particularly to their ability to express and understand affect and content without antagonizing each other by the style of their communication. Parents and adolescents who are effective problem solvers and positive communicators will have fewer conflicts than those who have not acquired these skills.

Cognitions

"Distorted thinking" refers to the tendency to jump to the worst possible conclusion about family events, to expect too much from another family member, or to adhere to fundamentally rigid, unreasonable beliefs about family life. Such absolutistic thinking promotes negative affect, which impedes rational conflict resolution. Parents may, for example, adhere to *ruinous* beliefs that their teenagers will get into serious trouble if given too much freedom; they may demand unflinching *obedience* or an unreasonable degree of *perfectionism*. They may attribute rebellious misbehavior to *malicious motives* ("He is doing it on purpose to hurt us"). Adolescents often have too keen a sense of injustice, adhering to the "injustice triad" of beliefs concerning *ruination, unfairness,* and *autonomy* ("My parents curfew rules are very unfair; I will never have a boyfriend and they will ruin my social life. I should be able to have as much freedom as I wish").

Structure

Family structure problems include difficulties in cohesion and alignment. "Cohesion" refers to the degree of involvement between parents and adolescents; it is very similar in meaning to what Patterson (1982) calls "monitoring." Disengaged families do not adequately monitor their youngsters' behavior and do not provide sufficient emotional nurturance for adolescent development to proceed normally; such youth engage in risky, delinquent behaviors and/or fail to acquire skills for intimate adult interactions. Overinvolved families smother their youth through too much emotional nurturance and hold them back from individuating with too much monitoring. A balanced degree of cohesion seems optimal. "Alignment" refers to the taking of sides: coalitions and triangulation. When parents work well as a team, adolescents adhere to limits. When one parent takes sides with an adolescent against the other, or places the other in the middle, discipline breaks down, and adolescents stretch the limits, escalating risky behaviors.

Overview of Training Procedures

When presented with a family experiencing parent–adolescent conflict, the therapist's task is to assess the extent to which the three factors discussed above account for the presenting problems, and to intervene to change these factors. We have developed, refined, and tested intervention modules designed to teach problem solving and communication skills, to change unreasonable belief systems, and to alter family structure (Robin & Foster, 1989). Others have discussed the application of these techniques with children who have disorders such as Attention Deficit Hyperactivity Disorder (ADHD) (Barkley, 1990). Not all families require all interventions; this depends upon assessment. It is not possible, however, within the confines of a linear manual, to cover all possible permutations. Instead, we have taken the approach of giving concrete advice for the practicing clinician about the modal case of parent–adolescent conflict, with some hints for branching in other directions as necessary. We have chosen to focus in this manual primarily on the first two factors: skill deficits and cognitions. It is difficult to cover the diverse interventions needed to address family structure; therapists need both written guidelines and live supervision to learn these techniques. Interested readers should consult the following references for introductions to modifying family structure: Alexander and Parsons (1982); Haley (1976, 1980); Madanes (1981); Minuchin and Fishman (1981); or Robin and Foster (1989).

Behavioral family systems therapy is a highly directive, psychoeducational intervention. Such an intervention demands a therapist skilled at structuring the therapeutic context and also skilled at building rapport. Previous experience with families and adolescents is necessary to implement the techniques outlined in this manual. The beginning therapist who wishes to implement these techniques will need to have supervision to become effective.

We have organized the manual in terms of the phases of therapy, and of the sessions within each phase (see table 4–1).

For each session, we have provided concrete information about goals and methods, using many clinical examples and paraphrases of possible therapist remarks. First, the therapist must engage the family in this funny dance we call "family therapy"—simultaneously establishing rapport, assessing problems and interactions, judging sources of resistance, and building a therapeutic contract. The therapist might be seen as a "gymnast" during this phase, juggling many factors to create an impression while not letting any one factor fall down. Second, the therapist must teach skills for

Table 4–1
Phases of Problem-Solving Communication Training

I. Engagement Phase
   A. Session 1: Assess family interactions; build rapport
   B. Session 2: Assess individual/couple characteristics
   C. Session 3. Build a therapeutic contract and prepare the family for change
II. Skill-Building Phase
   A. Session 4: Introduce problem-solving skills
   B. Session 5: Introduce communication skills
   C. Sessions 6 and 7: Build skills
III. Intense Conflict Resolution
   A. Session 8: Introduce Cognitive Restructuring
   B. Sessions 9 and 10: Apply problem solving, communication training, and cognitive restructuring to intense family conflicts
IV. Termination
   A. Sessions 11 and 12: Relapse prevention and fading-out therapy

problem solving and communication. Now the therapist assumes the role of "teacher," imparting new knowledge and motivating families to practice the skills. Third, the therapist must change cognitions and intervene to resolve intense conflicts. Fourth, the therapist must gracefully "butt out," permitting the family to move ahead without a relapse.

Session 1: Build Rapport and Assess Family

Goals

The goals for Session 1 are (1) to establish rapport with the family; (2) to build a picture of the family's deficits in problem-solving skills, cognitive distortions, and family structure problems; (3) to shape a shared view of the problem, such that family members perceive the interactional nature of the problem; (4) to motivate the family to work hard for change.

"Musts" for Interviewing Families

First, remain unaligned. Don't take sides, even if family members ask you leading questions. Second, involve all family members. Bring out silent family members, and nicely control monopolizers. Third, be accepting and noncritical. Don't get defensive if challenged. And fourth, don't give premature advice or suggestions for change.

Opening Social Phase

Escort the family into the room. Arrange the chairs in a semicircle. Make light conversation ("Did you have any difficulty parking?" "It sure is cold out"). Make positive comments, if possible, on some feature of the adolescent's appearance or clothing ("That's a great Detroit Piston shirt. How do you think they will do this season?"). This helps establish instant rapport.

Give Rationale for Engagement Phase

"We are going to get to know each other. I'm going to get a feel for how things are in your family. You will get a feel for how I work with families. It usually takes 3 sessions for me to learn enough to come up with a plan to help you change things. Today I will talk to you all together; next time, we will split up: I will spend half the session with _____(teen) and half with _____ (parents). In the third meeting I'll talk with you all together again and formulate goals for change and a plan of action to bring those goals about."

Give the Ground Rules for Controlling the Session

"As we talk, I've got several basic rules I need your help with. One person talks at a time. I will give you each a turn to talk. No hitting or getting physical. Say it in words. And by the way,_____(parents), is it okay for_____ (teen) to say whatever he wants without fear of punishment? (checking for teen to have permission to speak).

Problem Inquiry

1. Ask a family member to give you a brief description of the problem. Let them decide who will go first. "Whoever would like to start, tell me about the problems that are going on."
2. Listen attentively to the speaker for 4 or 5 minutes, blocking any interruptions from others.
3. Briefly paraphrase the speaker's problem, asking pinpointing questions to assess interaction sequences. Look for the antecedents and consequences of the adolescent problem behavior, and how the adolescent's behavior reflects family problem-solving and communication skills.
4. *Example:*

Mother: "Sally just doesn't listen to us anymore. She doesn't do her homework, talks back, comes in late, and has a bad attitude."
Therapist: "So you're upset that Sally does not listen in the sense of not minding what you request: homework, curfew, and so on. And you also don't like the way she communicates her opinions— she is disrespectful. Is that right?"

Mother: "Exactly."
Therapist: "Good. Now, recall a recent episode of not doing what you said around, let's say, homework. Give me a blow-by-blow description of the episode. How did it start? Who said what to whom? How did it end?"

5. After the first speaker has described the problem and you have commented upon his or her description, ask the other members of the family to give their perspectives. As you comment and pinpoint their problems, link the various perspectives into a chain of events. Comment upon any specific deficits in problem solving or communication you notice.

6. Control any angry outbursts or impulsive interruptions. Redirect comments that change the topic.

7. Maintain a neutral stance. Family members will try to get you to take their sides. Don't! Be neutral even if a member's position sounds ridiculous.

8. After obtaining a brief overview of the problem from each family member, reframe it in interactional terms, that is, as a sequence of events. This helps to shape a shared view of the problem, and prepares the family to accept a family intervention. For example, the therapist might say, "So when you and Sally have a problem with homework, several things happen. You ask her to start her math. She says 'in a minute.' You ask her more loudly. She accuses you of yelling. You deny it. She yells at you. Your husband threatens to ground her. She stomps out. Everyone feels angry. Is this the way it is?"

9. Continue with the problem inquiry until each family member has given his or her perspective, and you have reframed it in interactional terms. Don't get too convoluted. Stick to the "big picture."

Directly Assess Skill Deficits

1. Ask the family to what extent they engage in each of the following steps of problem solving when disagreements arise:
   a. "Do you clearly tell each other what is the problem?"
   b. "Do you try to think of several ideas to solve it?"
   c. "Do you discuss the good and bad points of each idea?"
   d. "Can you reach a decision you all can live with?"
   e. To teen: "Do you have a real say in such discussions?"
   f. To parents: "Does your teen try to dictate to you?"
   g. "Do solutions work? What happens if they don't?"

2. Review the Family Negative Communication Handout (see table 4–5) with them and ask which of the negative communication habits on the left side occur regularly in the family
   a. "What names do you call each other?"

    b. "How do you put each other down?"
    c. "Who criticizes?"
    d. Go through the other items on the handout.

Assess Cognitions

1. Ask what runs through their heads during arguments.
2. When a family member looks upset, ask what he or she is thinking at that moment.
3. Suggest common beliefs that parents and adolescents have (see Session 8, table 4–6) and ask whether these apply.

Assess History of the Problems

1. How did the family get along prior to the adolescence of this child?
2. When did the problem begin?
3. How have the problems changed?

Assess Assets

1. How does the family have fun together?
2. What does each member like about the others?
3. Don't assume everything is negative. Look for the positive too.

Summarize and Assign Homework

1. Make a summary statement of what you have learned, giving hope for change. For example, you might say:

> "At this point, I'd like to pull things together. I've learned today that in your family there are arguments every day about chores, homework, curfew, bedtime, and friends. Sometimes mom or dad pick a fight; sometimes Sally picks a fight. When you tell each other what's bothering you, the other person gets very defensive, and the complainer gets accusing, and before you know it, you are bringing up everything from the past. Sally, you seem to believe your parents are old fashioned and too strict. Mr. and Mrs. Jones, you seem to believe Sally will get herself in serious trouble if you don't watch her closely. It's all very unpleasant. But, I've seen many families like this, and the thing that impresses me about you is that you do care about each other. You have what it takes to change things. But it's going to take some hard work."

2. Assign self-report questionnaires as homework. You may select:
    a. Issues Checklist (Barkley, 1991; Robin & Foster, 1989).

   b. Conflict Behavior Questionnaire (Barkley, 1991; Robin & Foster, 1989).
   c. Parent–Adolescent Relationship Questionnaire (Robin, Koepke, & Moye, 1990).
   d. Other family measures (Robin & Foster, 1989).
3. Set next appointment and handle billing and payment.

Session 2: Individual/Couple Assessment

Goals

The goals for Session 2 are (1) to establish rapport with the adolescent; (2) to assess adolescent psychopathology and/or cognitive functioning; (3) to obtain a developmental history; and (4) to assess marital interaction and family impact of adolescent–parent conflict.

Introductory Comment

Collect the self-report measures before beginning the session. If the measures have not been completed, ask each family member to complete them while the others are being interviewed.

Part One: Adolescent Interview

   1. Do not begin by discussing the family problems since most adolescents will feel blamed, or alienated, and thereafter will not cooperate with you.
   2. Begin by asking the adolescent to tell you about his or her interests, favorite recreational activities, sports, or hobbies.
   3. Be genuine and convey your interest in getting to know the adolescent as a person. Don't be condescending. Don't try to be a peer to the adolescent either. Such approaches will turn off most teenagers. Be yourself: most teenagers are quick to spot a phony front.
   4. Look for similarities between the adolescent's interests and your own recreational interests. Point out any similarities in a genuine, matter-of-fact manner. This will help establish your credibility.
   5. Listen reflectively and do not criticize the adolescent or preach if you do not approve of the adolescent's recreational pursuits.
   6. Adolescents will often ask you personal questions. Honest self-disclosure is usually helpful in building rapport and establishing the therapist as a positive adult role model. However, know your own limits for self-disclosure and respect them. Tell the adolescent if a question crosses your limit for self-disclosure. Do so honestly and without hostility.

For example, if the adolescent asked, "Did you, Dr. Jones, ever have sex without a condom when you were a teenager?," you should reply in this manner: "Bill, there are some things about my life that are too personal for me as a therapist to talk about with my patients. We are just getting to know each other. If there is a time later in our sessions when I feel it would help you for me to go into detail about such things, I'll consider answering even these questions, but not now."

7. Spend about 10 minutes on this phase of the interview. Don't shortchange rapport building because adolescents often size up adults based upon initial impressions. Your ability to produce change may depend upon establishing a good relationship with the adolescent as quickly as possible.

8. Make a gradual transition into a discussion about the presenting problems. Use an aspect of your discussion of the adolescent's interests as an opening to shift gears to family and/or school problems. The following dialogue illustrates shifting gears.

Teen: "I get off on SuperNintendo. I could play that for hours."
Therapist: "Do your parents set limits on it?"
Teen: "Yep. That's a real bummer. Mom makes me turn it off after three hours!"
Therapist: "What do you do next?"
Teen: "We usually get in a big argument."
Therapist: "I'd like to learn more about all the arguments you and your mom have. What other topics do you argue about?"

9. Inquire about the adolescent's perspective on the family conflicts, problem-solving skills, and communication patterns. Do not repeat what you did in Session 1; briefly get the teenager's perceptions.

10. Translate adolescent gripes into goals for change. Take a hopeful stance about the possibility for change. Ask the adolescent to give specific goals for change for each family member, and inquire about perceived obstacles to change. Adolescents often perceive their parents' rigidity as the major obstacle to change. Take their concerns seriously, and indicate that you will be doing your own evaluation of the parents.

11. Assess the individual adolescent's psychopathology and/or cognitive functioning. This is the portion of the overall assessment where intellectual and/or academic testing is done, if called for. This is also the portion of the overall assessment where the therapist assesses the adolescent for formal psychiatric problems such as ADHD, mood disorders, anxiety disorders, and so on. A detailed discussion of such assessment goes beyond this manual. Consult Mash and Terdal (1988).

12. Assess preconceptions about therapy. Begin by saying something like this: "People have all kinds of ideas about what we therapists do. I'd like

to make sure we understand each about this. What are your ideas about my job as your therapist?"

    13. Correct common misconceptions about therapy:

        a. *Only crazy people go to therapy.* Point out how therapy is designed to help people with problems in daily living, and note that the teen is certainly not crazy.

        b. *My friends will find out about my problems.* Review the general principles of confidentiality.

        c. *Parents never change; therapy is a waste of time.* Point out past successes and help the teenager see that his or her parents may be hurting too.

Part Two: Couple or Single Parent Interview

    1. Open with a positive comment about the adolescent. Acknowledge with empathy the difficulties of parenting an adolescent: "He is a fine young man, but I certainly understand how his need for freedom can drive you nuts," for example, or "I was impressed by Sally's honesty. Sometimes I bet you must get pretty mad when she tells it like she sees it at home. There is a place for tact; teenagers just don't see that yet."

    2. Take a brief developmental history, focusing on parent–child interactions. You are looking to determine at what developmental stage significant oppositional behavior occurred. Many adolescents were very oppositional as young children, and their parents' responses set the tone for later conflict.

        a. What was the child's temperament as an infant?

        b. What were the "terrible twos" like?

        c. How did the child relate to the parents as a preschooler?

        d. To what extent was noncompliance a problem from ages 6 to 10?

        e. What management techniques did the parents use to deal with noncompliant behavior? How effective were these techniques?

        f. How did the child get along with siblings?

        g. What associated medical problems or developmental delays occurred?

    3. Make a smooth transition into taking a brief marital history. Remember, couples are often threatened if asked directly about marital problems. The developmental history provides the opportunity for a more indirect approach. In addition, focus your questions more upon the impact on the marriage of having a difficult teen, and how the couple would like to change this. Sample questions you could ask include:

        a. What was family life like before your child was born?

        b. How did you become a family? How did you meet?

        c. What were the early years of your life together like?

        d. How did the birth of your child influence your relationship?

    e. To what extent do you agree about how to handle conflicts with your adolescent at present?

    f. In what ways does your adolescent's rebellious behavior impact your marriage?

    g. In what ways does your adolescent take advantage of your disagreements to "divide and conquer"?

    h. How does the adolescent's problem behavior impact your social life?

    i. How does the adolescent's problem behavior impact the family's finances?

    j. How would improvement in parent–adolescent conflict benefit the couple?

4. Assess parental psychopathology. Follow conventional assessment procedures here. You are not attempting to do a detailed assessment; you simply want to get a quick feel for what is going on. If you uncover a major problem area, such as depression, substance abuse, or anxiety disorders, you may need to schedule an additional session. Often, these problems will be denied, but you will later learn of their presence and have to deal with them.

5. Make a brief summary statement and adjourn the session. Summarize what you have learned in this session and integrate it with the information collected in the previous session. For example, you might say: "Today I learned that the difficulties with Tom began as he turned 12; before then, family life was pretty peaceful and you were a close couple. As more conflict with Tom has occurred, it's made it more difficult for you to be close as a couple. This fits with the problem-solving communication skill deficits I learned about in the last session. All of this has been getting you, Mrs. Jones, down, and making you feel depressed recently."

Session 3: Contracting and Preparation for Change

Goals

The goals for Session 3 are (1) to establish goals for change which are salient and acceptable to the family; (2) to decide to what extent the family needs training in each component of the overall intervention; and (3) to give the family feedback about your conceptualization of their problems.

Tasks

First, present the Agreement for Action (see table 4–2) as a therapeutic contract. Second, complete this agreement, filling in the blanks, with the family's assistance. Third, provide information and answer questions as you go. This discussion sets the family's expectations for the remaining sessions.

Table 4–2
Agreement for Action

We, the _____ family agree with Dr. _____ that we need to take *action* in order to get along better with each other. We agree to take the following actions:

Problem Solving

_____ Learn to tell each other our problems clearly, without blame.
_____ Learn to think of many ideas to solve each problem.
_____ Learn to think through the effects of our ideas on each other.
_____ Learn to negotiate agreements we can all live with.
_____ Learn to follow up carefully to carry out our agreements.
_____ Learn to "stay cool" if our agreements don't always work at first.

Communication

_____ Learn to think before we start running off at the mouth.
_____ Learn to express anger/criticism fairly, without attacking the person.
_____ Learn to listen to each other respectively, even when we disagree.
_____ Learn to stick to the topic.
_____ Stop making snide, sarcastic remarks.
_____ Let bygones be bygones. Don't dredge up the past.
_____ Learn to make it short, not to lecture.
_____ Learn to answer each other, not clam up or say "I don't know.".
_____ Other:_____

Thinking Straight or Realistic Expectations

_____ Don't think the worst right away. Evaluate the evidence carefully.
_____ Accept our imperfections. Don't expect perfect behavior or obedience all the time.
_____ Don't assume more freedom always means more trouble. Evaluate the evidence.
_____ Don't assume rules are always unfair. Evaluate the evidence.
_____ Other: Improvement

Involvement

_____ Parents agree to take the time to monitor or keep an eye on the adolescent.
_____ Adolescents agree to monitor parental behaviors that may need change.
_____ Attend therapy sessions as scheduled.
_____ Carry out assignments between sessions.
_____ Pay _____ per session.
_____ Work hard for positive family change

Signatures

_____   _____
_____   _____

Introducing the Agreement for Action (AFA)

1. Give rationale and agenda. Distribute blank agreement forms. The therapist should say something like this: "Today I'm going to give you feedback about what I learned from the last two meetings. I hope to answer any questions and reach an agreement with you about our goals for change together. To make this easier, I've got an Agreement for Action. Here are copies for everyone. We will go over each section and check off the sections that apply to your family."

2. Read the opening paragraph of the AFA.

3. Give feedback about problem-solving deficits. Go over each step of problem solving. Assess reaction to feedback and check off the appropriate goals on the AFA.

4. Give feedback about communication skill deficits. Be specific. Check off appropriate goals on the AFA.

5. Discuss cognitions. Explain how absolutistic thinking can elicit excessive anger and impede rational conflict resolution. Note which distorted beliefs apply to this family and check off the applicable goals on the AFA.

6. Discuss involvement. These goals relate to general involvement and participation in therapy. All of the goals apply to all families. Explain and review them.

7. Obtain family members' signatures.

8. Answer any additional questions.

9. Adjourn the session.

Session 4: Introduce Problem-Solving Training

Goals

The goals for Session 4 are (1) to present the steps of problem solving to the family; (2) to guide the family through an initial problem-solving discussion; (3) to teach the family to use the problem-solving worksheet to organize their discussions; and (4) to give the family a success experience resolving a meaningful disagreement.

General Training Procedures

Teach problem-solving skills through instruction, modeling, behavior rehearsal, and feedback. First, give a brief rationale with instructions for each step of problem solving. Second, model appropriate verbalizations and each step. Third, ask each family member to rehearse the appropriate problem-solving response. Finally, praise appropriate statements and suggest corrective feedback for inappropriate behaviors. It is expected that family members' initial responses will not meet criteria. Therefore, you must be prepared to shape terminal responses through successive approximations.

Give Rationale for Problem Solving

The therapist should say something like this:

> "We are entering a new stage of treatment where you will learn new problem-solving and communication skills. It usually takes four sessions to

learn these new skills and start to apply them at home. These skills will help you reach solutions you can all live with for important disagreements."

"In problem solving, each of you will take turns defining a specific problem. You will then list some solutions, decide which ones you would like to try, and plan to carry them out. If you do not at first succeed, you will try again or renegotiate. We will learn to use these steps of problem solving to resolve disputes around specific issues such as curfew, chores, dating, and so on."

Give the Ground Rules for Controlling the Session

"We have several basic ground rules for this phase of our treatment, similar to before. One person talks at a time. No hitting or physical violence. Try to talk with respect. I will interrupt you if you break these rules."

Select an Issue for an Initial Problem-Solving Discussion

1. Select an issue rated with an anger-intensity level of two or three on the Issues Checklist, if the family has completed this measure. Such an issue will be meaningful but of moderate intensity. Moderate intensity issues are ideal for skill acquisition; high intensity issues arouse too much affect.

2. Ask the family to select a significant but not the most intense issue of disagreement.

3. Distribute the Problem Solving Outline for Families (see table 4–3) to each family member and/or post a large-print copy on the wall.

Teach Problem Definition

1. Issue the rationale and instructions: "We have selected curfew (substitute your issue) for discussion. First, we each must define the problem. We define the problem by starting with an "I", and making a short, clear statement of how we feel and what is happening that is a problem. Try not to be accusatory."

2. Model a plausible problem definition: "For example, Mr. Smith, if I were you, I might say, 'I am angry at you, Tom, because I have caught you coming home past curfew five times. I'm worried you could get in trouble being out late.'"

3. Conduct a behavior rehearsal. Ask Mr. Smith to define the problem: "Mr. Smith, please define the curfew problem, in your own words, following these guidelines."

4. Give feedback. If the problem is adequately defined, praise the family member and move on. If the problem definition is inadequate, give corrective feedback, accompanied by further modeling, culminating in another behavior rehearsal:

Table 4–3
Problem-Solving Outline for Families

I. Define the Problem
    A. Tell the others what they are doing that is a problem and explain why.
        1. Be brief.
        2. Be positive, not accusing.
    B. Repeat the others' statements of the problem to check out understanding of what they said.
II. Generate Alternative Solutions
    A. Take turns listing possible solutions.
    B. Follow three rules for listing solutions:
        1. List as many ideas as possible
        2. Don't evaluate the ideas
        3. Be creative; suggest crazy ideas.
    C. It won't have to be done just because it was stated.
III. Evaluate/Decide upon the Best Idea
    A. Take turns evaluating each idea:
        1. Would this idea solve the problem for the teen?
        2. Would this idea solve the problem for the parents?
        3. Rate the idea "plus" or "minus" on the worksheet.
    B. Select the best idea:
        1. Look for ideas rated "plus" by all:
            a. Select one such idea
            b. Combine several such ideas.
        2. If none is rated "plus" by all, see what ideas came closest to agreement and negotiate a compromise. If two parents are participating, look for ideas rated "plus" by one parent and the teenager.
III. Plan to Implement the Selected Solution
    A. Decide who will do what, when, where, and how.
    B. Plan reminders for task completion.
    C. Plan consequences for compliance or noncompliance.

Poor definition: "I get mad when you purposely come home late and show total disrespect for my feelings."

Therapist correction: "You started with an "I", but then you accused him of coming home late on purpose and failed to pinpoint the problem. It may or may not be done on purpose. It would be better to say, 'I get mad when you come home late because I feel as if you are disrespectful of me and not thinking of my feelings.' Now, please try again."

Teach Paraphrasing/Listening Skills

1. As each person states his or her definition, ask at least one family member to paraphrase the speaker to check for understanding. For example, you might say, "To make sure you heard what your dad said, Tom, I would like you to restate his words, without adding anything of your own."

2. Praise accurate paraphrases; coach the family member, involving

clarification from the speaker, for inaccurate paraphrases. The following sample dialogue illustrates the procedure.

Tom: "So you think I come home later than that Stone Age curfew that anybody knows is unfair."
Therapist: "Tom, you added a put-down and accusation to your dad's words. Repeat just what he said."
Tom: "He thinks I come home late and disrespect him."
Therapist: "Good!"

3. Have each person define the problem and then ask others to paraphrase these definitions.

4. Afterward, reiterate that it is natural for family members to have different opinions about an issue, but that it is not necessary to persuade the others to accept one's own opinion in order to discuss the issue.

5. Correct problem definitions, but don't require perfection in the first session. You want to get through the entire outline.

Teach Solution-Listing (Brainstorming) Skills

1. Begin by providing a rationale and instructions. You might say, "Now that we have defined the problem, we need to think of some solutions. You will take turns listing as many ideas as possible. Say anything that comes to mind, even if it sounds silly. Don't judge the ideas yet; that comes later. You don't have to do it just because you said it. This is called brainstorming."

2. Ask one family member to write down the ideas on a Problem-Solving Worksheet (see table 4–4). In the early sessions, it is often a good idea to ask the adolescent to write down the solutions to maintain his or her involvement. But if you expect the adolescent to refuse, you should at first ask another family member.

3. Prompt the family members to take turns suggesting ideas. Keep the floor open to all ideas. Block any attempts to evaluate the ideas, critically or positively. Keep the mood light, and keep the pace of the session moving.

4. While it is not your responsibility to generate the ideas, the therapist may make several suggestions to lighten the mood or keep things moving forward. Suggest outlandish, unusual ideas to lighten the atmosphere and spur creativity.

5. Continue listing solutions until you either have 8 to 10 ideas or you judge the family to have moved beyond their initial positions. Most families reiterate their initial positions through their first few suggestions for change; afterward, they begin to come up with novel alternatives.

Table 4–4
Problem-Solving Worksheet

Name _____ Date _____

Problem or Topic: _____

_____

_____

Solutions	Evaluations		
	Teen	Mom	Dad

Agreement: _____

_____

_____

6. Block attempts to manipulate solution listing to express anger and vent "hidden agendas."

Teaching Evaluation/Decision-Making Skills

1. Introduce evaluation/decision making by asking the family to review the ideas on the worksheet. Ask *each* family member to evaluate *each* idea, indicating whether it will solve the problem, whether it is practical, and whether he or she likes it. Then, ask the family members to rate the idea "plus" or "minus," recording the ratings in the appropriate columns on the worksheet. The therapist should say something like this: "Now that you came up with some ideas, we need to evaluate them and vote 'plus' or 'minus' if we like or dislike them. Take the first idea on the list. I want you each to say whether this idea will solve your problem, whether it will solve the others' problems, and whether it's practical. Then, rate it 'plus' or 'minus.' We will put your ratings in the correct column next to the idea on the worksheet."

2. Model a correct evaluation: "For example, the first idea to address the curfew problem is, 'Stay out all night.' As a teenager, I might say, 'That's a great idea; it solves my problem of missing out on late parties. Of course, I'd be dead meat if I tried it. So maybe it's not that great. I guess I'd give it a minus.'"

3. Guide family members to evaluate and rate each idea. Carefully control the interaction. Do not let it deteriorate into an argument. Directively help family members clarify ideas. Sometimes, additional solutions emerge; this is acceptable. Add them to the list and evaluate them.

4. Lead the family in the decision-making phase. After all the ideas have been evaluated, ask the secretary to read aloud any ideas rated "plus" by everyone. *If one or more ideas were rated "plus" by all,* congratulate the family on reaching an agreement and ask them to combine the ideas into an overall solution. Proceed to implementation planning. *If no ideas are rated "plus" by all,* you will have to help them negotiate a compromise.

5. Address negotiation/resolving an impasse. Why does the family seem to be stuck in an impasse? Possible explanations include:

1. A high level of mutual distrust and hostility
2. Extreme cognitions mediating refusal to compromise
3. Extremely coercive adolescent who typically controls the parents
4. Parent–child power struggle
5. The issue touches a basic value and is nonnegotiable.

In this manual, we cannot exhaustively cover techniques for handling each of these situations; readers should consult Robin and Foster (1989) for more details. We will offer a general outline of negotiation techniques: First, find an idea on which the family came close to an agreement. For example, in a two-parent family, this might be an idea rated positively by one parent and the teenager. In a single-parent family, use your judgment. Second, clearly state the gap between their various positions. Third, ask the family to bridge the gap by suggesting several additional ideas in-between their positions. And fourth, ask the family to evaluate these ideas and try to reach a consensus.

6. As an example of negotiation, let's use the issue of putting away clothing. The idea on which the mother and her teenage son came closest to agreement was: "Teen will put the clothes away daily." However, the mother wanted him to put his clothes in his drawers, but he insisted that he would fold them neatly and leave them on the bed. They were asked to generate alternatives to bridge this gap. They suggested:

1. Build a chute from the bed to the drawer
2. Take turns putting the clothes away
3. Earn money for putting them away
4. Put them away some but not all days of the week.

After evaluation, they agreed that on Monday, Wednesday, and Friday the teen would put the clothes in the drawer. On Tuesday, Thursday, and Saturday, he would fold them neatly and leave them on the bed. On Sunday, they would flip a coin to determine what he did.

7. Help the family plan to implement the solution. Guide the family to specify a detailed plan to put the agreed-upon solution into action. Such a plan indicates:

    a. Who will do what, when, and where
    b. Who will monitor compliance with the agreement, and how monitoring will be carried out (with charts or graphs, or verbally?)
    c. The consequences for noncompliance, for example, punishments
    d. What if any performance reminders will be given
    e. What constitutes compliance, for example, what do we mean by a clean room?
    f. What difficulties are anticipated in carrying out the plan.

8. As an example of an implementation plan, let's look at a solution to a curfew problem. The agreement was that Tom will select one weekend night to have a midnight curfew and the other weekend night will be home at 10:00 P.M. Weekday curfew will be 9:00 P.M.

    a. The family defined "midnight" to mean within 10 minutes of midnight.
    b. Mom and dad agreed to take turns waiting up for Tom.
    c. Everyone agreed that loss of weekend going-out privileges on the next weekend would be the consequence for noncompliance.

d. They anticipated problems such as "My watch is slow," or getting a flat tire. In emergencies, Tom was to call ahead to indicate that a problem had come up and he might be late. They also anticipated that if special event came up, such as New Year's Eve, Tom could ask for an extension on the curfew, but he had to ask at least 48 hours in advance.

Summary and Assignment of Homework

First, praise the family for getting through the steps of problem solving and reaching an agreement. Second, ask for their reactions to the process of problem solving. Third, assign as homework implementation of the agreement. Fourth, explain that you will be teaching them how to integrate problem solving into their daily life at home as a means of resolving conflict.

Session 5: Introduce Communication Training

Goals

The goals of Session 5 are (1) to increase family members' awareness of their negative communication habits and the deleterious impact of negative communication on parent–adolescent relations; (2) to pinpoint the most salient negative communication habits for this family; (3) to teach positive communication habits, using instructions, modeling, behavior rehearsal, and feedback; and (4) to assign home practice of positive communication skills.

General Procedures

Begin the session by distributing and reviewing the Family Negative Communication Handout (see table 4–5). Family members are asked to recall recent examples of specific negative communication habits on the handout, to consider the impact of these habits on each other, and to suggest more constructive approaches for expressing their thoughts and feelings. Next, the therapist should select several salient negative communication habits for intensive correction, and train the family to replace these habits with more positive responses. Homework is assigned to practice the new communication skills in daily conversations.

The success of communication training depends upon the persistence of the therapist. It is important to consistently correct every instance of a targeted negative communication pattern, assertively but respectfully. It is also important to "balance" targets across family members. Don't single out the father several times while ignoring the adolescent's problem behavior.

Table 4–5
Family Negative Communication Handout

Check if your family does this:		Try to do this instead:
1.	Call each other names	Express anger without hurt
2.	Put each other down	"I am angry that you did _____"
3.	Interrupt each other	Take turns; keep it short.
4.	Criticize too much	Point out the good and the bad
5.	Get defensive	Listen: calmly disagree
6.	Lecture	Tell it straight and short
7.	Look away from speaker	Make eye contact
8.	Slouch	Sit up, look attractive
9.	Talk in sarcastic tone	Talk in normal tone
10.	Get off the topic	Finish one topic, go on
11.	Think the worse	Don't jump to conclusions
12.	Dredge up the past	Stick to the present
13.	Read others' mind	Ask others' opinions
14.	Command, order	Request nicely
15.	Give the silent treatment	Say what's bothering you
16.	Make light of something	Take it seriously
17.	Deny you did it.	Admit you did it, or nicely explain that you didn't
18.	Nag about small mistakes	Admit no one is perfect; overlook small things

Review of Family Negative Communication Handout

1. Distribute the handout to each family member.

2. Explain the rationale: "Today we will work on how you communicate with each other. I've noticed that you sometimes get really upset about the way you talk to each other. This leads to a lot of anger, hassles, and unpleasant arguments, sidetracking you from the issues you are discussing. Look at this handout. On the left side are negative communication habits; on the right side are positive alternatives. Give me some recent examples of the negative habits which occurred in your family."

3. Prompt family members to take turns describing recent negative communication interchanges.

Increase Awareness of the Deleterious Impact of Negative
Communication on Family Relations

As the family presents examples of negative communication, help them to become aware of the impact of such habits on family relations. The following sample dialogue demonstrates this procedure.

Therapist: "What happens when your mom nags you about doing the dishes?"

Teen: "I get mad and put her down."

Therapist: "Mrs. Jones, what do you do next?"
Mother: "I start yelling."
Teen: "Then I never do the dishes."
Therapist: "So nagging spurs put-downs, yelling, and more defiance. You can see how one negative begets another, and before long everyone is very upset."

Suggest, Model, and Rehearse Constructive, Positive Communication Habits

1. Point out positive responses on the right-hand column of the handout.

2. Model the application of these responses to the examples under discussion.

3. Request the family to role-play the positive responses, coaching them as needed. The following sample dialogue demonstrates modeling, coaching, and role play:

Therapist: "Mrs. Jones, when it is time for Tom to do the dishes, you might start by saying assertively. 'Tom, I would appreciate it if you would now do the dishes; it's 7:00 P.M., the time we agreed upon.' "
Mrs. Jones: "And when he doesn't do it, then what?"
Therapist: "You clearly express your anger and frustration without put-downs or nagging. Start with an 'I,' say how you feel, and set forth conditions or consequences. For example, 'I am angry that you're not getting down to the dishes; I expect you to start now or I will put consequences into effect.' Now, Mrs. Jones, you try that in your own words, and let's see how Tom responds."
Mrs. Jones: "Tom, I expect you to start the dishes; it's 7:00 P.M."
Therapist: "Good."

Intense Correction of Selected Negative Communication Habits

1. Pick two or three habits to correct.

2. Ask the family to conduct a problem-solving discussion of a topic of their choice. Pick a topic likely to invoke the negative communication habits.

3. Indicate that you will stop the discussion whenever examples of the negative communication habits occur, and then request corrections.

4. Consistently interrupt the discussion.

5. Use feedback, instructions, modeling, and behavior rehearsal to coach the family to correct negative communication.

6. Continue this process for the remainder of the session.

7. Liberally praise positive efforts.

Communication Training Homework Assignment

1. Assign the family the task of practicing the newly acquired positive communication habits at home.

2. Give each family member permission to politely prompt the others to monitor and correct their communication at home. For example, the adolescent might be asked to call his mother's attention to nagging. The mother might be asked to call her son's attention to put-downs. If a family member encounters hostility when trying to call attention to negative communication, instruct him or her to back off and tell the therapist at the next session. Otherwise, the family may corrupt your assignment into an excuse for further arguments.

Sessions 6 and 7: Building New Skills

Goals

The goals for Sessions 6 and 7 are (1) to strengthen problem- solving communication skills through additional coached practice; and (2) to review homework and guide the family in applying the skills to their interactions throughout the week.

Procedures

Sessions 6 and 7 do not have a detailed content outline because they do not involve the introduction of new material. The therapist now works to help the family build upon the skills introduced in Sessions 4 and 5. Generally speaking, divide the session time between reviewing homework, conducting problem-solving discussions, and correcting negative communication. Additional homework to conduct problem-solving discussions throughout the week and to practice new communication skills should be assigned. Tailor the sequence of problem-solving and communication training activities to the idiosyncratic needs of each family.

We will give examples of the types of activities you might do to accomplish these goals.

Reviewing Homework/Problem Inquiry

1. Ask for a report of the past week's homework.
2. Ask whether the family successfully implemented solutions negoti-

ated in the past week's therapy session? If the answer is yes, praise them liberally and ask them to continue implementing that solution. If the answer is no, investigate what went wrong:

a. Did family members try to implement the solution?
b. Was there resistance from one member?
c. Did negative communication side-track them?
d. Was there mistrust and hostility?
e. Did they "forget" to do things?

3. Help the family straighten out any problems with the past week's solutions before beginning a new topic. You may need to coach them to renegotiate the original problem or discuss a new angle on it. Use problem-solving and communication skills flexibly in this process.

4. Did the family practice the skills at home? How did the practice work out? Ask for a report of any problem solving discussions. Also ask for a report of application of new communication skills.

5. Help them plan to practice the skills more effectively in the future. Identify any consistent themes that were problematic at home, and plan to incorporate them into today's session. For example, if problem definition deteriorated into a "free-for-all" accusation/defensiveness sequence, plan to work on problem definition. If the father dominated the discussion at home and failed to listen to the adolescent's ideas, concentrate on this problem during the session.

6. The family's ability to benefit from this type of therapy depends upon their success with such homework assignments. This is a very important part of Sessions 6 and 7, and may take most of the session.

Skill Practice

1. Conduct a new problem-solving discussion, using a moderate to severely conflictual issue. Focus on refining skills, as needed.

2. Target additional negative communication skills for correction, using feedback, instructions, modeling, and behavior rehearsal.

Homework and Summary

1. Assign increasingly complex skill-oriented tasks.

2. Ask families to set aside a regular time for family meetings. Suggest that they use problem solving to resolve accumulated gripes during these meetings. Suggest that they tape or videotape the meetings for your later review.

3. Assign implementation of any newly negotiated solutions.

4. Assign practice of communication skills.

Session 8: Introduce Cognitive Restructuring

Goals

The goals of Session 8 are (1) to increase family members' awareness of how their thoughts about their relationships can influence their feelings and mediate their responses to each other; (2) to teach family members to identify and challenge common unreasonable expectations and inaccurate attributions about parent–adolescent relationships; (3) to teach family members to generate reasonable cognitions and adopt them; and (4) to teach family members to reframe problem behavior in nonblaming, nonmalicious ways.

Increasing Awareness of the Role of Cognitive Processes

You can open the session by indicating that the focus of today's meeting will be on the role of thinking and feeling in parent–adolescent conflict, and that the format will differ from the previous sessions. Indicate that imaginal exercises, question-and-answer discussion, and role plays will be used to teach family members to become aware of how their thinking influences their feelings, which in turn may make it more difficult to deal with arguments.

An imaginal exercise is often useful for teaching clients the connection between thoughts, feelings, and behaviors. Pick a recent topic that the family has argued about. Construct an imaginal scene that depicts extremely absolutistic, unreasonable thinking about that issue. Tailor your imaginal scene to each family member, taking into account their idiosyncratic cognitive and communication style. Describe the scene in a lively, humorous fashion, blowing up or exaggerating the extreme thinking. After having them imagine the scene, inquire about their thoughts, affects, and likely actions in a manner that interlinks these variables. Keep your descriptions brief and involve family members in the exercise to maintain interest and attention.

As an example of an imaginal exercise, let's suppose that Andrew's parents forbid him to see his friend of many years, William, because they are afraid that Andrew might be corrupted by his friend because William was hanging out with a "bad crowd," smoking, drinking, and disobeying adults. The therapist was aware of this issue, and constructed the following imaginal exercise to introduce cognitive restructuring:

Therapist: "I'd like you to close your eyes and imagine this scene. Mr. and Mrs. Smith, you are walking past Andrew's room and you notice something that looks strange. You go in and see one of William's dirty T-shirts on the floor. You smell something funny—like beer. You look under the bed and find three empty beer cans, still damp from having recently been drunk. One of them has lipstick marks on it. Now, tell me, what would you be thinking?"

Mrs. Smith: "That's terrible. Andrew has been drinking beer, with William. And doing who knows what else with girls. Right in my very own house. I'll kill that disobedient kid. I knew William was a bad influence!"

Therapist: "Great. Sounds like you can relate to this. For one, sounds like you'd be thinking in a *ruinous* way all about how evil William is corrupting your innocent Andrew. We call this type of thinking *"Ruination."* Ruination refers to the idea that teenagers can ruin themselves and their future if they do the wrong things or have too much freedom. Also, you'd be upset about *disobedience*. Parents expect teenagers to *obey* them all the time and get very upset if they don't. Right?"

Mrs. Smith: "Right! I would be so mad I wouldn't know what to do next."

Therapist: "That's exactly my point. If you think such extreme thoughts, you will have strong angry feelings. And what would happen if Andrew walked in the door at that very moment?"

Andrew: "I'd catch hell. We would have the biggest argument in the world."

Therapist: "Thank you. Extreme thoughts leads to extreme feeling. Extreme feelings lead to fights and arguments."

The therapist can further develop such a rationale with Andrew, bringing out the themes of *Unfairness, Autonomy,* and *Ruination* by illustrating how his mother has unrealistically jumped to incorrect conclusions by misinterpreting the available evidence.

Identifying and Challenging Unreasonable Thinking

After showing the family the connection between situations, extreme thoughts, angry affect, and arguments, you should review the List of Common Unreasonable Beliefs (see table 4–6). Ask the family to give recent examples of how these beliefs apply to them. Have them specify the situation, the belief, their feeling, and their response. This exercise is designed to train them to identify unreasonable thinking in its many different forms: expectations, attributions, underlying assumptions, logical errors, and so forth.

Next, teach the family how to challenge the validity of unreasonable beliefs. Help them to apply the following types of questions to the examples of unreasonable beliefs they identified earlier in the exercise:

1. Does this belief really make logical sense?
2. What is the evidence that supports my belief?
3. What is the worst thing that could happen if my teenager keeps doing the things I think are terrible?
4. Did I feel the same way when I was a teenager? What, then, is the big deal?
5. Is it possible that my parents really have my best interest in mind?

Table 4–6
Common Unreasonable Beliefs

Parents

1. Ruination. "If I give my teenager too much freedom, he (she) will ruin his (her) life, get in serious trouble, and make serious mistakes."
   A. Friends: "If Andrew goes out with William and William does bad things, Andrew will become corrupted, a bum, an alcoholic, a sex addict, and a delinquent."
   B. Chores: "If she does not learn to do her chores now, she will grow up to be slovenly, aimless, unemployed, and a welfare case."
   C. Incomplete homework: "He will never graduate from high school, will never get into a good college, will never get a decent job, and will be dependent upon us forever."
2. Obedience/Perfectionism. "My teenager should always behave perfectly and especially obey me."
   A. Visiting relatives: "Doesn't she know Sundays are for visiting relatives. How dare she even think about going out with her friends? Such disobedience!"
   B. Doesn't follow directions: "He can't even put away the dishes without me bugging him 10 times. What disrespect! If I did this to my dad, I would have gotten the paddle."
   C. Curfew: "Why do we have to go through the same argument every Saturday? Can't she just do what I say and come home by 11:00 P.M."
3. Malicious Intent. "That rotten kid got in trouble on purpose just to get me mad."
   A. Playing the radio too loud: "He's just blasting the radio to get on my nerves."
   B. Withdrawing to one's room: "She's hiding out on purpose in her room to get even with me for asking her to do the chores."

Adolescents

1. Unfairness/Ruination. "My parents are totally unfair. They just don't understand me. They are going to absolutely ruin my life. I'll never have any fun because of their unfair rules."
   A. Curfew: "Why should I have to come home earlier than my friends? That's unfair. I'll lose all my friends and be an outcast."
   B. Chores and sibling rivalry: "Why do I always get stuck doing the dishes and trash? Why doesn't my brother get his fair share? My parents are always picking on me and letting him off easy."
   C. Bad teacher: "Mrs. Jones is a witch. She is going to ruin my whole school career. It's not fair that she always calls on me in class and is so strict about getting homework in on time."
2. Autonomy. "I ought to have as much freedom as I want. I should be able to do whatever I want."
   A. Sexuality: "It's my body and what right do my parents have to tell me not to have sex with my boyfriend? I can do whatever I want with my body."
   B. Homework: "I resent my mother asking about my homework. I can get it done all by myself. She has no right to interfere."
   C. Clothes and hair: "I'll dye my hair any color I like. And I'll wear any kind of jeans I choose. Parents shouldn't have anything to say about this."

---

6. Am I making a mountain out of a molehill? Am I overgeneralizing?
7. Am I seeing the trees but missing the forest? Am I focusing on one detail and missing the whole picture?
8. Am I viewing the world as black or white, all or none, when it really is many shades of gray?
9. What are some possible positive motives for my teenager's/parent's action that seems malicious to me?

10. What right do I have to expect life to be fair? Who said life is always supposed to be fair?
11. Does anyone really have as much freedom as I want? And would I really be happy if I had such freedom? After all, with freedom comes responsibility.

It may be helpful for parents and adolescents to write down challenges to particular beliefs. You may give them the list of challenging questions outlined here. Brainstorming can be used to generate a variety of creative alternative ways of thinking about situations. The goal at this stage is not to convince people to give up their favorite beliefs, but only to make them realize that there may be alternative ways to think about conflictual situations. Be careful to explain that you are not telling the family to change its beliefs; you may encounter resistance from rigid individuals, who will misinterpret exploration of alternative beliefs as being ordered to give up their cherished notions.

Disconfirming Unreasonable Beliefs

As you teach parents and adolescents to challenge their thinking about family relationships, the stage is set for disconfirming illogical reasoning, unrealistic expectations, or inappropriate attributions. Guide the family members to formulate more reasonable, alternative conceptualizations of the situation, and suggests an "experiment" to test out realistic versus unrealistic beliefs. The rationale for an "experiment" is to arrange for the family members to collect "evidence" that will convince them of the veracity of the realistic beliefs, so that they will not have to "take it on faith" from the therapist or any other authority figure. Several types of experiments have proven useful:

1. *Conduct a survey.* A parent might survey other parents or experts in similar situations to determine what they do or think. For example, parents who believe that failure to complete chores will lead to ruination in adulthood might survey five upstanding citizens and determine whether any of them ever failed to complete their chores during adolescence. Adolescents who believe that early curfews ruin peer relationships might survey five popular college students and determine whether they ever had early curfews. You must have some knowledge of the reference group to be surveyed, or the experiment can backfire.

2. *Collect archival data.* A family member might collect information from books, movies, videotapes, or other archival sources. For example, adolescents who believe parents are unfairly restricting their cigarette smoking might collect objective information about the dangers of smoking. Parents who believe teenagers who date will become promiscuous and pregnant

might read updated books about dating and adolescent sexuality. A father who believes a forgetful son purposely fails to turn the lights out in order to waste money might be given information on attention deficit hyperactivity disorder.

3. *Take another's perspective.* Ask a parent and an adolescent to put themselves in each others' shoes and to try to appreciate each others' perspectives on the problem. Reverse role playing might be used to facilitate taking another's perspective. For example, the parent could role-play an angry adolescent upset at an unfair curfew, while the adolescent role-plays a rigid parent insisting upon an early curfew. Prompt each role player to describe his or her thoughts and feelings throughout the exercise, guiding them to take each other's perspectives. Such exercises will sometimes help family members appreciate the need to think flexibly about rules and regulations.

Homework and Generalization

The exercises and tasks in this session interactively introduce cognitive restructuring to the family undergoing treatment for parent–adolescent conflict. They provide the family with a foundation upon which to build reasonable expectations, beliefs, and attributions.

In order for generalized change in thinking to occur, the family must apply cognitive change techniques outside of the therapy session. You can close Session 8 with one or more of the following homework assignments, designed to foster future use of cognitive restructuring techniques:

1. Pick a belief theme such as Ruination. Ask family members to monitor all occurrences of ruinous thinking throughout the week, log them, and give each other feedback designed to challenge such thinking.
2. Ask family members to eliminate extreme words such as "should" or "must" from family conversations, and make requests in a more tentative manner.
3. Ask family members to write down all of the challenges possible to a particular unreasonable belief.

Sessions 9 and 10: Skill Application

Goals

The goals of Sessions 9 and 10 are to teach family members how to (1) apply behavioral skills and cognitive change techniques to remaining intense family conflicts; and (2) learn how to manage crisis situations.

Procedures

You help guide the family to problem solve the remaining intense, anger-producing issues. Some of these issues may be discussed during the sessions; others may be discussed by the family at home, who then report back to you. It is preferable to have the family devote more time at home to such discussions, and use the therapy time to review problems that came up during the home discussion. However, the most severe issues may have to be discussed in your presence to avoid the discussion deteriorating into an argument.

Subtle aspects of communication should be targeted for change during these sessions. By this time, major patterns such as put-downs or accusations have probably been targeted. Negative voice tone, subtle sarcasm, and non-verbal communication habits may now need to be targeted. For example, one adolescent complained that her father's "English teacher smile" came across as sarcastic to her. The therapist learned that she was referring to the way her father curved up his lower lip as he was talking; the father, indeed an English teacher, was completely unaware of this pattern, but with feedback from his daughter and the therapist he agreed to monitor and change it.

You are likely to uncover cognitive distortions as more intense anger-producing issues are discussed. Unreasonable beliefs often mediate intense affect surrounding these issues. Cognitive restructuring will follow as a natural intervention. If affect runs very high, you may find it useful to talk with subunits of the family, particularly with regard to cognitive restructuring, only later bringing the family back together. For example, the Smith family was problem solving the issue of church attendance when John announced he was really an agnostic and had no plans to attend church again. The Smiths were a religious Catholic family; the parents became enraged and flew into a tirade. The therapist decided to discuss the matter with the parents separately from the adolescent, later bringing them together to work out a solution.

In this stage of therapy, siblings may be invited to join selected sessions. If the topic is sibling fighting, for example, siblings should be present. The adolescent can be appointed the "expert" who explains problem-solving steps to the siblings; this often enhances the adolescent's status in the session.

Crisis Management

A "crisis" refers to a situation in which a solution has broken down or a rule has been broken, and one family member is confronting another, with feelings running very high. We are referring to situations such as:

1. Dad greeting Sally at the door at 2:00 A.M. when her curfew was 11:00 P.M.
2. Mom discovering that John burned a hole in the rug with a match.
3. Sally learning one hour before her boyfriend is scheduled to pick her up for the prom that she is grounded for not doing her homework.
4. Mom denying Bill the use of the family car, and Bill refusing to leave mom's bedroom until she gives him the car keys.

Typically, parents and adolescents resort to yelling, screaming, ordering, power control, and a host of negative communication techniques in a crisis. Anger overwhelms family members and they lose control, even if they have learned positive problem-solving communication skills.

Crisis management is designed to help families calm down and avoid a physical or extremely hurtful violent confrontation. Problems are never resolved during crises, but only later after people have regained their composure. You need to help the family identify the most common types of crises they encounter, and to prepare to use anger management and related techniques to calm down and avoid a hurtful confrontation. In this manual we cannot exhaustively present such anger management techniques. Instead, we will outline in broad strokes the steps to be followed.

Steps for Managing Crises

1. Ask the family to describe the types of crisis situations they encounter. Mention crises that you observed throughout the earlier therapy. Pinpoint the sequence of escalating affect, and try to identify the points at which various family members lose control. What are the triggers for loss of control?

2. Explain that it is best to calm down and resolve the problems at a later time.

3. Incorporate cognitive-behavioral anger management techniques into the remaining discussion of crisis management.

4. Identify behavioral and cognitive "stop responses" that would permit family members to keep from "losing it" as a crisis escalates, for example, leave the scene, call a Time Out, or count to 10. Get a commitment from each family member to try one or more of these techniques.

5. Identify affect-dissipating responses that could take the edge off the anger during a crisis, for example, relaxation, exercise, or punching a pillow. Get a commitment from each family member to try one or more of these techniques.

6. Role-play a mock crisis, asking family members to use these techniques.

7. Ask them to try the techniques at home.

Summary

Most families will benefit from crisis management planning and resolution of intense conflicts during this stage of therapy. Some families also display unusual structural problems that need to be addressed: enmeshed parent/child relationships, disengaged parents, triangulation, blended family issues, coalitional patterns, and so forth. Such patterns should be addressed during this stage of therapy. Although it goes beyond the scope of this manual to provide the therapist with comprehensive techniques for changing such patterns, these patterns cannot be ignored. Readers should consult Robin and Foster (1989) for more detailed instructions for how to change such patterns.

Sessions 11 and 12: Termination/Disengagement

Goals

The goals of Sessions 11 and 12 are (1) to review the goals of therapy and assess the degree to which these goals have been achieved; and (2) to prepare family members to continue to apply the skills which they learned on their own in the future.

Procedures

You should space out the last two sessions, meeting every two or three weeks instead of weekly. This provides an opportunity for consolidation of session learning and additional generalization over time. During the sessions help the family consolidate and summarize what they have learned and plan for the future. We do not normally conduct problem-solving discussions or communication training during the last few sessions.

1. Give a rationale for termination. For example, you might say "I'm very impressed with the way things are going for your family. Things are not perfect, but you are coping effectively and have learned a lot. We are approaching the end of our contract together. You have been doing a lot between sessions to apply the skills we have worked on together. We need to review where we started, what we accomplished, and help you plan for the future."

2. Review the Agreement for Action introduced in Session 3. Go through each of the goals that were checked off, and ask each family member to comment upon the extent to which that goal has been accomplished.

3. Add your own comments about goal attainment. Be realistic. Point out to the family any goals that were too lofty for a short-term therapy.

4. Tell the family that it is rare for every goal to be accomplished to everyone's satisfaction.

5. Translate the goals that remain to be accomplished into concrete actions that the family can take on its own after termination of therapy.

6. You may find that their goals have changed somewhat as a function of working with you. Point out how therapy can change one's view of the world, and help them leave therapy with the flexibility to face future changes with courage and confidence.

7. You may also need to highlight additional therapeutic steps that you recommend. For example, if significant marital conflict was uncovered but not completely dealt with during problem-solving communication training, you may suggest a referral for marital therapy. If significant school learning problems or individual pathology was identified, you may need to suggest testing and/or individual therapy.

8. Leave the family with the idea that therapy is a mechanism for coping with periodic developmental crises. Make it clear that the family is welcome to return for another course of family therapy if they desire it.

Author's Final Comment

With the techniques outlined in this manual, a therapist who has had some general experience treating families and adolescents will be able to intervene to ameliorate parent–adolescent conflict. A number of clinical outcome studies have demonstrated the effectiveness of problem-solving communication training (see Barkley, 1990; Robin & Foster, 1989, for reviews) in reducing family conflict. While certainly not the only approach to such conflict, problem-solving communication training is an easily taught readily replicated, and clearly documented, intervention.

References

Alexander, J. F., & Parsons, B. V. (1982). *Functional family therapy.* Monterey, CA: Brooks/Cole.

Barkley, R. (1990). *Attention deficit hyperactivity disorder.* New York: Guilford Press.

Barkley, R. (1991). *Attention deficit hyperactivity disorder: A clinical workbook.* New York: Guilford Press.

Haley, J. (1976). *Problem solving therapy.* San Francisco: Jossey-Bass.

Haley, J. (1980). *Leaving home.* New York: McGraw Hill.

Madanes, C. (1981). *Strategic family therapy.* San Francisco: Jossey-Bass.

Mash, E. J., & Terdal, L. G. (1988). *Behavioral assessment of childhood disorders* (2d ed.). New York: Guilford Press.

Minuchin, S., & Fishman, H. C. (1981). *Family therapy techniques.* Cambridge, MA: Harvard University Press.

Montemayor, R., Adams, G. R., & Gullotta, T. P. (1990). *From childhood to adolescence: A transitional period?* Newbury Park, CA: Sage.

Patterson, G. (1982). *Coercive Family Process.* Eugene, OR: Castalia.

Robin, A. L., & Foster, S. L. (1989). *Negotiating parent–adolescent conflict: A behavioral family systems approach.* New York: Guilford Press.

Robin, A. L., Koepke, T., & Moye, A. (1990). Multidimensional assessment of parent–adolescent relations. *Psychological Assessment, 2,* 451–459.

5
Social Skills Training

Craig Winston LeCroy

Introduction and Overview

Social skills training is being increasingly used as a treatment method in working with children and adolescents. Teaching a young person social skills is a direct method of influencing how that young person is likely to interact with others in the future. The goal is to teach people the skills needed to sustain social interactions that will lead to positive outcomes. The strategy of social skills training is straightforward: identify the skills needed and select a method to teach those skills (Strayhorn, 1988).

This structured training approach is characterized by learning skills through practice. There are various methods for the "practice" to occur. Typically, young people are taught skills through the use of role-play practice with feedback from group members and the group leader. However, skills can also be learned by observing models, reviewing video tapes, reading stories that model the skills, playing games that emphasize the skills, and by many other methods.

The preferred method of teaching young people social skills is in a group setting. Social skills are interpersonal social behaviors and a group provides a natural environment in which to learn such skills. Group training is particularly effective because:

- Participants benefit from the opportunity to interact with others. Interactions that would not occur in individual training take place.
- Groups provide greater feedback to individuals, in terms of both positive feedback and encouragement about practicing the skills and negative feedback about how to make the skills appear more realistic or acceptable to others.
- Groups provide more motivation for young people to learn the skills. Young people prefer to interact with each other while learning social skills. Since they enjoy such interactions the group is more motivating than individual treatment would be.
- Better learning takes place in a group setting because participants can

126

practice their skills with different people and learn to respond to the unique qualities of various individuals.

Clearly, there are many good reasons to teach social skills in a group setting, but social skills training can also work for individuals. Since this manual provides a group treatment model, adaptations will need to be made when working with individuals. It is also good to remember that being an effective group leader will be critical to the success of a social skills training group. This manual does not address the skills needed to lead successful groups. For more information about group treatment and group leadership skills, see Rose and Edelson (1987), *Treating Children and Adolescents in Groups*.

Social Skills for Who?

Human service practitioners have found that social skills training is an appropriate method for helping many different young people with a variety of problems.

During adolescence many skills are needed by *all* young people, not just those in trouble. Many practitioners have used social skills training programs for prevention as well as treatment. For prevention, all young people can be offered a generic program of social skills training or young people identified as "at risk" can be offered a social skills training program. More troubled youth with specific difficulties can be thought of as having a deficit in certain skills and can be taught these skills to remedy their deficits.

Young people in today's society face many difficult demands. Many of these demands require certain social skills. For example, friendship is critically important to most young people, yet some young people have a difficult time starting and maintaining conversations. Also, as young people move into the dating stage, a more complex set of social demands require more advanced social skills. What do you do in a situation in which your boyfriend or girlfriend begins to pressure you about having intercourse, but you are not comfortable with that idea. Or more simply, what are the skills needed to get along better with friends, teachers, parents, and siblings? As a young person gets older, he or she will face more demands on his or her abilities to resolve conflict and negotiate with others. Without such skills interpersonal relationships will suffer and the young person may develop undesirable alternatives such as aggression or withdrawal. Social skills training can be helpful in each of these situations.

Through social skills training young people acquire more control and direction over their lives. It is a method that enhances their locus of control. Experiencing their ability to affect their world leads to a greater sense of self-esteem. Too often young people become discouraged because they believe they cannot be effective in their environment. Social skills training can help change that.

Settings for Social Skills Training

Social skills training programs are administered in various settings. School is a common training ground for social skills, for it affords such easy access to young people. Social skills programs can be part of the regular curriculum, an afterschool activity, or a night school course. Some social skills programs are implemented during the noon hour. Many social skills training programs become a regular part of a treatment protocol. For example, residential treatment centers often set aside group time for social skills training. Day treatment programs may include a period of time for skills training as well. Young people may be court-referred to a group social skills training program. Voluntary groups can also be formed, for example, in housing projects or at community-based agencies.

Evaluation and Research on Social Skills Training

Social skills training may be one of the more effective treatment procedures in working with a variety of child and adolescent problems. Social skills training methods are based on the notion of competence, which suggests that problem behaviors should be viewed as deficits in a child's repertoire of responses (Asher, 1983; Hops, Finch, & McConnell, 1985). The treatment model based on this conceptualization focuses on the teaching of prosocial skills and competencies that are needed for day-to-day living, rather than on understanding and eliminating pathological responses. Thus the emphasis is on teaching children how to respond effectively to new or difficult situations. The outcome is more positive consequences to their responses as compared to past behaviors that elicited negative consequences.

Some of the earliest applications of social skills training came from research conducted at Achievement Place, a behaviorally based residential treatment center for adolescents. These studies focused on conversational skills such as asking questions, volunteering information, and so forth (see Maloney et al., 1976; Minkin et al., 1976). These earlier successes in using a social skills intervention paved the way for more complex applications.

Perhaps the best experimental design evaluating social skills training with delinquents was reported by Sarason & Ganzer (1973). These researchers found that, compared to control group subjects, the delinquents in the social skills group had an increased locus of control and reduced recidivism rates at a three-year follow-up. Research on social skills training with delinquents continued with Goldstein and Glick (1987) and Hazel, Schumaker,

Sherman & Sheldon-Wilder (1981) conducting numerous studies that provided empirical support for this intervention model. Hazel et al. (1981) developed a well regarded program that focuses on eight essential skills: giving positive feedback, giving negative feedback, accepting negative feedback, resisting peer pressure, problem solving, negotiating, following instructions, and beginning conversations. Using a single-system research design, the researchers found that the target behaviors increased over baseline levels.

These early efforts to examine the effectiveness of social skills training led the way for increasing applications of this model to numerous other problems and client groups. For example, social skills training has been applied to:

Developmentally disabled adolescents (Matson, Monikam, Coe, & Raymond, 1988)

Conduct-disordered adolescents (Tisdelle & St. Lawrence, 1986)

Blind adolescents (Marshall & Peck, 1986)

Enhancing general social competence (LeCroy & Rose, 1986)

American Indian adolescents (Schinke et al., 1985)

Adolescents seeking employment (Hiew & MacDonald, 1986; Staab & Lodish, 1985)

School adjustment problems (Brown & Greenspan, 1984; LeCroy & Milligan, 1991)

Preventing unwanted pregnancy (Gilchrist, Schinke, & Blythe, 1985)

Preventing substance abuse (Pentz, 1985)

Studies support the varied application of this model to numerous social problems of children and adolescents. Research must now be directed toward refining the intervention components, examining the relative efficacy of social skills training with other alternative treatments, and evaluating the long-term effects of the intervention.

Considerations in Conducting the Social Skills Training Group

General Considerations

Who to Include in the Group. Since social skills training is a broad-based teaching method that is individualized for each group member, you will find that most young people can benefit from this type of group. Therefore, soliciting volunteers is one method of recruitment depending on the goals and purpose of your particular program. However, it may be necessary to limit participation to a certain number of young people. In this case you will want to institute a procedure whereby you can identify the young people who are likely to benefit the most from the program. Depending on your situation this could be done by administering assessment devices, conducting pre-group interviews, designing a referral system for teachers or other professionals to use to refer individuals directly to the group, or selecting young people who meet certain risk criteria. Discuss with other professionals in your area what would be the best and most practical method for obtaining young people to participate in the social skills group.

Group Composition. Factors influencing group composition include how well the young people in the group know each other, how heterogeneous the group is, and how large the group is. Too much intergroup familiarity can lead to problems with control. It is recommended that not too many "good" friends be involved in the same group. Heterogeneous groups appear to work well—some age variation (three to four years), gender mix, and cultural and ethnic mix create an interesting group for everyone involved.

Practical Considerations

One of the most important practical considerations is how big to make the group. Social skills groups are best when kept to approximately 6 to 10 members. Every member needs to be able to practice skills during the group meeting, so the group should not be too large. Groups tend to function better when there are two group leaders, especially if the group is as large as 10 members. Since participants practice different skills every week, it is important to find a desirable and easily accessible meeting place. Convenience is important since individuals should have as few barriers to participation as possible. These same considerations apply with regard to scheduling the group. Most social skills groups meet on a weekly or biweekly basis for about 1 to $2\frac{1}{2}$ hours. Groups can be longer if an activity is incorporated into the structure of the group (for example, a 30-minute basketball game).

Screening and Intake Considerations

All young people who are interested in the program should be screened individually to assess their potential to benefit from the group. Additionally, it may be desirable to hold a meeting for parents. During the screening the group leader can interview the young person to assess his or her social skills. Also, if desired, pretreatment assessment instruments can be administered (see Corcoran & Fischer, 1989, for examples). This meeting is seen as the working "contract" between the group leader and participant. In order to reach a mutual agreement the leader can describe the nature and goals of the group and the young person can describe how he or she might benefit from the group. Establishing appropriate expectations concerning the group should be an important goal during this time. For example, the leader may want to review the skills to be learned, the methods used, and the program rules, and provide handouts on the group. A group contract can be written and signed by the participating young person.

Social Skills Taught

A careful review of the literature, previous social skills programs, and extensive experience led to the selection of 11 social skills that are believed to be critical to the promotion of positive interactions with others. These skills provide a broad representation of skill areas but do not overlap each other too much. Of course, depending on the clients being served, some skills may need to be added and others deleted. However, the format is well specified and makes it easy for practitioners to expand and contract the social skills program to meet their unique needs. The social skills program consists of the following sessions: (1) Creating Positive Interactions; (2) Getting to Know Others: Starting Conversations; (3) Making Requests: Getting More of What You Want; (4) Expressing Your Feelings Directly; (5) Getting Out: How to Say "No"; (6) Asserting Your Rights: Tell It Like It Is; (7) Identifying How Others Feel: The Art of Empathy; (8) Dealing with Those in Authority; (9) Responsible Decision Making: Think about It; (10) Learning to Negotiate: Conflict Resolution; and (11) When You're in Need: Asking for Help.

Session 1—Creating Positive Interactions

Introduction and Overview

Today we are going to learn about how to create more positive interactions with others. One easy way to do this is to give another person a compliment or say something nice about that person. By giving someone a compliment you are creating a positive interaction. The other person will feel better about you and you will feel better about yourself. Just as you like to hear nice things about yourself, other people in your life—friends, parents, and teachers—like to hear nice things about themselves. In creating positive interactions it is important to learn how to both give and receive compliments. Many people have a difficult time receiving a compliment because they become embarrassed ("Gosh, are you talking about me?"), or they can't accept it so they reject it ("I'm really not that good a baseball player"). By receiving a compliment, you are letting the person who gave you a compliment know that you like what that person is saying. If we practice this skill it will be easy for you to give others compliments. But make sure that any compliments you give are true or sincere (don't say, "I really like those shoes" when you really think they are ugly). Think about what you really like about another person before you give him or her a compliment.

Discussion Questions

Why is it important to learn the skill of giving and receiving compliments? Encourage the group to recognize the truth of the following points:

1. Learning to give compliments can help you have more positive interactions with others because you are saying something nice about the other person. Also, giving someone a compliment may encourage the other person to give you a compliment later.
2. Learning to give compliments will let other people know what it is you like about them or why you think they are nice.
3. If you give a person a compliment when they do something nice for you, they are more likely to do other nice things for you.

Looking at Examples

Describe a recent situation in which you used the skill of giving and receiving a compliment.

Conduct a role play where the skill was *not* used appropriately to generate a discussion about why the skill is important (this will be especially important with the skill of receiving the compliment). Examine the situation according to the following questions:

1. What was the setting where this occurred?
2. Who was present?
3. What was the statement used to give the person a compliment?
4. Was the statement a compliment (positive, encouraging positive interactions)?
5. Was the compliment true or sincere?
6. What was the outcome of the compliment?
7. How did you feel afterward?

Have the group present their own examples.

Modeling the Skill

Although it is easy to learn how to give good compliments, many of us do not use this skill as much as we should. Therefore, it is important to practice so you will feel more comfortable giving and receiving compliments. By practicing it a lot we will be more likely to give compliments. I'll start by doing a role play to model how to give a compliment.

Giving Compliments.
Modeling Situation. When you arrive at school today you see that your friend has just gotten a new haircut—one that is much different than he or she had before. You like the change and decide to give a compliment to your friend.

You: "Hey, I really like your new haircut. It really looks good on you."
Peer: "Well thanks, I'm still getting used to it."
You: "Well, I think it looks great!"

Skill Review. "Let's look at what skills were demonstrated in this role play. The model was successful in using the following skills:

1. Looked the person in the eye and used good body language (smiled, was positive with an enthusiastic tone of voice).
2. Used an 'I' statement.
3. Gave a clear and specific compliment to the other person.
4. Followed up the compliment with another statement that reinforced the earlier compliment."

Receiving Compliments. It is also important to practice the skill of receiving compliments. Remember the goal here is to accept the compliment.

Modeling Situation. You worked very hard on a social science report that was due last week. Your teacher has graded the reports and you go to see her to pick up your report.

Teacher: "I really liked your social science report. You did an excellent job."
You: "Thank you! I really enjoyed doing the report and I spent a lot of time on it."
Teacher: "Well, it certainly shows."
You: "Thanks, I really learned a lot from this report."

Skill Review. In this role play the model demonstrated what specific skills needed to receive a compliment? Encourage the group to identify the following skills:

1. Looked the person in the eye and used good body language (smiled while accepting the compliment).
2. Said "Thank you" right away and did so in a manner that showed pride, not embarrassment ("Oh, gee, I guess so, thanks") or overconfidence ("I always do good on reports").
3. Followed up the first comment with a second thanks.

Practice Opportunities

Each group member should practice *both* giving and receiving compliments during the group session. First, practice giving compliments; next, using some of the same situations, practice receiving compliments. Select one team to observe the nonverbal skills and another team to observe the verbal skills.

Situation 1. Compliment your parents on a dinner that you really enjoyed. You would say:

Situation 2. Compliment a friend who you really enjoy doing things with. You would say:

Situation 3. Compliment a friend or parent on how they look. You would say:

Situation 4: Compliment someone who did a good job playing a team sport with you (basketball, football, softball). You would say:

Situation 5: Compliment a friend who discussed a problem that he or she was experiencing with you. You would say:

Extra Assignments

1. In the group practice giving compliments by having each member of the group give the person on their right a genuine compliment. The compliment doesn't have to be personal but does need to be sincere. The person receiving the compliment can practice skills at receiving compliments.

2. As an individual, make a point to give four different people compliments during the next week. In your diary keep track of who you gave a compliment to, what you said, what they said, and how you felt. Bring your diaries to the group next week for discussion.

Session 2—Getting to Know Others: Starting Conversations

Introduction and Overview

Getting to know other people is an important skill that we all need to learn. For some people this is easy, but for others it is more difficult. To be successful in life one needs to learn how to start conversations. Starting conversations is a way to meet other people, and also a way to get information. You may need information that another person has, and you must get to know the person who has this information in order to ask about the information. For example, let's say you need some information about how difficult it is to get accepted on the soccer team. If you didn't know anybody who was on the soccer team, you'd have to get to know someone in order to find out about how difficult it might be. Also, you could get other important information like how much time it takes, whether playing on the soccer team is fun or hard work, and so forth. There are three parts to a conversation that require skills. The first is *starting* a conversation, the second is *keeping the conversation going,* and the third is *ending the conversation.*

Discussion Questions

"Why do we need to learn skills for getting to know others?" Encourage the group to realize the following points:

1. Learning how to get to know others can help you meet new people and make new friends.
2. Learning how to get to know others can help you feel comfortable in a variety of situations (for example, at parties, or introducing yourself to someone you don't know).
3. Learning how to get to know others can help you get to know your friends better.
4. Learning how to get to know others can help you get information from other people that you may want.
5. Learning how to get to know others can help you share things about yourself so that you develop stronger friendships.

Looking at Examples

Describe a situation where you recently used the skill of starting a conversation.

Conduct a role play where the skill was *not* used appropriately to generate a discussion about why the skill is important (show what happens when a person does not know how to start, maintain, or end a conversation). Examine the situation according to the following questions:

1. What was the setting where this occurred?
2. Who was present?
3. What was the statement used to start the conversation?
4. How was the conversation kept going?
5. How did the conversation end?

6. What was the outcome of the conversation?
7. How did you feel afterward?

Have the group present their own examples.

Modeling the Skill

Starting, continuing, and ending a conversation can be a complex set of skills. I will model each aspect of conversation. Watch carefully how I model each separate part of the conversation.

Modeling Situation. You would like to get to know a new person that has recently moved to your neighborhood. You go outside and see this person walking toward you on the sidewalk.

You: "Hi, I'm _____. Hey aren't you new around here?"
Peer: "Yes, we moved here just about a month ago from California."
You: "Were you ever in an earthquake there?"
Peer: "Yeah, I've been in lots."
You: "What's it like to be in an earthquake?"
Peer: "Well, lots of times you can't tell they happened, but once I was eating breakfast and everything on the table started to shake."
You: "Wow! That must have been scary."
Peer: "Well, you get used to them after awhile."
You: "What kind of sports do you like to play?"
Peer: "I was on the soccer team at my old school."
You: "Great! I'm just learning to play soccer but I love it. Hey, I've got to get going to meet a friend. Nice to meet you— let's practice some soccer sometime."
Peer: "OK, see you later."

Skill Review

Let's look closely at this role play to see what skills the model demonstrated about how to get to know someone. What skills did the model show? Encourage the group to generate the following list of skills:

1. Looked the person in the eye and had good body language (showed interest and enthusiasm).
2. Greeted the person by saying his own name and asking a question.
3. Asked an open-ended question about the person.
4. Made a statement to follow up on the person's response.
5. Asked another open-ended question about the person.
6. Made another statement about the conversation.

7. Ended the conversation by letting the person know he had to leave. Made a plan to get together again.

The "You" in this model demonstrated the three skills used in conversations by:

1. Saying his own name and asking the newcomer a question to start the conversation.
2. Making statements about the conversation and asking additional open-ended questions to keep the conversation going.
3. Stating clearly that he had to leave and making a plan to meet again in the future to end the conversation.

It may be helpful to review with the group the difference between an open-ended and a close-ended question. A set of close-ended questions can be presented to the group and they can rephrase them as open-ended questions. Some close-ended questions you can use include the following:

1. Are you a new student here?
2. Do you like to play basketball?
3. Do you like art class?
4. Do you go home after school?
5. Did you read that book for English class?

Practice Opportunities

Each group member should practice the skill at least once during the group. Use the following situations or have the group itself generate situations members would like to practice:

Situation 1. Starting a conversation with a friend's parent you don't know very well.

Situation 2. Starting a conversation with someone you sit next to in school but haven't gotten to know.

Situation 3. Talking with your coach after a practice about how you are doing.

Situation 4. Talking with a student at a photography show to find out how they took a picture.

Situation 5. Talking with an uncle you don't know very well who has come to visit.

Situation 6. Joining a conversation with several friends who have been discussing a particular class in school.

Extra Assignments

1. Play 10 questions where every person in the group must think of 10 open-ended questions to ask another person in the group. You may need to practice distinguishing open–versus close-ended questions with the group.

2. Select someone you do not know very well and start a conversation with him or her. In your diary, record your thoughts about what happened and how it went.

3. Carefully observe two people having a conversation and record what you think they did well to make the conversation go better and record what you think they didn't do well to keep the conversation going.

4. Use the situations on starting conversations to practice conversations with the opposite sex. Set up the role plays so that it involves a boy–girl interaction. Have the group members discuss the differences encountered when the interactions are of mixed gender. Also, give the group members an assignment involving starting a conversation with someone of the opposite sex who they would like to get to know better.

Session 3—Making Requests: Getting More of What You Want

Introduction and Overview

If we learn to make requests well, we will be able to get along better with others and to get more of what we want. We all have to make requests of other people. Sometimes those requests aren't easy and sometimes we don't say them in the most appropriate manner. After a difficult math class you may want to ask another person in your class some questions about how to do the homework—this is an example of making requests of others. As you can see, this can be a critical skill. If you can ask for and receive help, you will get more of what you want—in this case help on your homework. Since making requests of others involves asking people for favors, you must make your request in a polite and appropriate manner. What would happen if you simply said, "Hey, you need to help me with this homework assignment, I don't understand it"? This type of demand could lead the other person to say, "Forget it, I don't have to help you do anything." So, as you can see, learning how to make requests includes learning how to do it in a polite and appropriate manner.

Discussion Questions

In your own words, why is it important to learn how to make requests of others? Encourage the group to grasp the following points:

1. Learning to make requests will help you get more of what you want because you will be asking for it directly.

2. Learning to make requests will help you feel more in control of your life because you will be taking charge of more things.
3. Learning to make requests in a polite and appropriate manner will help you get along better with others.

Looking at Examples

Describe a situation from your own life in which you had to use the skill of making requests, or give an example of a time when you could have used this skill but you didn't. Point out the consequences of not using this skill. Examine the situation in terms of the following questions:

1. What was the setting where this occurred?
2. Who was present?
3. What was the statement used to make a request?
4. Was the request made in an appropriate and polite manner?
5. What was the outcome of making a request?
6. How did you feel afterward?

Have the group present their own examples.

Modeling the Skill

Making requests is not always hard to do. Keep in mind, though, that it is important to make requests in a nice manner.

Modeling Situation. Your friend refers to you as "Big Toes" and you'd rather be called by your real name or by a different nickname.

Peer: "Hey, Big Toes, did you get out of class early?"
You: "I know you use nicknames for everyone—and most people like it, but I'd like you to call me by my name."
Peer: "Well, I didn't know it bothered you. I guess I can call you by your name but 'Big Toes' really fits you."
You: "There's just something about 'Big Toes' that I don't like—maybe you could come up with something different that I would like."
Peer: "That's cool."
You: "Thanks."

Skill Review

Let's examine how this skill was used in the role play. The model demonstrated the following:

1. Looked the person in the eye and used good body language.
2. Made a clear, direct request of the other person.

3. Used an "I" statement, if appropriate.
4. Showed appreciation, if the request was accepted, by thanking the person.

Practice Opportunity

Each member should practice the skill at least once during the group session. Select group members to evaluate each individual's performance according to the skill steps.

> *Situation 1:* You forget your lunch money and want to ask a friend if you can borrow some money from him or her.
>
> *Situation 2:* You have been working very hard on a paper for your science class. When you get your paper back you were disappointed that you received a C grade. You want to ask the teacher to please review your paper again because you feel it deserves a better grade than a C.
>
> *Situation 3:* Your friend has been teasing you a lot about your girl or boyfriend. You want to ask him or her to please stop teasing you.
>
> *Situation 4:* You get into a conflict with your parents and you believe they have not let you tell your side of the story. You want to ask them to please listen to your story.

Extra Assignments

1. Describe a situation in which you would like to make a request of another person. Try to think about an event from the last two weeks where you wish you would have used the skill of making requests. Write out a script of what you would say to the other person.

2. During the next week write down as many situations as you can think of where you either did make a request or could have made a request.

3. Ask group members to generate situations where a person needs to use the skill of making requests. Use these situations for continued role play practice or have group members write out responses of what they would say. Discuss the different responses in the group.

Session 4—Expressing Your Feelings Directly

Introduction and Overview

An important skill for all of us to learn is how to express our feelings directly. Often it is hard to directly state how you are feeling to another person. But if someone is doing something you don't like, it is important to let that person know how you are feeling. When we speak directly to others about our feelings we often avoid getting into fights or walking away with hurt feelings. When we express our feelings directly we often end up feeling better about ourselves. Expressing your feelings may help you cope better with your emotions. For example, if a friend does something that makes you really mad, it is better to express your feelings to that person directly than to walk away angry. Some people who express their feelings are labeled "complainers." Usually this is because they don't express their feelings in a very appropriate way. When you use this skill you must do it in an appropriate manner and at the right time. It is important to use this skill when you want to make things better, not as a way of making others feel bad.

Discussion Questions

Why is it important to learn how to express our feelings directly to others? Encourage the group to realize the following points:

1. Learning to express your feelings can help you avoid situations that could lead to trouble, like fights.
2. Learning to express your feelings can help you feel more in control of your life.
3. Learning to express your feelings can help you get along better with other people.
4. Learning to express your feelings will help other people listen to what you have to say.

Looking at Examples

Describe a situation from your own life in which you had to use the skill of expressing your feelings directly, or give an example where you could have used this skill but you didn't. Point out the consequences of not using this skill. Examine the situation using the following questions:

1. What was the setting where this occurred?
2. Who was present?
3. What was the statement used to express feelings?
4. How did you express your feelings in a direct manner?
5. What was the outcome of expressing your feelings?
6. How did you feel afterward?

Have group members describe their own examples.

Modeling the Skill

We are not taught to express our feelings in a direct manner, so often this can be difficult to do. I will do a role play to model how to express feelings and then we can do our role-play practice.

Modeling Situation. You are working on a project with a friend, you make a mistake, and your friend calls you "stupid."

Peer: "You just messed it up! You are so stupid!"
You: "When you call me stupid it makes me really mad. Anyone can make a mistake."
Peer: "I just say that all the time to people. I didn't mean to get you mad."
You: "Well, it does make me mad, so please don't call me that."

Skill Review

Let's look carefully at how this skill was used in this role play. The model demonstrated the following:

1. Looked the person in the eye and used good body language.
2. Stated feelings in a clear and direct manner.
3. Listened to what the other person had to say in response.
4. Stated how the other person can avoid the situation in the future.

Practice Opportunity

Each member should practice the skill at least once during the group session. Select group members to evaluate each individual's performance according to the skills steps. The group may want to help the role player identify the appropriate feeling to express in a particular situation.

The group can use examples of situations that were discussed earlier or select from the sample situations below.

Situation 1. Your friend keeps changing the channel and you are interested in watching a specific TV show.

Peer: "I'm going to see what else is on."

You: _____

_____

Peer: "I didn't know you wanted to watch that show."

Situation 2. Your teacher assigns you to work with two other classmates on an art project. You have been working hard to get the project completed but your classmates are just sitting around talking.

Peer: "I thought that was a really great movie."

You: _____

_____

Peer: "Well, OK, we'll pitch in."

> *Situation 3.* You have gone to the movie with several of your friends. This is a movie you really wanted to see. During the movie your friends are talking so loudly that you can't hear the movie.

Peer: "I can't believe your parents make you do that."

You: _____

_____

Peer: "Sorry, we'll be more quiet."

Extra Assignments

1. The focus here has been on expressing feelings directly to others. But this may be a good opportunity for young people to also learn how to respond when others are expressing feelings about them. It is difficult for young people to listen to others tell them about their feelings. They don't like to hear that someone feels hurt because of their words or deeds. Group members can practice listening to others and thinking about what others are telling them.

2. Describe a situation in which you would like to express your feelings more directly. Write out a script of what you would say to the other person. If you have an opportunity during the week to use this skill, make a note about it and report back to the group.

3. It is important to help the group members learn how to recognize feelings. Have each member take home an "assignment card" that says at the top of it, "Feelings I Had This Week." Have them list the feeling and then describe the situation in which that feeling arose.

Session 5—Getting Out: How to Say "No"

Introduction and Overview

We often hear people talking about the importance of saying "No." This is because we often end up doing things that we really don't want to do. Sometimes we get talked into something or pressured to act in a certain way. The "No" skill is important when you are being pressured into doing something you don't want to do. This can be one of the most difficult skills to learn, because all of us want to get along with our friends and we don't want them to dislike us because we refuse to get involved in something we don't want to do. Let's look at an example. What if a group of your friends all decided to cheat on an upcoming school test? If you *didn't* want to be involved, you would have to say "No" to them. Of course, you don't want to hurt their feelings, but at the same time you don't want to be involved in cheating. By learning to say "No" you will learn to have more control over your life. It will be easier for you to express your true feelings and it may help you avoid trouble.

Discussion Questions

Why is it important to learn the skill of how to say "No"? Encourage the group to recognize the following points:

1. Learning to say "No" can help you stay out of trouble.
2. Learning to say "No" will put you more in control of your own life.
3. Learning to say "No" can help you feel better about yourself because you won't do something that you don't want to do.
4. Learning to say "No" will help prevent others from taking advantage of you.

Looking at Examples

Describe a situation in which you had to use the skill of saying "No," or give an example of a time when you wish you had been able to say "No" but you were pressured into doing something you really did not want to do. Do a role play in which the "No" skill was *not* used and then generate a discussion about why the skill is important. The group leader may wish to use an example from his or her own life to share with the group. Examine the situation by using the following questions:

1. What was the setting of the situation?
2. Who was present?
3. What was the statement that put pressure on the person?
4. How did you say "No"?
5. What was the outcome of your saying "No"? Did your friends react positively? negatively?
6. How did you feel afterward?

Have group members present their own examples.

Modeling the Skill

Saying "No" is not as easy as it sounds! It takes a lot of practice and work to be good at this. I will do a role play to model how to say "No" and then we can all practice this skill.

Modeling Situation. You agreed with your parents that you would be home at 9:30 P.M. It is now 9:00 P.M., you are at a friend's house, and he says,

Peer: "Hey, lets go to the mall, I know Matt and Blake will be there."
You: "I'd like to go with you to meet them, Tom, but I can't because I promised I'd be home by 9:30."
Peer: "Come on—they won't care if you're a little late."
You: "No, I really can't do that Tom; let's plan to get together with them next week."
Peer: "Well, OK, I guess I'll just have to go without you."

Let's look at what skills were demonstrated in this role play. The model did the following:

1. Looked the person in the eye and used good body language.
2. Said "No" clearly and early on.
3. Said "No" in a way that was polite.
4. Kept saying "No" when continued pressure was applied.
5. Suggested an alternative activity.

Practice Opportunities

Have each group member practice the skill at least once during the group session. Select other group members to evaluate individual performances by giving feedback on one of the five skill steps. This will help the group members focus their feedback and observe the role play more closely. The group can use examples of situations that were discussed earlier or select from the sample situations below.

Situation 1. A friend comes up to you at school and wants to borrow a magazine you just bought and want to read during your break.

Peer: "Hey, can I borrow that magazine? I've been wanting to read it."

You: _____

_____

Peer: "Let me read it now; you can read it when you get home."

You: _____

_____

Situation 2. After some of your friends and you decide to go to the record store, they begin to talk about shoplifting some CD's. Everyone is expected to steal a CD. You decide you don't want to be involved in the stealing.

Peer 1: "Everyone take one CD when you are in there. It's easy; they never watch you—I took 3 CD's last week.

You: _____

_____

Peer 2: "Come on—we're all in this together, so we're all going to do it."

You: _____

_____

Peer 1: "You're a jerk. Let's go—leave him behind."

Situation 3: A good friend calls you at home and says he wants to come over. You have a lot of homework to finish before tomorrow and are really much too busy to see your friend right now.

Peer: "I'll be over in a half hour."

You: _____

_____

Peer: "You're always doing homework! Come on, take a break—how about getting together for only an hour?"

You: _____

_____

Extra Assignments

1. During the week keep track of situations in which you need to say "No." Pay attention to how difficult or easy it is for you. Prepare a situation for role plays next week.

2. Interview at least two people outside the group about situations they have faced where they had to say "No." What were the situations? What did they do? Were they able to resist the pressure? What did they say? Do they think they could have handled the situations better? If so, how?

3. Have the group members pair up. Provide the pairs with situations to act out or allow each pair to invent a situation. Have one person make a demand of the other and instruct the other person to practice saying "No" loudly and clearly. Repeat this exercise several times so that each person becomes familiar and comfortable with the act of saying "No."

Session 6—Asserting Your Rights: Tell It Like It Is

Introduction and Overview

Asserting your rights is an important skill to learn. We all have certain rights. We need to learn both to identify our own personal rights and to assert them when needed. Asserting your rights means letting people know you want to be treated fairly. To assert our rights effectively, we need to be able to know when we are being assertive as opposed to being aggressive or passive. People react to the same situation in different ways. For example, let's say someone borrows something from you without asking. You could react in one of three ways: you could be aggressive by demanding or physically taking the borrowed object from the person; you could be passive by deciding to just forget about it and not let the person know that it isn't right to borrow without asking; or you could be assertive by letting the person know that if they want to borrow things from you they need to ask you first.

Discussion Questions

Why do you think it is important to learn about asserting your rights? Encourage the group to recognize the following points:

1. Learning to assert your rights can help you increase your own self-respect. Because you are standing up for your own rights you can develop greater self-confidence.
2. Learning to assert your rights can help you get more of what you want. By being direct and honest about what you want you are more likely to be successful in getting what you want.
3. Learning to assert your rights can help you feel more in control of yourself.
4. Learning to assert your rights can help you avoid situations in which other people treat you unfairly.

Looking at Examples

Describe a situation from your own life in which you had to use the skill of standing up for your rights, or give an example of an experience in which you should have been assertive but were not. Emphasize the consequences of not using assertiveness appropriately. Examine the situation by addressing the following questions:

1. What was the setting where this incident occurred?
2. Who was present?
3. What was the statement used to stand up for your rights?
4. Was the statement assertive, not passive or aggressive?
5. Was the statement a direct, honest, and appropriate expression of your concerns and feelings?
6. What was the outcome of standing up for your rights?
7. How did you feel afterward?

Have the group present their own examples.

Modeling the Skill

Many of us are not comfortable about standing up for our own rights. Lots of us are taught not to demand our rights but instead to react passively and do nothing. Other people learn to be aggressive about their rights instead of assertive. I will do a role play to model how to stand up for your rights and then the group can do role plays to practice the skills.

Modeling Situation. One of your friends asked to borrow one of your favorite books. You let the person borrow it, but asked that it be returned within two weeks. When two weeks had passed you reminded the person to return the book, but she still has not returned it.

Peer: "Hi! How are you today?"
You: "I'm fine. Would you please bring back that book I let you borrow? I'd like you to bring it back to me tomorrow."
Peer: "I'm sorry. I keep forgetting."
You: "Well, it is important to me to get it back, so please remember. Why don't you write a note to yourself so you don't forget."
Peer: "OK. I'll do that right now."

Skill Review

Let's examine how this skill was used in the role play. The model demonstrated the following:

1. Used good body language and looked the person in the eye.
2. Asserted rights in a direct, honest, and appropriate manner.
3. Asserted rights in a way that would not get the other person upset.
4. Listened to what the other person had to say in response to what was said.
5. Offered a suggestion to help deal with the situation.

This model was a good example of appropriate assertiveness. How is this different from an aggressive response and a passive response?

An aggressive response might be, "You're so dumb, why can't you remember to bring back my book!" This is aggressive because it makes the other person upset and probably angry. A likely outcome is a fight with this person.
A passive response might go something like this:

You: "Do you think you could bring back my book?"
Peer: "Well, I'd really like to keep it until the end of the school year."
You: "Well, I guess that would be OK."

This is passive because the person is not being honest and direct about how she feels. She will probably end up being angry at her friend and may end feeling angry at herself for not standing up for her rights. A passive response does nothing to resolve the situation.

Practice Opportunity

Each member needs to practice this skill once during the group session. Select group members to evaluate their peers' performance by using the skills discussed in the skill review. Make sure that each performance includes a direct, honest, and clear response and that the other person involved in the role play is not upset by what is said.

> *Situation 1.* A teacher asks you to come in from recess even though you have permission to stay outside from the teacher who is responsible for you at that time.

Teacher: "Recess is over. You have to come in now."

You: _____

_____

> *Situation 2.* A friend of yours has gotten in the habit of calling you names. You don't like it and it makes you feel bad.

Peer: "Come on, Bozo, let's go outside."

You: _____

_____

Situation 3. You have been waiting in line a long time to see a movie that you really want to see. A group of five people cut in front of you in the line.

Peer: "This is going to be a great movie, we have to get in."

You: _____

_____

Extra Assignments

1. During the group time have group members brainstorm about the different rights that young people have. For example, I have the right to be treated with respect by not having others call me names. Have each member select one right and express to the group what that right is: "I have a right to. . . . " Each member can discuss how comfortable he or she was with the exercise.

2. Have group members invent situations for asserting their rights. For each situation have them write down an assertive, an aggressive, and a passive response. Use these responses in the group to discuss the differences between passive, aggressive, and assertive behavior.

3. Have each group member describe a difficult situation in which to stand up for his or her rights. Use these situations for role plays during group practice.

Session 7—Identifying How Others Feel: The Art of Empathy

Introduction and Overview

The skill of empathy is a very important skill to learn. Empathy means being able to understand how another person feels— not just the surface feelings but the deep-down feelings the person has inside of them. If a teacher gets mad at your friend and she gets into trouble, how do you feel? If you feel bad for her, then you are using empathy. To express empathy you have to be able to feel what it is like to be another person. This skill does not come naturally, but you can learn how to be more empathic. In the situation described above you might say, "I'm sorry you got in trouble. You seem really upset over it." Sometimes people do not express their feelings but we can sense what they are feeling. To be able to sense another person's feeling is using the skill of empathy.

In learning how to be empathic we have to learn how to identify others' feelings. Once we can do this, we can express to the other person that we understand how he or she feels. The key to this skill is learning to perceive how others feel. When we use the skill of empathy our friends feel like we really understand them and we can help them feel better about themselves. People like to feel understood; using empathy can help others feel this way.

Discussion Questions

Why is it important to learn the skill of empathy? Encourage the group to identify the following points:

1. Learning to use empathy can help you understand and get along with others better.
2. Learning to use empathy can help others feel better because they know that someone understands them.
3. Learning to use empathy can help you feel better because you helped someone else by understanding them.
4. Learning to use empathy can help you get to know another person better because you have shared feelings with them.

Looking at Examples

Describe a situation where you recently used the skill of empathy. Conduct a role play where the skill was *not* used appropriately to generate a discussion about why the skill is important (show what happens when one person ignores another person's feelings). Examine the situation by answering the following questions:

1. What was the setting where this occurred?
2. Who was present?
3. Did you listen carefully to what the other person said?
4. What were the other person's feelings?
5. Why was the person feeling this way?
6. What empathic statement was made to the other person?

Have the group present their own examples.

Modeling the Skill

Learning the skill of empathy takes practice, because it is hard to learn how to identify what another person is feeling. I will do a role play to provide an example.

Modeling Situation 1. Your best friend is really looking sad. You ask him how things are going.

Peer: "My parents have been fighting a lot and now they are going to get a divorce."
You: "I'm really sorry. This must be very hard on you. I know I'd be real upset."
Peer: "Well, I'm just going to have to learn how to deal with it but, gosh, I really want to live with both of them."

Modeling Situation 2. Not all feelings are sad. Empathy can also be used for happy feelings. Suppose your friend is a good speller and she has been studying hard to do well on the big spelling test coming up. She wins and is very happy.

Peer: "Guess what? I won! I beat everybody on the spelling test."
You: "Great! I knew you could do it. I was really rooting for you. I'm happy for you."

Skill Review

Let's look at this role play to see what skills the model demonstrated about how to show empathy for someone. What skills did the model show? Encourage the group to generate the following list of skills:

1. Looked the person in the eye and had good body language
2. Listened carefully to the other person's situation or problem
3. Identified the other person's feelings
4. Identified a reason for the person's feelings
5. Stated an empathic response.

Practice Opportunities

Each group member should practice the empathy skill at least once during the group meeting. Use the following situations or have the group itself generate situations that they would like to practice.

Situation 1. Your friend plays on the basketball team and they made it all the way to the finals. Last night they lost. He comes up to you in the hall and is looking sad.

Situation 2. Your friend really wants to have the lead role in the school play. She has been practicing every day for the rehearsal. Yesterday was the competition for the role. When she sees you she says, "I can't believe it—I got the lead role!"

Situation 3. A friend of yours got into a big fight with another kid at school. This is someone your friend really likes and now she is mad at her. She says to you, "I know she really hates me now. I'm never going to be able to work this out."

Situation 4. Your dad decided he wanted to be in a community play and has been practicing to try out for the part. He just found out that he didn't get the part and is very disappointed.

Situation 5. Your friend comes to school and is looking very sad. When you ask what's going on, he says, "My cat died last night."

Extra Assignments

1. Read a story to the group and have the group members identify the feelings that the different characters were experiencing. Discuss how one could use skills of empathy in the story.

2. Act out a play that includes expression of a lot of different feelings. Use the play as a modeling experience to coach the group members about how to be empathic.

3. Develop a work sheet that includes different statements from different people (friends, teachers, parents, and so forth). Have group members practice identifying the feelings involved in each statement.

4. Ask each group member to write down an experience he or she had in which he or she either used empathy skills or could have used them. Have them write down the situation, feelings, and what was said. Use these for group discussion.

Session 8—Dealing with Those in Authority: Staying Out of Trouble

Introduction and Overview

As we are growing up we all have to deal with others who are in a position of authority, people who are responsible for us, like parents, teachers, coaches, police, bosses, and so forth. Sometimes it is difficult to deal with those who have authority over us. However, these people often ask for your respect and want to get along with you. As a result, we may have to treat those in authority differently than we treat our friends. Learning how to deal with those in authority is important if you want to avoid arguments and stay out of trouble. If a teacher asks you, "Why aren't you in your class? Recess is over," and you snap back, "I'll get to class—when I want to," you will get into even more trouble. It is also important to realize that how we say something can sometimes get us in trouble.

Discussion Questions

Let's examine why it is important to learn skills involved with dealing with people in authority. Encourage the group to remember the following points:

1. Learning to deal with authority can help you get along better with adults.
2. Learning to deal with authority can help you avoid problems caused by an inappropriate response.
3. Learning to deal with authority will show adults that you are mature, and they may give you more responsibility in the future.
4. Learning to deal with authority will increase the likelihood of more positive interactions.

Looking at Examples

Describe a situation from your own life in which you had to use the skill of dealing with authority. It is helpful if the group understands that even adults must deal with those in authority. Also, give an example where you could have used this skill but you didn't. Point out the consequences of not using this skill. Examine the situation by answering the following questions:

1. What was the setting where this occurred?
2. Who was present?
3. How did you listen to the person in authority?
4. Did you apologize to the person, if necessary?
5. Did you ask for suggestions, if appropriate?
6. How did you feel afterward?

Have the group present their own examples.

Modeling the Skill

Dealing with those in authority can be difficult for many people. As children we have to learn to deal with parents, as adults we have to deal with bosses. Whatever one's age, it is often difficult to accept what someone in authority has to say to us. I will do a role play to model how to deal with those in authority, and then the group can practice these skills.

Modeling Situation. You went to spend the afternoon with some friends but agreed to be home by 4:00 P.M. since your family has plans to have dinner with some friends. You lost track of time and did not get home until 4:45 P.M.

Parent: "You were suppose to be home by 4:00— you're 45 minutes late! You're going to lose weekend privileges for two weeks."

You: "I'm sorry I was late. I know you were counting on my being home at 4:00. I'm sorry I let you down. I should have paid more attention to what time it was but I didn't."

Parent: "That's right; you let me down! You are going to have to learn how to be more responsible."

You: "I know I am. Maybe you can help me come up with some ways that will help me remember better."

Skill Review

An examination of the skills used in this role play show that the model:

1. Looked the person in the eye and used good body language.
2. Listened attentively to what the person had to say.
3. Apologized directly to the person.
4. Took responsibility for his behavior.
5. Offered a suggestion to avoid the difficulty in the future.

Practice Opportunity

Each member of the group should practice dealing with authority at least once during the group session. Select group members to evaluate individuals' performances according to the skill steps described in the skill review.

Situation 1. You arrive late for class because you were talking to someone.

Teacher: "You were late for class and I expect you to be here on time."

You: _____

_____

Situation 2. Your boss asks you to do something and you forget exactly what he wanted you to do. When he comes by to check your work he complains that you have done it all wrong.

Boss: "That's not the way I asked you to do it."

You: _____

_____

Situation 3. A teacher catches you throwing something at another student during class.

Teacher: "You know that such behavior is not allowed in my classroom."

You: _____

_____

Extra Assignments

1. Change the role plays so that the person in authority displays considerable anger. Discuss in group how these types of situations may call for different skills.

2. Ask group members to record any situation they encounter in which they have to deal with someone in authority—either successfully or unsuccessfully. Use the situations for group discussion and role plays.

Session 9—Responsible Decision Making: Think about It

Introduction and Overview

In this session we are going to learn about how to make decisions. All of us have to make decisions everyday. But often we don't make the best decision and as a result the outcome isn't always positive. The focus in learning decision making is making *responsible* decisions. To make responsible decisions you have to think about the decision and evaluate both the positive and negative outcomes or consequences involved in that decision. Often, what happens is that we simply make a decision without *thinking* about what the decision means for us. Making responsible decisions is a skill just like the other skills we have been learning. However, it is different in that it is a thinking skill, not a skill that involves other people. Once you've made a decision you might need to use some of the other skills we've been learning in order to act on that decision. For example, your friends have planned a party that you really want to go to, but your mom has asked you to stay home because she isn't feeling well and needs help with your younger brothers. You have to decide what to do in this situation. Should you go to the party, or should you stay home to help your mother? Each choice has its own consequences. In order to make the best, most responsible decision you need to think about what the alternative choices are, what the positive and negative outcomes might be, and then decide on a plan.

Discussion Questions

Why is it important to learn how to make decisions? Encourage the group to discuss the following points.

1. Learning to make decisions can help you make better, more effective decisions.
2. Learning to make decisions can help you think about situations and choices more carefully so that you don't follow the first idea that comes up.
3. Learning to make better decisions now can help you prepare for future decisions that will be difficult, like choosing a career.
4. Learning to make decisions can help you feel better about the choices you do make because you will have thought about them carefully.

Looking at Examples

Describe a recent situation in which you had to make a difficult decision. Share with the group how you went about thinking about the choices you had, how you considered the negative and positive consequences, what choice you finally made, and how you acted on that choice. If possible, explain how you could have arrived at a different conclusion if you had not carefully used decision-making skills. Also, share with the group a situation where you didn't use good decision-making skills and discuss the consequences that followed.

Examine the decision-making situation using the following questions:

1. What was the setting where this occurred?
2. Who, if anybody, was present?
3. What process did you use to make the decision:
   a. generating alternative choices
   b. describing the positive and negative outcomes of each choice
   c. choosing one or a combination of choices
   d. acting on the decision
4. How did you feel afterward?

Have group members describe an example from their own life.

Modeling the Skill

Since this is a thinking skill, I'll model for you the thinking process that you go through when using responsible decision making.

Modeling Situation. It's the beginning of the school year and you are interested in being involved in two afterschool activities whose schedules conflict.

You want to be on the basketball team but you are also interested in the computer club. Most of your friends will be playing basketball and this activity would probably be more fun, but your parents are pushing you to join the computer club, especially since they just bought you an expensive new computer.

1. Generate alternative choices.
   a. You could sign up for basketball.
   b. You could sign up for the computer club.
   c. You could do one this year and the other next year.
   d. You could look into a different basketball or computer club option—one not connected with school but with the YMCA, your church, and so on.
2. Describe the positive and negative outcomes of each choice.
   a. Basketball would be the most fun because your friends are involved in basketball, but your parents would be disappointed because they want you to learn more about computers.
   b. Computer club would please your parents but wouldn't be much fun; however, you do have a few friends in the computer club.
   c. As a compromise, you could join the computer club, but let your parents know that next year you want to try out for basketball.
   d. You could join the basketball team at the YMCA or take a computer course at the community center. But in either case, you'd have to find transportation, and the computer course would cost money. Also, do you really have the time to play basketball and do computers?
3. Choose one or a combination of choices.
   a. You decide on choice "c" since this one serves to solve most problems. You will please your parents and make use of the new computer they bought for you. Computer club will probably be fun since a few of your friends also belong. And you will also let your parents know that you really want to play basketball and that you will do that next year.
4. Act on the decision.
   a. You make a plan to sit down with your parents and discuss your decision and how you arrived at the decision. Ask them for their support in your decision. Sign up for the computer club. Discuss your decision with your basketball friends.

Skill Review

Let's review the steps involved in responsible decision making. In this example the model demonstrated the following skills:

1. Generating as many alternatives as possible.
2. Examining each alternative or choice for positive and negative outcomes.
3. Deciding on one or a combination of choices.
4. Developing a plan to act on the decision.

Practice Opportunity

Each member of the group should practice this skill at least once during the group meeting. Have various group members think out the decision-making process aloud so others can examine and evaluate the skills being used. The group may want to use examples shared by the group or they may want to select from the sample of situations below.

> *Situation 1.* Two different people have asked you to go to a football game with them. One person is a good friend you really like and want to keep and the other person is someone new that doesn't know many people and you want to get to know her better. You already know enough about both the old friend and the possible new friend to think that they wouldn't get along.
>
> *Situation 2.* You are out with two of your friends who decide they want to soap someone's car windows. You like these friends a lot and don't want to offend them, but you don't want to get into trouble.
>
> *Situation 3.* Your parents are going out and ask you to stay home this afternoon because they are expecting a delivery. After your parents leave the delivery person calls and says he can't come today. Next your friend calls and invites you over. Your parents expect you to be home but now there is no reason you really have to stay at home.
>
> *Situation 4.* You are trying to do well in your math class. Last week you got sick with the flu and missed several days of classes. You have a midterm exam coming up and want to do well but are afraid you might not understand some of the material that was covered when you were sick.

Extra Assignments

1. Use some problem situations to practice decision-making skills with the group. Present each problem and work with the group to generate alternatives, think of consequences, and plan a course of action. Praise the group for creative thinking and their abilities to examine consequences.

2. Make a game out of the process. Present a problem situation and see if each group member can generate two alternative choices. You may want to divide the group in half and have teams independently work through a problem.

3. Have each group member identify a problem situation in which they had to use decision-making skills. Have each describe the process and evaluate his or her performance in using responsible decision making. Another option: ask each person to discuss a time when he or she made a bad decision and explain how that decision could have been made better.

Session 10—Learning to Negotiate: Conflict Resolution

Introduction and Overview

We all have to face conflict situations in our lives. Everyday we come into contact with people who we don't always get along with. When we don't get along with someone, it is usually because of a conflict. A conflict may be a misunderstanding about something, a disagreement about something, or a different viewpoint about something. The important thing about a conflict is that the people involved are not happy with what is going on. Let me give you some examples. A conflict might arise between friends over whether to invite another friend along on a planned trip. A conflict might arise with parents about how late you can stay up on weekend nights. A conflict might arise with a teacher about whether the homework you turned in is acceptable. As you can see, there are a lot of ways you can get into conflicts! Therefore, it is important to learn ways to resolve conflict. The best way is through negotiation. That means learning to compromise and "talk it out" when you have a conflict. Negotiation is better than getting mad at the other person because of the conflict. When you get mad, the other person often responds by also getting mad. Then an argument or even a fight could happen. Everyone needs to learn "conflict-resolution" skills, which include learning to negotiate or compromise. That involves making suggestions to the other person about how to solve the conflict and working with the person to reach an acceptable solution for all people involved.

Discussion Questions

Why is it important to learn how to negotiate with other people? Encourage the group members to recognize the following points:

1. Learning to negotiate can help you get along better with other people since you can solve conflicts.
2. Learning to negotiate can help you understand other people better since you have to listen to the other person's viewpoint.
3. Learning to negotiate can help you get more of what you want in a situation since you can reach a compromise with the other person.

4. Learning to negotiate can help you earn the respect of the other person or help you keep your friendship with the other person since you are working together to solve the problem.

Looking at Examples

Describe a situation from your own life in which you had to use the skill of negotiation, or give an example of a situation in which you should have used this skill but didn't. Point out the consequences of not using this skill. Examine the situation by addressing the following questions:

1. What was the setting where this occurred?
2. Who was present?
3. What statement was used to begin the negotiation?
4. Did you offer an alternative solution?
5. Was an alternative solution offered by the other person?
6. Did both people try to reach a compromise?
7. Was a compromise accepted or did both people agree that, although they had tried to compromise, no clear solution was available to them?

Have group members describe their own examples.

Modeling the Skill

We all have conflicts with other people so we need to be good at negotiating with them to solve those conflicts. There are a couple of things to remember if you want to use negotiation successfully. First, think about some solutions before you attempt to solve the problem. Second, remember to stay calm. Never get angry when trying to negotiate. I will do a role play to model how to negotiate and solve a conflict with another person.

Modeling Situation. A new television series has started this fall and you really want to watch it. Unfortunately, your sister regularly watches another show that comes on at the same time as the show you want to watch.

You: "Can we discuss our plans for watching TV?"
Sister: "Sure."
You: "You know that show that you always watch at 7:00 P.M.? Well, there's a new show on at the same time that all my friends watch and they say it's really great. I'd like to be able to watch that new show. Do you have any ideas about how we can solve this conflict?"
Sister: "Well, we've been watching the other show and I really like that show, so I'm not sure what to do."

You: "What do you think about us taking turns? I could watch my show one week and you could watch your show the next week."
Sister: "Well, then I would miss half the shows!"
You: "I know, but that seems fair—and we both get to see some of our shows. Maybe we could also ask Mom for another TV."
Sister: "Sure! That would be great. I guess for now we can take turns."
You: "Thanks for helping solve this problem."

Skill Review

Let's look carefully at how this skill was used in this role play. The model demonstrated the following:

1. Looked the other person in the eye and used good body language.
2. Asked to speak with the person about the conflict.
3. Explained the conflict in a clear and relaxed manner.
4. Listened to the other person's ideas for possible solutions.
5. Proposed a compromise solution.
6. Thanked the other person for helping to work the conflict out.

Practice Opportunity

Each member should practice the skill at least once during the group session. Select group members to evaluate individuals' performances by using the skill steps listed above. The group may want to help the role player think of different solutions to propose prior to doing the role play. The group can use examples of situations that were discussed earlier or select from the situations below.

Situation 1. You would like to be able to stay out later on weekends. You have had the same curfew for over a year. Since you're older now and most of your friends can stay out later, you'd like to have your curfew changed.

You: (Ask to speak with the parent about the problem)
Parent: "Sure."
You: (Present the conflict)
Parent: "Just because other kids stay out later that doesn't make it right."
You: (Ask for suggestions to solve the conflict)
Parent: "I don't think that's possible."
You: (Propose a compromise, negotiate a solution)
Parent: "Well, I'll think about it."
You: (Thank parent for listening)

Situation 2. You are discussing your plans for the weekend with your best friend. You have already invited another friend to go out with you on Saturday night. However, your best friend doesn't really like this person and says that she does not want to go if the other person is going to go with you.

You: (Ask to speak with your friend about the problem)
Friend: "OK."
You: (Present the conflict)
Friend: "I don't really like that girl."
You: (Ask for suggestions to solve the conflict)
Friend: "Well, I don't know—I was just planning on us going."
You: (Propose a compromise, negotiate a solution)
Friend: "Well, I'll give that a try."
You: (Thank friend for listening)

Situation 3. You are playing a new game that you learned in school with two friends. A conflict starts because each of you have a different understanding of what the rules are.

You: (Ask to speak with your friend about the problem)
Friend: "OK."
You: (Present the conflict)
Friend: "Well, that's the way I remember learning it."
You: (Ask for suggestions to solve the conflict)
Friend: "I am sure that's the way it's played."
You: (Propose a compromise, negotiate a solution)
Friend: "Well, we can try that for now, until we ask the teacher."
You: (Thank friend for listening)

Extra Assignments

1. Present a number of conflicts for group work or as individual homework assignments. Have participants practice brainstorming to find solutions to the various conflicts. Point out that arriving at a solution will be easier if they work at thinking up alternative choices as solutions.

2. As a homework assignment have each group member recall a conflict that could have been solved with conflict resolution skills. Have each person write out the situation, what happened, and what the result was. Now have each person go back over the situation and write out a script for how he or she could have used conflict resolution skills.

3. Have each group member write a story about conflict resolution. Have them fantasize or make up a conflict, describe what happened, and

then continue the story by describing how the conflict was resolved using negotiation skills.

4. Develop a series of conflict situations as stories about interesting people and circumstances. Use guided imagery as you describe how the person in the story resolved her conflict through her use of negotiation skills.

Session 11—When You're in Need: Asking for Help

Introduction and Overview

Today we are going to learn about what to do when we need help. All of us face difficulties that are sometimes too much for us to handle alone. When this happens we need to ask for help, even though it may not be easy to do so. Asking for help is a critical skill because you may be dealing with a problem that is serious and needs to be brought to another person's attention. For example, some kids get really down on themselves, even to the point of wanting to commit suicide. Other kids get abused or are physically punished to the point of serious injury. Kids may end up addicted to drugs. In all of these situations, you need to ask for help. You may find yourself in other situations that may not be as serious, yet you still may need to ask for help. For example, you may be feeling lonely and want someone to talk with, or you may be having a conflict with your parents and want to check it out with someone else. As you can see, knowing who to talk to and how to ask for help can be an important skill to learn.

Discussion Questions

Why do we need to learn skills for asking for help? Encourage the group members to recognize the following points:

1. Learning to ask for help can assist you in dealing with serious problems that may be too much for you to handle by yourself.
2. Learning to ask for help can assist you in feeling better about yourself.
3. Learning to ask for help can assist you in feeling more in control of your circumstances.
4. Learning to ask for help will lead to increased respect from others because you asked for help when you needed it.

Looking at Examples

Describe a situation from your own life in which you had to ask for help (if it is not too personal), or describe a situation involving someone you know who had to ask for help. Examine the situation by addressing the following questions:

1. What was the setting where this occurred?
2. Why is there a need to ask for help?
3. What kinds of help are needed?
4. Who are some people you could go to for help?
5. Who should you see to get help?
6. How would you describe your problem to the person helping you?
7. How do you think you would feel afterwards?

Have the group present their own examples.

Modeling the Skill

Asking for help and knowing what kind of help to get can be difficult. I will model how to ask for help. However, most of what I model will be what you need to think to yourself so I will just be thinking out loud.

Modeling Situation 1. Your parents fight all the time, but their fights have become worse in the last six months. They just told you that they are going to get a divorce. You are very upset and have been crying for several days. You just can't get it off your mind.

You: "I need to ask for help—I'm really feeling upset. I've been upset before but now I just can't keep from crying and I can't stop thinking about their divorce. I'm not doing well at school either because I just can't concentrate. I could use some help with this problem."

You: "I could get help from a number of people. I could talk with my friend, I could talk to my teacher, I could call that kid's help line, I could see a school counselor, and I could talk with my aunt."

You: "I think I'll see a school counselor because they deal with these kinds of problems. But if I'm still feeling bad today when I go home, I'm also going to call that kid's line, just to talk with someone."

You: (You make an appointment to see a school counselor and when you go to your appointment you describe your situation). "I'm really upset because my mom and dad are getting a divorce."

Modeling Situation 2. You and a couple of friends start goofing off during P.E. class and the teacher gets really mad and starts yelling at you. He calls you names and tells you to go to his office. When you get there he starts yelling at you again and then says he's going to spank you. He gets out a wooden paddle and makes you bend over and really spanks you hard.

You: "He really hurt me with that spanking—I can't even sit down. I think what he did was wrong. We weren't really doing anything that bad and he just lost his temper and took it out on us. Also, I heard that kids weren't suppose to get spanked anymore. I know they suspend kids from school but spanking them isn't right."

You: "I need to ask for help—what he did wasn't right and I should tell somebody so this doesn't happen again or so it doesn't happen to somebody else."

You: "I could ask for help from my other friends, my homeroom teacher, the school counselor, or my parents."

You: "I think I should talk with my parents first. I'll tell them what happened and see what they think. I might also mention it to a school counselor but I'm not sure he can help me with this."

You: (When your parents get home from work you tell them you need to discuss something with them). "Something happened to me in school today and I just wanted you to know about it. We were goofing off in class and the teacher got really mad at us—so mad he yelled at us and gave us a spanking. But it really hurt—I can't even sit down because he hit me so hard. I just don't think this was fair—we weren't doing anything that bad, he just lost his temper and took it out on us."

Modeling Situation 3. You and your best friend get into a really big fight. She is not talking to you anymore. You feel really bad about this because you really like her and you want to be friends again.

You: "I really like her and I don't think we should stay mad at each other. This isn't helping anybody. I've tried to talk with her and she won't speak to me. I feel hurt and at the end of my rope."

You: "I need to ask for help—we haven't been able to solve this problem and she won't talk to me. I'm feeling more upset each day."

You: "I could discuss this with another friend of mine, my teacher, my parents, or the school counselor."

You: "I think I should talk with my mom first. She knows my friend and she might have some ideas about what I can do."

You: (After getting home from school you tell your mom you need some help). "Mom, I need your help. I'm really upset because my best friend and I had a fight and she won't talk with me. I just don't know what to do."

Skill Review

Let's look closely at this role play and see what skills the model demonstrated about how to ask for help. The model demonstrated the following set of questions:

1. Why is there a need for me to ask for help?
2. What kinds of help could I use?
3. Who are some people I could see to get help?
4. Who should I see to get help?
5. How would I describe my problem to the person helping me?

Practice Opportunity

Let's practice how you might prepare yourself to ask for help. Using the situations below, think out loud how you would use the skills of asking for help.

Situation 1. You are having a difficult time in one of your classes. On the last test you got a D. You really want to do better. How would you ask for help in this situation?

Situation 2. Your parents got in a really big fight last night and your mom left and hasn't come home. You are very upset and want to talk to someone. How would you ask for help in this situation?

Situation 3. You feel very shy and have a hard time meeting people. Also, there are some kids at school that make fun of you because you are shy and don't know what to say at times. Having your schoolmates pick on you is really getting to you. How would you ask for help in this situation?

Situation 4. Your friend is very down on himself. He has been getting more and more depressed. Lately he has been talking about making life easier by not being around. You are afraid he is serious about committing suicide. How would you ask for help in this situation?

Extra Assignments

1. Write a story about someone who was having a difficult life and needed help. Describe how that person got help. Each person in the group will then share their story with the group.

2. Present a number of situations to the group in which a person needed to ask for help. Have the group brainstorm about who they would ask for help and discuss why this person would be the best person to choose.

3. Ask each group member to share an example about someone they knew who should have asked for help to solve a problem. Discuss how these people could have received help by asking for it.

References

Asher, S. R. (1983). Social competence and peer status: Recent advances and future directions. *Child Development, 54*, 1427–1434.

Brown, G. M., & Greenspan, S. (1984). Effect of social foresight training on the school adjustment of high-risk youth. *Child Study Journal, 14,* 61–77.

Corcoran, K., & Fischer, J. (1987). *Measures for clinical practice: A source book.* New York: Free Press.

Gilchrist, L. D., Schinke, S. P., & Blythe, B. J. (1985). Preventing unwanted adolescent pregnancies. In L. D. Gilchrist & S. P. Schinke (Eds.), *Preventing social and health problems through life skills training.* Seattle, WA: Center for Social Welfare.

Goldstein, A. P., & Glick, B. (1987). *Aggression replacement training.* Champaign, IL: Research Press.

Goldstein, A. P., Sprafkin, R. P., Gershaw, N. J., & Klein, P. (1983). *Skill-streaming the adolescent.* Champaign, IL: Research Press.

Hazel, J. S., Schumaker, J. B., Sherman, J. A., & Sheldon-Wilder, J. (1981). The development and evaluation of a group skill training program for court-adjudicated youths. In D. Upper and S. M. Ross (Eds.), *Behavioral group therapy, 1981: An annual review.* Champaign, IL: Research Press.

Hiew, C. C., & MacDonald, G. (1986). Delinquency prevention through promoting social competence in adolescents. *Canadian Journal of Criminology, 28,* 291–302.

Hops, H., Finch, M., & McConnell, S. (1985). Social skills deficits. In P. H. Bornstein & A. E. Kazdin (Eds.), *Handbook of clinical behavior therapy with children.* Homewood, IL: Dorsey Press.

LeCroy, C. W., & Milligan, K. B. (1991). Promoting social competence in the schools. In R. Constable, J. Flynn, & S. MacDonald (Eds.), *School social work: Practice and research perspectives,* Chicago: Lyceum Press.

LeCroy, C. W., & Rose, S. D. (1986). Evaluation of preventive interventions for promoting social competence in adolescents. *Social Work Research and Abstracts, 22,* 8–17.

Maloney, D. M., Harper, T. M., Braukmann, C. J., Fixsen, D. L., Phillips, E. L., & Wolf, M. M. (1976). Teaching conversation-related skills in pre-delinquent girls. *Journal of Applied Behavior Analysis, 9,* 371.

Marshall, M. J., & Peck, C. A. (1986). Facial expression training in blind adolescents using EMG feedback: A multiple-baseline study. *Behaviour Research & Therapy, 24,* 429–435.

Matson, J. L., Manikam, R., Coe, D., & Raymond K. (1988). Training social skills to severely mentally retarded multiply handicapped adolescents. *Research in Developmental Disabilities, 9,* 195–208.

Minkin, N., Braukmann, C. J., Minkin, B. L., Timbers, G. K., Timbers, B. J., Fixsen, D. L., Phillips, E. L., & Wolf, M. M. (1976). The social validation and training of conversational skills. *Journal of Applied Behavior Analysis, 9,* 127–139.

Pentz, M. A. (1985). Social competence skills and self-efficacy as determinants of substance use in adolescence. In S. Shiffman & T. A. Wills (Eds.), *Coping and substance use.* New York: Academic Press.

Rose, S. D., & Edelson, J. L. (1987). *Working with children and adolescents in groups.* San Francisco: Jossey Bass.

Sarason, I. G., & Ganzer, V. J. (1973). Modeling and group discussion in the rehabilitation of delinquents. *Journal of Counseling Psychology, 20,* 442–449.

Schinke, S. P., Schilling, R. F., Gilchrist, L. D., Barth, R., Bobo, J. K., Trimble, J. E.,

& Cvetkovich, G. T. (1985). Preventing substance abuse with American Indian youth. *Social Casework, 66,* 213–217.

Staab, S., & Lodish, D. (1985). Reducing joblessness among disadvantaged youth. In L. D. Gilchrist & S. P. Schinke (Eds.), *Preventing social and health problems through life skills training.* Seattle, WA: Center for Social Welfare Research, University of Washington.

Strayhorn, J. M. (1988). *The competent child.* New York: Guilford Press.

Tisdelle, D. A., & St Lawrence, J. S. (1986). Interpersonal problem-solving competency: Review and critique of the literature. *Clinical Psychology Review, 6,* 337–356.

6
Cognitive-Behavioral Anger Control Training

Eva L. Feindler
Jennifer Guttman

The Rationale and Development of Anger Control Training

The antisocial behavior of children and adolescents presents a significant challenge to the clinical community. Prevalence rates of aggressive behaviors and criminal acts are high, and conduct disorders in childhood and adolescence portent problems in adulthood (Kazdin, 1987). Further, aggression in children, if untreated, appears to be stable over time (Olweus, 1984) and results in significant social adjustment difficulties. Since cognitive processes, such as attributions, self-statements, and problem-solving skills, play a major role in the development of anger and the sometimes resultant aggressive response to provocation (Novaco, 1975), and since the correlated social and problem-solving skills deficiencies of antisocial children and adolescents have been documented, cognitive-behavioral anger control training programs for such children and adolescents have been developed.

Novaco's (1975) cognitive-behavioral conceptualization of anger and anger control problems functions as the basis for the anger control procedures described by Feindler and her colleagues (1984, 1986, 1987, 1989, 1990). Based on Meichenbaum's (1975) stress inoculation model, Novaco (1975) identifies anger as a stress reaction with three response components: cognitive, physiological, and behavioral. The cognitive component is characterized by one's perception of social stimuli and provocation cues in the social context, by one's interpretation of these stimuli, by one's attributions concerning causality and/or responsibility, and by one's evaluation of oneself and the situation. This component represents the most significant area for intervention with aggressive adolescents as their perceptions and attitudes serve to prompt most behavioral responses to provocation. In addition to cognitive deficits and distortions, aggressive adolescents display high states of emotional and physiological arousal as well as other social and self-control skill deficits.

Recent reformulations of the frustration-aggression hypothesis indicate that the cognitive aspects of the hypothesis need further emphasis (Berkowitz, 1989). It may be that cognitive processes account for the *absence* of overt aggression because of their inhibitory potential. Explosive adolescents may in fact lack inhibitory self statements and accompanying belief systems. Dodge's (1985) studies of attributional bias have demonstrated that the individual's perception of whether his or her goals have been thwarted and how they have been thwarted are critical to the prediction of an aggressive reaction. Further, there seem to be specific cognitive deficiencies and distortions such as a hostility bias, a legitimacy of retaliation bias, and belief in aggression, that characterize aggressive children and adolescents and that are targeted for remediation in current anger control programs (Feindler, 1991).

Finally, recent evidence from developmental psychology points to cognitive scheme as a key ingredient in the development of stable behavior patterns. As Olweus (1984) and others (Huesmann, Eron, Lefkowitz, & Walder, 1984) have indicated, children who display angry and aggressive behavior patterns are quite likely as adults to display aggression more frequently and more intensely. Early aggressiveness in school was found to be predictive of later serious antisocial behavior, including criminal behavior, spouse abuse, traffic violations, and self-reported physical aggression, in a follow-up study of 600 subjects (Huesmann et al., 1984). Slaby and Guerra (1988) suggest that these aggressive behavior patterns might be changed by addressing those cognitive factors (that is, beliefs, attributions, and moral judgments) that may play a central organizing role in social-emotional development.

This chapter will present a complete anger control intervention designed for a group of aggressive adolescents. Particular attention will be paid to cognitive deficits and distortions that have been identified and treatment strategies that directly target misattributions, misperceptions, and poor problem-solving ability. Anger control strategies designed to effect change in the physiological and behavioral components will also be described in this detailed manual. Further, recommendations for assessment and development of the group intervention and clinical issues in the areas of generalization enhancement, diagnostic decision making, and group process will be made.

A General Description of Anger Control Training

Based on the premise that adolescents who lose control over their anger do so because of particular behavioral and cognitive skill deficits, Feindler and her colleagues (Feindler, Ecton, Kingsley, & Dubey, 1986; Feindler, Marriott, & Iwata, 1984) have developed an anger control training program that is appropriate for adolescents in a variety of settings. The program focuses on the control of emotional and impulse responding, as well as on the appropriate expression of anger in an assertive and rational manner, by teaching arousal-management skills and cognitive strategies designed to promote the enhancement and generalization of self-control skills. As the adolescent builds a repertoire of skills, he or she begins to experience greater satisfaction from effective communication in interpersonal conflicts, and as a result suffers less from the punishing consequences of aggressive responding.

The Chill-Out program (Feindler & Ecton, 1986) uses a self-regulatory coping skills approach with special emphasis on the cognitive components of anger. Adolescents are taught to recognize, moderate, regulate, and prevent anger and its often accompanying aggressive component and to implement problem-solving actions in response to interpersonal provocation. Behavior change, in specific terms of reduced physiological arousal, aggressive responding, and negative anger sustaining attributions and self statements is the desired outcome of the intervention program.

Whether administered on an individual client basis or to a group of adolescents, the intervention program consists of interrelated training strategies and therapeutic goals designed to help adolescents achieve self-regulatory skills. Throughout, the youth are educated about (1) interaction between the cognitive, physiological, and behavioral components of their anger experience; (2) the adaptive and maladaptive functions of their anger; (3) the situational triggers that provoke their anger; (4) the concept of choice and self-responsibility in their responses to provocations, and (5) the importance of appropriate verbal expression of affect.

During each treatment session adolescents learn specific cognitive-behavioral skills such as the use of coping statements, reattribution of blame, assertiveness, arousal reduction, self inhibition, problem solving, and self analysis of anger control. Each skill is practiced through the use of role-played provocations, in-session group exercises or games, and is structured to enhance the anger control intervention approach which is strongly recommended.

Introduction to the Treatment Protocol

Cognitive-behavioral anger control training is generally presented as a didactic program in which skills training for the adolescent is emphasized. The three main components, arousal management, cognitive restructuring, and prosocial skills, correspond to hypothesized deficiencies implicated in the development and maintenance of anger outbursts and aggressive behavior patterns. For each component, specific skills are presented in an educational format, modeled, rehearsed through repeated role-played provocations scenes, and then applied to the natural environment. The program is designed to teach the adolescent to assess each anger-provoking incident and to implement the most effective response from his or her repertoire of anger control skills (Feindler & Ecton, 1986). A general emphasis on interpersonal problem solving and communication of emotional arousal is designed to reduce aggressive behaviors.

Prior to implementation of the following 10-session treatment protocol, a number of clinical issues need to be addressed. First, clinical assessments must be made to determine the adolescent's appropriateness for intervention. The behavioral history and psychological profile of an adolescent must be examined, since anger control strategies seem more effective with the impulsive and reactive adolescent who requires skills acquisition with appropriate cognitive mediation during a provocation (Feindler, 1990).

Other factors that must be taken into consideration include psychiatric diagnosis, level of cognitive functioning, emotional maturity, and additional psychopathology. These issues are discussed and recommendations are made in an article by Feindler (1987).

Next, there are several assessment methods that may be considered to further delineate the adolescent's anger control difficulties. Self-report inventories recommended for anger assessment with adolescents include the 44-item State-Trait Anger Inventory and Anger Expression Scale (Spielberger, 1988), the 128-item Cognitive-Behavioral Anger Control Inventory (Hoshmand & Austin, 1987), the 71-item Children's Inventory of Anger (Finch & Nelson, 1978), or the 33-item Assertiveness Scale for Adolescents (Lee, Hallberg, Slemon, & Haase, 1985). Pre–post measurement employing any of these inventories will help to evaluate the effectiveness of an anger control intervention. For research purposes, clinical investigators are encouraged to use additional measures such as direct observation, ratings by others, analogue measures, and self-monitoring to enhance both the reliability and validity of measured behavior change. (Refer to Feindler, 1990, and Feindler & Ecton, 1986, for a detailed review of assessment issues.)

Once a group of adolescents who may benefit from anger control have been identified, there are additional clinical issues to consider. The following represents a set of typical questions asked by those planning a program.

Issues to Consider When Planning Anger Control Interventions for Adolescents

How long should the sessions be? Given that adolescents typically have short attention spans, sessions should last no more than 45 minutes, so a maximum amount of material can be digested. However, sessions can be extended for mature adolescents and in groups that form a cohesive bond.

How long a period should elapse between sessions? There should be approximately one week between sessions. This will give the students time to process the information they have learned and practice their new skills. However, with less mature or frequently disruptive adolescents, sessions might need to occur more than one per week.

Should there be a cotherapist? Yes. Having two therapists to lead a group can be very helpful. First, the two therapists can role play provoking incidents together for the students. Second, having two therapists attending to the actions of the students is valuable when assessing progress. Third, the therapists can take turns introducing the content and in-group exercises, *and* monitoring in-group behavior.

Should both therapists be the same sex? If possible, it would be useful to have therapists of opposite genders to colead the group. This will increase diversity and the members of the group can witness both a man and a woman acting in a controlled manner.

How many adolescents should be in a group? Approximately eight adolescents per group. With this size group each adolescent does not feel too conspicuous and yet a feeling of intimacy and openness can develop among the group members. Also, in a group this size there will be fewer distractions between group members.

What's better, same-sex or mixed-sex groups? Same-sex groups are better when initially teaching anger control. Adolescents may attend better when they are not distracted by members of the opposite sex. However, in abusive relationships, anger control is often a problem. So, if possible, after the students have gone through the program in same-sex groups, review groups could be implemented as mixed-sex groups.

Can staff members who may continue to run this type of training program at the residence sit in on the session? Yes, but there should never be more adults than adolescents in a group. For a group of eight adolescents with two therapists no more than two staff members should sit in at a time. Also, if at all possible, the same staff members should sit in on every group. The reasons for this are twofold. First, it would help to maintain consistency for the adolescents in the group. Second, if the staff members are participating in order to learn how to implement this type of program, they should see it through from start to finish.

Would it be useful to use video equipment? Yes. It would be particularly helpful if other staff members will be learning the anger control techniques. This way, when staff watch the video, they can see the skills being taught and watch the students implement the techniques in the exercise portion of the treatment. However, if the group coleaders determine that video equipment will distract the group members, it should not be used.

What should the leader do about noncompliance to in-group tasks and to homework assignments? First, explore the reasons for noncompliance and clear up any possible misunderstandings concerning requirements or rationales. Second, make sure that the student understands the contingency system in place. That is, if he or she does not comply with the program rules, he or she will not be able to participate as an actor in role play situations and he or she will not be given reinforcers. This will effect his or her chances of participating in the lottery at the end of the program. Finally, if the student continues to be oppositional, the leader maintains the option of dismissing him or her from the group.

Are there any adolescents who would definitely not *benefit from anger control training?* Yes. Adolescents experiencing extreme depression and/or suicidal thoughts may not have the motivation to participate. Also, adolescents who are currently abusing substances will not benefit from the program, since the substances reduce their motivation and dampen their cognitive functioning. Finally, adolescents with thought disorders or delusions will be unable to glean much from the program, since they will have difficulty understanding the cognitive restructuring components. These issues would need to be addressed prior to the adolescent's involvement in anger control training.

What about using individual therapy concurrently with group anger control training? This would not pose a problem, as long as there is consistency between what the individual is expected to accomplish in his or her individual therapy and the skills being taught in the anger control treatment. Theoretical orientation between both needs to be compatible.

What ages should group members be? This program is designed for adolescents. Thus, the group members should be between the ages of 13 and 18. However, the treatment program's pace and content can be scaled down for children of younger ages.

Is it acceptable for all the group members to know each other, or be in the same classroom, or living unit? Yes. A benefit to having the students know each other is that they can monitor each other's behavior. As the students implement the techniques outside of the training setting, their peers can reinforce and give feedback regarding how effectively the anger control skills were used. One cautionary note: in-group role plays are less likely to be of a hypothetical nature and may be more volatile.

Is there any optimal setting for this type of skills training program? It would be optimal to hold the group training sessions in a number of different settings (for example, a classroom, a residence hall lounge). In this way generalization would be increased, since the students would be practicing their skills in different surroundings.

The Treatment Manual: Group Adolescent Anger Control Training

Presession: Intake and Screening

1. Intake and screening should be designed as an individual session with each potential member of the group.

A. Any pretraining assessments should be given at this time, such as the STAXI, the State Trait Anger Expression Inventory (Speilberger, 1988), the Children's Anger Inventory (Finch, Saylor, & Nelson, 1983), and/or the Anger Inventory (Novaco, 1975).

B. A history of each participant should be taken, including some background about any conflictual relationships they are in currently, and information about their history of anger control problems.

C. Give each student the rationale for the training program:
   i. We will teach a variety of techniques that will assist the student in controlling his or her anger in provocative situations
   ii. We will increase personal power by teaching the students the skills necessary to communicate their needs and desires effectively.

D. Describe the nature of the training program:
   i. New skills will be taught each session that will enable the student to control his or her anger.
   ii. Participation in exercises and role play will be required.
   iii. Group discussions will be encouraged.
   iv. Homework assignments will be assigned.

E. Define program rules:
   i. Set up meeting times, discuss length of program and length of sessions, explain rules for participation.
   ii. Introduce In-Session Checklist for following instructions, staying on task, cooperation, doing homework assignments.
   iii. Introduce In-Session Checklist Chart. Points range from zero to five points per session. Reinforcers (candy, soda, and the like) will be contingent upon in-session behaviors. Students must accumulate a minimum of four points to earn a reinforcer. Checklist includes: coming on time, handing in homework assignments, first 15 minutes of cooperation, second 15 minutes of cooperation, third 15 minutes of cooperation.
   iv. Explain the end-of-program lottery. Person(s) with the most checks for each behavior will have the opportunity to win prizes (For example, music tapes).
   v. Ask students to summarize the rules.

2. During this session participants should be screened for their ability to profit from this type of group. Adolescents with a history of mild-to-moderate forms of reactive aggression will certainly benefit. Students who have average intellectual functioning, who have engaged in few antisocial acts, and who lack psychiatric contraindications are also good candidates for improvement in anger control.

3. Before the end of the session each participant should sign a Voluntary Consent form.

Session 1

1. Group orientation:
   A. Have each of the members of the group introduce himself or herself.
   B. Reiterate the rationale for the training program: to teach the group members how to control their anger. For students who deny they have a problem with anger control, explain that the skills they will learn are useful for anyone who experiences anger.
   C. Review the rules of the program: meeting times, participation in role plays and group discussions, the In-Session Checklist, homework assignments, and so on.
2. Introduce *Brief Relaxation Technique.*
   A. *Deep Breaths:* Explain to students that taking a few slow deep breaths can help to maintain a controlled response to anger provocations. Give students examples of athletes (for example, figure skaters, gymnasts, baseball players) who visibly use a few deep breaths before attempting some event. Remind students about their physiological cues, for example, muscle tension in the neck, lower back, or shoulders, or heart palpitations. Other cues include fist clenching, cursing, or gritting of the teeth. Explain that deep breathing will function to reduce physiological tension, refocus attention away from external provoking stimuli to internal control, and provide a time delay before making a choice of how to respond.
3. Exercises:
   A. Have the students think about a situation in which they were very angry. Students may need to be prompted with questions such as "Think, for a moment, of the last time someone really got you steamed," or "Can you remember the last time you were in a situation when you wanted to hit someone who was really pushing your buttons?" Have students enumerate what physiological and other cues they noticed. Write these cues on the blackboard. Participating students get one point.
   B. Model for the students how, when they first notice that they are beginning to get angry, they should stop and remind themselves to relax and take one or two deep breaths.
   C. Have the students provoke each other. For example, one student might say to another, "Just get out of my face." Ask them to say "Relax" aloud and take the deep breaths. In this way the leader can determine if the students understand this procedure. Participating students get one point.
   D. Have the students practice diaphragmatic breathing. Tell them to imagine they have a balloon in their stomachs and they have to blow it up without moving any other part of their bodies. Check to make sure they are not lifting and tensing their shoulders.

4. Introduce the *Hassle Log:*
    A. Hand out Hassle Logs (see table 6–1) to students and ask various students to read the separate items in the log aloud.
    B. Run through an example of a hypothetical conflict with students and demonstrate how to fill out the Hassle Log.
    C. Give the rationale for using a Hassle Log: It is a self-monitoring device that will provide each student with an accurate picture of how he or she handled conflict situations during the week. It is a learning device for students regarding what sets them off. It provides an opportunity to report situations that were different and that were handled well. Finally, it provides scripts for in-session role play. Explain to each student the contingency: if they complete the Hassle Log appropriately, then it will be used as a script for role plays.
    D. Explain the positive consequences for students who complete Hassle Logs: they will earn points that can be exchanged for reinforcers. Also, they can participate as actors in role plays.
5. Summarize:
    A. Explain Hassle Log requirements: Present mechanics of completing Hassle Logs: they will earn points that can be exchanged for reinforcers. Also, they can participate as actors in role plays.
    B. Tell the students to fill in their Hassle Logs, and to record examples of their use of the deep breathing technique during a conflict situation.
    C. Give out session points and contingent reinforcers.

Session 2

1. Collect and review Hassle Logs and homework assignments. Students who did not comply will not earn session points and will not be permitted to be actors in role plays. Further, explain to the noncomplying student that he or she is a member of the group and in order to learn the skills being taught he or she needs to complete the homework assignments.
2. Recap. Review the brief relaxation techniques. Ask students if they had any difficulty implementing this strategy in the past week. Field any questions. For example, the relaxation technique may not have been effective if the student continued to focus his or her attention on the provocative stimuli instead of on the deep breaths he or she was taking.
3. Introduce *self-assessment of anger* and the concept of *ABC's* (that is, antecedents, actual behavior, consequences). Hand out the ABC's Worksheet (see table 6–2) so the students can visualize what is discussed.
    A. *Provoking Stimulus:* What gets the adolescent angry? Situational variables are assessed in terms of what is going on in the environ-

Table 6–1
Hassle Log

Name: _____   Date: _____

Morn. _____ Aft. _____ Even. _____

WHERE WERE YOU?

Class _____   Specialty Class _____
Cottage _____   Dining _____
Gym _____   Outside/On Campus _____
Off Campus _____   Other _____

WHAT HAPPENED?

Somebody teased me. _____
Somebody took something of mine. _____
Somebody told me to do something. _____
Somebody was doing something I didn't like. _____
Somebody started fighting with me. _____
I did something wrong. _____
Other: _____
_____

WHO WAS THAT SOMEBODY?

Another student _____   Teacher _____
Counselor _____   Parent _____
Another Adult _____   Sibling _____

WHAT DID YOU DO?

Hit Back _____   Told Supervising Adult _____
Ran Away _____   Walked Away Calmly _____
Yelled _____   Talked It Out _____
Cried _____   Told Peer _____
Broke Something _____   Ignored _____
Was Restrained _____   Other _____

HOW DID YOU HANDLE YOURSELF?

1	2	3	4	5
poorly	not so well	okay	good	great

HOW ANGRY WERE YOU?

1	2	3	4	5
burning mad	really angry	moderately angry	mildly angry	not angry at all

Table 6–2
ABC's Worksheet

Instructions: Write a statement about the antecedents, behaviors and consequences.

Antecedents	Behaviors	Consequences
Indirect Trigger:	Cognitive:	Positive: (if any)
Direct Trigger:	Physiological:	Negative:

ment (overt antecedents) and physiological states of fatigue, hunger, and so on. (covert antecedents).

B. Introduce the idea of *triggers:* these are the identification for the anger-provoking antecedent event. In this discussion, focus on the beginning of the anger/aggression sequence. Prompt group members to identify things that trigger an anger cue in them. Define and focus on:

    i. *Direct triggers:* Direct aversive provocations by another person. These may be in verbal (being told what to do) or nonverbal form (a kick, push, obscene gesture, or the like).

    ii. *Indirect triggers:* These aversive stimuli include misperceptions or misattribution of events such as feeling blamed or feeling like someone is disapproving. Most of these events involve a faulty appraisal of what is going on, such as: "He put me on restriction because he doesn't like me." Help students to identify different ways of interpreting provoking incidents.

C. *Actual Behavior/Reaction:* How do you know when you're angry? Focus on cognitive or physiological covert or overt cues that occur:

    i. *Negative statements to self* (for example, "I'm an idiot") or statements of intention to harm the other person (for example, "I want to kick him in the face").

    ii. *Physiological cues:* muscle tension, rigid posture, angry stare, butterflies in stomach, tense facial muscles, and so forth.

D. *Consequences:* Ask students, "What happened to you as a result of not controlling your anger? Did you get into trouble?" Also, there may be positive consequences of temper loss in that the individual may feel personal satisfaction or achieve some desired goal or object.

4. Exercises:

A. *The Trigger Finger:* Break into two teams of equal number. Ask the students to see which team can come up with the longer list of antecedents or triggers that typically result in an angry reaction. Each team has five minutes. Each member of the winning group gets two points.

B. Model for the students how direct triggers and indirect triggers in the form of negative self-statements (misattributions or misperceptions) can heighten a conflict. Then have students provoke each other. The student being provoked should relate the cognitive self-statements he or she generated in response to the provocative antecedent event. One point for participation.

C. *Going Head to Head:* The students break into two teams (A and B). One member from Team A states a physiological covert or overt cue and a team member from Team B must come up with a cognitive covert or overt cue. If both members give plausible cues, then a member of Team B must come up with a cognitive cue this time, and a member from Team A a physiological cue. If one team member cannot respond, the other team has an opportunity to steal the point and come up with a cue. For example, a member from Team A states that a physiological cue is "getting hot" and a member from Team B says a cognitive cue is "I'm going to kill him." These are both correct answers. Now a member from Team A must state a cognitive cue, for example, "She better not take another step toward me," and a member from Team B must state a physiological cue, for example, "heart palpitations." Again both teams are correct. Team A continues by stating a physiological cue and Team B offers a cognitive cue. This time Team A incorrectly identifies a physiological cue as "I'm going to smash him," so Team B has a chance to steal a point. Team B does this by stating both a correct cognitive cue, since Team A was wrong, and stating the physiological cue, which is what they were supposed to identify. One point is given for each correctly identified cue.

D. Working as teams again, the students now compete to see who can develop the longer list of both positive and negative consequences for the provoker. The leader will supply a vignette of a provocative situation. The members of the winning team get four points.

E. Have the training staff role-play a provocative event, for example, thinking a peer or adult is lying with regard to something promised to the adolescent. Demonstrate the identification of antecedents, behaviors, and consequences.

F. Ask two students to role-play a provocative event of their choice or one supplied by the leader. Have the "actors" and other members from the group identify antecedents, behaviors, and consequences. One point for participation.

5. Summarize:
    A. The ABC Model (antecedents, behaviors, consequences).
    B. For homework, ask the students to write down two incidents and to identify the associated A's, B's, and C's. Have them do this on two ABC's Worksheets that the leader distributes.
    C. Hand out additional Hassle Logs.
    D. Give out session points and contingent reinforcers.

Session 3

1. Collect and review Hassle Logs and homework assignments.
2. Recap.
3. Introduce *Refuting Aggressive Beliefs.*
    A. Explain that sometimes we have beliefs about why people act in certain ways toward us. These beliefs can lead a person to think another person is acting aggressively or nonaggressively.
    B. Explain that there are both aggressive and nonaggressive ways to interpret situations. For example, an aggressive belief would be, "If someone looks at me differently or acts differently toward me, I should beat him up"; A nonaggressive interpretation might be, "If someone looks at me differently or acts differently toward me, maybe she is having a bad day."
    C. Explain that interpreting situations in a nonaggressive way will help us control our anger.
4. Exercises:
    A. *All the Reasons Why:* Have the students brainstorm and write down the attributions they make about why people do things. For example, tell the students to write down why someone might have passed them in the hall and put his or her foot out, causing them to trip. The students will probably generate a list of aggressive beliefs regarding what happened: "He did it on purpose," "He wants to start something with me," and so on. After the list is generated move onto part B. One point for participation.
    B. Have the students brainstorm and write down alternative, nonaggressive explanations about why the person in the above example might have put his or her foot out. Some examples might be: "It was an accident" or "He was having a bad day." After this is done move onto part C. One point for participation.
    C. Have the students debate whether the nonaggressive interpretations they generated are or are not plausible explanations. One point for participation.
5. Summarize:
    A. The difference between aggressive and nonaggressive beliefs or interpretations of situations.

   B. Hand out additional Hassle Logs.

   C. Give out session points and contingent reinforcers.

Session 4

1. Collect and review Hassle Logs and homework assignments.
2. Recap. In particular, review the process of refuting aggressive beliefs and the differences between aggressive and nonaggressive beliefs. Field any questions.
3. Introduce *assertion techniques* as alternative responses to aggression. Instruct group members to use these assertion techniques in response to provoking stimuli that require action. These responses are designed to deescalate conflict situations while maintaining rights and an appropriate level of self-control.

     i. *Broken record:* This response involves a calm, monotone repetition of what you want, for example, "Please give me my radio back." The student is trained to continue to repeat the response in the same calm manner until the property is returned. There is no escalation in terms of increased voice volume, threatening gestures, or the like.

     ii. *Empathic assertion:* This is a form of assertion that involves sensitive listening on the student's part to the other person's feeling state. This method is particularly useful when dealing with authority figures who are angry. For example, if a staff member complains, "This room is a mess. I can't believe you guys are such slobs! Start cleaning immediately," the student who learns how to use empathic assertion might answer, "I know you're upset with the mess, but we just got back from the rec room and haven't had time to clean up yet." Discuss how the staff member in this situation would have felt better because his or her feelings were heard.

     iii. *Escalating assertion:* This is a sequence of responses that increases in assertiveness in order to obtain a desired outcome. Begin with a minimal assertive response and escalate to final contract option in which a threat to the other person for noncompliance to original demand is presented. For example: (1) "Please return my radio"; (2) "I asked you to return my radio"; (3) "I want my radio *now*"; (4) "If you don't give me my radio *now*, I will go tell the staff and they will come and get my radio for me."

     iv. *Fogging:* This is a technique used to short-circuit an aggressive verbal conflict by confusing the provoker. The individual being provoked should appear to agree with the provoker, but not really agree. For example, the provoker might say, "You are stupid," and the target student might reply, "I know you think I'm stupid." Explain to group members that such an agreement does not indicate truth, but rather a way to turn things into a joke.

4. Exercises:

  A. Model the above assertion techniques with the coleader. Then have the students sit in a circle and make provoking remarks (for example, "You're a liar!") to different students. Ask two students to use the broken record, two to use the empathic assertion, two to use escalating assertion, and two to use fogging. One point for correctly using the assertion technique.

  B. The leader should provoke the students (or have the students provoke each other), but tell them they can use any of the assertion techniques. After they use an assertion technique they must identify which technique they used in order to get one point. Tell the students no technique can be used more than two times. In this way you prevent the students from copying each other and using the same technique.

  C. *Circle of Criticism:* Have students sit in a circle. One by one, they are instructed to turn to the person on their right and make a direct criticism (for example, "Your hair is dirty," or "Where did you find those shoes—in the gutter?"). The person receiving the criticism should respond immediately with a fog (for example, "Thanks so much," or "I know you think so.") Continue until all have given and received criticism several times. The situation need not be relevant to the person on their right. One point for participation.

5. Summarize:

  A. Discuss with students when to use assertive responses rather than withdrawal or aggressive responses. Assertion is optimal when the adolescent is certain of his or her rights in a situation and when there is a high probability of a nonaggressive, successful outcome to the problem situation.

  It is not a good idea to use an assertive response when the individual is unclear about his or her rights (for example, the student is not sure if a radio another person has is his or hers or not). Also, an assertion technique should not be used if there is a good chance that it will lead to further aggression or harm.

  B. Give out more Hassle Logs. Also, ask the students to write down at least two incidents when they use one or more of the assertion techniques.

  C. Give out session points and contingency reinforcers and provide students with positive feedback concerning their cooperation and commitment.

Session 5

1. Collect and review Hassle Logs and homework assignment. Give the students clear feedback on their choice of assertive responses to particular situations.
2. Recap:
    A. Review the four assertion techniques: broken record, empathic assertion, escalating assertion, and fogging.
    B. Field any questions regarding how the students felt about implementing these techniques in the conflict situations they encountered in the past week. Discuss effective and noneffective responses as well as situational outcomes.
3. Introduce *Self-Instruction Training.*
    A. Define *reminders* as things we say to ourselves to guide our behavior or to get us to remember certain things. Ask group members to think of specific things they say to remind themselves to bring certain items to class, and so forth.
    B. Give examples of situations where reminders can be used in pressure situations, such as at the foul line during a very close basketball game.
    C. Describe how students can implement reminders by recognizing they are getting angry and then stopping themselves by pausing, kicking back, looking away for a moment, and then saying to themselves "Stay calm." Thus, the key components are *Stop, Press the Pause Button, Kickback,* and *Remind.*
    D. Describe how reminders can also be helpful in situations in which the adolescent has to try to stay calm. Reminders or internal self-control statements are key ingredients of increased personal power. Thinking before acting gives students control over their anger arousal and helps them determine their choices in response to provocation.
4. Exercises:
    A. Have the group members generate a list of reminders that they use in those pressure-type situations. Write them on the blackboard. Some examples include: Slow down, Take it easy, Take a deep breath, Cool it, Chill out, and Ignore this. One point for participation.
    B. *It's Hot in the Middle:* Have students choose the best reminders and write them on index cards. Then shuffle the cards and have the students sit in a circle with one student in the middle. Have another student(s) provoke him or her and have the student being provoked practice aloud using the reminder on the index card, and any others she or he might generate. One point for participation.
5. Summarize:

A. Use of reminders: Discuss how reminders work best if they are implemented as soon as we recognize ourselves getting angry and not later in the chain of anger-provoking events.

B. Give out more Hassle Logs. Also, ask the students to write down some incidents in which they practiced using reminders.

C. Give out session points and contingency reinforcers.

Session 6

1. Collect and review Hassle Logs and homework assignments.
2. Recap:
   A. Review use of reminders. Review rationale for using reminders: Things we say to ourselves to guide our behavior or to get us to remember certain things. Explain that reminders are a cornerstone of self-control. Review the sequence of effective reminder implementation.
   B. Field any questions that arose after the students tried to implement this technique in the past week.
3. Continue *Self-Instruction Training*.
   A. Application of reminders procedure:
      i. *Overt to covert:* Model the use of overt reminders: role-play a situation in which one student is cursing-out another who is emitting *audible reminders* in order to ignore this behavior. Suggest the use of reminders instead of reacting to the direct provocation.
      ii. Fully describe the *substitution procedure,* whereby a youth has a choice after recognizing the antecedent anger trigger. She or he can either react in an angry or aggressive way, which may lead to receipt of negative consequences, or she or he can emit *covert reminders* to remain calm and uninvolved in the conflict situation. Emphasize the personal power inherent in not responding to anger provocation.
      iii. Demonstrate use of covert reminders, and review rationale for maintaining this level of self-control.
      iv. Emphasize the idea that the timing of reminders is critical. Give examples of someone who uses reminders before any actual provocation (too soon) and after she or he has received a punishment for explosive behavior (too late).
      v. Discuss candidly with the students situations in which they would be unwilling or unlikely to ignore a direct provocation.
4. Exercises:
   A. Have one student stand in the middle of the group. Have another student provoke him or her. Have student in middle use self-gener-

ated reminders to calm himself or herself down. One point for participation.

B. Have two students role-play one of the situations below, while the other students observe the role play and record all the anger control techniques used. These would include any that have been taught thus far (for example, deep breathing and assertion responses). The students should record this on the worksheet entitled All Together Now (see table 6–3). After the role play, the students should discuss what skills they saw the actors use. One point for participation as an actor in a role play or as an active observer.

    i. A student is trying to complete school assignments quickly, so that she does not have to remain after school. While she is busy at her desk, a classmate comes up behind her and begins to tease her about having to stay after, about being dumb, about being the last one finished, and about missing the ball game because of it.

    ii. As a student is returning to his room, he sees somebody sneaking out of it with something under his arm. The student quickly goes into his room and checks to see if anything is missing. He immediately notices his radio is gone. He runs out to find the student and a confrontation takes place.

    iii. The teacher of a class returns to the room after a phone call. She notices the target student is out of her seat. She was actually picking up her pencil which another student threw across the room. But the teacher remarks that she broke the rule and will now lose her school check, which may mean that she will lose her home visit.

5. Summarize:

A. Self-instruction training: Use and timing of reminders.

B. Hand out more Hassle Logs and also, ask the students to write down examples of their use of *reminders*.

C. Hand out another All Together Now worksheet and have the students record the anger control techniques of one of their peers. This assignment would only be possible if the students were in some of the same classes or living in a residential unit together.

D. Give out session points and contingency reinforcers.

Session 7

1. Collect and review Hassle Logs and homework assignments. Have the students give examples of peer observations. This will model the use of direct peer social reinforcement for improved anger control outside the therapy room.

Table 6–3
All Together Now

Behaviors and Skills	Describe a Behavior or Describe How A Skill Was Used
Direct Triggers:	
Indirect Triggers:	
Reaction Cognitive:	
Physiological:	
Consequences Positive (if any):	
Negative:	
Faulty Reminders (Beliefs):	
Deep Breaths:	
Assertion Techniques Broken Record:	
Empathic Assertion:	
Escalating Assertion:	
Fogging:	
Overt Reminders:	
Thinking Ahead Procedure:	
Problem-Solving Strategies:	
Self-Evaluative Statement:	

2. Recap:
   A. Deep breathing
   B. ABC's (antecedents, behaviors, consequences)
   C. Assertion techniques (broken record, fogging, empathic and escalating assertion)
   D. Self-instruction training: reminders (overt to covert)
   E. Field any questions related to implementing self-instructions (reminders) over the past week.
3. Introduce *Thinking Ahead* procedure as another self-control technique to use in conflict or anger-provoking situations.
   A. Define thinking ahead as using problem solving and self-instructions to estimate future negative consequences for a possible current aggressive response to a conflict situation. For example: "If I slap her in the face, I will get a restriction and not be able to go home this weekend."
   B. Explain thinking ahead procedure by stressing the importance of using future negative consequences as a reminder to not get involved in acting-out behaviors, and discuss the relevance of appropriate timing when using the thinking ahead procedure.
   C. Define covert and overt consequences of aggressive behavior. Covert examples: people not liking you, people not trusting you, losing your friends, or being burdened by the reputation of acting out so everyone assumes you were involved in any given conflict. Overt examples: having your privileges removed or being placed in a more restricted environment.
   D. Explain to students that they should *remind* themselves of negative consequences, stop the possible misbehavior, and substitute an alternative behavior such as deep breaths, assertion, or reminders. Again, this process underscores the principle of *thinking before acting*.
4. Exercises:
   A. Have the students break into teams and develop a list of covert and overt, short-term and long-term, internal and external punishing consequences for aggressive behavior (for example, hitting another student, talking back to a staff member). Have them order the list hierarchically from the least punishing consequence to the most punishing consequence. Each member on the team with the longest list is given four points.
   B. Have the students sit in a circle. Have them provoke each other. During the provocation, have them use the thinking ahead procedure by saying aloud the statement "If I (misbehave) now, then I will (future negative consequence)." One point for participation.
   C. Have two students role-play a provoking event from their Hassle Log. During the role play have them identify the course of action they would normally have taken for the audience. Then have them

remind themselves aloud what the negative consequences would be for such an action, have them substitute an alternative behavior (for example, assertion, reminders), and have them identify which alternative behavior they are using. Have the "actors" and the group discuss the positive consequences of the alternative behavior. One point for participation.

5. Summarize:

A. Thinking Ahead procedure: Have students identify negative consequences that might occur in the future that they can use to control their present behavior. Also, discuss the future positive consequences for achieving better anger control (for example, more privileges).

B. Hand out more Hassle Logs. Also, ask the students to implement the thinking ahead procedure and write about its effectiveness.

C. Give out session points and contingency reinforcers.

Session 8

1. Collect and review Hassle Logs and homework assignments.

2. Recap:

A. Review thinking ahead procedure.

B. Field any questions regarding difficulties encountered implementing this procedure.

C. Prompt students to name and describe the anger control techniques taught so far: deep breaths, assertion, reminders, and thinking ahead.

3. Introduce *Self-Evaluation* process:

A. Define self-evaluation as a method of providing oneself with feedback on how a conflict situation was handled. Basically, these self-evaluation responses are reminders that occur *after* a conflict situation to provide the individual with immediate feedback on behavior and feelings during a conflict. Thus, these are *after reminders*. Discuss how positive and negative after reminders might affect the behavior that preceded it (basically, this is a lesson in the power of self-reinforcement).

B. Using an example from a student's Hassle Log, help the students to focus on a "coping statement" used by the student before, during, and after conflict situations. A coping statement is a statement made to oneself when self-control fails (for example, "I'll be able to control my temper better next time").

   i. Focus on whether the self-evaluative statement is reinforcing or punishing, regardless of whether the conflict situation was resolved or not.

    ii. Define self-evaluation as another reminder that can guide personal behavior.

   iii. Provide examples of positive and negative self-evaluation statements. Leaders can provide examples of their own internal self-statements that serve either to reinforce or to punish behavior. An example of a positive statement: "I'm learning these skills and getting better every time. I'm proud of myself." An example of a negative statement: "I'm never going to get this exactly right. I might as well give up."

   iv. Model positive/reinforcing self-evaluation statements.

    v. Give sequential examples of coping statements used before, during, and after provocation. For example:

Before: "I can remain calm."

During: "Good for me, I'm staying calm."

After: "I knew I could stay calm and I deserve something special as a reward."

4. Exercises:
  A. Have students develop a list of:
    i. Positive feedback statements for use during and after a conflict. For example: "I handled myself really well" or "I'm getting better at this all of the time."
    ii. Have the students develop a list of coping statements to be used when self-control fails. For example: "I'll be better at this next time" or "At least I didn't lose it completely."
  B. Have students role-play. Possible role plays are given below, or incidents can be taken from the students' Hassle Logs. Have the other students fill in the All Together Now worksheet and discuss what skills the actors use. One point for participation as an actor in a role play and one point for participation as an active observer.
    i. It's a nice Saturday afternoon. You want to go outside and do something. You've finished all your chores and you have free time. You see a group of girls standing around in the parking lot. As you approach them, they start to tease you and call you names. "Look who's coming over here," "Dumbo," "Get a load of how she's dressed," and worse. You decide to turn around and walk away, but one of the girls starts to follow you, saying "What are you afraid of?" and still calls you names.
    ii. You loaned your radio to another student in your class during lunch. Now, you have finished all of your assignments and have earned free time. You would like to have your radio back, but you see that the other person is still listening to it. You ask to have it back and the other student says "No."

       iii. You and another student are supposed to sweep and mop the floor of the laundry room. You both begin to do it, when the other student puts his broom down and says, "(Name), you better finish this whole thing because I'm too tired." You say that it is his job too and he replies, "Shut up and do it or there will be big trouble for you." After the role play have the students give positive accurate feedback about the student's performance and demonstration of self-control. One point for participation.

  C. *Face to Face:* Have a student stand in the middle of the circle while others provoke him or her. After the student handles the situation in a way that demonstrated self-control, have him or her explain what strategies he or she used to control his or her anger. Also, have him or her generate a positive self-evaluative statement about his or her anger control performance. Then ask the group to give him or her positive feedback. One point for participation as an actor or active observer.

5. Summarize:
  A. Review the use of self-evaluative statements as reminders that come after you have done something. These statements can affect the way the student feels about himself or herself and the way in which he or she behaves in a situation like that again.
  B. Hand out Hassle Logs and also ask the students to note some self-evaluative statements they use during conflict situations in the coming week (these can be positive feedback statements or coping statements).
  C. Give out session points and contingency reinforcers.
  D. Provide feedback to group participants about their continued cooperation and enthusiasm during group meetings and on any behavior changes that have been noted.

Session 9

1. Collect and review Hassle Logs and homework assignments.
2. Recap:
  A. Review self-evaluative statements: They are reminders used after a conflict situation to provide the individual with immediate feedback on behavior and feelings during a conflict. Self-evaluative statements are another reminder that serves to guide personal behavior.
  B. Field any questions related to difficulties using self-evaluative statements in the past week.
3. Introduce *Problem-Solving Training:* Making choices between anger control alternatives. Emphasize that the following questions cannot be generated unless the student is able to *recognize* that she or he is angry,

stop, pause, and *think.* Present the following sequence to students on a blackboard and review each step, giving examples from the Hassle Logs they have presented in this session.

A. Problem definition: *"What Is the Problem?"* Identify the antecedent stimuli, including provoking stimulus, situational variables, and internal anger cues. Combine all of these components into a clear problem statement. Example: An innocent student is accused of stealing money from another student. The problem definition is that the innocent student is getting angry (heart palpitations, burning cheeks), because she or he has been accused unfairly of stealing.

B. Generation of alternative solutions: *"What Can I Do?"* This phase requires individuals to brainstorm all of the possible responses to the problem situation. The process of brainstorming precludes the evaluation or critique of any responses generated until a later time.

C. Consequent evaluation: *"What Will Happen If . . . ?"* Using methods similar to those incorporated in the thinking ahead procedure, identify positive and negative consequences for each response. These consequences should be overt and covert, and long and short term.

D. Choosing a problem solution: *"What Will I Do?"* This phase involves rank ordering all solutions generated according to the desirability/undesirability or severity of the consequences enumerated above. The solution that optimizes positive consequences, minimizes negative consequences, and solves the presenting problem is the one to implement first.

E. Feedback: *"How Did It Work?"* The final step in this problem-solving procedure involves the evaluation of the solution based on its effectiveness in solving the problem. Use of self-evaluation reminders should be prompted at this stage also. If a chosen solution is not effective, then a second-choice solution should be implemented.

4. Exercises:

A. *When There's a Will, There's a Way:* Have the students generate solutions to a problem in which there are few or no solutions. The vignette should not have an interpersonal component. For example: What should Susan do if she is stranded on a highway alone, 20 miles from civilization, and she has no radio? Through this exercise the students will be able to differentiate between problems that really have few solutions and those where there are alternatives. One point for participation.

B. Use a number of examples from students' Hassle Logs. Have the students:
   i. In a group identify the problem.
   ii. Break into teams and generate alternative solutions.

      iii. Come back to the group and discuss positive and negative consequences of all the possible solutions generated by both groups.

      iv. Choose a problem solution by majority vote.

      v. Help the students determine its effectiveness.

5. Summarize:
   A. Review the problem-solving sequence:
      i. What is the problem?
      ii. What can I do?
      iii. What will happen if . . . ?
      iv. What will I do?
      v. How did it work?
   B. Give out more Hassle Logs and ask the students to also write down incidents in which they used this sequence in order to solve a problem.
   C. Give out session points and contingency reinforcers.

Session 10

1. Collect and review Hassle Logs and homework assignments.
2. *Program Review:* Before class write the name of each skill taught in the program on a separate index card. When class begins asks each student to select one index card at random. Give the students a few minutes to think about (1) how to describe/define the strategy; (2) how to demonstrate the strategy; and (3) when is the best time/situation to implement the strategy. The students, using the outline above, will discuss the skill they chose with the group.
   The skills taught include:
   A. *Deep breaths.* Remind students about their physiological cues and how the deep breath technique can be used to reduce tension and stress, redirect their attention away from external provoking stimuli to internal control, and provide a time delay before making a choice how to respond.
   B. Concept of *ABC's*
      i. *Antecedents* are provoking stimuli. Overt antecedents are situational variables in one's environment that provoke anger. Covert antecedents are physiological states, such as fatigue.
      ii. *Triggers* are provoking stimuli. Direct triggers are direct aversive provocations by another person. These may occur in verbal or nonverbal form. Indirect triggers are the adolescent's misinterpretation or misattribution of events, the result of a faulty appraisal system. Indirect triggers may also include observed injustice or unfairness.

     iii. *Faulty Reminders* or beliefs need to be replaced with statements directing the student to let go of personalized anger and look at other ways to view the situation less aggressively.

     iv. *Behavior* is the individual's actual reaction to the provoking stimuli, which can involve a variety of cognitive, physiological, covert, and/or overt responses.

     v. *Consequences* are events that happen as a result of controlling or not controlling anger. Consequences can either be rewarding or punishing.

  C. *Assertion techniques* include broken record, empathic assertion, escalating assertion, and fogging.

  D. *Reminders* are things we say to ourselves (overt and covert) to guide our behavior or to help us to remember certain things.

  E. The *Thinking ahead* procedure is another type of reminder that utilizes problem solving and self-instruction to estimate future negative consequences for current misbehavior to a conflict situation.

  F. *Self-evaluation statements* are reminders that are used after a conflict situation to provide immediate feedback on behavior and feelings during a conflict.

  G. *Problem solving:*

What is the problem?

What can I do?

What will happen if . . . ?

What will I do?

How did it work?

3. Discuss situational and personal elements that would help the student determine which strategy to use.

  A. Introduce *Barbs:* A "barb" is a provocation statement made directly to the target adolescent in situations other than the actual training one. The adolescent is issued a warning first: "I'm going to barb you" Then the barb is delivered. (Example: "Why are you watching TV when you are on restriction?") The person delivering the barb notes the adolescent's response and gives both positive and constructive feedback. Gradually the barbs should more closely approximate realistic inquiries made by staff members. The students should be told that the barbs will be provided by a variety of staff members, in a variety of stimulus situations, and on an intermittent schedule. Eventually barbs can be given without warning.

  B. The leader should barb the students at this point so they get used to the procedure. Since this is phase 1 the barbs should all start with a warning.

4. Ask students to describe in detail several conflict situations that have occurred. Ask them to describe the various anger control techniques

they used during the provocations. Another option is to have the students role-play several scenes using the anger control skills they have learned. Pass a hat filled with pieces of paper that identify a certain anger control technique. Whatever technique is selected, the student has to try to use that skill in his or her role play. Other students observing have to guess which technique(s) are being implemented.

5. In closing:
   A. Provide students with feedback on:
      i. His or her cooperation during the program.
      ii. His or her performance during exercises and role plays.
      iii. His or her enthusiasm and/or interest in various components of the program.
      iv. His or her motivation for change; being on time, completing homework assignments and Hassle Logs, and so on.
      v. Observable changes in behavior, including any anecdotal observations from other persons involved with the student.
   B. Let the student know what you have learned by participating in the group and tell the student that you enjoyed working with him or her.
   C. Ask each group member to review his or her participation. Have each of them give self-evaluative praise statements regarding their participation and improvement in anger control. Prompt students to reinforce observed changes in each other.
   D. Institute the end-of-program lottery. The three students who have accumulated the highest session points are allowed to participate. Those student's names are placed in a hat and one student's name is chosen. That student wins a gift certificate to a record store.
   E. Remind them before they leave that the responsibility for appropriate behavior and consequences (positive or negative) lies with the individual student and that she or he makes her or his own choices.
   F. Make appropriate referrals for any students still exhibiting difficulty controlling their anger.

Optional Booster Session

This session may be given approximately one month after termination of the formal anger control program. The program will be reviewed during this session.

1. Emphasize that these techniques work only when the student is able to *recognize* an anger reaction, *stop, pause,* and *think before acting.*
   A. Deep breaths
   B. ABC's

     i. Antecedents
    ii. Triggers
  iii. Faulty beliefs
  iv. Behaviors
    v. Consequences
  C. Assertion techniques
     i. Broken record
    ii. Empathic assertion
  iii. Escalating assertion
  iv. Fogging
  D. Reminders
  E. Thinking ahead
  F. Self-evaluation
  G. Problem solving
2. Remind the students that the responsibility for appropriate behavior is theirs. They make their own choices. Thank them for coming.

Future Considerations for Anger Control Intervention

Research has demonstrated sufficiently that anger control training results in specific behavioral changes in children and adolescents. However, explicit efforts to enhance generalization certainly should be included in the planning and implementation of any anger control training intervention such that change extends to other environments and across time (Feindler, 1990). Some authors have indicated that anger control programs may only be useful in demonstrating short-term reductions in aggressiveness and disruptiveness (Lochman & Lampron, 1988), and therefore may be considered only as an adjunct to more traditional therapeutic approaches.

Lochman and Lampron (1988) suggest that cognitive-behavioral interventions for aggressive behavior disorders are most effective when more operant behavior procedures, including reinforcement for goal attainment, are used to augment the training and to ensure maintenance of change. Clearly, the interdependence between the various cognitive skills training strategies and contingency management approaches needs further investigation.

Kazdin's (1987) review of interventions for conduct disordered youth emphasizes a need for alternative models of treatment, such as the high-strength intervention model of the broad-based intervention model. This might necessitate an increase in the amount and duration of the anger control treatment as well as the incorporation of other treatment models. In fact, anger control interventions may take several forms.

It would seem that there are five basic components of anger control training: (1) arousal reduction, (2) cognitive change, (3) behavioral skills development, (4) moral reasoning development, and (5) appropriate anger expression; and at least six modalities in which treatment could be provided: (1) individual therapy, (2) group skills training, (3) family anger control, (4) dyadic anger control training, (5) parent-only anger control, and (6) classroom anger control training/affective education. A careful determination of which therapeutic components and which modalities would be most effective for these adolescents must be made following a comprehensive clinical assessment and an optimal client–treatment modality match.

Finally, a review of maintenance and generalization of change resulting from anger management interventions has indicated that changes in verbal behavior assessed via self-report and changes in cognitions (in particular, during hypothetical conflict negotiations) can be obtained (Feindler, 1990). However, there is still an important note of caution to be heeded. Few, if any, of the published anger control studies have produced change in actual rates and intensities of aggressive behavior as directly observed or as recorded in a reliable and continuous baseline fashion and most studies are too brief to adequately assess maintenance. Although we agree that some change, and certainly internal change, is noteworthy, these procedures can really only be considered effective if we can impact rates of family violence, self-destructive behavior, property damage, interpersonal aggression, and any other by-product or end product of anger arousal. Certainly, longer interventions and treatments that are interwoven into family, school, and community systems are needed in order to prevent the continued escalation of youth anger and aggression.

References

Berkowitz, L. (1989). Frustration-aggression hypothesis: Examination and reformation. *Psychological Bulletin, 106*(1), 59–73.

Dodge, K. A. (1985). Attributional bias in aggressive children. In P. C. Kendall (Ed.), *Advances in cognitive-behavioral research and therapy* (Vol. 4). Orlando, FL: Academic Press.

Feindler, E. L. (1987). Clinical issues and recommendations in adolescent anger control training. *Journal of Child and Adolescent Psychotherapy 4*(4), 267–274.

Feindler, E. L. (1990). Adolescent anger control: Review and critique. In M. Heisen, R. M. Eisler, & P. M. Miller (Eds.), *Progress in Behavior Modification* (Vol. 26). Newbury Park, CA: Sage.

Feindler, E. L. (1991). Cognitive strategies in anger control interventions. In P. C. Kendall (Ed.), *Child and adolescent behavior therapy: Cognitive-behavioral procedures*. New York: Guilford Press.

Feindler, E. L., & Ecton, R. B. (1986). *Adolescent anger control: Cognitive-behavioral techniques*. Elmsford, NY: Pergamon Press.

Feindler, E. L., Ecton, R. B., Kingsley, D., & Dubey, D. (1986). Group anger control training for institutionalized psychiatric male adolescents. *Behavior Therapy, 17,* 109–123.

Feindler, E. L., Marriott, S. A., & Iwata, M. (1984). Group anger control training for junior high school delinquents. *Cognitive Therapy and Research, 8*(3), 299–311.

Finch, A. J., & Nelson, W. M. (1978). *The Children's Inventory of Anger: A self-report measure.* Unpublished manuscript available from the author at the Medical University of South Carolina, Charleston, SC.

Hoshmand, L. T., & Austin, G. W. (1987). Validation studies of a multifactor cognitive-behavioral anger control inventory. *Journal of Personality Assessment, 51,* 417–432.

Huesmann, L. R., Eron, L. D., Lefkowitz, M., & Walder, L. (1984). Stability of aggression over time and generations. *Developmental Psychology, 20,* 1120–1134.

Kazdin, A. E. (1987). Treatment of antisocial behavior in children: Current status and future directions. *Psychological Bulletin, 102*(2), 187–203.

Lee, D. Y., Hallberg, E. T., Slemon, A. G., & Haase, R. F. (1985). An assertiveness scale for adolescents. *Journal of Clinical Psychology, 41*(5), 51–57.

Lochman, J. E., & Lampron, L. B. (1988). Cognitive-behavioral interventions for aggressive boys: 7-month follow-up effects. *Journal of Child and Adolescent Psychotherapy, 2,* 21–25.

Meichenbaum, D. (1975). A self-instructional approach to stress management: A proposal for stress inoculation training. In C. Speilberger & I. Sarason (Eds.), *Stress and anxiety* (Vol. 2). New York: Wiley & Sons.

Novaco, R. W. (1975). *Anger control: The development and evaluation of an experimental treatment.* Lexington, MA: Lexington Books.

Olweus, D. (1984). Development of stable aggressive reaction: Patterns in males. In R. J. Blanchard & D. C. Blanchard (Eds.), *Advances in the study of aggression* (Vol. 1, pp. 103–137). New York: Academic Press.

Slaby, R. G., & Guerra, N. G. (1988). Cognitive mediators of aggression in adolescent offenders, part 1: Assessment. *Developmental Psychology, 24*(4), 580–588.

Spielberger, C. D. (1988). *State-Trait Anger Expression Inventory Professional Manual.* Odessa, FL: Psychological Assessment Resources.

7
Adolescent Relapse Prevention

Mindy Hohman
Gary Buchik

Introduction

Those who work in the field of adolescent chemical dependency know that our patients bring to us an assortment of problems alongside their addictions. A follow-up study of chemical dependency treatment by Hoffman and Kaplan (1991) found that in a sample of 826 adolescents 66 percent used one or more drugs during the week prior to admission, with the drugs used being (in descending frequency) marijuana, cocaine, alcohol, and stimulants. The adolescents also presented with problems involving abuse, depression, suicide ideation and attempts, poor self-image, and learning problems. In view of these statistics and problems, it should come as no surprise that this same study revealed that 60 percent of the adolescents sampled either relapsed or did not remain abstinent during the year following treatment. Adolescent relapse following addiction treatment continues to be a difficult issue to address.

This manual was born from our clinical experience with chemically dependent teens and is based upon the relapse prevention models of Marlatt (1985, 1990), Annis (1986, 1988), and others. These researchers studied relapse in adult sample populations, and they developed coping skills training as a method of reducing such relapse. A study by Chaney, O'Leary, and Marlatt (1978) found that skills training reduced both the severity and duration of relapse. Moreover, Annis and Davis (1988) found that coping skills training helped to reduce the number of drinking episodes and also helped to increase adjustment in other problem areas.

The purpose of this chapter is to outline a coping skills training program designed specifically for adolescents. This model is appropriate for use in any kind of chemical dependency treatment, but it was designed to be a relapse prevention model for use in aftercare programs or in outpatient treatment. This program can be adopted in its entirety or used in segments, depending on the needs of the treatment provider. We believe that clinicians who use this model will be able to customize it to serve particular individual client or group needs.

The Cognitive-Behavioral Model of Relapse Prevention

Marlatt (1985, p. 128) writes that three cognitive factors are "interactive determinants" of relapse in abstinent alcoholics: self-efficacy, outcome expectancies, and attributions of causality. *Self-efficacy* is one's belief that one can carry out a specific task (or not engage in certain behaviors such as drinking). *Outcome expectancies* are the beliefs one has regarding the outcome of certain behaviors or actions. ("If I don't drink, I will feel better"). Another important aspect of outcome expectancies is defined by Marlatt as the alcoholic's perception of the effect of alcohol and/or other drugs. *Attributions of causality* define how one explains behavior, for example, the alcoholic may view a relapse in terms of his or her belief that "I am a weak person."

The first and most important ingredient in behavioral change is the individual's motivation to change. While Marlatt indicates that the alcoholic must make a commitment to reaching a desired goal (usually, complete abstinence), the ability to achieve this goal is contingent on possessing the coping skills for dealing with high-risk situations as well as the self-efficacy that the person can employ to use these skills effectively. Abstinence maintenance requires much more than willpower.

Marlatt writes that abstinent alcoholics maintain a relatively stable sense of self-efficacy that they can remain abstinent, stable, that is, until they run into a high-risk situation. He (1985, p. 37) defines a high-risk situation as "any situation that poses a threat to the individual's sense of control and increases the risk of potential relapse." Cummings, Gordon, & Marlatt's (1980) study of 311 initial relapse episodes from patients with a variety of addictive disorders found three categories of high-risk situations: negative emotional states, interpersonal conflicts, and social pressures. A similar study of an adolescent sample conducted by St. Mary and Russo (1989) found these risk categories: grief/loss, social/recreational, and emotional/intrapersonal.

If the alcoholic can cope effectively with the high-risk situation, she or he will experience an increased sense of self-efficacy based on performance accomplishments, and will be more likely to continue maintaining abstinence. If, however, the alcoholic finds that she or he has no coping skills available, decreased self-efficacy and failure to maintain abstinence may well result. As the person feels a loss of power or perceived control, positive attributions regarding the effect of the abused substance can occur. ("I may as well drink—at least I felt better drunk than sober").

Once the alcoholic has taken that first drink (or drug), Marlatt (1985) writes that she or he experiences the "abstinence violation effect." The recovering person develops a belief system in which any alcohol or drug use if "taboo" because such use will lead to a complete return to drinking or drug using. This belief may be supported by other people, such as the recovering person's therapists and her or his peers in recovery. The intensity of the abstinence violation effect depends on two cognitive-affective factors: cognitive dissonance and personal attribution effect (Marlatt, 1985). Cognitive dissonance is the experience of guilt and conflict, stemming from behavior that does not match one's self-image. Personal attribution occurs when one holds oneself totally responsible for a problem and an inability to cope with it. The greater these effects, the more likely it is that the alcoholic will proceed into full-blown relapse.

Marlatt (1985) proposes many interventions in his Relapse Prevention model. They focus on the three areas where he sees the alcoholic being most at risk: lack of coping skills leading to decreased self-efficacy, positive outcome expectancies of alcohol use, and attributions of causality regarding relapse when it does occur.

Adolescent Relapse Prevention

After studying relapse among adolescent alcoholics, Brown, Vik, and Creamer (1989) concluded that, to date, little is known about this problem because prior research has tended to focus on prevention issues or prediction of heavy drinking.

Brown, Stetson, and Beatty (1989) studied abstinence coping skills in three groups of teens: those who were alcohol abusers and in alcoholic treatment, those who were not abusers themselves but who came from alcoholic families, and those who were not abusers who came from nonalcoholic families. They found that alcohol and drug abusing teens tended to use more external cognitions, such as worrying about parents or other authority figures. Nonabusing teens were more likely to adopt behavioral responses, such as engaging in alternative activities. Brown, Stetson, and Beatty (1989, p. 51) write, [of] "further potential significance to clinicians is the finding that no single strategy was employed in a majority of situations. Therefore, a broad coping repertoire with multiple strategies may be most useful in making responsible decisions regarding alcohol consumption."

In another study Brown, Vik, & Creamer (1989) followed 75 adolescents who had completed alcoholism treatment. They conducted interviews at three and six months posttreatment. They found abstinence rates similar to those of adult alcoholics as well as similar characteristics of the relapse episodes. Adolescents, however, differed significantly from adult relapsers in that a majority of the former's relapses occurred because of direct social pressure to drink. Risk tended to vary with the context as well, in that the adolescents were more likely to drink with older, pretreatment friends. Brown, Stetson, and Beatty (1989 p. 229) conclude that "further research is needed to clarify which coping skills are most effective in high-risk situations and determine whether coping skill training efforts influence adolescent treatment outcome."

Coping Skills Training for Relapse Prevention

As we indicated above, this training outline is meant to be used as a guideline. Clinicians will need to develop session outlines that fit the needs of their individual clients. In our treatment plan we help our clients to develop their own individualized lists of high-risk situations and then to develop specific coping skills to deal with those situations. Our outline provides information regarding common high-risk situations for dependent adolescents, but it is not intended to be an exhaustive list. The situations and coping skills described are drug-specific. Clinicians may choose to add other general skills training, such as assertiveness training, problem-solving methods, dealing with grief, and communication skills training, to help their clients.

Many of the adolescent clients who attend the kind of group therapy outlined here may be expecting a more process-oriented mode of therapy, one similar to groups most treatment programs provide. Therefore, all clients need to be advised at the outset about the goals, objectives, and structure of the group. Members will be working on learning new skills more than on expressing feelings. Expression of feelings at certain times in the group is appropriate; however, if clinicians find that group members keep trying to make this a process-oriented experience, they may then want to offer such a group separately or refer the client(s) to concurrent individual therapy.

Who is appropriate for this group therapy? Any adolescent who has made a commitment to abstinence is a candidate for this group. Participants can include those who have completed treatment for chemical dependency or adolescents who have quit using drugs or alcohol on their own and wish further help. These sessions can be adapted for adolescents who are currently in inpatient treatment and are preparing for discharge.

What should occur in the pre-screening interview? Prior to entering the group, potential clients should be interviewed. The therapist should investigate the client's background information and motivation for maintaining abstinence. This is also the time to explain the format for the group, stressing the participation required for behavioral rehearsal. At this time the therapist administers two scales: the Adolescent Self-Efficacy Scale (St. Mary & Russo, 1989) and the Adolescent Alcohol Expectancy Questionnaire (Brown, Christiansen, & Goldman, 1987).

The Adolescent Self-Efficacy Scale (see Scale 7–1) was developed to

Scale 7–1
Self-efficacy Scale for Chemically Dependent Adolescents

Below each stressful situation is a series of numbers, 1 through 10. This is your ranking scale, you are to read each situation carefully and then *rank each one according to your belief in your ability to deal with each situation without using drugs.* A rank of 5 or below would indicate that you are unlikely to use drugs to help you cope. A rank of 6 or above would indicate that you are probably going to use drugs in that situation.

1	2	3	4	5	6	7	8	9	10

use drugs
0% of the
time to cope

use drugs
30% of the
time to cope

use drugs
100% of the
time to cope

Assess

1. When I can't handle anything anymore.

   1 2 3 4 5 6 7 8 9 10

2. When I'm bummed out.

   1 2 3 4 5 6 7 8 9 10

3. To feel good.

   1 2 3 4 5 6 7 8 9 10

4. When I lose someone really close.

   1 2 3 4 5 6 7 8 9 10

5. To help cope with things.

   1 2 3 4 5 6 7 8 9 10

6. When I'm frustrated.

   1 2 3 4 5 6 7 8 9 10

7. When I feel like no one cares about me.

   1 2 3 4 5 6 7 8 9 10

8. When I feel like I don't count anymore.

   1 2 3 4 5 6 7 8 9 10

9. When I'm sick of everything.

   1 2 3 4 5 6 7 8 9 10

10. To hide from my feelings.

    1 2 3 4 5 6 7 8 9 10

11. To have a good time.

    1 2 3 4 5 6 7 8 9 10

12. When someone I'm close to dies.

    1 2 3 4 5 6 7 8 9 10

13. To forget about my problems.

    1 2 3 4 5 6 7 8 9 10

14. When I lose a boyfriend/girlfriend.

    1 2 3 4 5 6 7 8 9 10

15. After an argument with my parents.

    1 2 3 4 5 6 7 8 9 10

16. When I'm at a concert.

    1 2 3 4 5 6 7 8 9 10

17. To celebrate.

    1 2 3 4 5 6 7 8 9 10

18. When I'm sad.

    1 2 3 4 5 6 7 8 9 10

19. When I feel guilty.

    1 2 3 4 5 6 7 8 9 10

20. When I don't feel good about myself.

    1 2 3 4 5 6 7 8 9 10

Source: St. Mary and Russo (1989).

measure the amount of confidence that an adolescent feels in terms of his or her ability to resist using drugs or drinking in a given situation. This scale was tested in a hospital setting with chemically dependent adolescents. A factor analysis showed that the test measures confidence in three areas: intrapersonal/emotional, social/recreational, and grief/loss. A split-half test for reliability produced a correlation coefficient of .8912, indicating that the test has high reliability.

The Adolescent Alcohol Expectancy Questionnaire (see Scale 7–2) is a 10-item scale designed to measure expectations of general and specific ef-

Scale 7–2
Alcohol Expectancy Questionnaire—Adolescent (Revised)

Please read the following statements about the effects of alcohol. If you think the statement is true or mostly true, then mark "true". If you think that the statement if false, or mostly false, or rarely happens to most people, then mark "false". When the statements refer to "drinking alcohol", you may think in terms of any alcoholic beverage such as beer, wine, whiskey, liquor, rum, scotch, vodka, gin, or various alcoholic mixed drinks. *Whether or not you have had actual drinking experience yourself, you are to answer in terms of how you think alcohol affects the typical or average drinker.* It is important that you respond to every statement. There are no right or wrong answers to the following statements.

	True (1)	False (0)
1. Drinking alcohol makes a person feel good and happy.	____	____
2. Alcohol makes sexual experiences easier and more enjoyable.	____	____
3. Drinking alcohol can get rid of physical pain.	____	____
4. People are apt (likely) to break and destroy things when they are drinking alcohol.	____	____
5. People become harder to get along with after they have a few drinks of alcohol.	____	____
6. Drinking alcohol creates problems.	____	____
7. People feel sexier after a few alcoholic drinks.	____	____
8. It is easier to open up and talk about one's feelings after a few drinks of alcohol.	____	____
9. A person can talk with people of the opposite sex better after a few drinks of alcohol.	____	____
10. Drinking alcohol makes a bad impression on others.	____	____
11. People drive better after a few drinks of alcohol.	____	____
12. Drinking alcohol can keep a person's mind off his/her problems at home.	____	____
13. Teenagers drink alcohol in order to get attention.	____	____
14. It is hard to reason with a person who has been drinking alcohol.	____	____
15. Parties are *not* much fun if people are drinking alcohol.	____	____
16. People are more creative and imaginative (can make-believe better) when they drink alcohol.	____	____
17. People feel more caring and giving after a few drinks of alcohol.	____	____
18. Drinking alcohol makes it easier to be with others and, in general, makes the world seem like a nicer place.	____	____
19. It is easier to play sports after a few drinks of alcohol.	____	____

	True (1)	False (0)

20. Drinking alcohol makes the future seem brighter.
21. A person can do things better after a few drinks of alcohol.
22. Drinking alcohol makes people more friendly.
23. A person may have a few drinks of alcohol in order to be part of the group.
24. When drinking alcohol, people are more apt (likely) to insult and make fun of others.
25. People are more sure of themselves when they are drinking alcohol.
26. When drinking alcohol, people do not feel in control of their behavior; they are apt (likely) to do something that they do not want to do.
27. Drinking alcohol makes people feel more interesting.
28. Drinking alcohol is O.K. because it allows people to join in with others who are having fun.
29. Drinking alcohol makes a person happier with himself/herself.
30. When talking with people, words come to mind easier after a few drinks of alcohol.
31. People feel powerful when they drink alcohol, as if they can get others to do what they want.
32. Drinking alcohol makes people worry less.
33. People drink alcohol because it gives them a neat, thrilling, high feeling.
34. Drinking alcohol makes people feel more alert.
35. Alcohol increases arousal; it makes people feel stronger and more powerful and makes it easier to fight.
36. Sweet alcoholic drinks taste good.
37. A few alcoholic drinks make people less shy.
38. Drinking alcohol makes men more aggressive or pushy.
39. After a few alcoholic drinks, people are less aware of what is going on around them.
40. Most alcoholic drinks taste good.
41. Most people think better after a few drinks of alcohol.
42. Alcohol helps people stand up to others.
43. People do not worry as much about what other people think of them after a few drinks of alcohol.
44. When drinking alcohol, people are more apt (likely) to be taken advantage of by others.
45. People do not drive as well after a few drinks of alcohol.
46. People understand things better when they are drinking alcohol.

	True (1)	False (0)
47. Drinking alcohol gets rid of aches and pains.		
48. People are apt (likely) to become careless after a few drinks of alcohol.		
49. A person enjoys people of the opposite sex more after she/he has been drinking alcohol.		
50. Drinking alcohol makes a person feel less up-tight.		
51. People act like better friends after a few drinks of alcohol.		
52. Alcohol makes people feel more romantic.		
53. Drinking alcohol makes a person more pleased with himself/herself.		
54. Drinking alcohol loosens people up.		
55. Drinking alcohol causes hangovers.		
56. Most alcohol tastes terrible.		
57. People do stupid, strange, or silly things when they drink alcohol.		
58. Alcohol makes people more relaxed and less tense.		
59. People laugh a lot and do silly or crazy things when they have been drinking.		
60. Having a few drinks of alcohol is a nice way to enjoy holidays.		
61. When drinking alcohol, people are more apt (likely) to take advantage of others.		
62. It's fun to watch others act silly when they are drinking alcohol.		
63. People drink when they have problems.		
64. Drinking alcohol makes a person feel healthier.		
65. People feel less alone when they drink alcohol.		
66. People feel dizzy and are apt to fall down when they drink alcohol.		
67. Drinking alcohol makes a person feel close to people.		
68. Teenagers drink alcohol because they feel forced to do so by their peers.		
69. Alcohol changes people's personalities.		
70. People often have trouble remembering what they did while they were drinking alcohol.		
71. A few drinks of alcohol makes it easier to talk with people.		
72. People can control their anger better when they are drinking alcohol.		
73. People have stronger feelings when they are drinking alcohol.		
74. Alcoholic beverages makes parties more fun.		
75. Drinking alcohol does not get rid of problems, it just pushes them aside.		
76. Alcohol makes people better lovers.		

	True (1)	False (0)
77. People don't feel so alone when they drink alcohol.	_____	_____
78. After drinking alcohol, a person may lose control and run into things.	_____	_____
79. Drinking alcohol gets rid of a person's feelings that he/she is not as good as other people.	_____	_____
80. Drinking alcohol relaxes people.	_____	_____
81. Drinking alcohol allows people to be in any mood they want to be.	_____	_____
82. People become loud and noisy when they drink alcohol.	_____	_____
83. Drinking alcohol can keep a person's mind off his/her mistakes at school.	_____	_____
84. It is easier to speak in front of a group of people after a few drinks of alcohol.	_____	_____
85. People get in better moods after a few drinks of alcohol.	_____	_____
86. Drinking alcohol helps teenagers to do their homework.	_____	_____
87. Drinking alcohol leads students *not* to do their homework.	_____	_____
88. Alcohol seems like magic.	_____	_____
89. People don't worry about the things they are in charge of when they are drinking alcohol.	_____	_____
90. People become more interested in people of the opposite sex after a few drinks of alcohol.	_____	_____
91. Alcohol makes it easier to stand up for what one thinks is right.	_____	_____
92. People have more courage after drinking alcohol.	_____	_____
93. People become less afraid after drinking alcohol.	_____	_____
94. Feelings become more intense after drinking alcohol.	_____	_____
95. People fight after drinking alcohol.	_____	_____
96. After drinking alcohol, people can argue a point more forcefully.	_____	_____
97. Drinking alcohol brings out the humorous or sarcastic side of people.	_____	_____
98. People become more outspoken or opinionated when they drink alcohol.	_____	_____
99. Women become more aggressive when they drink alcohol.	_____	_____
100. People become more aroused or excited when they drink alcohol.	_____	_____

Adolescent AEQ 100-item Revised Scoring System

Scale 1: Global Positive Change	1, 3, 16, 18, 20, 25, 27, 29, 47, 53, 64, 65, 77, 81, 88	At least 14 items must be complete
Scale 2: Changes in Social Behavior	5*, 6*, 10*, 13*, 15*, 17, 22, 28, 36, 40, 51, 56*, 60, 62, 68*, 74, 85	At least 15 items must be complete
Scale 3: Improved Cognitive and Motor Abilities	11, 19, 21, 30, 34, 41, 46, 72, 76, 86	At least 9 items must be complete
Scale 4: Sexual Enhancement	2, 7, 9, 49, 52, 67, 90	At least 6 items must be complete
Scale 5: Cognitive and Motor Impairment	4, 14, 23, 24, 26, 31, 38, 39, 44, 45, 48, 55, 57, 59, 61, 63, 66, 69, 70, 75, 78, 82, 87, 89	At least 22 items must be complete
Scale 6: Increased Arousal	35, 42, 73, 84, 91, 92, 94, 98	At least 7 items must be complete
Scale 7: Relaxation and Tension Reducation	8, 12, 32, 33, 37, 43, 50, 54, 58, 71, 79, 80, 83	At least 12 items must be complete

AEQ Total: Total of scales 1, 2, 3, 4, 6, 7 minus scale 5.

Items followed by * are to be scored negatively (i.e., an answer of "false" is scored as +1 and an answer of "true" is scored 0.)

Source: Brown, Christiensen, & Goldman (1987).

fects of alcohol. The scale has a mean internal coefficient alpha of .72, suggesting internal consistency. Discriminant validity analysis indicated that this scale does discriminate between alcohol expectancy and measures of delinquency.

These scales should be readministered every four weeks, and individual scores charted. The purpose of these scales is to determine areas of concern in self-efficacy and attitudes toward alcohol and drugs. As clients participate in these sessions and practice coping skills, their scores should reflect an increase in self-efficacy and a decrease in positive attributes toward alcohol and drugs. The scores can be shared with the clients as part of an ongoing evaluation of their skills in maintaining sobriety and their readiness to terminate treatment.

What is the setting for the group? These sessions are designed for outpatient treatment but can be used in an inpatient setting. They may be used in conjunction with an aftercare program or at a school, as part of a student assistance program.

What is the size and structure of the group? Ideally, the group should be kept small, with perhaps six to eight adolescents. The group can be open or closed, depending on the setting. Before entering the group clients should know that the group is specifically designed for relapse prevention and will require active participation and role playing.

This outline contains 10 sessions, with an additional generic "High-Risk Situation Coping Skills Training" model. The therapist can schedule this group to run as long as he or she wants. Many sessions are models for a series of sessions. We expect that additional coping skills will be necessary for most adolescent clients. If this is an ongoing group, such as an aftercare program, the sessions can be repeated every three months. *Remember:* coping skills sessions must be specifically geared to the particular needs of the individual group members.

Sessions can be scheduled to run for 60 to 90 minutes, depending on the maturity level of the group members.

What are the rules of the group? Clients are expected to attend all group sessions and must notify a facilitator ahead of time if they are going to be absent. They must participate during group, and they must maintain group confidentiality. Clients are to treat one another with respect and are expected to be honest. If a relapse occurs, clients must disclose this to the group and make a recommitment to abstinence. The group facilitators must decide ahead of time how a second relapse will be handled. A second relapse may be grounds for termination. It has been our experience that actively involving group members in the development of behavior expectations is quite successful.

Dishonesty and denial are hallmarks of chemical dependency. Urinalysis screening, both random and scheduled, is a physiological indicator of a client's progress. If this monitoring device is available to the therapists, we suggest using it.

Clients may also be expected to concurrently attend Alcoholics Anonymous (AA) meetings and to participate in other aspects of an aftercare or treatment contract. Referral to AA is fairly standard practice for alcoholism treatment programs. While the efficacy of AA is debated in the empirical sense literature, it has been found that adolescent participation in formal, organized groups is associated with reduced drug and alcohol use (Selnow & Crano, 1986).

Who are the facilitators? Ideally, there should be a female and male facilitator for the group. These facilitators should be very familiar with alcoholism treatment; ideally, at least one of them should be a recovering alcoholic and active in AA. This provides the kind of modeling that Bandura (1977) suggests is important in the attainment of self-efficacy. In a study conducted by Argeriou and Manohan (1978), it was found that young males who had a recovering alcoholic counselor made more positive changes in their drinking behaviors than those who had a nonrecovering therapist.

What is an ideal sequence to present skills training? It is assumed that other coping skills will be included with the presentation of these relapse-specific sessions. Recovering adolescents will need training in social skills (communication, listening, giving and receiving feedback), assertiveness, anger management, negotiation skills, life-style adjustment, and so on.

The first two sessions of this series of sessions should be presented in the order given below. This will introduce the concepts. Other sessions may be offered in the order that the therapists feel are most appropriate.

How should parents be involved? It is very important that the entire family participate in the treatment process. While not much research has been completed, one study (Hoffman & Kaplan, 1991) found a correlation between parent involvement and length of sobriety.

Ideally, weekly multifamily sessions should be offered, using the agenda from the coping skills groups. High-risk situations involving the family are an excellent agenda. The same tools used in the coping skills groups (brainstorming, role playing, group problem solving, and feedback) should be used with the families. Family members should be included from the beginning and should receive the same orientation concerning group expectations as did the adolescents. Family members should be expected to remain abstinent during the course of treatment.

In our experience it is common for family members to have limited knowledge regarding chemical dependency and treatment approaches. Education in community self-help groups (AA, NA, Al-Anon) may also be lacking. Separate education classes for families are often helpful.

What are the gender issues? To date, no empirical studies have investigated whether female and male adolescents experience recovery in different ways. It is our experience, however, that females and males do have different issues in maintaining abstinence. We advise that whenever possible groups be allowed to split into female/male subgroups for investigation of these issues specific to gender.

Relationships, romantic and otherwise, that occur in group can provide an important learning tool for the group. It will depend on the skills of the therapist to create an environment where sensitive issues can be addressed.

Session 1—Relapse Map

I. Concepts
   A. Relapse results from a series of choices that an individual makes.
   B. Relapse occurs not because of moral weakness but as a result of a lack of coping skills for high-risk situations.
   C. Identifying the series of events, thoughts, feelings, and behaviors (high-risk situations) that lead to relapse is important in building specific coping skills.

D. Irrational beliefs about ourselves, the effects of chemical use, and relapse lead to out-of-control actions.

E. Relapse or slips are no crime; *giving up on sobriety* is the only mistake a group member can make.

II. Objectives

  A. Clients will learn the rules of the group and meet each group member.

  B. Clients will create their own lists of high-risk situations.

  C. Clients will produce a written "map" of their relapse or near-relapse.

III. Materials Needed

  A. Art supplies: colored pens, paint, ink, pen, and pencil

  B. Blank paper, 8.5 × 11 or larger

  C. Copy of Relapse Map example for each participant (see table 7–1)

  D. Greaseboard/chalkboard

  E. Folder for each participant

  F. Posterboard or other large paper for "High-Risk Situation List," to be posted on wall

IV. Procedure

  A. Introduction

    1. Introduce therapist and pair up clients to introduce each other to the group. Have clients stand when doing introductions. Give basic guidelines for introduction on the board. Brainstorm these introduction basics with the group. Providing an explanation of the rules for brainstorming may be necessary. The therapist will need to be very involved at this point: early modeling of active participation may make role playing easier in later sessions. Keeping clients actively involved is very important.

    2. Share the goals of the program.

      a. Develop positive thoughts and behaviors to address relapse prevention.

      b. Develop individualized evaluations of participants patterns of relapse.

      c. Develop individualized evaluation of high-risk situations for each group member.

      d. Teach specific coping skills for high-risk using situations.

    3. Review all the rules for the group. Each program will need its own set of rules.

  B. Begin the session. Have each participant complete a Relapse Map. First, distribute the Relapse Map example. Then, show group members how to complete one worksheet, using a cotherapist or client volunteer as an example. Next, have clients complete their personal Relapse Maps. A friendly competition can help clients focus on their

Table 7–1
Relapse Map

This purpose of this worksheet is to draw a map of your relapse or using patterns.

Instructions: On a separate piece of paper, draw a picture map of your relapse. Work through the events, thoughts and feelings that led up to your relapse. Draw a square around your behaviors. Draw a circle around your thoughts. Write in your feelings where they belong. Include how you felt then and how you feel now. Be creative, use pictures, symbols and designs to Map the course of your relapse.

Example: Feeling sad
     and lonely

          Avoided calling
          my sponsor

               He would be mad
               at me for being sad

                    Got in a stupid fight with
                    my mom and left the
                    house mad.

                         Went to video arcade
                         knowing there would
                         be old friends there

                    My old friends are the only
                    ones that understand me
                    because they've had the same drug
                    experiences
             non-users can't
             understand.
         Ran into old friends

    Accepted an
    invitation to a
    party
Avoided meetings and
sponsor for two days
      I won't use and my
      friends won't pressure
      me to use because
      they like me.
              Noticed some non-users at
              party and avoided them.
                 Didn't leave when the non-
                 users left the party

                    Thought the non-users
                    were boring and stupid
                    for leaving.

                         Sat down with my old
                         friends while they
                         smoked a bong.
               I can handle this
               no problem
            One hit wouldn't hurt
      Smoked a hit on the bong
      with old friends
Smoked pot and
drank beer

work. Therapists should move through the room assisting clients, praising their work, and showing work in progress to the group. Always ask permission to share a client's work with the group. Stress the use of colors and art to express feelings.

C. After each client has completed his or her Relapse Map, have each member share his or her map with the group. One of the therapists should have a map prepared to model to the group. Hold each presentation to a short amount of time, perhaps 2 or 3 minutes. One effective way to add impact to this procedure is to promote group sound effects as the presenters go through their maps. "Oh no's," boos, and cheers can help reinforce the idea that relapse is not a sin.

D. After the presentations are completed, the therapist leads a brainstorming session to generate a list of high-risk situations that are important to this particular group of adolescents. Drawing on the pretest information and the Relapse Map exercise, clients should generate 10 to 15 high-risk situations. When the list is completed, reach a group consensus on which high-risk situation should be addressed over the next several sessions. This list of high-risk situations should be maintained as a working list for the group. Keep the list posted during the group meeting and regularly review all the high-risk situations, crossing out situations group consensus feels are no longer high-risk and adding new high-risk situations to the list as they come up in the group discussion. As new members join the group old issues will reappear on the list.

Have adolescents place their maps in their folders, and remind them to bring these folders to each group meeting.

E. Close the group. Ask each member to share one thing he or she learned during this exercise. Form a group circle, place your arms around each other, and say the "Serenity Prayer." This is a pleasant way to support 12-step attendance and gives group members the opportunity to hug each other. Hugs are good therapy.

Session 2—Stress and Problem Solving

I. Concepts
   A. Stress is a high-risk situation that is common in recovery. Learning relaxation techniques is helpful in coping with stressful situations (Gorski & Miller, 1986).
   B. Problem solving is a process during which we evaluate our choices and consequences.

II. Objectives
   A. Clients will learn four ways to manage stress through relaxation training.

    B. Clients will learn a structured problem-solving strategy.

III. Materials Needed

    A. Clients' folders

    B. 3 × 5 index cards

    C. High-Risk Situation List developed by clients

    D. Problem-Solving Worksheet

IV. Procedure

    A. Begin this session and all other sessions with a relaxation exercise as follows:

       1. Explain the relaxation process to clients, including the benefits of learning to center and relax.

       2. Instruct clients to sit up comfortably and slowly inhale to the slow count of 1–2-3. Repeat this process three times.

       3. Complete a progressive large muscle relaxation by having clients tense their muscles, hold for a brief count of 1–2-3, and then relax their muscles. (We advise therapists to research progressive relaxation techniques.) In this session we suggest doing a complete relaxation exercise. In subsequent group meetings a shorter version will be less time consuming, yet still very effective. After an introduction most clients appear to effectively apply the relaxation technique in the shortened version.

       4. When the clients have completed the muscle relaxation, complete a short visualization (3–5 minutes). Ask the clients to visualize a safe, quiet place for themselves. This is not guided imagery: allow the clients to visualize on their own.

       5. Bring the clients slowly back into the present and close this exercise by having them give themselves affirmations. Ask clients to state the affirmations out loud.

    B. Introduce problem solving.

       1. Hand out the Problem-Solving Worksheet (see table 7–2)

       2. As a group, have clients select on high-risk situation from the list developed in previous group sessions. The therapist will use this situation to model problem solving.

       3. Solve the problem on the board. Stress the ideas that:

          a. There is no perfect solution.

          b. The solution may be different for each person.

       4. Use the following decision-making formula:

          a. Identify the problem, the feelings, and the person's needs (what do they want?).

          b. Generate possible solutions without evaluating them (brainstorm).

          c. Evaluate each possible solution as to possible outcomes and consequences.

Table 7–2
Problem Solving

The purpose of this exercise is to learn an organized approach to solving everyday problems.

The Problem is:

Identify: Identify as many parts of the problem as you can.

The feelings
Your thoughts and beliefs
What outcome do you want?

Generate: Brainstorm, think of all possible solutions to your problem.

Include the funny, stupid, questionable and reasonable solutions.
Let your mind work without limit. You are not in the action stage.
Let it all loose.

Evaluate: You had your fun in the Generate section. Now it is time for reality. Evaluate
eachof your solutions.

What are the negative and positive consequences to me?
How will it effect the other people in my life?
Am I willing to pay the price?
Is it possible for me to do the solution?

Practice: You've picked your solution and now it is time to put it into action. Consider:

Is it the right time?
Where is the right place?
Are these the right people?

---

      d.   Pick a solution and role-play it in the group. Make the situations as real as possible and allow only positive performances.

  C. Ask clients to individually pick another high-risk situation. Tell them to use the Problem-Solving Worksheet to develop their own solutions. This activity may be done in pairs, with solutions shared with the group by means of a role play.

Session 3—Making Sober Friends

This session would be appropriately coupled with more extensive coping skills training in relationship skills such as making conversation and listening. The therapists will need to judge the skills of the group to determine at what pace to proceed. An effective strategy would be to introduce the Making Sober Friends session to determine the group's comfort and skill with relationship skills. If needed, use communication and listening skills sessions as part of a series on Making Sober Friends.

Skills in making friends is likely to be an area in which many recovering adolescents have large deficits. Past relationships may have been built primarily on the commonality of drug or alcohol use (Ellis, 1986). Mijuskovic (1988) writes that a large factor in adolescent alcoholism is loneliness. Indeed, alcohol and drugs are often used as a "social lubricant." All this may be complicated by the self-deception of many addict/alcoholics that they are socially adept.

I. Concepts
   A. Adolescent relapse research (Brown et al., 1989) indicates that pressure from using peers is a major reason for relapse.
   B. The adolescent's self-image as a user of drugs and/or alcohol makes it difficult for him or her to both give up old using friends and to make new sober friends.
   C. Affiliation with 12-step programs offers quick entry into a social network of people with positive self-images.
   D. For clients resistant to AA/NA, other community support groups, clubs, churches, teams, and so on, can fulfill the need for a new social network.
   E. Making new friends is only one part of a necessary life-style change.
II. Objectives
   A. Clients will demonstrate the social skills necessary for making friends.
III. Materials Needed
   A. High-Risk List
   B. Greaseboard/chalkboard
IV. Procedure
   A. Begin the group with the relaxation procedure.
   B. Next the therapist asks the group for their personal experiences in making new friends, in school, at meetings, and in the community. Divide the greaseboard in two. List the difficulties in making new friends on one side and the thoughts and beliefs about making new friends on the other side. Typical beliefs include "If you've never used drugs, you can't relate to me," "Non-users are boring," and "If we don't discuss drugs or recovery, what is there to talk about?"
      Note: "I'm not changing my friends" will be the position of many clients. We suggest avoiding conflict over this issue. We take the stance that the group is learning a skill, and the decision to use the skill rests with the individual client.
   C. When the brainstorming session is complete, the therapist leads the

clients to discuss and list the behavioral and cognitive skills necessary to overcome the difficulties listed.

D. The therapist may need to add a didactic presentation on the basic skills of conversation. These will include: small talk, eye contact, body language, listening skills, showing interest, introducing yourself, not swearing, and avoiding drunk-a-logs (bragging about your drinking habits).

E. The therapists can then model these skills by role-playing a scenario such as meeting someone at an AA meeting. Clients should then role-play situations of their own choosing from the list generated earlier.

F. For additional practice, pair the group members and have them pretend to meet each other for the first time. Have them change partners after 10 minutes. Have the role play occur in various contexts, such as meeting at school, on a bus, or at a social function. Therapists should include themselves in this exercise to assist the adolescents in practicing the same skills with adults. This is an effective exercise to use periodically throughout the program.

G. When complete, review the session with the clients. Ask for feedback on the original list of difficulties and cognitions.

H. Close the group with homework assignments: group members are to start a conversation with someone at school, at work, or at a meeting, and they are to contact another member of this group to share a social outing during the week. Group members will need to be willing to exchange phone numbers to accomplish this assignment. The therapist notes that the next session will begin with a review of the homework assignment.

Session 4—Dealing with Relapse

In aftercare and relapse prevention groups relapse should be expected. How this issue is dealt with by the therapists is critical to the ultimate success of the group. The group must establish an atmosphere that allows clients to self-disclose their relapses and at the same time protects other group members in their commitment to sobriety. Clearly stating the therapy policy and response to relapse should be undertaken at the first meeting of the group.

I. Concepts
   A. Relapse may be the result of a lack of appropriate coping skills for high-risk situations.
   B. An individual's cognitive and affective response to a relapse can determine how quickly she or he reestablishes sobriety.
   C. "One drink, one drunk" does not need to happen.

  D. Reestablishing sobriety may require a specific set of skills that can be learned before the fact of relapse.

  E. By changing thoughts and beliefs regarding relapse a client can greatly increase his or her likelihood of returning to sobriety.

  F. A single incident of alcohol or drug use is a mistake, not a failure.

II. Objectives

  A. Clients will receive information regarding relapse.

  B. Clients will design a likely scenario of their own relapse.

  C. Clients will evaluate their feelings, thoughts, and beliefs about their "relapse."

  D. Clients will develop a problem-solving strategy for the prevention of their "relapse."

  E. Clients will develop a problem-solving strategy for recovering from their "relapse."

III. Materials Needed

  A. Greaseboard/chalkboard

  B. Problem-Solving Worksheets

  C. High-Risk List

  D. Create Your Own Relapse Worksheet (see table 7–3)

  E. Prepared relapse story to use as an example for the group

IV. Procedure

  A. Open the group with the relaxation procedure.

  B. The therapist begins by discussing relapse. Generate a list of attitudes and beliefs regarding relapse from the group. Discuss the group's beliefs about why relapse happens and what can be done about relapse once it happens. Typically, adolescents view sobriety as an all-or-nothing proposition. Relapse means that they have failed themselves, their parents, their peers, the treatment center, and their therapists.

  C. The therapists need to reframe these beliefs about relapse by providing clients with accurate information, including the information in the concepts section of this lesson (see Marlatt (1985) for more information). Some of this information differs from what is traditionally communicated in AA/NA. We, however, view AA/NA concepts of "Keep coming back, it works" as supporting our model.

  D. Using the Create Your Own Relapse Worksheet the therapist will read the model relapse story. The therapist will then instruct the clients to use about 15 minutes to create their own relapse stories using the worksheet. Clients are to create an "if relapse were to happen to me" story in which they explain how relapse would happen. Emphasize that individuals should make their stories as detailed as possible.

  E. When the relapse stories are completed, break into two groups and have group members share their stories. As the stories are delivered, the therapist lists the high-risk situations on a greaseboard. Feelings

Table 7–3
Create Your Own Relapse

The purpose of this exercise is to imagine your own relapse in order to avoid it.

Your imagined relapse will need to be as detailed as possible. Put your knowledge of your personality, using triggers, strengths and weaknesses to work. In your relapse story include friends, places, thoughts and beliefs. You may want to review your RELAPSE MAP. Visualize the whole story before you begin writing.

_____

_____

_____

_____

_____

_____

_____

_____

_____

_____

_____

_____

_____

_____

_____

_____

and thoughts that accompany the high-risk situations and the actual relapse should also be listed.

F. Using the Problem-Solving Worksheet, the small groups evaluate feelings, thoughts, and high-risk situations and then brainstorms alternative coping strategies. Alternative cognition regarding the relapse are developed. For example, "I relapsed because I'm weak" becomes "I relapsed because I didn't have the skills to deal with my anger toward my dad." Attributions regarding the effects of the drugs or alcohol used are also reframed. For example, "I need drugs to escape" becomes "Drugs will make my problems worse."

G. After each member participates the group reforms. Group members are asked to share what they learned in the session and to identify their level of confidence in dealing with a relapse.

H. Close the group by having clients give affirmations about themselves and specific positive feedback to another member of the group.

Sessions 5 and 6—Dealing with Parents

This theme can be addressed over two or more sessions. Clients will need to think about areas of difficulty that they experience with their families. These areas can then be categorized according to several themes. Two common themes we have chosen are "Misunderstandings about Recovery" and "If Mom or Dad Is an Alcoholic." Readers may wish to refer to other chapters in this book for examples of sessions regarding anger management, negotiation skills, assertiveness training and the like. We recommend that these general skills be addressed in sessions prior to these specific examples.

Session 5—Dealing with Parents: Misunderstandings about Recovery; or, Whose Recovery Is This, Anyhow?

 I. Concepts
   A. Recovery is a new process for everyone, including parents.
   B. Parents may or may not choose to change their old behaviors.
   C. If a client can detach from the problem in order to understand it, he or she will be more likely to utilize successful coping skills.
 II. Objectives
   A. Clients will identify situations in which they experience problems with their parents regarding their recovery program.
   B. Clients will demonstrate a coping skill—detachment—by describing their parents' thoughts and feelings about the problem.
   C. Clients will label their own feelings in response to parents and state ways to reframe these feelings.

D. Clients will demonstrate the ability to manage their anger through detachment, reframing, and other appropriate coping skills.

III. Materials Needed
   A. Greaseboard/chalkboard
   B. Problem-Solving Worksheet
   C. High-Risk List

IV. Procedure
   A. Open the meeting with relaxation exercises.
   B. Ask the clients about their difficulties in relationships with their parents and other family members, particularly in regard to their recovery programs. Some possible responses may be: "My mom never believes me when I come home late, she thinks I may have been out getting high"; "My dad always wants to know about my AA meetings—who was there, who I sat with, and so on"; and "My parents insist on meeting my AA friends." Another common concern many have is that mom and/or dad will not attend any self-help meetings.
   C. The therapists write several different examples of difficulties on the greaseboard. The therapists can empathize with each situation, for example, by saying, "Yeah, I know that's hard."
   D. Under one of the examples, the therapist writes "Behaviors" and "Feelings." The client who identified this particular situation is then asked to discuss further how the parent behaves and/or what is said, and then is asked to discuss what he or she thinks the parent might be feeling. This exercise will probably require some prompting. Group members should be encouraged to help the client identify feelings he or she wasn't aware of, for example, fear, worry, curiosity, or concern. Try to get to the "bottom-line" feelings. Maybe mom just wants to be in control. Ask the client to probe further: What do you suppose she fears about losing control? What does she think will happen? List answers under behavior.
   E. Next to the parents' behavior and feelings, list the client's behavior and feelings. How does he or she typically respond to this situation—how does he or she act, how does he or she feel? Does this help solve the problem or does it perpetuate it?
   G. Have the group generate alternative behaviors and list them. Ask the client how he or she might feel if an alternative behavior was tried.
   H. After several examples have been generated, ask the group to recall (from previous sessions) what they know about anger in general. Then ask for other ways of handling anger that haven't been discussed, and list these. Discuss detachment, or "putting yourself into another's shoes." Highlight other coping methods, such as reframing the anger: Is anger really hurt, sadness, or fear? Other coping methods include sharing feelings, using "I" statements, keeping a

journal, discussing with others, and exercise. Sometimes it is not appropriate to ventilate anger, and it must be dissipated in other ways.

I. Ask group members to role-play these scenarios. Discuss afterward and add to the previous lists of coping skills and feelings. Begin with the therapist role-playing one of the situations as a model.

J. Have the clients fill out a Problem-Solving Worksheet and have them place it in their notebooks. Ask the clients to select a current problem with their parents to problem solve.

K. Close the group. Ask each client to give himself or herself an affirmation and tell the group their number of days of sobriety.

Session 6—Dealing with Parents, or, What if Dad or Mom Is an Alcoholic?

There are an estimated seven million children of alcoholics in this nation (Woodside, 1983). Children of alcoholics are found to have more depression, to experience lower self-esteem, and to have a higher risk of becoming heavy drinkers themselves (Roosa, Sandler, Beals, & Short, 1988).

If this is an issue for even one group member, it is worth addressing. Most likely there will be hidden alcoholism in group members' families that the clients are reluctant to address. If a client seems to be struggling with this issue, a referral for individual therapy would be appropriate. This could run concurrently or be initiated after the end of these sessions. Referrals can also be made to Alateen (Al-Anon for teens) or Coda-teen, (Codependents Anonymous for teens).

When the issue of parents' alcoholism or drug abuse is addressed, therapists should expect disclosures of sexual or physical abuse. The therapist should meet with the client individually to notify him or her that an abuse report must be made, and to gather further details if needed.

I. Concepts
   A. If an adolescent who is in recovery lives in the home of an active alcoholic, his or her chances for relapse are much higher.
   B. While the adolescent may, in the past, have adapted to the alcoholism and any concomitant violence or abuse by drinking or using drugs, this coping skill is no longer suitable. Therefore, these adolescents need to develop specific skills and methods for dealing with the dysfunction of alcoholism.
   C. The purpose of this group is not to label or diagnose alcoholism in parents. It is to provide "Action Plans" for those who identify with this problem.
II. Objectives
   A. Clients will review definitions and symptomatology of alcoholism and drug addiction.

B. Clients will review the impact alcoholism has on a family, and discuss how they themselves have been impacted.

C. Clients will identify what individual high-risk situations the parents' alcoholism caused for the client.

D. Clients will develop an "Action Plan" that outlines specific coping skills and resources they can utilize.

III. Materials Needed

A. Greaseboard/chalkboard

B. Action Plan Worksheet (see table 7–4)

C. High-Risk List

IV. Procedure

A. Open group with the relaxation exercise.

B. Ask group members to describe the symptoms of alcoholism and drug addiction. List these symptoms. (It's interesting to see what their level of awareness is at this point.) Fill in symptoms they leave out. Then ask the group to describe how alcoholism impacts the family and list their thoughts on the board. Fill in as appropriate.

C. Review the previous sessions, that is, remind the group that several members had mentioned difficulties with their parents' drinking. Ask, "How might having an alcoholic, or any other type of dysfunctional parent, set you up for a relapse?" List the group's replies. Their answers may include: "They drink right in front of me but tell me not to"; "We have all kinds of alcohol [or drugs] in the house"; "My mother gets so irrational when she's drunk that she won't let me out of the house to go anywhere, even AA"; and "I get slapped and called a loser." These situations can be added to the posted High-Risk Situations List.

D. Point out that these high-risk situations are indeed high risk! Many times clients will need a plan that involves more than the everyday coping skills they have already learned. These are called "Action Plans," plans created in the event that a problem situation occurs that will enable the person to take care of himself or herself.

E. Next, ask a specific client if he or she would like to develop an individualized Action Plan in front of the group. With his or her permission, begin by identifying his or her resources. List these on the board. Resources are anyone the client believes he or she can talk to or go to for help. Make sure some adults are included on the Resource List. Then ask him or her to described several typical high-risk situations. The adolescent usually starts with minor ones and might need encouragement to disclose those situations with potential for violence or abuse. The therapists may need to probe for these.

F. Ask the group for help brainstorming specific coping responses to these situations. If the replies are, "Call someone" or "Crawl out my

Table 7–4
Action Plan

The purpose of this worksheet is for you to design a plan of action for High Risk Situations you will encounter in your recovery.

Here is the Problem:

Here is how I feel about the problem:

These are My resources:

People

Places

Skills

Beliefs

Things

To make this plan I will decide who, what, where and when. The why is that I want to be safe and sober.

The Plan is:

bedroom window," make sure that the therapists remind group members about the Resource List. Who would be called? Where could the client go? The therapists should stress the idea that they do not advocate running away from home, but should also point out that if an adolescent feels that he or she must leave home for his or her personal safety, then the non-drinking parent should know about this decision. He or she should tell the parent where he or she will be and for how long.

As the clients devise these Action Plans, the therapists should continually check to make sure that these plans are realistic, that is, does the client believe that he or she could or would carry out these plans?

G. Split the group in half. Each therapist takes half of the group and each group picks a high-risk situation to role-play. Use the Action Plan as a guide. Clients can rehearse the role play, and then present it to the other group. The group should be encouraged to provide feedback regarding the coping skills previously taught, such as body language, eye contact, voice, right time, place, and person.

H. Close the group by asking members to share one strategy that they learned they that see as being effective for them.

Sessions 7, 8, and 9

The next three sessions are based upon cue exposure, or responding to objects, thoughts, or feelings—anything that reminds an alcoholic or drug addict of drinking or using drugs. Marlatt (1990) recommends that coping skills rehearsal should always take place in the presence of drinking and using cues. Session 7 focuses on triggers, which are external objects or sounds that bring on thoughts of using. Session 8 deals with refusal skills, or how to deal with others who ask the alcoholic to drink or the addict to use drugs. Session 9 deals with urges and cravings, which are internal desires to drink or use.

Session 7—Cue Exposure/Trigger Identification

Cue exposure has been found to be important in relapse prevention, particularly with drug addicts. A study by O'Brien, Childress, McLellan, and Ehrman (1990) found that cocaine addicts had physiological responses when shown drugs, paraphernalia, and other cues. They also found that clients utilizing cue exposure tended to remain in treatment longer and report less use of cocaine.

I. Concepts
  A. Exposure to drug cues, including paraphernalia, occurs frequently in the adolescents' daily environment.
  B. Direct practice with refusal skills in simulated, safe (low risk) settings increases ability to apply refusal skills.
II. Objectives
  A. Clients will identify their individual drug and alcohol stimulation cues and triggers.
  B. Clients will practice visualization skills to use in "practicing" coping skills.
III. Materials Needed
  Materials are to be individualized according to the drugs of choice of group members. Remember, these are props only and are not to be used or consumed in group! Some examples might be:
  A. A six pack of canned beer on ice if possible. Nothing beats a Bud.
  B. Marijuana substitute, oregano, or other herb will be close enough. Also, rolling papers, pipes, or bongs can be included.
  C. Cocaine substitute and a mirror to line it on (Sugar, flour, saccharin, any white powder will do.)
  D. Greaseboard, chalkboard
IV. Procedure
  A. This session requires good rapport between clients and therapists. It should be conducted *only* after the group members and therapists have demonstrated that degree of rapport.
  B. In this session the relaxation procedure should be delayed until later.
  C. The therapists should enter the group room a bit late the "fake drugs" and a cooler of beer in their hands. They sit down and begin rolling a "joint," and lining out the "cocaine." One of the therapists reaches into the cooler, withdraws a beer, and opens it. The therapists should make no attempt to explain their actions.
  D. Open the group by asking each member to share his or her feelings. The therapists can use the reaction of the group members to lead into E below.
     Note: In our experience the clients have always had the same reaction. First they deny that the therapists have brought real drugs and alcohol into the group. Many clients attempt to laugh off the event. Then anger begins to surface along with the thought that they are being toyed with or that our actions are somehow unfair. Many clients begin to acknowledge feelings of craving, while others stick with the denial that this exposure bothers them. Recalling euphoric feelings (Euphoric recall) gets the group excited and prompts members to narrate "using" stories. Many times group members also express depressive thoughts about how impossible it is to stop using.

E. As the therapists continue to play with the "fake" drugs, they lead the group members into recalling how they spent their "using" days thinking about, preparing to use, and using drugs and/or alcohol.

F. A very specific story can be built by the group or an individual in the group. Push the clients to detail their "using" experience, ask them to recall feelings and thoughts from the past experiences. Make sure they discuss the settings they used in, who they used with, what time of day they used, what music they listened to, and any other experience that could be later identified as a cue or trigger. The excitement and euphoric recall should neither be discouraged nor encouraged.

   Note: At this point, it is our experience that the group often becomes polarized. A portion of the clients get sad and hopeless and perhaps angry. The other clients get into a euphoric recall mode. Both reactions—or any other reaction—are okay.

G. Ask the clients to discuss current triggers and cues that they have experienced since entering sobriety, and to discuss how they have (or have not) coped with these.

H. The therapist then asks the group to brainstorm individualized lists of cues and triggers, based on present and past stories. These are written on the greaseboard.

I. At this point, the therapists prepare to close the group. By consensus, one of the identified using triggers is picked. The therapists then uses the relaxation exercise combined with guided imagery. The imagery should focus on a successful application of coping skills for the identified cue. Upon completion of this exercise, close the group by checking with each client on the current feelings about urges or cravings. (We owe a note of thanks to David Halchishick for his contribution to this exercise.)

Session 8—Cue Exposure/Refusal Skills

This session is based on the work of Monti, Kadden, Abrams, and Coney (1989). This session is a model for a series of sessions using the same format. The therapist will need to determine the number of sessions that are appropriate.

I. Concepts
   A. Behavioral rehearsal of refusal skills, in a safe and secure setting, improves one's ability to apply refusal skills in the natural environment.
   B. Successful practice raises self-efficacy and increased the likelihood that refusal skills will be applied.

II. Objectives
  A. Clients will demonstrate coping skills (refusal) for their specific high-risk situations.
  B. Clients will have the opportunity to observe others role-play refusal skills, thus enhancing the modeling effect.
III. Materials Needed
  A. Any of the drug and/or alcohol props used in the previous session
  B. Music and any other trigger previously identified by the group
  C. A Cues and Triggers List generated in the last session, preprepared on a poster board
  D. High-Risk Situation List
  E. Greaseboard
  F. Refusal Skills Worksheet (see table 7–5)
IV. Procedures
  A. Use the relaxation procedure to open the group meeting.
  B. Presents information on coping with environmental cues and triggers, especially being asked to get high or drink.
    1. Being asked to use is a common experience.
    2. While you can avoid parties, using hang-outs, and other obvious places, you will still be confronted with offers to use at school and work.
    3. Beyond just saying "No" you must have specific skills in refusing the request to use. Practice of these skills will increase the likelihood you will be successful in such high-risk situations.
    4. Review skills necessary for refusing a request.
      a. Do a in-your-head rehearsal.
      b. Ask yourself what does a person look like when he or she means what he or she says? (Generate list on board)
        1. Maintain eye contact.
        2. Use a strong voice.
        3. Maintain a strong posture: face the person, sit or stand straight.
      c. What does a person say when he or she means it? (Generate list on board)
        1. Say "No"—avoid "Maybe" or beating around the bush.
        2. State your position such as "I don't drink," "Not today," "I am in recovery."
      d. What does a person do?
        1. Suggest an alternative activity or go to an alternative activity.
        2. Leave the situation.
        3. Evaluate yourself: should you contact your sponsor? Go to a meeting? Are you experiencing cravings?

Table 7–5
Refusal Skills Worksheet

High Risk Situation	My Coping Strategy
1. _____	_____
_____	_____
_____	_____
2. _____	_____
_____	_____
_____	_____
3. _____	_____
_____	_____
_____	_____
4. _____	_____
_____	_____
_____	_____
5. _____	_____
_____	_____
_____	_____

C. Review the posted Cues and Triggers List with the clients and pick one for the therapists to role-play. Use the props in the role play. The therapists should model each of the above skills.

D. Have one client at a time select a cue or trigger and set up a role-play situation using peers as players. Remember to use the props. The therapists should assist the nonparticipants in evaluating the application of the refusal skills from the lesson.

   Note: It is important for the therapists to focus the clients on keeping the situation as real as possible. Unrealistic practice will not serve the client well in his or her real world. Clients can be used to evaluate the "realness" of each situation.

E. Introduce the Refusal Skills Worksheet. Complete one worksheet using the entire group. Then ask each client to complete a worksheet by himself or herself. This worksheet should be added to the client's folder.

F. The therapist then leads the clients into a visualization. Each client selects a refusal skill he or she feels he or she could apply and use in personal visualization. This is not a guided imagery: clients should have the opportunity to create their own scenario.

G. Close the group by asking each client to share a coping skill that he or she feels he or she can use.

Session 9—Cue Exposure/Internal Urges

I. Concepts
   A. Urges and cravings are defined as thoughts concerning alcohol and drug use and desires to use. Often they are a reaction to stress engendered by high-risk situations.
   B. Urges and cravings are not necessary physiological in origin. They may also be due to attributions the client makes concerning drugs and alcohol.
   C. Reframing urges and cravings as thoughts that can be managed provides strategies for the client to successfully cope with the urges and cravings.

II. Objectives
   A. Clients will identify personal experiences, thoughts, and beliefs related to cravings.
   B. Clients will demonstrate knowledge of coping skills for dealing with cravings.

III. Materials Needed
   A. Urges and Cravings Handout (see table 7–6)
   B. Refusal Skills Worksheet
   C. High-Risk Situations List
   D. Cues and Triggers List

Table 7–6

Myths and Facts About Urges and Cravings

Myths	Facts
Abstaining from using alcohol/drugs is either easy because of no cravings or it is impossibly difficult because of cravings.	Some people have very few urges or cravings and others may experience urges and cravings that make staying clean more difficult.
Learning to manage cravings does not take any extra effort or time.	It is usually helpful to allow extra time and energy to learning how to manage cravings.
Cravings for drugs or alcohol lasts forever.	Individual cravings are usually short and happen less and less as time goes on. The intensity of the cravings and urges may or may not change.
If the initial quitting of alcohol/drug use is difficult, maintaining abstinence is equally difficult.	Quitting the use of alcohol or drugs and maintaining abstinence are different behaviors and may require different strategies.
If you have any difficulty in managing cravings, it probably means you cannot quit or didn't really want to quit.	Most people have some trouble managing cravings and urges in the beginning.
Feeling proud or successful after getting through a difficult time of craving is a waste of time. After all the battle is not over!	It is important to be proud of your successes and progress rather than to think craving is a sign of failure.
There is not much to know about cravings and how to manage them to stay clean and sober	There are coping skills and strategies you can learn AA/NA/CA can support you in building new skills.
If you have had a difficult time in the past dealing with cravings, you can expect it to be hard in the future.	Each time you have cravings is a new chance and may need a different strategy than the last craving. You can learn from each situation what works and what doesn't.

Source: Mary Downs, MA. Ron Downs and Associates, 1208 East Broadway Road. Suite 120, Tempe, Arizona 85282

IV. Procedure
  A. Ask clients to discuss their experiences with cravings and urges. The clients should identify the feelings, thoughts, and beliefs associated with their cravings.
  B. The therapist provides accurate information regarding cravings, such as people experience urges and cravings differently, not all recovering people have cravings, and sometimes urges come out of nowhere. Review the Urges and Cravings Handout with the group.
      Present interventions for dealing with cravings:
    1. Changing thoughts: Remind self of positive aspects of recovery, negative aspects of using; Remind self that urges are temporary and will pass.
    2. Changing behavior. Avoid high-risk situations. Develop alternative activities, such as going to meetings, reading AA literature, exercising, or calling a friend.

   C. The therapist sets up a role-play situation to model cognitive interventions. One therapist portrays someone experiencing an urge or craving. The other therapist acts as the urge by giving cognitive messages to the person such as: "A drink would really taste good," "No one here knows I'm recovering, one wouldn't hurt," or "I need a drink to fit in." Have the therapists face each other in chairs. Have therapist 1 counter each cognition, utilizing information from the lecture. To end the role play, therapist 1 announces that she or he has successfully managed the cravings.

   D. Ask for feedback regarding the role play. Get client feedback on how realistic the role play was and the effectiveness of the cognitive restructuring.

   E. Select clients to role-play their own craving experiences. Peers should serve as the craving cognition. Instruct the clients to end their role play when they feel they have successfully managed their craving. Repeat for each group member.

   F. Close the group. Ask group members to share feedback about the exercise, including what was most meaningful to them.

Session 10—Coping with Loss: Saying Goodbye to Drugs and Alcohol

According to St. Mary and Russo (1989), adolescent alcoholics predict lower levels of self-efficacy in dealing with grief and loss situations. We suggest that a general session on coping with loss be conducted prior to this specific lesson. We believe this session is important because addictions counselors have known for years that clients experience a grief reaction upon entering abstinence and recovery. Many times this reaction is termed "the death of a relationship" or "the death of a best friend or lover—drugs." Jennings (1991, p. 221) writes that the "dynamics of mourning that are specific to the loss of drugs can be observed in the behaviors of recovering persons."

   I. Concepts
     A. Recovering people feel a sense of loss when entering abstinence, which itself can be a high-risk situation for relapse.
     B. Coping with loss can occur in a variety of healthy and unhealthy ways.
     C. Methods of healthy coping include acknowledging one's feelings, sharing them with others, and letting them go.
   II. Objectives
     A. Clients will examine their feelings concerning abstinence and recovery.

B. Clients will brainstorm past and present methods of coping.

C. Clients will actively participate in a structured coping method exercise.

III. Materials Needed

A. Greaseboard/chalkboard

B. Blank notebook paper and pencils

C. Matches or a lighter, and a place for a small fire.

IV. Procedure

A. Open with the relaxation exercise.

B. Begin group by discussing the theme of grief and loss. The therapist can stress the idea that this issue is very common for teenagers and especially for those in recovery. If ignored, these feelings of grief and loss can create high-risk situations.

C. Solicit from the group situations that cause grief and loss. Write these situations on the greaseboard. The answers will probably include death of a parent, death of a friend, loss of a pet, and breaking up with a boyfriend or a girlfriend. After these "traditional" losses, explore those special losses that may be related to alcohol and drug use: loss of friendships, jobs, family relationships, trust, self-respect. Then ask the group to name the "losses" that came from getting sober. They may be puzzled or have difficulty answering this questions, they may need to be led. Possible answers include: loss of drug-using friendships, loss of cash (from dealing), loss of power and prestige, and *most importantly*, loss of the relationship with the drugs or alcohol.

D. Explain to the group that although getting sober is usually a happy event, many times addicts feel a great deal of sadness that they don't know how to communicate, or don't want to communicate. Ask group members how they felt when they either decided to be abstinent or came to grips with the fact that they were an alcoholic or an addict. List these answers next to "Loss of Drug/Alcohol Relationship."

E. Ask the group how they dealt with this sadness. If some members state that they didn't feel sadness, ask them if it was possible that they "stuffed" their feelings. Suppression can be a coping method. List all the members' responses in a column next to the feelings. Review the coping responses; ask which worked and which didn't work.

     Note: Some members may have a difficult time with this topic. They may indicate that AA tells them not to focus on the past or future but to "Live One Day at a Time." Reinforce the idea that using slogans can be a great coping method, but also point out that feelings still must be explored so that they lose their power. There is always a sense of loss in coming to terms with addiction.

F. Ask the members of the group if they are experiencing any sense of loss now, a loss related to their recovery. Think of examples that might bring up their loss or grief feelings. For instance, if someone says, "What do you mean, you don't drink?," how do they cope with their feelings? Emphasize responses regarding sharing the feelings, writing them down, and "turning them over" to their Higher Power.

H. Have group members write a short letter in which they say good-bye to drugs and alcohol. Be sure to have them include their feelings. Break into two groups. Have each member read his or her letter. When all are finished, take them outside to a parking lot or other open area. Put the letters in a pile and set them on fire. Stand in a circle, hugging, to watch the pile burn.

I. Close the group by indicating that burning their letters doesn't necessarily mean that individual members will never use alcohol or drugs again. What it does mean is that sad feelings lose their power as they are acknowledged, shared, and let go.

High-Risk Coping Skills Session

I. Concepts
  A. Application of social learning theory principles of modeling and behavioral rehearsal increase coping skills rapidly.
  B. Receiving feedback on behavioral rehearsal of coping skills will improve performance.
II. Objectives
  A. Clients will demonstrate mastery of specific coping skills to deal with high-risk situations.
  B. Clients will demonstrate mastery of techniques for visualization practice of coping skills.
III. Materials Needed
  A. High-Risk Situation List
  B. Greaseboard/chalkboard
  C. Problem-Solving Worksheets
IV. Procedures
  A. Begin the session with the relaxation procedure.
  B. Next have the group select a high-risk situation from the list. Select an individual member of the group to be the subject of the situation. Using the group, problem solve the situation. Design a workable solution for the subject.
  C. The therapists should then role-play the situation using the group's solution. Ask the group to evaluate the role play. Is it a real-world

solution? Have the group give feedback on the role play. Areas to evaluate include (1) body language, (2) eye contact, (3) clear message, (4) select the right time, (5) chose the right place, and (6) do it with the right person. Assist the clients in discovering that not only must they develop the appropriate coping skill but they must develop the judgment to determine when is the *right time* to use the skill, where will be the most effective *right place* to put the skill into practice, and whether the coping skill is matched to the *right person*.

D. Instruct the clients to complete a role play of the same situation and have the group evaluate the role play and the subject as in part C. All role plays should have positive outcomes.

E. Break the group into two smaller groups and repeat the above process with each member of the smaller groups. It is not necessary for the therapist to model each role play. Have the clients pick their own high-risk situation and use the Problem-Solving Worksheet to design a solution. The clients and therapists should participate in the role plays, but ensure that participation of each group member. Have the group evaluate each role play using the criteria in part C.

F. Reconvene the larger group. Ask the client to select a high-risk situation for which they feel they have a successful solution. The therapist next conducts a visualization exercise, asking each client to rehearse his or her coping skills solution. Ask the clients to relax and try to see themselves successfully carrying out the successful application of the coping skill solution they had designed and role-played earlier.

The relaxation procedure that has been repeated in each group should enable visualization exercises to be accomplished in a brief time span. The therapist is trying to accomplish two things. First, the clients are practicing the coping skills for a specific high-risk situation. Second, they are practicing a useful coping strategy, visualization. Once again the therapist will need to determine the skills level of the group and make adjustments. Some groups of adolescents may not make effective use of visualization or may require more time on the exercise. Relaxation and visualization training skills will be necessary for the therapist. Those not familiar with the techniques should seek further information and training.

G. Close the group by asking for feedback on the session.

References

Annis, H. (1986). A relapse prevention model for treatment of alcoholics. In W. Miller & N. Heather (Eds.). *Treating Addictive Behaviors: Processes of Change.* NY: Plenum Press.

Annis H. & Davis, C. (1988). Self-efficacy and the prevention of relapse: initial findings from a treatment trial. In T. Baker & D. Cannon (Eds.), *Assessment and Treatment of Addictive Disorders*. NY: Praeger Press.

Argeriou, M. and Manohan, V. (1978). Relative effectiveness of nonalcoholics and recovered alcoholics as counselors. *Journal of Studies on Alcohol, 39,* 793–799.

Bandura, A. (177). Self-efficacy: toward a unifying theory of behavioral change. *Psychological Review, 84,* 191–215.

Brown, S., Vik, P., & Creamer, V. (1989). Characteristics of relapse following adolescent substance abuse treatment. *Addictive Behaviors, 14,* 291–300.

Brown, S., Stetson, B., & Beatty, P. (1989). Cognitive and behavioral features of adolescent coping in high-risk drinking situations. *Addictive Behaviors, 14,* 43–52.

Brown, S., Christiansen, B. & Goldman, M. (1987). The alcohol expectancy questionnaire: an instrument for the assessment of adolescent and adult alcohol expectancies. *Journal of Studies on Alcohol, 48,* 483–491.

Chaney, E., O'Leary, M. & Marlatt, G. (1978). Skill training with alcoholics. *Journal of Consulting and Clinical Psychology, 46,* 1092–1104.

Coleman, S. (1985). An aftercare group model for adolescent substance abusers. *Journal of Alcohol and Drug Education,* 53–59.

Cummings, C., Gordon, J., & Marlatt, G.A. (1980). Relapse: Strategies of prevention and prediction. in W.R. Miller (ed.), *The Addictive Behaviors*. Oxford: Pergamon Press.

Ellis, D. (1986). *Growing Up Stoned*. Pompano Beach, FL: Health Communications, Inc.

Gorski, T. & Miller, M. (1986). *Staying Sober: A Guide for Relapse Prevention*. Independence, MO: Independence Press.

Hoffman, N. & Kaplan, R. (1991). *One Year Outcome Results For Adolescents: Key Correlates and Benefits of Recovery*. St. Paul. MN: CATOR/New Standards, Inc.

Jennings, P. (1991). To surrender drugs: a grief process in its own right. *Journal of Substance Abuse Treatment, 8,* 221–226.

Mackay, P. & Marlatt, G. (1991). Maintaining sobriety: stopping is starting. *The International Journal of Addictions, 25,* 1257–1276.

Marlatt, G. A. (1985). Cognitive factors in the relapse process. in G.A. Marlatt & J. R. Gordon (Eds.), *Relapse Prevention: Maintenance Strategies in the Treatment of Addictive Behaviors*. New York: Guilford Press.

Marlatt, G. A. (1990). Cue exposure and relapse prevention in the treatment of addictive behaviors. *Addictive Behaviors, 15,* 395–399.

Mijuskovic B. (1988). Loneliness and adolescent alcoholism. *Adolescence, 23,* 503–516.

Monti, P., Kadden, R., Abrams, D. & Conney, N. (1989). *Treating Alcohol Dependence*. New York: Guilford Press.

O'Brien, C., Childress, A., McLellan, T. & Ehrman, R. (1990) Integrating systematic cue exposure with standard treatment in recovering drug dependent patients. *Addictive Behaviors, 15* 355–365.

Roosa, M., Sandler, I., Beals, J. & Short, J. (1988) Risk studies of adolescent children of problem drinking parents. *American Journal of Community Psychology, 16,* 22–239.

Selnow, G. & Crano,W. (1986). Formal versus informal group affiliations: implications for drug use among adolescents. *Journal of Studies on Alcohol, 47,* 48–52.

St. Mary S. & Russo, T. (1989). *A Self-Efficacy Scale for Chemical Dependency in Adolescents.* Unpublished thesis, University of Wisconsin, River Falls.

Woodside, M. (1983). Children of alcoholic parents: inherited and psychosocial influences. *Journal of Psychiatric Treatment and Evaluation, 5,* 531–537.

8
A Treatment Program for Children with Conduct Disorders

Brian A. Glaser
Arthur M. Horne

Introduction and Overview

By definition, conduct disordered youth violate family, school, and societal rules. Social incompetence, peer rejection, substance abuse, depression, academic failure, suicidal behavior, and an increased probability of physical injury and premature death are frequent complications. Family, school, and community resources are strained by the repercussions of the chronic nature of this disorder. In 1986 more than 1.4 million juveniles were arrested for nonindex crimes (vandalism, drug abuse, running away) and almost 900,000 for index crimes (larceny, theft, robbery, assault, forcible rape). The cost to society includes not only the funds required for repair and/or replacement of material goods and the health services necessary for victims, but also the $1 billion per year that is necessary to maintain the juvenile justice system (Feldman, Caplinger, & Wodarski, 1983). And, of course, the number of antisocial acts resulting in monetary loss and/or victim suffering committed by children and adolescents far exceeds the number of reported crimes. It is estimated that about 4 percent of boys under age 18 exhibit diagnosable disorders of conduct, and approximately two-thirds of those boys will continue to display antisocial behavior into adulthood (American Psychiatric Association, 1987).

The present intervention was designed to be a flexible, multidimensional approach that addresses the problems of academic characteristics, individual child characteristics, family factors, and social resources. Due to the refractory nature of this disorder, we have chosen several delimitations (or druthers) to our work. First, we prefer to work with children at the elementary and middle school level, where conduct problems appear to become firmly entrenched through association with deviant peers. We feel that early identification is imperative. As a result, we work with elementary and middle schools to identify aggressive/disruptive children. Second, we want the intervention to be effective at home and at school. Further, we want treatment effects to be maintained. As a result, treatment is not clinic-bound. We recommend that clinicians become very familiar with schools and neighborhoods. They should also be comfortable with the notion of entering the home. Third, we have found a social learning family therapy approach to be most effective (Horne & Sayger, 1990; Sayger, Horne, Passmore, & Walker, 1988). Of course, we don't always get our druthers. We often work with older children and encounter roadblocks and detours throughout treatment. Our effort here is to describe the intervention process in general, as well as some specific applications for particular types of conduct problems.

Theory and Research

Treatment of conduct disorders may take a variety of forms, depending upon the mission and setting of the service provider (private practice, school, court, community mental health center, child protective service). The most common models of intervention include individual therapy, group therapy, behavior therapy, problem-solving skills, pharmacotherapy, residential treatment, family therapy, parent training, or community-wide interventions (Kazdin, 1987). Conduct disorder is very stable and difficult to change, so a variety of interventions are called for. The existence of so many interventions reflects the experimentation and diversity of approaches to a most difficult problem, but is also indicative of the lack of a clearly defined intervention that has been demonstrated to be consistently effective with a high rate of success. Some treatment providers use only one approach, but most providers use a combination of approaches, in part because there is considerable overlap among the interventions. At the core of effective interventions is a behavioral focus.

Behavior therapy has been the intervention of choice in the majority of empirically based evaluations of treatment programs focusing on conduct disorders. Behavior therapy emphasizes the learning of new behaviors and the reduction of maladaptive ones through reinforcement of successive approximations of the desired outcome, and either extinction or punishment for dysfunctional behaviors. The structure for the learning experience has ranged from maximum security in a tightly controlled correctional environment utilizing token economies and elaborate systems of punishment, to group and individual interviews in clinic or school settings utilizing social reinforcement and role playing.

Extensive reviews of the effectiveness of behavioral intervention programs have been written. Summaries of early work in a variety of settings have been provided by Costello (1972), Braukmann and Fixsen (1975), Burchard and Harig (1976), and Stumphauzer (1973). These reviews provided information about the effectiveness of behavior therapy, primarily in structured settings characterized by close control over the delivery of services and the general environment. An example is Achievement Place in Lawrence, Kansas, a community setting program of group foster care for adjudicated juveniles. The system utilized professionally trained teaching parents who attempted to correct behavioral deficits through modeling, practice, and instruction, using a token system. While these early systems of behavioral intervention demonstrated the effectiveness of behavior change while clients were involved in the system, there were several drawbacks to the approach. First, the process was usually quite expensive and required the development of a delivery service that provided for control and security. Second, the behavior changes that occurred frequently did not generalize beyond the treatment center.

In reviewing the treatment programs completed through 1975, Patterson, Reid, Jones, and Conger (1975) found behavioral/social learning family therapy approaches to be effective for reducing conduct disorder behaviors of the child identified as the problem in the family, and also found that treatment had generalized to other family members, including siblings. Further, parents began to see their child's behavior as more positive, and parents became more effective at providing rewards for appropriate behavior and punishments for acting-out behavior. Overall, mothers seemed more satisfied with their children and rated the family as happier, and fathers developed a more influential role in the family by controlling coercive actions of the child.

In the years since, Patterson has continued to examine treating families with antisocial children, including examining specific treatment conditions. He has conducted carefully controlled studies to examine the effects of treatment versus control group outcome, treatment versus placebo controls in working with families with stealers, and treatment with other forms of deviant behavior (Patterson, 1982). In addition, other researchers have carried out programs to replicate his research with equally positive results (Fleischman & Horne, 1979; Sayger et al., 1988), and some have extended his work by addressing additional components of treatment and evaluation (Fleischman, Horne, & Arthur, 1983; Forgatch & Patterson, 1989; Horne & Sayger, 1990; Kazdin, 1987).

Attempts to intervene during adolescence have resulted in minimal success. While some treatment programs targeting early-to-late adolescents have shown some initial success, the follow-up results have been less encouraging (Kazdin, 1987; Patterson, 1986). Interventions that have demonstrated more effectiveness aim at influencing children at an earlier age and address others involved in the child's life: parents, teachers, and sometimes peers (Fleischman, Horne, & Arthur, 1983; Forehand, Wells, & Greist, 1980; Patterson et al., 1975).

Although the picture looks rather unencouraging for changing well-established patterns of antisocial behavior in older adolescents, research in the last decade has provided some grounds for optimism about our ability to prevent the development of full-blown chronic conduct disorder in younger children. First, well-designed empirical research studies have provided information about the developmental progressions likely to result in chronic conduct disorder, as well as correlates of the developing disorder. They have also identified clear markers of high-risk status in children. Second, a number of researchers have demonstrated the efficacy of several interventions in making at least short-term changes in specific types of conduct problems and antisocial behavior.

Attempts to treat conduct problems in children and adolescents can be categorized into three major areas: individual child characteristics, behavior and learning problems of the child in the academic setting, and family management.

Individual Child Characteristics

In treating the individual child, the four areas of social competence outlined by Dodge, Pettit, McClaskey, and Brown (1986)—encoding of social problem interpretation, response search, response decision, and behavioral enactment—have been the primary targets of intervention. Chalmers and Townsend (1990) demonstrated that perspective-taking skills could be successfully taught to conduct-disordered girls. Attempts to teach social problem-solving strategies have been successful, with decreases in antisocial behavior maintained for up to a year (Guerra & Salby, 1990; Kazdin, Bass, Siegel, & Thomas, 1989; Lochman, Burch, Curry, & Lampron, 1984). Guerra and Salby's (1990) study also involved cognitive behavior modification of the youth's outcome expectancies for antisocial behavior and their value of importance to the youth. Lochman and Curry (1986) and Kazdin et al. (1989) showed that these children can benefit from learning strategies for controlling their anger. On the other side, increasing social skills has not always been accompanied by reductions in antisocial behavior (Kazdin, 1987), and maintenance of learned prosocial behavior beyond a year has not been widely documented.

Focusing on a peer approach, Feldman, Caplinger, and Wodarski (1983) demonstrated that involving conduct-disordered youth with well-adjusted boys in social activities that stressed group participation resulted in decreased antisocial behavior. Bowman and Myrick (1987) also reported positive effects of a peer facilitation program in reducing behavior problems in middle childhood children.

Academic Setting

Interventions in the academic setting have shown mixed results. Some evidence exists that suggests that academic remediation has been associated with decreased levels of conduct problem behavior (MacMillan & Kavale, 1986). Wilson and Herrnstein (1985), though, have noted that while academic skills may improve, antisocial behavior is not always reduced. However, instructing teachers in behavior management strategies has been effective both in reducing problem behavior and improving academic performance (Kelley, 1989).

Family Management

Treatments aimed at helping parents manage and discipline their problem children and at altering systemic functioning of the family have shown positive levels of success in decreasing oppositional and conduct problem behaviors in preschool and elementary school-aged children (Kazdin, 1987; McMahon, Forehand, & Greist, 1981). In fact, Forehand and Long (1988) determined that their treated subjects were indistinguishable from normal controls at a seven and one-half year follow-up during adolescence. Sayger et al. (1988) demonstrated the effectiveness of a family intervention utilizing social learning family therapy, which resulted in positive behavioral changes in conduct problem children and improvement in family relationships, family environment, problem solving, and other systemic factors.

Developmental Considerations

Recent research has provided valuable information about specific causal, correlational, and risk factors for chronic antisocial outcome and has set the stage for an even more sophisticated approach to the problem. It is apparent that models of the development of chronic conduct disorder must consider not only the developmental trajectory of the child, but also the possible impact of various parental and family characteristics on each point in the trajectory. A conceptual framework developed by Horne, Norsworthy, Forehand, and Frame (1990) addressed the development of conduct disorders and intervention points to help prevent antisocial behavior from developing. Using a developmental axis, going from birth to adolescence, the model breaks the development of delinquency into two components. The first component, the child's individual developmental progression, depicts the child as having certain genetic predispositions, cognitive potential, and temperament, which may lead to initial conduct problems directly or indirectly through the development of coercive parent–child interactions. If a coercive interactional style develops and is maintained, the child develops only weak bonding to conventional societal norms, increasing the probability of rejecting, and being rejected by, normal peers. At the same time, the child's conduct problems develop into displays of poor social competence (including attributional bias of hostility toward peers, lack of perspective taking, failure to consider alternative solutions to social problem situations, and selection and enactment of inappropriate behaviors), which also result in the child being rejected by normal peers. When peer rejection is sustained over several years, the child will seek a commitment to a deviant peer group in early adolescence. If the child has also failed to develop appropriate academic skills over the grade-school years due to time spent off-task (and perhaps preceding cognitive deficits), by the time she or he reaches adolescence the student will not be invested in school, nor will the adolescence have a successful experience there. The combination of academic failure and association with a deviant peer group provides the final impetus for serious antisocial and illegal behavior.

The second component of the developmental factors contributing to the development of conduct disorders includes the environmental and systemic factors that influence families. Parental and family factors may contribute to the development of chronic conduct disorder in youth, such as existing psychopathology (for example, paternal antisocial behavior), poor family management practices, economic stressors, and marital conflict.

The development of this delinquency model has been presented as though delinquency develops in a linear fashion. In actuality, the factors that contribute to the development of delinquency do not develop linearly; rather, they are interactive in nature and acting at different levels of intensity at different times. These factors occur across time, conditions, and family characteristics and may differentially influence the child's development in various ways at different points.

Each point in this multidimensional model is proposed to be amenable to intervention, resulting in many possible treatments. However, in contrast to previous research that has tended to concentrate on one specific problem area, it is proposed that *every one of these areas in which a child and his family exhibit difficulties must be treated,* in order to reduce the risk of chronic antisocial behavior beyond only temporary time periods. It must be noted, though, that to maximize the probability of detecting treatment efficacy, children and their families should receive treatment only for those areas in which they demonstrate deficits. This underscores the importance of thorough and accurate assessment. In addition, the timing of the intervention must be such that the problem has been consistently present for some time, to minimize the probability of the false-positive identification (a costly error in this type of intervention), but such that the problem has existed for a short enough time to keep the probability of effecting change high. In this model, then, it would appear imperative to intervene with children who have repeatedly been identified as showing conduct problems in the home and school *before* they finish the fourth grade, when such behaviors appear to become firmly entrenched through association with deviant peers.

Previous research has further demonstrated two problems that must be addressed for an intervention to be successful: generalization of treatment effects to the home and school environments, and long-term maintenance of treatment gains. One method for enhancing generalization of treatment effects is home-based and school-based interventions. These appear to be more useful than clinic-based programs. Second, given the resistance of conduct problem behavior to change, it would appear to be necessary to adopt the chronic disease model of treatment suggested by Kazdin (1987). In this case, the child and his family are assumed to require "booster" intervention treatment sessions on a regular basis to prevent the recurrence of past problems and the development of new ones.

In sum, the existing research on the causes of, correlates to, and interventions with conduct disorder in children and adolescents has been synthesized to develop a multidimensional model of development of chronic antisocial behavior. Based on this model, a multifaceted, flexible intervention program is recommended. The intervention utilizes treatment components previously demonstrated to be effective for each of the problems of academic characteristics, individual child characteristics, family factors, and social resources. The intervention components are empirically based, are carefully timed to occur after risk has been established but before antisocial behavior patterns have become entrenched, and are designed to enhance generalization across settings and time.

Treatment Program Overview

The treatment program outlined in this chapter includes the following sessions: Initiation of Therapy, Establishing an Environment for Change, Self-Control Skills, Communication Skills, Discipline, and Generalization and Termination. School Interventions occur throughout the program. Optional sessions regarding Stealing, Elopement, and Truancy are also included.

Presenting therapy in manual form gives the appearance of structure and perhaps rigidity to a program. While we acknowledge the importance of structure, and recognize that it is an important part of the contribution that behavioral and social learning interventions have made to psychotherapy, we pride ourselves on the flexibility of this program, both in tailoring specific interventions for each family and in how the program components are presented. For example, we rarely, if ever, carry out the program as presented here. We have labeled each treatment component as a "session" here for convenience because we often view each component as taking about a session. However, in actual practice the order of presentation changes, not all components are presented to each family, time spent on each component varies depending on the skill level of the parent(s), and content is altered to meet the needs of the family. We have found that the number of sessions required to carry out this program ranges from about 8 in a university-based training clinic with fairly motivated parents to about 26 for home-based family therapy with child protective services–referred physically abusive families (Horne & Sayger, 1990; Sayger et al., 1988).

Session 1—The Initiation of Therapy

Overview

A. Assessment Tasks:
   1. Gather information about *what* people do regarding the presenting problem ("What," not "why," is of interest).
   2. Gather information about cognitive/emotional reactions.
   3. Gather information about sequences and patterns. For example, ask what happens before, during, and after.
   4. Determine what alternative behaviors would be acceptable to the family.
   5. Explore solutions the family has attempted.
   6. Explore family myths.
   7. Establish the strengths of the family.
B. Initial Interview Clinical Skills:
   1. Use open-ended questions.
   2. Paraphrase and summarize.
   3. Communicate empathy.
   4. Provide reassurance and normalize problems.
   5. Acknowledge each family member's position and perspective.
   6. Refuse to accept helplessness and hopelessness.
   7. Break complex problems into manageable units.

The therapeutic intervention process begins with interviewing the identified child or adolescent and the family to determine that the treatment program is appropriate and relevant to the family. At this stage a number of considerations enter into the process, including ascertaining that the family has sufficient personal and family resources to begin work. Families that are experiencing high levels of substance abuse, physical abuse and/or neglect, and/or the lack of basic necessities (food, shelter) will not be able to participate until those shortcomings and problems are addressed. Further, therapist knowledge of the child's level of involvement with other agencies is crucial at this point, for if the child is about to be incarcerated or removed from the home, this will require different levels of intervention. If it is determined that the child is appropriate for the program, then family and individual assessment begins.

Assessment

A thorough assessment of the child's history and current behavior is a critical component of treating conduct disorders. There are four primary areas for assessment of conduct disorders: the child, the family, the school, and the community (see Horne & Sayger, 1990). We routinely collect the Family Environment Scale (Moos & Moos, 1984) and Child Behavior Checklists (Achenbach & Edelbrock, 1983) from the parent and from the school, and other instruments as needed, for example, the Revised Children's Manifest Anxiety Scale (Reynolds & Richmond, 1985), the Self-Description Questionnaire (Marsh, 1988, 1990), the Children's Depression Inventory (Kovacs, 1981), the Personality Inventory for Children (Wirt, Lachar, Klinedinst, & Seat, 1984), and clinical instruments for the parent(s).

It is also crucial to collect information from various settings. For example, academic problems and peer rejection are often associated with conduct disorders. Improving academic performance and peer relations must be an integral part of the treatment program, or the intervention will be less likely to experience success. We feel very strongly that the therapist must consult with the school and community agencies as well as with the family.

Intervention Principles for Assessment

The following is the minimum for beginning therapy:

1. Release of information to consult with teacher(s)
2. Release of information to consult with community agencies (court services, child protective services, other counseling agencies, the Boys Club, and so on).
3. Release of information for medical history from family physician and/or other health care providers
4. Release of information for information from previous treatment efforts
5. Completion of the clinical instruments discussed above.

Maternal depression, substance abuse, poverty, childcare issues, therapist characteristics, and many other factors can contribute to lack of success in therapy. We have become increasingly convinced that there are several common issues and events that serve to interfere with treatment. We attempt to address them from the start of therapy instead of waiting for the family to drop out of treatment.

A component of the assessment process is to have parents and children share positives within the family interaction process. So much time is spent on describing coercive or negative interactions that little time is spent on the positive characteristics of family members. We ask: "If we were to assign you the task of catching your child being good, what would you describe him as doing?" or "What are your child's best qualities?"

Another part of the assessment or intake process is to have each family member describe how they would like things to be different, that is, more positive. This is a particularly important aspect for working with the children, for by having them define positive goals to which they would like to aspire it is possible to have those goals serve as motivators during stressful times. When asking a child to participate in "time out," for example, we can explain that it isn't fun to do, but that they had requested their parents to spend less time yelling and hitting them, and that time out will help accomplish the goal they had established.

Session 2—Establishing an Environment for Change

Overview

We use the handout presented in table 8–1 during our second sessions with parents. It provides the best overview for this session.

Establishing an environment for change, or setting up for success, is part of the initial intervention process of treatment. The major theme of this component is getting started in such a way that the therapeutic process becomes successful from the beginning. This involves some initial activities the families engage in to change the family structure, and targeting a behavior that can be addressed successfully early on in therapy. We have found that helping families achieve a small success early in the therapeutic process, participants become more fully committed to the process. Such a success hooks the participants, and gives them hope. It also provides the therapist with a sample of problem-solving behavior. The initial phase has two parts. The first is to establish with the adolescent and the parents steps to follow to begin experiencing more success in family living. The second part is to define clearly problems to be addressed and initiate the process of carrying out the program.

Intervention Principles Initiating Change

Part I: Improving Family Experiences. 1. Change the environment. This involves having parents and the child work together to identify ways in which the environment might be altered to remove the likelihood of problems. This can range from providing afternoon snacks for children so that they aren't as irritable after school, to putting in a room divider to provide two adolescent children with separate spaces in their bedroom. Most adolescents and families we work with are not particularly insightful when it comes to identifying environmental problems. Thus it becomes a responsibility of the therapist to facilitate the problem solving necessary to develop needed environmental changes.

Table 8–1
Handout for Parents: Establishing an Environment for Change

Before tackling a problem, it sometimes helps if we can step back and look at what may be contributing to the situation. We can then work on changing those things first. Here are some ideas you might want to consider.

1. *Rearrange the environment.* Are there items you could acquire or ways you could rearrange your home to make the desired behavior easier to do?

   _____

   _____

2. *Develop consistent routines.* Children are more comfortable if they know what to expect. Take a look at the most common problems and see if a set routine might help resolve them.

   _____

   _____

3. *Make sure your commands are clear, polite, and understood.* The way we tell children to do something has a big impact on their compliance. Key things to do are: (1) get the child's attention; (2) say exactly what you want; (3) say when you want it; and (4) be polite but firm.

   _____

   _____

4. *Teach new skills.* Sometimes children don't perform the way we'd like because they lack the skills, not the motivation. In what areas could your children use instruction?

   _____

   _____

5. *Treat each other with care, respect, and love.* This may mean biting your tongue, or, conversely, mentioning behavior that may otherwise be taken for granted.

   _____

   _____

6. *Strengthen marital ties.* When your marriage is strong, it is easier to work together to solve child-management problems. What are some ways you could strengthen your relationship?

   _____

   _____

7. *Improve parental coordination.* How can you share responsibilities and support each other's efforts?

   _____

   _____

8. *Encourage parental growth and well-being.* We all need time for ourselves, away from our children. What are some personal interests you could pursue?

   _____

   _____

2. Develop consistent routines. The term that most typically identifies conduct-disordered children and their families is chaos. There frequently is little or no order to family activities, and routines are haphazardly followed, if at all. Teaching families and children the importance of providing structure in their lives is one of the more difficult tasks, but one of the most important and influential therapeutic activities. It is important to help families to understand that routine is necessary for the initiation of therapy, but that they will not have to live with such order forever. Most families have room for considerable flexibility in their lives, but chaotic families need a heavy dose of structure and order during the early stages of treating children with conduct disorders.

3. Make sure parental commands are clear, polite, and understood. Much of the time that parents talk with their children they use abusive or punitive communication styles. It is important to help them learn basic communication patterns that will facilitate having the children cooperate and participate in making positive change. Most families need considerable modeling and structured rehearsal time to effectively apply these skills. Examples include teaching parents to: (a) say what they mean and mean what they say—"Billy, I want you to stop watching television and come to dinner now"; (b) put time limits on what they do—"Frankie, you may watch TV until the end of this program and then it is to be turned off and you are to take a bath"; (c) make statements instead of asking questions—"Aaron, turn off the TV now," *not* "Aaron, will you turn off the TV now?"

4. Teach the child(ren) any requisite skills necessary to perform the desired task or behavior. We find that children frequently lack the skills and/or ability to do what parents want done because the parents have never taken the time to carefully instruct the children in what is wanted and how it is to be done. Cleaning the bathroom has many steps that young people may not have considered. This activity also includes having parents begin to learn to give operational definitions of tasks they want completed: "I want you to straighten up your room" is vague, whereas "I want the clothes put in drawers or hung in the closet, the bed made, and all things picked up off the floor and put away before you go out for the day" is specific.

5. Treat each other with care, respect, and love. We find that families with aggressive children or conduct-disordered children frequently treat each other very abusively, both physically and verbally. Teaching family members to speak to each other with the same regard and caring that they would employ in the presence of a stranger or a valued neighbor can be an important activity. Just as parents wouldn't likely yell at and hit a neighbor coming into the house with dirt on his shoes, so they should learn to talk to their children in a tone of voice that communicates caring but also firmness and an expectation of responsible behavior: "You tracked dirt into the house. I want you to take off your shoes now, then get the broom and dust

pan and clean the entryway." We encourage family members to treat each other better than family—to interact as nicely as most strangers do!

6. Strengthen marital ties. Our research indicates that approximately half of all two-parent families with conduct-disordered children are experiencing marital difficulties. It is important in the early stages of treatment to explore the marital functioning of the parents and determine if there are ways of improving on the degree of satisfaction each has with the relationship. It is also important, if the family is a single-parent family, to explore how relationships with the estranged parent functions and then to work toward improving parental interactions if they are not satisfactory. Forehand and Long (1991) found that marital separation does not cause conduct disorders, but a highly conflictual divorce or separation contributes to emotional problems for children, including aggressive behavior. It is important that parents, while choosing not to live together, avoid carrying out their conflicts in a manner that impairs their children.

7. Improve parental coordination. Whether parents are together or divorced/separated, it is important that their consistency and cooperation be developed while addressing problems related to conduct-disordered children. This does not have to last forever, but particularly during the initial stages of intervention it is crucial that parents not actively sabotage each other in their efforts to help the children.

8. Encourage parental growth and well-being. During the initial phase of take-off in airplane flight, flight attendants explain that if it is necessary to use oxygen on the plane, parents should always attend to themselves first and then attend to their children, for if parents become incapacitated they will be unable to help their children in any meaningful way. The same is true when working with families with conduct-disordered children. Frequently it is clear that parents have not taken care of themselves or their children very well, and so it is very important for the adults to receive assistance in this area. Of particular importance are the lack of positive feelings about themselves, resulting in poor abilities to care for self or others, as in the case of depression, alcoholism, or other substance abuse. Often, mothers have become isolated and insulated from the outside world and become lethargic and incapacitated, unable to care for themselves or others. Helping them to develop and become stronger is an important function in the early stages of therapy.

Part II: Defining the Problem

1. Target a minor behavior that you as the therapist feel can be addressed quickly and efficiently.
2. How does the family approach the problem?
3. How does the family deal with the problems that emerge?
4. How is the problem resolved?

5. Teach them how to generalize the skills developed and used in setting up for success to more major issues. That is, how does the family approach the issue, where do problems emerge, and how does the family resolve conflict?

6. Let us offer an example: One family we were working with had been referred by child protective services. There was a great amount of dysfunction in the family, with many, many issues to address. The first behavior targeted was the family involvement surrounding the washing of the youngest child's hair. This seven-year-old girl protested loudly and cried profusely when her long hair was being washed. Hair washing inevitably evolved into a loud, angry argument between mother and daughter. The live-in boyfriend would join in. Oldest sister, aged 15, would then begin arguing with the live-in boyfriend. Soon, everyone in the household was screaming and shouting. This ritual took place every Tuesday and Saturday night. Setting aside all other issues, the therapist and family worked together to make Tuesday and Saturday evening less conflictual. By successfully addressing this escalating chain of events, conflict within the home was lessened, all parties to therapy benefited, and credibility for the therapeutic process was established. Therapy was off to a good start.

Session 3—Self-Control Skills

Overview

1. Teach problem-solving sequence.
2. Explain the role emotions play in everyday life.
3. Explain how thoughts/beliefs/attitudes determine emotions and behavior.
4. Teach parents to modify their self-talk.
5. Teach relaxation skills.
6. Teach self-control skills to the target child and siblings.

People who are not able to control themselves very effectively are generally not efficient at helping control others either. This is the case with families with conduct disorders: parents generally lack self-control skills themselves and so are unable to pass them on to their children. There are several steps in teaching families with a conduct-disordered child how to develop more effective self-control skills.

Problem-Solving Sequence

One of the most important steps to take is to teach family members a problem-solving sequence modified from reality therapy: (1) What is my goal?; (2) What am I doing?; (3) Is what I'm doing helping me to achieve my goal?; and (4) If not, what can I do differently? This exercise is generally very helpful because it assists parents to get in touch with the fact that what they are doing isn't working. If it was working, they wouldn't be coming in for assistance and wouldn't be having conflicts with community agencies.

The following sample dialogue illustrates how to introduce the idea of a problem-solving sequence.

Therapist: Mr. Jones, exactly what do you want out of your son?"
Jones: "I want him to cooperate, to mind. I want him to get along with the rest of the family."
Therapist: "And what do you do?"
Jones: "Well, I yell at him and tell him he's got to do it or I'm gonna whack him."
Therapist: "Is it working? That is, does he do what you want, is your goal being met?"
Jones: "No, but he can't just get away with what he does. He minds for a little bit, but then goes back to the same old stuff."
Therapist: "So what you do works briefly, but in the long run doesn't and so you would be willing to consider some other steps that might get him to cooperate more?"
Jones: "Yeah, but I don't know what else to do."

At this point, family members are amenable to learning other things to do that will prevent the same cycle from continuing.

Explain the Role Emotions Play in Daily Life

The role of an emotion is to motivate us to do something. Sometimes, though, the emotion is so strong, as with anger, or so debilitating, as with depression, as to cause people to act in ways they later regret. Putting emotions in the context of the problem and determining how to manage the emotion is very important.

Explain How Thoughts/Beliefs/Attitudes Determine Emotions and Behavior

Most parents attribute their emotions and behavior to the environment: "He was so bad he made me so angry I had to hit him." Helping parents see that how we perceive the situation, how we evaluate the environment, influences our thinking and behavior, is crucial to helping them establish better self-control skills. We teach them that thoughts lead to emotions:

Thought	*Emotion*
He's mean and selfish and always has to have his own way.	Anger, hurt, depression
He's not able to do the things he wants and so he acts out; I'll need to help him get his work done so he will be calmer.	Calm, helpful

At this point, it is important to generate examples of what has been said in earlier session(s). During the assessment session and the session on environmental change, observe family interactions. If possible, film or tape interactions and play back sections for the family to illustrate family interaction patterns. Take specific comments from earlier sessions and play them back, then discuss with all the family members the way in which they each think about a situation, how they emotionally react consistent with their feelings, and how they behave consistently with their feelings. This helps them learn the ABC's of emotions:

A. A situation occurs.
B. Parents think about the situation, or have beliefs about what they observe.
C. They develop emotional responses consistent with their thoughts: angry thoughts lead to angry feelings, depressed thoughts lead to depressed feelings, and so on.
D. People behave consistently with how they feel: angry people act angry, depressed people act depressed.
E. There are consequences for the way people behave. This outcome frequently leads to a "family dance" in that the family members experience an ongoing cycle of emotion, behavior, consequence, emotion, behavior, consequences without breaking the cycle.

Teach Parents to Modify Their Self-Talk

Helping parents to see how their self-talk contributes to their emotional and behavioral distress, then practicing new ways of framing the situation, is crucial. At this point, it is useful to introduce a homework assignment, the listing of upsetting and calming thoughts for the week.

Upsetting Thoughts	*Calming Thoughts*
Anger	Be consistent. It will get better.
This is too much work. I can't handle this.	Take one day at a time. It will get easier.

In this exercise, parents list the thoughts that upset them on the left side of the paper, and on the right they write down thoughts that they could have had that would have been more calming to them. If they were able to generate the calming thoughts to begin with, they simply write those down.

Teach Relaxation Skills

Once parents have learned that their previous attempts weren't working, have learned to identify their self-talk, and have learned to challenge their upsetting thoughts with calming thoughts, they are ready to replace their former actions with an alternative: relaxing and calming down. The goal of this level of intervention is not to immobilize parents, but to break the coercive cycle that has existed in the family. The point here is that families can learn to respond even to negative situations in a more calm and reasoned manner. There are numerous relaxation programs available, but we use a very brief one:

> "Close your eyes, get comfortable."
>
> "Attend to your breathing."
>
> "As you breathe in and out, slow your breathing down."
>
> "As you inhale, do so deeply, and slowly count from 1 to 10; when you reach 10 exhale fully."
>
> "After you have exhaled, slowly count from 1 to 10; when you reach 10 inhale fully."
>
> "Continue this cycle until you feel calm, relaxed. Then open your eyes."

Teach Self-Control Skills to the Target Child and Siblings

We like to work with the entire family as much as possible. Our experience has been, though, that for the self-control skills section, the children are often so disruptive that teaching self-control skills is not possible because there is too much confusion to be effective. We frequently separate the children and their parents, working first with the parents, then with the children. If the family is one that can focus on the activity together, though, it is good to address the entire issue with all family members at once.

The techniques for teaching self-control vary depending upon the age of the child. For very young children (and some adults) we use the turtle technique. For older children and adolescents, we may use the Coke machine technique or the Nintendo technique. The following is an example:

Therapist: "Do you always do what others tell you to do?"
Adolescent: "No, man, nobody tells me what to do."

Therapist: "Even other kids?"

Adolescent: "Nobody. I don't take nothing off of nobody."

Therapist: "Tell me what starts a fight."

Adolescent: "Somebody gets into my face. I don't like it when somebody gets into my face."

Therapist: "Is it usually somebody you know?"

Adolescent: "Sure."

Therapist: "And they know you don't like them in your face."

Adolescent: "Yeah, they know. Everybody knows."

Therapist: "So they know that when they get in your face, there's going to be a fight?"

Adolescent: "Yeah."

Therapist: "So you let them tell you what to do?"

Adolescent: "No. What do you mean?" (adolescent grins)

Therapist: "You're like Super Mario."

Adolescent: "Huh?"

Therapist: "You know how when you push the B button and Mario jumps? That's what your friends do. They push your button and you jump. When they want to watch you fight, they push your B button and get down into your face and you do just what they want you to do. If they want to, they'll push the right button and run you off a cliff like Mario because you don't think for yourself. You're like Mario: you let someone else decide for you. You just obey others, not yourself. You put on a show for them when they want it."

Adolescent: "It's not like that. I just fight to defend myself."

Therapist: "OK. I'm not telling you not to fight. If you get something from the fighting, let me know. From where I stand, it looks like the fighting causes lots of trouble. Trouble with the school. Trouble in your family. Trouble from your probation officer. Do your want to keep fighting?"

Adolescent: "No man. I only fight because they get down in my face."

Therapist: "So how would you like to learn to push your own buttons?"

Adolescent: "Yeah."

Therapist: "During the next week I want you to pay attention to what happens when you think there may be a fight. I want to know what happens before, during, and after. What are you thinking when a fight starts?"

Adolescent: "Nothing."

Therapist: "So you just put it on cruise control?"

Adolescent: "Yeah."

Therapist: "Well, I want you to practice saying something to yourself. I want you to say something like, 'I'm in charge of myself here. I won't let him blow my cool. Only I can blow my cool.' In your own words, what would you say or rap to yourself?"

(Adolescent and Therapist collaborate on the individualized self-talk, and then practice it.)

Therapist: "O.K. Now that you have that down, I want you to practice it this week. I also want you to practice it when things get tense. Now, I'm not telling you that you can't fight. I know that you may need to defend yourself. All I want you to do is to make the decision yourself, not let others push your B button."

The following are the intervention principles for anger control for children:

1. Attempt to illustrate to the child or adolescent that others are currently controlling his or her temper, and that there are definite advantages to controlling one's own temper.
2. Collaborate with the child or adolescent in developing an individualized cognitive structure or strategy of calming self-talk to employ when child becomes angry.
3. Teach relaxation behaviors that are incompatible with anger and acting-out behavior.
4. Do all of the above in the child's own words. That is, have the child tailor his or her own anger control program.

Session 4—Communication Skills

Overview

A. Do:
   1. Speak your piece.
   2. Use "I" messages instead of "You" messages.
   3. Be specific.
   4. Be brief.
   5. Check to see that others are listening.
   6. Find out what others are thinking.
   7. Show that you're listening.
   8. Ask questions if you're confused.
   9. Stop and let others know when communication is breaking down.
B. Avoid:
   1. Put-downs
   2. Blaming
   3. Denial
   4. Defensiveness
   5. Communicating hopelessness
   6. Mindreading

7. Talking for others
8. Sidetracking (Fleischman, Horne, & Arthur, 1983, pp. 175–181).

The activities in the therapeutic process thus far have included (1) assessment, (2) changing the environment, and (3) developing self-control skills. Each of these activities had a specific focus, but there was also an emphasis at each level of learning better communication skills. At this point, we move to directly teaching more effective communication skills among the parents and children. The process works best if in previous sessions audio and/or video tapes have been made of the family interacting so that excerpts may be used with family members to demonstrate how their past and current communication style has led to coercive interactions that have been painful and less effective for satisfying family living.

Intervention Principles for Child Communication Skills

1. The therapist observes interaction between parent and child, and between therapist and child. The therapist then determines their level of social and communication skills. If deficiencies are noted, then basic communication skills, such as maintaining eye contact, using the appropriate tone of voice, and so on, must be taught.

2. Parents are informed of all techniques.

3. "I" statements are taught to all children. The rule is that the word "you" is banned.

4. Children are taught to respond to the parental inquiry "why?" with "There is no answer to that question."

5. These behaviors are taught in a lighthearted, fun manner. For example, the therapist "conspires" with the child in an alliance to carry out the generalization of the behaviors.

The following is a dialogue that illustrates the intervention principle for teaching communication skills to children.

Therapist: "Does your parent think you are a polite kid?"
Child: "No. She's on me all the time about being rude."
Therapist: "OK. I want you to try an experiment this week. Are you willing to try a trick on your parent? You have said that your parent doesn't notice when you're doing good. Let's check it out. Here's what I want you to do. I want you to be super polite this week, but I don't want you to tell your parent what you're doing. When she asks you to do something, I want you to jump up and do it right away. I want you to say 'please' and 'thank you.' No yelling. No lip. I want you to smile and make eye contact with your parent. Do you know how to do these things?"

Child: "Yeah, but . . . "

Therapist: "Yeah but . . . what?"

Child: "All the time?"

Therapist: "Oh no! Just one week. Just from right now until I see you next week. I wouldn't ask you to do this all the time. I just wonder if anyone would notice. What do you think?"

Child: "She won't know."

Therapist: "Are you willing to try?"

Child: "Yeah."

Session 5—Developing Positive Family Interactions

Overview

1. Encourage statements of thanks, praise, or appreciation.
2. Teach appropriate touching.
3. Teach selective attending skills.
4. Consider instituting a point system.
5. Consider instituting an allowance.
6. Consider developing a behavioral contract.

In general, families with children demonstrating conduct disorders are not pleasant. They have had a lifetime cycle of coercive interactions which, hopefully, have been broken to some extent by this time in the therapeutic process. Thus far parents and children have participated in the intake interview, in which they described positive aspects of each other's behavior; in the process of changing the environment, in which they learned to prevent many problems from developing; and in the communications skills training, in which they learned to develop better communication patterns. During the next step, developing positive family interactions, parent and children again move toward making the family environment a more positive, less coercive experience.

Specific steps in the process of developing positive family interaction are described in the sections below.

Statements of Thanks, Praise, or Appreciation

First, teach parents to be as sincere as possible. Second, teach them not to mention any history of poor performance in reference to current success. Third, teach them to focus on what was done well. Never say, "You did a good job, but . . . " If the task is incomplete or needs more attention, the parent should substitute a pause for the "but." Fourth, teach parents to use specific and general praise. Specific praise lets the child know what exactly is expected. General praise strengthens relationships

Physical Contact

One of the research projects associated with our work was done by Leslie James. Whereas she had predicted that highly functional families would touch much more frequently than highly aggressive families, in her study of touch we learned that both types of families *touch the same amount*. But there were dramatic differences in *how family members touched*. In functional families family members used affectionate or affirming touches whereas in aggressive families family numbers used touch to control, direct, or reprimand. Touch is very important to family members, but aggressive family members need to be taught specific methods of positive interaction. Teaching physical contact between parent and child is a tricky business. Trust is an issue. Children who have been struck do not necessarily appreciate uninvited touch. Education is often called for. For example, one mother was referred by child protective services as abusive and neglectful. The target child was a 6 year old boy. His 5 year old sister was also in the home, but was not the target of abuse. Therapy was conducted in the family's home. The boy presented many behavioral problems, both at home and at school. The younger sister was quite well behaved. Though there were many contributing factors to the boy's behavior problems, the therapist noticed that the little girl often snuggled with her mother, and the mother offered her much affection. The little boy frequently approached his mother, but she rebuffed him. At one point, the therapist asked her to hold the boy. She did so with obvious distress. She grimaced and appeared most uncomfortable. When asked about this, she admitted that she was concerned about affecting his sexual orientation by offering him too much attention. This myth was readily dispelled in therapy.

Attention

Teaching parents to attend selectively to their children is a very important skill for them. Most parents of conduct-disordered children attend to the children most often when the children are misbehaving. Oftentimes by attending to the child's aggressive behavior, the parents inadvertently reinforce the behavior they would like to reduce or extinguish. A mother, for example, who asks a child to straighten up his room, and then goes and helps the child when he begins to whine, may be teaching the child to whine in order to get attention and also that he doesn't have to do the work alone if he whines enough. Teaching parents to "catch the kid being good" is a skill taught to parents to help them learn that they can use their interpersonal interactions to increase the positives, rather than the negatives.

Point Systems

In addition to teaching the social reinforcement procedures described above, it is important to include more formal systems of increasing positive behaviors within the family. For younger children, point systems are very powerful incentives. Point systems are developed to help the parents and children keep track of a desired behavior, its frequency of occurrence, and the consequence for engaging in the desired behavior. Point systems are very powerful for establishing the behavior that parents would like to see demonstrated, but may be tedious and time-consuming to carry out. The positive aspect about point systems, though, is that they are perceived very positively by children and have an immediate impact if carried out properly. Point systems may use social reinforcers (time to read together, time to play together), tokens (stickers, poker chips), may be immediate (earn points for the next hour) or distant (save up points for summer vacation), and will always be designed to meet the specific interests and abilities of the family members. To institute an effective point system, the parents must:

1. Decide which behaviors earn points.
2. Determine how many points can be earned for each desirable behavior.
3. Select a list of special treats or privileges as rewards.
4. Decide how many points must be earned to receive a special privilege or treat and how often it can be earned.
5. Monitor the child's behavior and award points.
6. Review points and either reward the child or withhold privileges.

Allowances

A more advanced form of the point system is the allowance. Money is a very powerful motivator for young people and serves to very effectively increase positive behaviors when they too are contingently related. The steps for instituting an allowance system include:

1. Determine how much allowance may be earned on a daily or weekly basis.
2. Select chores or tasks the child will be responsible for completing to earn the allowance.
3. If need be, assign cents or dollar values to each task.
4. Develop a system for tracking the daily or weekly chores.
5. Determine how often the allowance will be given.

Contracts

Another form of reinforcer, and one that is more sophisticated than point systems or allowances, is the contract. Contracts involve having the parents and child negotiate what is acceptable and agreeable to each party. For example, "We agree you may go out on Friday and Saturday nights if you get your homework done during the week, have no fights reported at school, and will be in by midnight" or "You may use the car on Friday night if you cut the grass by Friday afternoon."

An important component of the contract system is that each member of the family stands to benefit from the process.

Intervention Principles for Developing Positive Family Interactions

1. The therapist must carefully consider the history and specific characteristics of the family and its members before initiating interventions during this session. Some of these interventions, such as touching, require special sensitivity.

2. The developmental level of the child must be considered when selecting interventions during this session.

3. As with all interventions described in this chapter, each must be specially tailored to fit the family. In the end, the family must design the intervention so that they can take responsibility for it.

Session 6—Discipline

Overview

1. Teach parents to use natural and logical consequences.
2. Teach parents about Grandma's Law.
3. If time-out is indicated, develop a detailed plan tailored for the specific needs of the family.
4. Consider other logical consequences such as assigning extra work and taking away privileges.
5. As with all interventions in this chapter, it is important to anticipate problems by troubleshooting.

To this point in the therapeutic process little attention has been directed specifically at discipline, even though behavior problems were the motivating factor for families to initiate involvement in therapy. The intent of the treatment program is to reduce coercive interactions and increase positive aspects of living in families. At this point we go back to the original reason for referral and review the initial requests for help and desired changes sought in the family. Generally, we can expect more than half of the coercive behaviors of the children to have been either significantly reduced or totally eliminated by this point, and many of the changes the family members indicated they desired during the assessment stage are now in operation within the family. Our experience is that defining the problem and desired changes, establishing an expectation for success and changing environmental conditions within the family, learning effective communication skill patterns, and reinforcing positive behaviors results in changes in the family, with the entire environment of the family becoming more positive. When we increase positive interactions, we cause a corresponding decrease in negative interactions. There will, however, still be problems to be addressed, and the disciplinary process addresses those areas more directly than we have to this point.

There are several specific disciplinary approaches that have been very effective for working with conduct-disordered children. While there is considerable overlap among them, certain methods are most appropriate for particular problem areas.

Natural and Logical Consequences

Natural and logical consequences involves teaching parents and children that there are consequences for their actions. Natural consequences are what occurs naturally: if a child goes out into the cold without a jacket, he will get cold, a natural consequence. A child who stays up too late at night will be sleepy the next day. A logical consequence is one that is determined by people: a child who does not study will not pass a test. The child who drives too fast gets a speeding ticket. These are logical since a rule has been established and people are informed of the rule and the consequences for not fulfilling the requirements of the rule or for violating the rule.

Natural and logical consequences are very powerful and readily available, but family members often do not use them effectively. This is often because family members are feeling they must be punitive more than the circumstances will provide, or they are interested in demonstrating their parental power and want to do it forcefully. Natural and logical consequences are particularly appropriate for irresponsible or immature behaviors and help children learn that there are consequences for their behavior.

An example of a logical consequence that is frequently used in homes is the "Saturday Box." The rule is that any item left around on the floor or anyplace else it does not belong will go into the Saturday Box. It remains in the box until Saturday, at which time the Saturday Box is emptied and all things are put away. When children have to wait until Saturday to get their favorite sneakers, they remember the next week to put them away instead of leaving them on the living room floor.

Grandma's Law

A form of logical consequences is Grandma's Law, or the Premack Principle. The rule is that the person must engage in a less desirable task before being able to engage in a more desirable one:

> You must eat your peas, *then* you may have dessert.
> Do your homework, *then* you can go out and play.
> Clean up the kitchen, *then* you may watch television.

Our experience with Grandma's Law is that almost every parent knows the law, but applies it in reverse order. We regularly encounter parents who say: "OK, you can have some cookies now, but you have to eat your dinner later." Or: Ok, you can watch television for a while, but then you have to do your homework." Teaching parents to be consistent and predictable on this one is the toughest part of implementing the method.

Time Out

Another example of a logical consequence is Time Out. This is perhaps the most powerful of disciplinary methods and works exceptionally well, even though many family members (and therapists!) argue that it doesn't work.

Parents come to therapy to learn how to control their child's behavior, the punishment has a certain face validity to them. Though we fully understand the importance of consequences to behavior, we value the other components of treatment. Time Out is our "fat lady" in that it comes near the end of treatment. First, we want parents to learn how to talk with their children, how to touch their children, how to monitor their behavior, and how to be supportive.

Much has been written about Time Out, and it is rare in therapy that a parent does not report already having tried it unsuccessfully. We have had much luck in tailoring Time Out for the specific family. That is, Time Out in general does not seem to work for any family. Time Out tailored for the specific family being seen seems to work well. The plan must include a detailed description of the target behavior(s), the Time Out location, what will be said, length of time, what behaviors might extend the time, what to say when Time Out is over, and what might go wrong. The following is a partial transcript that illustrates the importance of tailoring the Time Out procedure.

Mother of 7 year old: "Yes, we already tried Time Out. Fact of the matter is, our last counselor recommended it, but it was a disaster. We used the bathroom and he smashed the porcelain toilet. He totally destroyed the bathroom, and the remodeling job was very expensive. I'm afraid that we're just not up to it."

Therapist: "Wow! Yeah, it sounds like it wasn't very effective. It helps me to learn by talking about what went wrong. It would really help me to go step by step with what happened there so that we don't make the same mistake."

Mother: "Well, the damage aside, it does not seem to work well because I can't do it when his stepfather isn't home."

Therapist: "Why?"

Mother: "Because I can't get him into Time Out."

Therapist: "Why?"

Mother: "Because his behavior gets so out of control that he would harm me if I attempted to put him somewhere."

Therapist: "Do you mean that you generally attempt to place him in Time Out when the tantrum is going on?"

Mother: "Of course!"

Therapist: "Why of course?"

Mother: "Because it wouldn't be fair to put him in Time Out for minor behavior problems. I always wanted to be certain that he was really headed for a tantrum before I'd do it."

Therapist: "So you would only put him in Time Out when he was already in the middle of a big one?

Mother: "Yes. I think it's important to be fair."

Therapist: "When he throws big ones, do you usually see them coming, or do they happen out of the blue?"

Mother: "Oh no. I see them coming for miles. I just keep hoping that I can say something or that something will happen to avert it."

Therapist: "Is there something you notice early on, like a sinking in your heart or a feeling in your gut that he's going to have one?"

Mother: "Oh yeah!"

Therapist: "This week, I have an assignment for you. I want you to err on the side of unfairness. Every time you feel a little queasy about his behavior, and a few times even when you don't, I want you to send him to Time Out. Now let's troubleshoot about what might go wrong with the Time Out plan . . .

Therapist: (to child)"I want you to help by rehearsing the Time Out procedure with your parent. Sometimes you will be asked to go to Time Out during the next week. I want you to cooperate. When you come back next week, I want you to tell me how it went." (For young children, we ask them to report on how well the parent follows our directions. Children seem to really enjoy the opportunity to report on the parent's behavior.)

Trouble Shooting. When following up on the previous week's assignment, it is important to determine what happened before, during, and after the implementation or application of the assigned intervention or technique. We trouble shoot all areas of the treatment program. We have included this process under this section because the following example illustrates what we mean by "trouble shooting." With the Time Out assignment described above, the mother reported that her child cooperated well with the exercise. Only one major tantrum had occurred during the week, and he had cooperated with the procedure. We proceeded to explore the before, during, and after descriptions of the major tantrum incident as well as the rehearsal and other applications of the time out procedure. The mother in this case noted that when she announced that Time Out had ended, the misbehavior would reerupt. She found this frustrating and confusing. Apparently, her announcement cued further misbehavior. We encouraged her to let the bell sound of her kitchen timer signal the end of Time Out, and for her to explain that once he heard it, Time Out was over. She tried this, and then finally settled on just opening his door without saying anything when the Time Out was over.

We encourage parents not to talk with the child or to lecture the child about misbehavior after Time Out. Rather, the parent is encouraged to open the door or otherwise signal the end, and then proceed with a "business as usual" attitude.

The intervention principles for Time Out include the following steps:

1. The rationale behind Time Out must be explained to the parent. It is important that parents not misuse this technique.
2. The plan must include a detailed description of the target behavior(s) that will result in Time Out.
3. The Time Out location must be determined and safety-proofed.
4. What will be said before putting the child in Time Out must be determined.
5. The length of time in Time Out must be determined. We recommend three to five minutes of quiet behavior before ending Time Out. This, of course, varies with the age of the child.
6. Agreement on what behaviors might extend the Time Out must be determined.
7. How to signal the end of Time Out, that is, what to say or what not to say, must be determined. Scolding must *not* follow Time Out.
8. If the child makes a mess of the Time Out location, the child must clean it before coming out.
9. If the child was sent to Time Out for noncompliance, the child must complete the requested task immediately upon leaving Time Out.

10. The Time Out procedure should be rehearsed with the child before there is a reason to use it. Rehearsal should occur in the session and at home with the children both pretending to cooperate and pretending to resist.
11. Troubleshoot what might go wrong.

Assigning Extra Work

This is another form of a logical consequence, and is particularly useful when children do not comply with earlier disciplinary techniques. When a child refuses to comply with Time Out and disregards Grandma's Law, it is often useful to assign him work to do, with the understanding that he cannot engage in more desired activities he would like to do until he finishes his work. This has been an effective disciplinary method to use with more serious behavior problems such as lying, stealing, or damaging property. This method also provides an opportunity for the child to provide some form of restitution for the trouble caused by the behavior.

Taking Away Privileges

Another logical consequence to be considered is taking away privileges. This is an important method to use since Time Out, Grandma's Law, and assigning extra work will not always work with all problems. Taking away privileges is particularly relevant if the child tests the parent's use of Time Out or Grandma's Law. It involves disengaging from any power struggle that may occur, and instead informing the child that you want him to comply at once, and that if noncompliance continues, there will be a loss of a privilege, for example, "I want you to take out the garbage now. If you don't you will lose TV privileges for the evening" or "If you come home late from visiting with John, you will lose the use of your bike (Nintendo or whatever) for a day."

The tendency of many parents is to extend the period of time too long ("You'll lose TV privileges for a year", or to do this in a threatening manner ("If you don't behave, I'll . . ."). The parents should be calm, steady, and nonaversive, but firm.

Some Final Comments on Discipline, Punishment, and Aggression

The hallmark of conduct disorder is aggression. We believe that gaining control of the child's behavior depends on the accumulation of skills in several parenting areas. These include communication skills, anger control techniques, use of praise and other forms of social reinforcement, knowledge of natural and logical consequences, and effective use of Time Out. We value punishment, but teach it last because we think these parents often need to learn how to listen, to control their own emotions, and to accentuate the positive. For example, Wolfe (1985) discussed the "not necessarily more aversive but less positive" hypothesis regarding abusive parents. He cited research in which no differences in aversive interactions between parent and child in abusive and nonabusive homes have been found. On the other hand, a striking paucity of positive interactions in the abusive homes has been observed. Some of the data from our research suggest that this is true for cognitive patterns, at least for the child (Glaser, 1989). Thus, we teach the communication skills, anger control techniques, use of praise, and other forms of social reinforcement before moving into the more aversive contingencies. Further, we contract with each family not to use any type of corporal punishment while in therapy.

Concurrent to Therapy Sessions— School Interventions

Improving academic performance may be one of the most elusive goals of intervention. Making contact with the child's teacher is obviously important, and we recommend doing it early in treatment. In fact, many of our referrals originate with the teacher, and our clinic is often flooded with referrals in the fall following the initial parent–teacher conferences in our area.

When we contact the teacher, we want his or her concrete descriptions of the behavioral problems observed by the teacher. Getting a concrete description is essential. We asked one very good teacher to give us a simple behavioral goal for a disruptive child in her classroom in order to set up for success. She told us that she would be very happy if the child would just come to the mat during storytime, and not be disruptive. Apparently, he had been wandering about the classroom being disruptive during storytime. We chose this goal because we thought we could get a quick behavioral victory that would seal the alliance among all of us: the teacher, the parent, the child, and the therapist.

We worked with the child individually and encouraged him to go to the mat during storytime, and soon he began to report to the therapist that he was going to the mat. We waited for the teacher to confirm this report, but she did not. After several days, and several indications from the child that he was indeed going to the mat, the therapist asked the teacher if progress was being made toward the goal of going to the mat during storytime. She responded in a regretful tone that although he was indeed going to the mat and that he was not being disruptive, he was not attending to the story. Silly us. We quickly added attending to the child's repertoire, and finally had the "quick" success we were hoping for. The point we wish to make is that concrete descriptions of behaviors, goals, and what it means to meet the goals must be carefully addressed.

We also rely on teacher assessments of academic strengths and weaknesses, and we always ask the teacher whether he or she thinks psychological testing would be helpful. Finally, we ask the teacher how *we* can be of help.

It is extremely important for the clinician to use the best clinical skills during this consultation. Active listening, eye contact, and appropriate use of empathy are essential. We often want to link up the school and the home in order to improve parental monitoring of behavior. One way of doing this is to ask the teacher to send a Daily Report Card home to the parent which gives an account of the child's behavior as well as the homework assignment. The parent and teacher thus can communicate by means of this card. The child is required to be responsible for the card. The report is generally easy to develop, time-efficient for teachers, and communicates well with the parents. Table 8–2 offers a Sample Daily Report Card.

Optional Session—Stealing

Stealing without confrontation of the victim is the top discriminator of conduct disorder according to the DSM-III-R. It is also the most difficult to treat because of the sneakiness of the behavior. Most of it goes undetected, and the behavior itself is very rewarding. The adolescent's explanation for the presence of contraband is almost always plausible: "It belongs to a friend," "I saved for it and got it on clearance," "I've had it for a while," "I traded lunch money for it." Parents want to be reasonable and fair, and they are often willing to accept a plausible explanation. When addressing stealing in treatment, parents must be willing to commit to active monitoring of the child's possessions. To the parent(s), the therapist might say: "You have indicated that your child may be stealing. I know that this is a hard thing to accept. Research tells us that, in general, there is much more stealing going on than parents are aware of, or ever will be aware of, for that matter. If you want to help your child, if you want this behavior to stop, you must make a

Table 8–2
Sample Daily Report Card

Billy Thompson	Math	Social Studies	Science
Desired Behavior			
Attends to and stays on task			
Works independently			
Completes assignments			

0=Did not comply   1=Did comply
Total Points: _____
Comments:

strong commitment to follow through on this simple program that requires daily attention." To the child, the therapist might say, "You have protested that stealing is not a problem, and that there was only the one 'misunderstanding.' Whether or not this is true, your mom is implementing a new program. Here are the rules:

Rule 1. Your mom is going to inventory all of your possessions and make a master list. Then she is going to check off on all of your possessions on a daily basis. This includes all of your money. If you have an item that is not on your list, you must have a receipt. If there is no receipt, then the item will be considered to be contraband. Therefore it will be confiscated and disposed of appropriately. If something is missing, then a full accounting must be made.

Rule 2. You must also account for every penny of your money. Again, if money is missing, you had better have a receipt. If you have too much money, then your mother takes the excess.

Rule 3. Your pockets, wallet, and backpack will be spot-checked. Expect this on a daily basis.

Rule 4. When it is determined that stealing has taken place, you are to face the victim, apologize, and make restitution."

Optional Session—Elopement

Leaving home without permission, or staying out all night, is a common problem encountered by parent's of conduct-disordered children. Obviously, this is a serious, and at times dangerous, behavior. Gaining control of it quickly is essential. An 11 year old in a juvenile detention center recently told the second author that he would wait until his mother went into the bathroom before sneaking out. She had control of him as long as he was in her physical presence, but out of sight, out of mind, so to speak. He reported that the consequences to leaving (being grounded or chewed out) simply weren't effective because when he saw an opening, he would simply skedaddle.

Oftentimes, there are secrets associated with running away. Therapists need to explore the possibility of sexual or physical abuse. Sometimes the secret is the child's sexual orientation. Gay teenagers often meet with parental rejection and harsh punishment. Some of these children chose to run. Therapists need to explore this possibility. The therapist should raise the issue of elopement by saying something like this: The authorities have indicated that continued running from home will lead to _____(child's name) being removed from the home. Neither of you want this. You, _____ (parent's name) have demonstrated control of your child's behavior when he is present. Do you have any ideas how to stop this behavior?" Then brainstorm with the parent and the child.

The intervention principles for elopement include (1) improving parental monitoring skills; (2) improving parent–child communication; (3) determining what events surround elopement, that is, the before, during, and after; and (4) delineating appropriate, potent contingencies.

Deciding whether to hunt for the child must be determined by the individual circumstances and experiences of the family and the child. In some cases it is appropriate to let the child stay out and experience the negative consequences of his or her behavior. One conduct-disordered child came home sadly disappointed that no one came to find him when he hid out in a field and a cold rain fell on him all night long. Another adolescent who spent the night in a detention center experienced the process as frightening and benefited because his parents did not come after him. On the other hand, there are times when the child may be in such dangerous or precarious situations that it would not be appropriate to leave him out in the circumstances. One family we worked with learned their son was staying with a prostitute who provided sex and drugs—it clearly would be inappropriate to not respond to that situation.

An important component to this aspect of treatment is to return to the initial interview. Conduct-disordered adolescents generally want their family lives to be more pleasant and cooperative. When they develop a sense of trust and predictability, which occurs during the first few sessions, they are more amenable to participating in treatment for the various problems encountered. In this area, for example, we encourage the parents to provide a more hospitable living environment and to combine that effort with a sincere threat of placement in an alternative housing situation, such as a group home or a detention center. Faced with the carrot-and-stick approach, most adolescents with whom we have worked have selected the carrot.

Optional Session—Truancy

Hopping school is a common problem. We believe that basic principles of parenting can address this problem.

Intervention Principles for Truancy

Step 1: The parent must talk to school officials. The parent must insist on being notified personally if the child is not present at any point during the school day. In some situations, it may be necessary for the parent to call the school periodically to determine if the child is present. It is important for the parent to form relationships with school officials in order to address this problem. It has been our experience that schools are most responsive when they think the parent cares and is putting forth good-faith effort. We have also intervened as therapists by attending meetings or conferences at school regarding such issues.

Step 2: When notified about an absence, the parent will attempt to locate the child and return him or her to school. Many parents are unable to follow through on this because of employment requirements or lack of resources to conduct a search for the child. However, it is very important to interrupt the behavior and to return the child to school.

Step 3: The parent should escort the child to the appropriate school authority and determine what should happen next.

Tardiness or Refusing to Go to School

Though less serious, this problem is related to the problem of truancy. The disciplinary approaches presented earlier generally work well with the problem.

One student we worked with was unable to wake up in the morning, did not get dressed, failed to fix his breakfast, and was never ready for the bus when it came. We decided to use natural and logical consequences to prepare him for school. We explained that he would have to get up in the morning, get dressed, eat if he wanted to, and be on the front porch when the school bus came, and that if he wasn't ready, his mother would place him on the porch to catch the bus regardless of his state of dress (or undress). The next morning he failed to get up on time, did not dress, and was surprised with his mother put him on the porch. He immediately ran behind the house and hid until the bus was gone. His mother, having anticipated this, went and got him, put him in the car, gave him a sack that had some clothes in it, and told him: "Today only I am driving you to school. When we get there I am putting you out in front of the school regardless of what you are wearing. You may get dressed in the back seat if you wish. This is the only day I am driving you to school. After today, I will walk you to the school bus regardless of how you are dressed." The next morning the student was up and dressed and tardiness disappeared from the repertoire of problems.

Final Sessions—Generalization and Termination

Overview

1. Encourage family to address remaining problems within the family, and to consider addressing some outside the family (for example, work-related or neighborhood-related problems, in order to practice their new skills.

2. Steadily reduce the amount of direction you offer.
3. Help the family broaden its grasp of basic social learning concepts.

After successfully addressing the major targeted behavior, the parents can begin to practice their newfound skills by addressing other behaviors. This may involve the same child, or other children in the home. Some clients have been able to generalize the communication skills to extrafamilial people such as employers.

We address generalization in several ways. First, we want to be certain that parents are able to apply techniques to other problem areas. If we reduce noncompliance at home, can we also increase appropriate playground behavior at the school? Second, we want to be certain they are able to apply a variety of skills in several settings, and so we go from problem area to problem area until it is clear the family members are in control. Third, we reduce the role of the therapist from being an active teacher, to becoming a coach for the family, to finally serving as a consultant. Fourth, we reduce our number of meeting times and attempt to put greater periods of time between sessions. The steps include:

1. Parents begin to decrease formal monitoring of behavior.
2. Parents begin to appropriately use reinforcement and discipline techniques on nontargeted behaviors (generalization).
3. Parents begin to decrease the amount of treatment contacts.
4. The family develops a preventive program.
5. The therapist predicts relapses and prepares clients to reinstate the program.
6. The therapist links the family to other community resources.

Conclusion

Our experience with implementing this program is that considerable clinical acumen is required on the part of the therapist involved. Helping families feel motivated to change, directing critical issues of behavior while providing support and encouragement, and challenging family traditions and beliefs while supporting the family unit, can be very difficult tasks. Therapists considering implementing the program are encouraged to work with another person as a cotherapist or support person for the initial instances of working with aggressive families.

The procedures presented in this chapter are described in a number of sources in the literature related to working with conduct-disordered children, but the material provided here has largely been adapted from two sources, Fleischman, Horne and Arthur (1983) and Horne and Sayger

(1990). Readers are referred to those excellent sources for more extensive elaboration on methods and procedures, as well as research data providing support for the intervention model.

References

Achenbach, T., & Eldelbrock, C. (1983). *Manual for the child behavior checklist and revised child behavior profile.* Burlington, VT: Department of Psychiatry, University of Vermont.

American Psychiatric Association (1987). *The diagnostic and statistical manual of psychiatric diagnoses* (3d ed., rev.). Washington, DC: American Psychiatric Association.

Bowman, R. P., & Myrick, R. D. (1987). Affects of an elementary school peer facilitator program on children with behavior problems. *School Counselor, 34,* 369–378.

Braukman, C. J., & Fixsen, D. L. (1975). Behavior modification with delinquents. In M. Hersen, R. M. Fisher, & P. M. Miller (Eds.), *Progress in behavior modification* (vol. 1). New York: Academic.

Burchard, J. D., & Harig, P. T. (1976). Behavior modification and juvenile delinquency. In H. Leitenberg (Ed.), *Handbook of behavior modification and behavior therapy* (pp. 405–452). Englewood Cliffs, NJ: Prentice-Hall.

Chalmers, J., & Townsend, M. (1990). The effects of training in social perspective taking on socially maladjusted girls. *Child Development, 61,* 178–190.

Costello, J. (1972). *Behavior modification and corrections.* National Technical Information Service, no. PB 223–629/A5. Washington D.C. Law Enforcement Assistance Administration.

Dodge, K. A., Pettit, G. S., McClaskey, C. L., & Brown, M. (1986). Social competence in children. *Monographs of the Society for Research in Child Development, 51* (2, Serial no. 213).

Feldman, R. A., Caplinger, T. E., & Wodarski, J. S. (1983). *The St. Louis conundrum: The effective treatment of antisocial youths.* Englewood Cliffs, NJ: Prentice-Hall.

Fleischman, M., & Horne, A. (1979). Working with families: A social learning approach. *Contemporary Education, 50,* 66–71.

Fleischman, M., Horne, A., & Arthur, J. (1983). *Troubled families: A treatment program.* Champaign, IL: Research Press.

Forehand, R., & Long, N. (1988). Outpatient treatment of the acting out child: Procedures, long term follow-up data, and clinical problems. *Advances in Behavior and Research Therapy, 10,* 129–177.

Forehand, R., & Long, N. (1991). Prevention of aggression and other behavior problems in early adolescent years. In D. Pepler & K. Rubin (Eds.), *The development and treatment of childhood aggression* (pp. 317–330). Hillsdale, NJ: Lawrence Erlbaum Associates.

Forehand, R., Wells, K., & Griest, D. (1980). An examination of the social validity of a parent training program. *Behavior Therapy, 11,* 488–502.

Forgatch, M., & Patterson, G. (1989). *Parents and adolescents living together: Part 2, Family problem solving.* Eugene, OR: Castalia.

Glaser, B. A. (1989). *A bidirectional study of functional, distressed, and abusive families.* Unpublished doctoral dissertation, Indiana State University, Terre Haute.

Guerra, N. G., & Salby, R. G. (1990). Cognitive mediators of aggression in adolescent offenders: Part 2, Intervention. *Developmental Psychology, 26,* 269–277.

Horne, A., Norsworthy, K., Forehand, R., & Frame, C. (1990). *A delinquency prevention program.* Unpublished manuscript. Athens: Department of Counseling Psychology University of Georgia.

Horne, A., & Sayger, T. V. (1990). *Treating conduct and oppositional defiant disorders in children.* New York: Pergamon Press.

Kazdin, A. E. (1987). *Conduct disorders in childhood and adolescence.* Newbury Park, CA: Sage.

Kazdin, A. E., Bass, D., Siegel, T., & Thomas, C. (1989). Cognitive-behavioral therapy and relationship therapy in the treatment of children referred for antisocial behavior. *Journal of Consulting and Clinical Psychology, 57,* 522–535.

Kelley, M. L. (1989). *School-home notes: A behavioral intervention for parents and teachers.* New York: Guilford Press.

Kovacs, M. (1981). Rating scales to assess depression in school-aged children. *Acta Paedopsychiatrica, 46,* 305–315.

Lochman, J. E., Burch, P. R., Curry, J. F., & Lampron, L. B. (1984). Treatment and generalization effects of cognitive-behavioral and goal-setting interventions with aggressive boys. *Journal of Consulting and Clinical Psychology, 52,* 915–916.

Lochman, J. E., & Curry, J. F. (1986). Effects of social problem-solving training and self-instruction training with aggressive boys. *Journal of Clinical Child Psychology, 15,* 159–164.

McMahon, R., Forehand, R., & Griest, D. (1981). Effects of knowledge of social learning principles on enhancing treatment outcome and generalization in a parent training program. *Journal of Consulting and Clinical Psychology, 49,* 526–532.

MacMillan, D. L., & Kavale, K. A. (1986). Educational intervention. In H. C. Quay & J. S. Werry (Eds.), *Psychopathological disorders of childhood* (3d ed.). New York: Wiley.

Marsh, H. W. (1988). *Self-Description Questionnaire—I [SDQ-I].* San Antonio, TX: Psychological Corporation.

Marsh, H. W. (1990). *Self-Description Questionnaire—II [SDQ-II].* San Antonia, TX: Psychological Corporation.

Moos, R. H, & Moos, B. S. (1984). *Family Environment Scale Manual.* Palo Alto, CA: Consulting Psychologists.

Patterson, G. R. (1982). *Coercive family process.* Eugene, OR: Castalia.

Patterson, G. R. (1986). Performance models for antisocial boys. *American Psychologist, 41,* 432–444.

Patterson, G., Reid, J., Jones, R., & Conger, R. (1975). *A social learning approach to family intervention.* Vol. I, Families with aggressive children. Eugene, OR: Castalia.

Reynolds, C. R., & Richmond, B. O. (1985). *Revised Children's Manifest Anxiety Scale manual [RCMAS].* Los Angeles: Western Psychological Services.

Sayger, T. V., Horne, A. M., Passmore, J. L., & Walker, J. M. (1988). Social learning family therapy with aggressive children: Treatment outcome and maintenance. *Journal of Family Psychology, 1*(3), 261–285.

Stumphauzer, J. (1973). *Behavior therapy with delinquents.* Springfield, IL: Thomas.

Wilson, J. Q., & Herrnstein, R. J. (1985). *Crime and human nature.* New York: Simon & Schuster.

Wirt, R. D., Lachar, D., Klinedinst, J. K., & Seat, P. D. (1984). *Multidimensional description of child personality: A manual for the Personality Inventory for Children.* (1984 revision by David Lachar). Los Angeles: Western Psychological Services.

Wolfe, D. A. (1985). Child-abusive parents: An empirical review and analysis. *Psychological Bulletin, 97,* 462–482.

9

A Treatment Program
for Adolescent Bulimics
and Binge Eaters

Lillie Weiss
Sharlene Wolchik
Melanie Katzman

Introduction and Overview

Bulimia, or binge–purge eating, once considered a rare disorder, has recently received a great deal of attention in both the popular and the professional press. It is defined in the *DSM-III-R* (*Diagnostic and Statistical Manual III-Revised* [1987]) as recurrent episodes of binge eating, marked by a feeling of lack of control during the eating binges, and associated with such weight-control measures as self-induced vomiting, use of laxatives, strict dieting or fasting, and vigorous exercise. A person has to engage in a minimum average of two binge-eating episodes per week for at least three months to be diagnosed as a bulimic. An additional feature of the diagnosis is persistent over-concern with body shape and weight. The typical bulimic can be characterized as a white, single, college-educated woman from an upper-class or middle-class family, and the age of onset is typically the late teens. It is estimated that 8.3 percent of high school girls fill the diagnostic criteria for bulimia (Johnson, Lewis, Love, Lewis, & Stuckey, 1984) and that one in five regularly engages in binge eating (Levine, 1987).

This manual is a therapist's guide for working with bulimics. It is intended as an accompaniment to the program for controlling bulimia described in the workbook and self-help guide *You Can't Have Your Cake and Eat It Too: A Program for Controlling Bulimia* (Weiss, Katzman, & Wolchik, 1986). This manual is designed to help the clinician who is working with bulimics and binge eaters individually or in groups.

278

As we note in our book, our seven-week program is based on research findings that bulimics are depressed, have low self-esteem, suffer from poor body image, exhibit perfectionistic tendencies and a high need for approval, experience difficulty in handling negative emotional states such as anger and anxiety, and set unrealistic goals for thinness (Katzman & Wolchik, 1989). Each session in our program addresses one of these clinical features associated with bulimia.

Basic information and homework assignments are described in detail in our book and will not be repeated in the same detail here. This manual will focus on providing practical guidelines for working with bulimics and binge eaters that we have found to be very useful.

This program can be used to work with clients either individually or in groups. There are advantages and disadvantages associated with both group and individual treatment, and we do not necessarily endorse one over the other. Such practical matters as time considerations frequently necessitate the use of one mode instead of another. In this manual, we will mainly describe group treatment, but modifications in our program can easily be made when working with a client individually. For example, a therapist seeing a client individually can adhere to the basic format but can schedule more than seven sessions, taking more time with each one, if needed.

We have used this program with both individuals and groups, with very encouraging results (Wolchik, Weiss, & Katzman, 1986). In comparison with no-treatment controls, bulimics in the program made significant improvements not only in controlling their bingeing and purging but also in terms of improving body image and self-esteem, and decreasing depression, and maintained those gains at follow-up. We have replicated these results with other therapists and found the same encouraging results. We have also found that most of the bulimics that we have been able to contact maintained their progress several years after treatment was over.

Description of the Program

In the following pages we will describe our program in step-by-step fashion. We will begin by describing the preliminary interview and then describe each session. For each week, we will discuss the purpose of the session, summarize the therapist's role, and provide the homework assignments. A more detailed description of the program is presented in our book *Treating Bulimia: A Psychoeducational Approach* (Weiss, Katzman, & Wolchik, 1986). At the end of this manual we will discuss some issues the therapist should be aware of when treating bulimics.

General Information

Outline of the Program

Week 1: Education and Overview

Week 2: Eating as coping: Developing Alternative Coping Strategies

Week 3: Self-esteem, Perfectionism, and Depression

Week 4: Anger and Assertiveness

Week 5: Cultural Expectations of Thinness for Women

Week 6: Enhancing Body Image

Week 7: Summing Up: Where Are You Now and Where Do You Go from Here?

Format

The weekly group is led by two cotherapists and generally has between five to eight members, with group sessions scheduled to run approximately one and a half hours. In addition, two individual sessions are scheduled with each member, one after the second session and one after the fourth or fifth session. Each individual also receives a 10-week follow-up session. The individual sessions are intended to be "booster" sessions and do not replace group treatment. They are used to ensure us that each member's unique problems are addressed, for the group sessions themselves tend to be so "packed."

All sessions generally follow the same format. Except for the initial session, we spend the first 15 or 20 minutes reviewing homework, then we present new material, using a lecture-discussion-therapy format, and last we give homework. It is primarily a psychoeducational format, so that the clinician has to constantly juggle the provision of material and adaptations of it to fit members' needs with encouraging group cohesiveness and dealing with group process issues.

Materials

It is not possible to include all of the materials in this manual. The therapist can either use the materials from the workbook or obtain them in our book *Treating Bulimia: A Psychoeducational Approach* (1985). The basic materials needed include:

1. A flipchart or blackboard to integrate lectures with members' responses. (A flipchart is preferable because one can save responses and refer to them later).
2. The workbook *You Can't Have Your Cake and Eat It Too: A Program*

for Controlling Bulimia for each member. (All assignments are included in this workbook.)

3. (Optional). The test battery of pre- and postmeasures (only if the therapist wants to assess improvements in other areas than the eating behavior). The workbook and the assessment measures (which take about 15 minutes to complete) are available from the authors.

4. Binge Diaries. (Although these are included in the workbook, it is a good idea to provide extra copies for the members so that the group leader can collect these and review them. An example of a diary is provided in Figure 9–1.

5. At times, certain readings are assigned as part of the homework. These are usually materials that are readily available at bookstores and/or libraries, and we have included the appropriate references.

Preliminary Interview

The interview session is intended to screen for bulimia, to take a history and information on current behavior, and to present the program to the client.

Screening for Bulimia

An initial interview of roughly an hour is scheduled to assess whether the client fits *DSM-III-R* criteria for bulimia. For our purposes, we have defined a binge as something other than a meal that involved at least 1200 calories. Although we have not included them in our research samples, we have had females in our groups who binged less than twice a week and/or did not purge. These kinds of binge eaters have also benefited from the program.

We have had treatment problems, however, when we have inadvertently included anorexics or females with strong anorexic tendencies in our group. Their dynamics are very different from those of bulimics, and the issues of control around food can lead to acting out anorexic tendencies and getting into power struggles, thus undermining treatment. We have described such a situation in another paper (Weiss & Katzman, 1984). The therapist may be able to screen out adolescents with anorexic tendencies by taking a detailed inventory of daily food intake and having the client give examples of specific foods consumed during a binge. These clients report "binges" of much less than 1200 calories. One of our clients considered five almonds a binge! In addition, if the therapist feels that the main issue is not gaining weight versus trying to control her binges, that may be another clue of anorexic tendencies. Similarly, if the therapist senses either much resistance or a power struggle going on, further questioning may be in order before including a suspected anorexic in the group.

Binge Diary

Name:_____ Week No:_____

	Time	What I ate	Purge	Feeling and thoughts prior to eating	Alternative coping skills
MONDAY					
TUESDAY					
WEDNESDAY					
THURSDAY					
FRIDAY					
SATURDAY					
SUNDAY					

Total Binges:_____   Total Purges:_____

Figure 9–1.

Taking a History and Information on Current Behavior

After establishing that the adolescent is a bulimic or at least a binge eater, the therapist should try to understand her behavior, and establish rapport. Figure 9–2 presents a version of the intake form we use to gain information about a client's current and past binge eating behavior, as well as a weight, family weight, and psychiatric history.

Presenting the Program to the Client

Afterward the therapist describes the program to the adolescent, telling her that it is a seven-week program based on research findings that bulimics have certain difficulties in addition to their eating problems—that they tend to be depressed, perfectionistic, and to have low self-esteem, a poor body image, difficulty expressing anger, and unrealistic expectations of thinness. Clients are told that each session focuses on one of these topics, and that they will have homework after each session. It is important to stress the idea that the program focuses on *feelings,* not only on eating, and that the main emphasis is on teaching other ways of coping besides bingeing.

Several features should be emphasized in this initial meeting and throughout the program. The therapist can provide hope by presenting bulimia as a learned habit within one's control rather than a disease that is outside one's control. The therapist should stress that the adolescent has control and *responsibility* for her treatment and should use the client's statements to reinforce the idea that she is in charge of her eating behavior. Statements such as "You told me that when your Mom is home, you don't throw up" or "You don't binge or purge at school" or "You didn't binge and purge the whole time you were in Europe because you were on the road all the time," for example, can be used to demonstrate client control of her bingeing. The therapist needs to point this message: "All this lets you know that this is a behavior within your control and that you are *choosing* to binge to cope with some of your feelings. We are going to teach you other ways of coping with those feelings." The therapist should reassure the adolescent with statements such as "Even if you *feel* you don't have control, the truth is you do."

It is very important to reinforce the bulimic's own responsibility for achieving successful treatment—otherwise, she will feel helpless, seeing herself as a *victim* and losing hope. When the therapist places the responsibility for change in the client's hands, the client begins to realize that she has the power to make changes. Therapists should convey by their words and actions their sincere belief that the client is capable of making changes and they should also be ready to challenge her excuses. This frequently requires getting into an adult–adult mode rather than a parent–child one with the client, and requiring the client to do most of the work. A loving but firm, no-

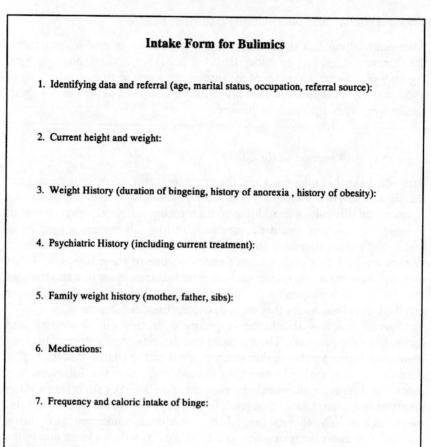

Intake Form for Bulimics

1. Identifying data and referral (age, marital status, occupation, referral source):

2. Current height and weight:

3. Weight History (duration of bingeing, history of anorexia , history of obesity):

4. Psychiatric History (including current treatment):

5. Family weight history (mother, father, sibs):

6. Medications:

7. Frequency and caloric intake of binge:

8. Description of binge (antecedents, function of binge, where and when):

9. Purging (kinds, duration, frequency):

10. Motivation:

11. Fee Arrangements:

Figure 9–2.

nonsense attitude helps the client take herself seriously and use her own resources to make changes.

It is also very important to convey attitudes that encourage commitment and regular group attendance. When clients seem ambivalent, therapists should not try to pressure them into joining the group. Instead, therapists should make statements such as: "It sounds like you are not sure this is for you. Maybe you would like to think it over before you make a commitment. The program *does* take a great deal of work on your part, and you should be certain that you want to participate before you commit yourself. But if you should decide to work in this program, we can guarantee that you will make very dramatic changes, as have many others." Sometimes we encourage clients to read the workbook to see if the program fits their needs. This attitude prompts the client to question her motivation and helps to ready her to do some work in the group once she gets stated.

The therapist should stress the importance of attending every session. In some situations, we have even required clients to pay the fee for the entire program at the beginning of the group. Of course, this is not possible to do in certain settings, but therapists can use whatever options are available in their own settings to encourage regular attendance.

Summary of Preliminary Interview

First, screen for bulimia, using operational DSM-III-R criteria (1200 calories, not a meal, twice a week or eight times per month). Binge eaters who do not strictly fit these criteria can also benefit from this program. Clients with anorexic tendencies should *not* be included in the group.

Second, take a history current and past eating behavior. Third, present the program to the client: (a) describe the structure and format; (b) emphasize feelings and learning other ways to cope than bingeing; (c) instill hope and emphasize the adolescent's responsibility for her own behavior; and (d) encourage regular attendance and commitment to the program.

Week 1—Education and Overview

Purpose

The purpose of the Week 1 class is to develop group cohesiveness and to provide clients with an overview of bulimia.

Introductions and Goal Setting

Leaders start out by introducing themselves and then requiring each client to tell the group a little about herself and what she would like to gain from her group experience. To increase cohesiveness, therapists should point out similarities between group members who share common experiences. Most members state that their reasons for entering the group include depression, guilt, and a sense that their lives are. Many mention feeling abnormal, different, and ashamed of their secretive behavior. They report how bulimia has affected their relationships, their schoolwork, their health, and their finances.

Developing Group Cohesiveness

Therapists should encourage the sharing of *feelings* rather than specific purging techniques. As with work in any group, therapists need to discuss issues of confidentiality and use basic therapeutic skills to encourage ventilation of feelings and development of group cohesiveness. Group cohesiveness can be encouraged by asking, "Does anyone else feel like that?" or "Has anyone else had a similar experience?" or "What do other people think about that?" The therapist's role is to help clients discuss their feelings of shame, disgust, guilt, anger, and hurt concerning their behavior. The ability to share these feelings, often for the first time, helps bulimics realize that they are not alone. Not every group member has to express these feelings to deal with them, for all group members can benefit from listening to each other.

It is very important that the feelings of anger and shame are dealt with so that clients can get beyond these feelings and begin to develop a sense of hope. Hope is an important part of the program; it is encouraged by stressing each member's ability to make changes. Bulimics frequently bring a sense of hopelessness and a "What's the use?" attitude to the group. Thus it is important for therapists to remind them that others with much longer bingeing histories *have* made successful changes. It is also important to remind them to set *realistic* goals for change. Their goal should not be the total elimination of binge eating and purging but instead a decreasing frequency of such behaviors. Many clients *will* stop bingeing completely, but setting a lower goal helps to prevent relapses in view of the bulimics' perfectionistic tendencies.

Providing an Overview of Bulimia

Following introductions and a discussion of feelings, the therapists should offer some basic information on bulimia: what it is and what it is not. Much of this session should be devoted to helping group members develop a sense of cohesiveness while providing educational information. Therapists should integrate the experiences of group members with the information they provide and use these experiences as a springboard for discussion. A blackboard or flipchart makes the procedure of providing information personal and informal.

Definition, Advantages, and Disadvantages. Therapists should first provide a definition of bulimia. Much of this information is provided in the workbook under the heading "Bulimic Basics." Therapists can define bulimia as eating large quantities of food, followed by either vomiting, use of laxatives or water pills, fasting, or very strenuous exercise to maintain a certain weight. They can state that this behavior usually starts in the late teens, particularly for females who are high achievers and perfectionistic about their bodies.

Therapists should then ask, "What are some of the advantages of bulimia?" Some clients may state that it is an easy way to eat and stay slim. Group leaders can respond to the effect that it is not an "easy" way, and may have serious consequences. Next the therapists can ask, "What are some of the disadvantages of bulimia?" and note some of the responses on the board, augmenting client responses with additional information. They should write down both the psychological and health hazards of bulimia, many of which the group members have already mentioned by now as they have talked about themselves. The psychological problems associated with bulimia include depression, withdrawal, anxiety, guilt, and shame. Some bulimics may already be experiencing some of the physical accompaniments of bulimia which include rotting teeth, electrolyte imbalance, throat blisters, anemia, ruptured stomach and esophagus, and a host of other problems. This part of the session is an eye-opener for many women. If a group member is already experiencing some medical problems, this too can have a profound effect on the group. Therapists should give this information matter-of-factly, not so much to scare clients and add to their sense of depression, but to point out some of the adverse effects of their behavior. It is important not to glamorize bulimia, for many bulimics feel it is the easiest way of dieting. It is important to emphasize that bulimia is *not* having one's cake and eating it too, as many people think. When noting some of the disadvantages of bulimia, therapists can also try to appeal to the adolescent's vanity, for example, by mentioning "chipmunk cheeks" or "rotting teeth" as unattractive consequences of constant vomiting. It is also a good idea to refer some clients to physicians for a check-up, particularly if they are experiencing some physical problems. Heavy laxative users should definitely be referred to a physician.

Myths and Misconceptions. Therapists should encourage discussion by asking, "What have you heard about bulimia?" or "What do other people think it is?" They need to dispute some of the popular myths and misconceptions about bulimia: that it is chronic, that it is incurable, that it is beyond one's control, and that it is a mental illness. They should present bulimia as a habit—a bad habit—that can be unlearned just as it was learned. By dispelling the myths, therapists provide a sense of responsibility and control of the bulimic over her own behavior. This gives her hope and also helps her to keep from "copping out" by disclaiming responsibility.

Cop-outs. Leaders then examine group members' "cop-outs," which are primarily related to abdicating control over their behavior. They ask group members to list what they tell themselves to give themselves permission to binge. These answers are written on the board next to each client's name. Group members frequently smile when they read the list of "cop-out" statements in the workbook because they have been using the same ones themselves. Awareness of their cop-outs helps them gain more control over their behavior, and they are less likely to use these as excuses for bingeing in future group discussions. Group leaders should encourage group members to identify each others' cop-outs. In future sessions, they should identify cop-outs whenever they occur. For example, if a group member states, "I had such a bad week, I had to binge," the therapists can ask the group members, "Are you going to let her get away with that?" or "What cop-out is Jane using?" This encourages group interaction and lets group members rather than therapists do the confronting.

Preview of the Coming Sessions and Homework

A brief preview of the topics they will be covering during the next six sessions is presented. For homework, they are to read chapter 1 in the workbook and to fill out the Binge Diary. They are told, "We know this will be difficult to do, but you need to look at what is happening with you before a binge so that you can change it." They are to record only *binges.* A binge has to be at least 1200 calories and cannot be a meal. Many bulimics have a tendency to write down any oversized portion or snack as a binge. They are also to note the number of purges and *exactly* what they were thinking and feeling before the binge.

Summary of Week 1

First, have group members introduce themselves and state their goals for treatment. Help them set realistic goals for change. Second, develop group cohesiveness by letting group members talk about feelings of guilt, anger, and shame. Third, provide an overview of bulimia including definition, psychological and physical hazards, myths, and cop-outs. Fourth, describe the program, emphasizing feelings rather than food. Fifth, give homework.

Week 2—Eating as Coping: Developing Alternative Coping Strategies

Purpose

The purpose of Week 2 is to help women identify the cues that lead to binge eating and to develop other responses to these cues. This is a very important session and serves as a basis for future sessions.

Identifying Cues for Bingeing

Group leaders ask each group member how her week went. Each adolescent identifies her own "triggers" for binge eating, and the therapists write these on the board. Sometimes group members are very vague. Therapists should push them to be specific and to find out *exactly* what happens prior to bingeing. The triggers for bingeing fall into three categories: eating habits ("I skipped meals and was starved"), thoughts ("I blew my diet already . . . I might as well pig out"), and feelings ("I was bored, sad, angry, lonely"). Therapists use the clients' responses to say that our cues for bingeing are threefold: eating behavior, thoughts, and feelings. They tell them that eating has been used to cope, and today they will learn some new ways of coping.

Changing Eating Habits

Although the program deals primarily with feelings, it is essential to start with good eating habits first, particularly for adolescents who need to be educated about proper nutrition. Learning good eating habits is one of the basic coping skills, and eating three meals daily is one of the ABC's of our program. The "Fat Facts" in the workbook provide the framework for discussion.

Therapists ask each woman to find her recommended weight in the 1983 Metropolitan Height and Weight Table for Women (p. 22 in the workbook). Most set their ideal weight at least 10 or 20 pounds below these norms. Therapists challenge the notion that every woman should weigh 103 pounds and stress that many females are trying to achieve unrealistic goals that are neither ideal nor healthy. There is usually some resistance to this idea, with many group members stating the weights in the table are too high. In our experience it is best not to fight them on this issue but to say something like "Okay, even if according to the charts you should be 130 pounds, we'll take your word that that weight feels too high for you and 110 pounds feels better. Let's see what you can eat to maintain 110 pounds."

The therapist can continue the discussion by saying, "If you multiply 110 pounds by 12, you can eat 1320 calories daily without gaining weight and even more if you exercise. Let's see how much that is." The therapists then write sample menus on the board. They ask: "If you had your druthers, what would you have for breakfast?" Then the therapists list several healthy choices, for example, cereal, milk and juice, eggs and toast; cream cheese and bagel; and so on. They then do the same for lunch, dinner, and a snack. They put down the approximate calorie count for each meal to come up with a total figure, usually around 1300 calories. Contrary to popular belief, most bulimics do *not* list calorie-laden foods as choices.

Therapists review some of the "Fat Facts" listed in the workbook and encourage the eating of healthy and regular meals. Group members are told to include a protein and a carbohydrate in each meal. A review of the basic four food groups is provided. Group members are told not to weigh themselves daily and to use exercise rather than starvation to reduce. Many group members are skeptical that they can eat so "much" and still maintain their weight. They are encouraged to try eating regular meals for just one week and see what happens. They are frequently surprised to see that they are not going to become obese overnight by developing a regular eating pattern.

Therapists should stress the importance of eating three meals a day, as starvation invariably leads to excessive hunger and bingeing. Bulimia is a natural physiological consequence of starvation: eating regularly is one of the best prevention strategies. Clients need to be urged to make this basic change in their eating habits. There is usually much resistance to this idea. We generally deal with this resistance by asking clients to just try our way for one week. After all, they are in a program to help themselves. Let them experiment and see what happens if they eat regularly for a week.

With adolescents, it is also important to provide information that continued dieting can lead to a weight problem later on because it affects the metabolism. Sometimes we give clients Kelly Brownell's article "Yo-Yo Dieting" to read (*Psychology Today*, January 1988, pp. 20–23).

I COPE

In addition to developing new eating habits as a coping response, clients learn some other coping skills to deal with their feelings of stress prior to bingeing. The acronym I COPE is used to illustrate other coping skills besides bingeing. Therapists write the words I COPE on the board and state that in this acronym, "I" stands for identifying stress, and each of the other four letters stands for a different stress management skill; Communication, Organization, Perception, and Enhancement. Therapists can give the following example of how this can be applied to binge eating. As you head for the refrigerator while studying for a test, you can first *identify* your feelings. You may be anxious, bored, or scared. You can then use one of the coping skills to deal with the stress. You can call a friend and talk about your feelings (*communication*), organize your materials and feel more prepared (*organization*), see the test as a small event rather than as a monumental task (*perception*), or exercise or nap to feel renewed (*enhancement*). After discussing the I COPE skills, therapists can ask group members to identify skills they could use more often.

Changing Thought Patterns

Therapists also discuss the effect that our thinking has on eating behavior and illustrate how negative monologues encourage bingeing. The workbook section on "Changing the Way You Think" is used to provide examples of how negative monologues can be replaced with more appropriate ones. Therepists should elicit each client's negative monologues and encourage her to replace them with more positive ones. A negative monologue that frequently leads to bingeing is "If I'm going to purge anyway, I might as well binge." We call this the purging cop-out. Therapists tell group members *not to purge no matter how much they eat.* ("You eat it—you keep it!"). They are told that this is clearly a behavior within their control—in fact, many had to *learn* to throw up, and as long as they continue *choosing* to vomit, then they are not really choosing to stop bingeing. Not purging frequently reduces the size of the binges. Laxative users are told to get rid of their laxatives. Therapists can also discuss research findings (Bo-Linn, Santa Ana, Morawski, & Fordtran, 1983) that indicate that despite laxative use 88 percent of food is absorbed, so women are fooling themselves when they think that laxatives are an effective weight loss help.

Developing Individual Coping Responses

After discussing all the different coping responses, each adolescent is asked to focus on one new coping response for the next week. Therapists enlist the aid of the group in generating some coping strategies for each member. We also use the "Strategies for Confronting an Oncoming Binge" in the workbook to generate responses. Therapists may wish to make Xerox copies of all the different coping responses listed by the group members and hand them out at the next session.

At the end of this session, Binge Diaries are collected. They will be returned, with written comments from the therapists, during the next session. This procedure is followed in *each* session.

This is a very "packed" session, one in which we attempt to cover a great deal of material. Obviously, one session is not sufficient for each member to identify all of her triggers for bingeing. This session, however, lays the groundwork for future sessions. Therapists need to frequently repeat the basic information provided here at future sessions. This is a good time to schedule an individual session with each of the clients.

Homework

For homework, group members read chapter 2 in the workbook and develop their own list of coping responses. As noted before, clients are *strongly* encouraged to eat three meals a day and to make a decision not to purge even if they binge. Each client is asked to try at least one new alternative coping response this week. As she continues filling out the binge diary, she lists alternative coping skills she could have used so she can use those the next time she is in a similar situation.

Summary of Week 2

First, go over the homework and help each group member identify her thoughts and feelings prior to bingeing. Write on the board the triggers for binge eating, which are usually feelings, thoughts, and excessive hunger due to starvation. Second, review "Fat Facts" and demonstrate how much a person can eat and still maintain her weight. Encourage group members to eat three meals daily and not to purge regardless of the size of their binge. Tell laxative users to throw away their laxatives. Third, discuss alternative ways of coping, using the I COPE acronym to illustrate basic coping strategies. Fourth, teach group members to change their thoughts that lead to bingeing, using "Changing the Way You Think" as a guide. Fifth, briefly review "Strategies for Confronting an Oncoming Binge" to help each woman generate her own alternate coping responses. Sixth, collect Binge Diaries, give homework for the week, and schedule individual sessions if you are doing group treatment. The purpose of the individual session is to solidify what has been learned to this point and to monitor the development of good eating habits and coping skills.

Week 3—Self-Esteem, Perfectionism, and Depression

Purpose

The purpose of Week 3 is (1) to help clients understand the relationship between self-esteem, perfectionism, and depression and how these relate to the binge cycle; (2) to help them become aware of the stringent demands they place on themselves and learn to lower their expectations; (3) to teach adolescents to nourish themselves in ways other than food; and (4) to raise self-esteem. They engage in three exercises, one to make them aware of their "shoulds," one to encourage nourishing behaviors, and one to raise self-esteem.

Homework Review

At the beginning of this and every session, each member's Binge Diary and homework are reviewed, together with a discussion of specific problems and success. In both group and individual therapy, therapists should pay attention to "cop-outs" and point them out when they occur.

Perfectionism and Bulimia

Therapists elicit a discussion on the relationship between depression, self-esteem, and perfectionism in view of research findings that bulimics set higher self-expectations, are more perfectionistic, have lower self-esteem, and are more depressed than other females. David Burns's article, "The Perfectionist's Script for Self-Defeat" (*Psychology Today*, November 1980, pp. 34–52) is used as a springboard for discussion. It is important that therapists read this article before the session. The article reviews the pitfalls of setting extremely high standards and describes some of the unpleasant consequences of perfectionistic behavior. Contrary to popular thought, the setting of unrealistic goals leads to poorer performance and frequently results in depression, low self-esteem, and other negative psychological states. The thought and behavior patterns of perfectionists are described very well in this article.

Therapists can begin the discussion by asking; "What do you think perfectionism is?" After allowing some discussion, they define it as the setting of *impossible* goals, goals set so high that nothing is ever good enough. Leaders should ask group members for examples of how they set unrealistic goals for themselves—both personal and weight goals. Most bulimics set impossible weight goals (one is *never* thin enough) as well as impossible personal ones and become depressed and lose self-esteem when they don't obtain these goals. Group leaders should talk about the costs and benefits of perfectionism. Perfectionists do not perform better just because they set high goals. The disadvantages are many. They should discuss in detail how perfectionism affects the binge–purge cycle and demonstrate with examples from the group. They can illustrate how all-or-nothing thinking and over-generalization, characteristic of perfectionists, lead to bingeing. For example, bulimics are either "on" or "off" a diet. When they are "on" a diet, they starve; when they are "off," they binge. When they eat a cookie after starving all day, they say to themselves, "Well, I blew it. I'm off my diet now. I might as well eat the whole bag." Many bulimics see eating in extremes—dieting or binge eating—with no happy medium. The all-or-nothing thinking is also used to label themselves as "good" or "bad" in relation to their eating habits. A "good" day means not eating; a "bad" day means the day started with a doughnut. Food is also labeled "good," for example, carrots, cottage cheese, and celery, and "bad," for example, pizza, dessert, and everything else! All-or-nothing thinking and overgeneralization frequently lead to binges and to feeling depressed afterward.

"I Should"

Another type of thinking characteristic of perfectionists is the "should" statements. Therapists ask clients to write down their "shoulds," and these are put on the board. Therapists can help group members challenge their "shoulds" (for example, "Why *should* you make friends with everyone in your class?") and to lower their expectations so that they can meet their goals more readily and have a feeling of accomplishment (for example, "Why don't you shoot for exercising only 15 minutes daily instead of two hours? You are much more likely to do that and then feel good about what you have done"). If any clients have attained their high goals for their eating behavior, for example, by not bingeing and purging at all during the past week, therapists should caution them that they are "human" and predict that they will slip from time to time. This prevents discouragement and depression when a binge occurs, which may then lead to reverting to the old cycle ("If I slipped, I may as well go back to my old ways.").

Nourishing Ourselves without Food

Therapists can encourage women to replace their "should" statements with "wants" and discuss how they can "nourish" themselves in ways other than by using food. Group members list which situations make them feel good, which relationships are nourishing, and what they can *say* and *do* to make themselves feel good (for example, "You did a good job"). These alternative sources of nourishment are written on the board.

Raising Self-Esteem

In this and in the following exercise, therapists are trying to raise the adolescents' self-esteem. They ask each client to list all of her positive qualities. In groups, they can do an exercise called Ego-Tripping (Morris & Shelton, 1974) in which each member lists five qualities she likes about herself and receives feedback from others as to what they like about her.

Homework

For homework, they are to read chapter 3 in the workbook and add to their "I should," nourishing activities, and positive qualities lists. Each member is to pick one thing from her list of nourishing activities and do it. In addition, she is to ask three people (one who knows her at school, one family member, and one friend) to tell her what they like about her and to record the answers.

Summary of Week 3

First, go over homework for Week 2. Second, discuss the relationship between depression, self-esteem, and perfectionism and how it applies to the binge–purge cycle. Third, have group members list their "shoulds" and discuss how these affect their behavior. Fourth, help them find ways of "nourishing" themselves without using food, through discussion of situations, people, thoughts, and actions that raise self-esteem. Fifth, have each group member list at least five positive qualities about herself. Sixth, give the homework for Week 3.

Week 4—Anger and Assertiveness

Purpose

The purpose of Week 4 is to teach clients basic assertive skills, particularly how to say "No" and to express anger.

Homework Review

In reviewing the homework and Binge Diaries, therapists can look for examples when clients binged instead of expressing themselves assertively. These situations can be used in discussions and role play.

What Is Assertiveness?

Therapists review the differences between assertive, nonassertive, and aggressive behavior (Alberti & Emmons, 1970). Assertiveness is standing up for oneself in such a way that one does not violate the basic rights of another person. It is a direct, honest, and appropriate expression of one's feelings and opinions. Nonassertion is failing to stand up for oneself, or standing up for oneself in such an ineffectual manner that one's rights are easily violated. Aggression is standing up for oneself in such a way that the rights of the other person are violated in the process. It is an attempt to humiliate or put down the other person. Some examples may be provided.

Human Rights

Group leaders can state that behaving assertively means exercising our rights and point out how rights are central to the definition of assertiveness. Leaders ask adolescents, "What are some of our basic human rights?" and write the answers on the board. Therapists may wish to read over the list of assertive human rights that appears in Manuel Smith's book *When I Say No, I Feel Guilty* (1975). These include the right to judge our own behavior, to make mistakes, to change our minds, and to say "I don't know," "I don't care," or "I don't understand." Many bulimics do not express themselves because they are not aware they have those rights. Below are two lists of human rights that therapists can use to augment client's responses.

Some Basic Human Rights

1. The right to express yourself and to feel good (not guilty) about doing so, as long as you do not hurt others in the process
2. The right to refuse a request without feeling guilty
3. The right to decide the ordering of your own priorities
4. The right to feel and express anger
5. The right to seek self-actualization of your potential
6. The right to feel competitiveness and achievement drive
7. The right to decide and judge for yourself
8. The right to have your opinions respected
9. The right to feel capable and adult—not to be patronized and treated like a child
10. The right to tell someone what your needs are

A List of Assertive Human Rights

1. You have the right to judge your own behavior, thoughts, and emotions, and to take responsibility for their initiation and consequences upon yourself.
2. You have the right to offer no reasons or excuses for justifying your behavior.
3. You have the right to judge if you are responsible for finding solutions to other people's problems.
4. You have the right to change your mind.
5. You have the right to make mistakes and be responsible for them.
6. You have the right to say, "I don't know."
7. You have the right to be independent of the goodwill of others.
8. You have the right to be illogical in making decisions.
9. You have the right to say, "I don't understand."
10. You have the right to say, "I don't care" (Smith, 1975).

After listing some basic results on the board, therapists can discuss how group members might exercise those rights more often.

Saying "No."

One assertive right that clients do not exercise is that of saying "No." Therapists should discuss the fears behind saying "No" (for example, "No one will like me"; "I don't want to hurt her feelings," and so on) and use role playing to help group members with specific situations.

Expressing Anger

Another right that bulimics do not exercise is that of anger expression. The research shows that bulimics have difficulty expressing anger appropriately. Many either "eat their feelings," "stuff them," or "swallow their anger," later "spitting it out." Therapists ask group members to think of a specific situation in which they were angry and did not express their anger the way they wanted to. They are to record their responses to the following questions: To whom was my anger directed? What did I actually do or say? What did I want to do or say? What were my fears behind saying or doing what I wanted to?

Therapists can ask, "What are your fears behind expressing anger?" and then suggest ways of expressing anger appropriately. They can use role play to help adolescents with specific situations.

Homework

For homework, they are to read chapter 4 in the workbook which reviews the material on assertiveness, basic human rights, saying "No," and expressing anger. One of the homework assignments is called "Yes's and No's," adapted from Lonnie Barbach (1975). This exercise both encourages assertive behavior and reinforces some of the "nourishing" exercises they have been given in the past. The exercise involves saying "No" to three things they didn't want to do but feel they *should* do and saying "Yes" to three things that they really want to do but would not usually let themselves have or ask others for. In addition, they are to record situations in which they felt angry and how they handled those situations. This exercise is designed to help them get in touch with their anger. Some clients may need their second individual session at this point, particularly if they are having a great deal of difficulty expressing anger to others. Everyone is to continue with their Binge Diary.

Summary of Week 4

First, review the homework from the previous week and focus on examples where clients binged instead of expressed their feelings assertively. Ask them what was "eating" them. Briefly discuss the relationship between binge eating and assertiveness and anger. Second, review basic assertiveness concepts and differentiate between assertive, nonassertive, and aggressive behavior. Third, ask group members to list their human rights and encourage them to exercise those rights. Fourth, discuss the right to say "No" without feeling guilty and help them explore their reasons for saying "Yes" when they wish to say "No." Role-play when appropriate. Fifth, ask them to list situations in which they did not handle anger appropriately. Discuss guidelines for expressing anger and role play if needed. Sixth, give homework for Week 4, and schedule an individual session for those who may need extra work at this point. (Those who do not have an individual session this week will be scheduled next week.)

Week 5—Cultural Expectations of Thinness for Women

Purpose

The purpose of Week 5 is to make bulimics aware of how societal expectations of thinness for women lead to bingeing and purging, of the heavy price they are paying to adhere to these expectations, and of how these societal expectations affect how they relate to the opposite sex.

Homework Review

Therapists review the homework from Week 4 and go over group members' "Yes's" and "No's," as well as do general problem solving with bingeing situations.

Societal Expectations for Thinness

Group leaders can elicit a discussion by asking group members what society tells us about being slim and how this affects our eating behavior. The next three exercises are designed to "wake them up" and to make them aware of society's unrealistic expectations of thinness. This is frequently an eye-opening session for group members, as well as being humorous at times. Therapists can use humor to exaggerate the absurdities of these expectations and of trying to live up to them.

The "Perfect" Woman

Therapists ask adolescents to list the qualities of the "Perfect Woman" and write these on the board. Slimness is usually mentioned as well as other physical features such as flawless complexion, long legs, white teeth, and so on. In addition to looking "gorgeous," a "perfect" woman is expected to achieve; be a wife, mother, and a gourmet cook; and do everything "effort-lessly." Therapists should encourage discussion of some of the unrealistic expectations females set for themselves and how these goals are impossible to reach.

Homework

For homework, they are to read chapter 5 in the workbook and do the homework exercises, which are geared to enhancing body image. The first exercise is adapted from Lonnie Barbach's Body Mirror Exercise (1975): clients are asked to examine their bodies without any clothing in front of a full-length mirror and to list what they like about what they see. The second exercise is to help them become aware that factors other than weight define a person's attractiveness to the opposite sex. They are to ask three males which females they consider sexy or attractive (movie stars and models excluded) and why. The third exercise is designed to help them become aware of some distortions in their body image. They are asked to find a magazine photo of someone whose body they think looks like theirs and one of someone whose body they wish to look like. They are to bring these to the group for feedback. When seeing the client in individual therapy, she can ask her friends for feedback. Continuation of the Binge Diary is also given for homework.

Summary of Week 5

First, review the homework for Week 4 and go over "Yes's" and "No's." Second, briefly discuss how societal expectations of thinness for females lead to bingeing and purging. Third, ask group members of list the qualities of the "Perfect Woman" and write those on the board. Fourth, ask about the payoffs and price of trying to live up to this ideal and write these answers on the board. Discuss the implications for them. Fifth, to help group members become aware of how societal expectations to be the perfect woman extend to their relationships with the opposite sex, ask how they act around other females and how they act around males they find attractive. Discuss the implications for them. Sixth, encourage them to stop trying to live up to an impossible ideal and to learn to accept their bodies as they are. Seventh, give the homework for Week 5 which is designed to enhance body image and to prepare for next week's topic. Schedule a second individual session with each client if you have not yet done so.

Week 6—Enhancing Body Image

This session is more effective when done in a group because feedback and confrontation from others are important for group members to gain insight into their distorted body images and to see how others perceive them, which is usually much less critical than the way they perceive themselves. They gain insight into their own behavior by observing other group members. When the client is seen individually, anecdotal material and feedback from her therapist and friends help her see her body more realistically and feel better about it.

Purpose

The purpose of Week 6 is to enhance body image, to help adolescents realize that weight is not the only criterion for attractiveness, and to decrease distortions in body image.

Enhancing Body Image: Review of the Body Mirror Exercise

The homework exercises from the previous week and exercises in the group during this session are done to help group members correct their negative perceptions of themselves and to feel better about their bodies. Members recount what they liked about their appearance when they looked in the mirror. They are asked to stand in front of the group and validate their bodies, telling what they liked about them. They are not to mention anything they did not like. Sometimes the therapist can model as she stands up and goes through each body part, starting from the top of her head and ending with her toes. It may help the group if the therapist does not mention weight when doing this exercise, but focuses more on the "functional" qualities of her features: "I love my hair because it is so easy to manage," "I like my hands because they are so agile." "I like my eyes because they are so expressive," "I like my breasts because they feel so good when they are touched," and so on. What we hope to accomplish here is to have clients "own" their bodies, imperfections and all, and feel comfortable with them. If the adolescent skips certain body parts, therapists can encourage her to go back to those parts and validate them. If she qualifies her statements—for example, "My hair is nice *when I set it*" or "My smile is pretty *except for my crooked teeth*"—therapists should point out that a feature does not have to be "perfect" to be liked. Clients should be encouraged to go back and say, "I like my smile," "I like my pretty hair," and so on. When she mentions a nice feature, for example, "I have nice ankles," she should be asked to talk about it and show the group what it looks like from all angles. Essentially, therapists attempt to reinforce positive responses.

This exercise obviously poses some difficulty when one or both therapists are male. It has not presented much of a problem in some of the groups we have supervised involving both a male and a female cotherapist. Therapists can use their own judgment and modify this exercise so that it feels comfortable for them and for their clients.

Some members may have a very difficult time not saying anything negative about their bodies. Therapists can state that they are not asking them to lie about their feelings, only to focus on positive aspects since they have "tunnel vision" and usually only focus on negatives. If clients have a real problem with a certain body part, therapists can ask them to exaggerate that part, both in the group and in doing the homework exercises, until they can feel comfortable with it. For example, they are to stick out their stomach or wiggle their thighs and keep looking at them until some desensitization takes place. They do not have to necessarily like every body part, but they need to feel comfortable with all their parts. Some aspects of their appearance can be changed, others they have no control over, so it is time for them to make friends with their bodies.

After each group member validates her body, group members and therapists give her feedback on what they see as her attractive features. It is important for the therapists not to focus on the woman's thinness except if she has a very distorted body image and sees herself as fat. They should also attempt to give feedback on her attractive *behaviors,* such as friendliness, certain mannerisms, bubbliness, and the like, and not focus solely on *appearance.*

What Is Sexy?

The next exercise is designed to bring to their awareness the reality that features other than weight constitute attractiveness to the opposite sex. Group members are asked to tell what the males they talked to said they considered sexy or attractive in females, and therapists write these answers on the board. They are asked to think of what is sexy to them and therapists write these answers on the board also. Although thinness is sometimes mentioned, more frequently personality and behavioral characteristics are noted with more frequency than physical features. Group members are made aware that they spend an inordinate amount of time focusing on one aspect of their appearance—weight—whereas other physical and personality features may be more important.

Correcting Distortions in Body Image

Leaders ask members to show the photos they had cut out from magazines of what they *thought* they looked like and what they *wanted* to look like. There is invariably much distortion in how they perceive themselves. Slim or normal-weight females often bring in pictures of obese women. Group members provide each other with feedback about their distortions. Frequently, bulimics are unable to see their own bodies realistically, but are incredulous at the distortions of other group members. This exercise can provide them with insight into their own perceptions even though they may still "feel" fat. Therapists should tell adolescents that even if they "feel" as though they have "humongous thighs" or "pregnant stomachs," they need to intellectually accept what they look like and take at face value what others tell them. Obviously, one session is not sufficient to correct distorted perceptions of the body. Therapists should ask adolescents to do the Body Mirror Exercise regularly until they feel more comfortable with their bodies and to trust the feedback from others and act on it rather than on their own perceptions.

Homework

They are to read chapter 6 in the workbook and to the homework which reinforces the work in the group and is again designed to help them like their appearance more and to focus on factors other than weight to feel good about themselves. They are to write down what they like about their appearance, what others like about it, and what their "attractive behaviors" are. This exercise is intended to reinforce the feedback they received in the group so that they can refer to it in the future. They are also told to pick one of their "attractive behaviors" from the list and exaggerate it, that is, to change something *behaviorally* that will improve their attractiveness, for example, to smile more often if their smile is attractive, to exaggerate certain movements, and so on. They are to record the reactions of others when they deliberately exaggerate these behaviors. They are frequently surprised and delighted to see how much attention they get from males when they are more verbal, smile more, or listen more, when no one notices if they gained or lost a few pounds! They are also asked to change something in their *appearance* aside from losing weight and to record other people's reactions to this change. Again, a change in hairstyle or makeup is likely to bring more comments than the loss of a pound or two. In addition, they are to continue their Binge Diary.

Summary of Week 6

First, review the Body Mirror Exercise for each group member. Let her tell the group what she likes about her body and have her receive feedback from other group members. In providing feedback, focus on the "functional" aspects of the features and on "behaviors," not only on appearance. Help clients "own" and accept their bodies. Second, review what is sexy for others and what they find sexy. Make it clear that features other than weight define attractiveness. Third, review the photos and help clients correct distortions in body image by getting feedback from others. Encourage group members to go by the feedback rather than by their own perceptions and feelings. Fourth, give homework for this week.

Week 7—Summing Up: Where Are You Now and Where Do You Go from Here?

Purpose

The purpose of Week 7 is to review progress and to prepare for relapses.

Homework

In the last session women usually come in with a very visible change in appearance, and this is reinforced by therapists and group members. Group members are asked to relate the reactions others had to the exaggeration of their attractive behaviors and the change in their appearance. Therapists should reinforce the truth that factors other than weight constitute attractiveness and get more attention.

Reviewing Progress

The rest of the session is spent on reviewing each client's progress and what she still needs to work on. Members can write down answers to the questions in chapter 7, of the workbook, to help them assess this. Leaders review each member's progress and what she still needs to work on.

Preparing for Relapses

Even though some group members may have stopped bingeing entirely by now, they should be told to expect relapses. Relapse should be defined in positive terms. Members are told that it is a cue that they need to work on something and to practice their new skills. Therapists should point out that progress seldom goes upward in a straight line but has ups and downs. Above all, they should be told not to panic when they relapse. They are to see each relapse as an opportunity to come up with new coping skills. They are not to engage in all-or-nothing thinking: "I messed up—I guess I will never be able to give up bingeing." Relapsing does not take away all the progress they have made so far. It is a cue to review their skills and nourish themselves with things other than food. Therapists should encourage clients to refer to their workbooks and reread them from time to time.

Follow-up

In addition, they are to continue filling out the Binge Diary and to use the alternative coping responses. A follow-up session can be scheduled for 10 weeks after the group is over. The follow-up session will be used to review progress, work on current problems, and suggest directions for growth. In individual treatment, therapists can schedule follow-up sessions according to the client's needs.

Closure

Leaders can end the group with a closing exercise in which every member tells each group member what she perceives that member has given to the group and what kind of a gift she would like to give that group member. For example, "You have given this group courage for trying new behaviors, and if I could give you a gift, I would like to give you the ability to see how beautiful you really are." This helps group members say goodbye. It also reinforces the gains made in the group so far and suggests future directions for each individual.

Summary of Session 7

First, discuss the homework from the last session. How did others react to the changes in appearance other than weight and the exaggeration of attractive behaviors? Second, review each person's progress and ask what changes she sees in herself and others. Third, prepare them for relapses. Fourth, schedule a follow-up session and ask them to continue filling out the Binge Diary. Fifth, do a closure exercise to help them say good-bye.

Process Issues in Treating Bulimia

In addition to the specific topics in each week, there are some specific issues for the therapist to be aware of across sessions. Below is a list of these tips and traps for therapists.

1. Vagueness versus Specificity:
   a. Ask where, when, how much, and the like. Find out *exactly* what occurs during a binge.
   b. Keep records of the client's number of binges and purges at each session so that you know what is happening.
2. *The Purging Cop-out:* THERE IS NO EXCUSE FOR PURGING.
   Purging is a behavior clearly within the client's control, and if she chooses to continue doing it, it must be addressed in the early stages of treatment.
3. *Commitment:* Set up expectations of commitment and work.
   a. Have clients make both a monetary commitment and a commitment to attend all of the sessions.
   b. Screen out noncommitted clients.

4. *Responsibility:* This is the most important issue and at the core of all of the other issues.
   a. The client should do at least 50 percent of the work.
   b. Get into an adult–adult mode rather than a parent–child mode whenever possible.
   c. Convey a firm but loving attitude in your words and actions.
5. *Being a Victim Versus Choosing:* Similar to above.
   Let the client know by your words and actions that she is in charge and that her behavior is a *choice.*
6. *Disease versus Learned Habit:* Related to issues of responsibility and choice. Bulimia is a learned behavior within one's control rather than a disease that leaves you with no hope of control.
7. *Hope versus Hopelessness:*
   a. Convey positive expectations of change.
   b. Do not get hooked into the client's negative, all-or-nothing thinking.
8. *Process versus Convent:* Use the group to do some of the work, particularly in identifying each other's cop-outs.
9. *Medical Issues:* Refer for a good medical check-up, especially for heavy laxative abusers.
10. *Family Issues:* Be aware of some possible rebellion in adolescents if they are coming to group because of parental pressure. Some family education and/or treatment may be necessary.
11. *Anorexia versus Bulimia:* Screen carefully beforehand. Refer adolescents with anorexic-type behavior for alternative treatment.

References

Alberti, R. E., & Emmons, M. L. (1970). *Your perfect right: A guide to assertive behavior.* San Luis Obispo, CA: Impact.

American Psychiatric Association (1987). *Diagnostic and statistical manual of mental disorders: III-Revised.* Washington, DC: American Psychiatric Association.

Barbach, L. (1975). *For yourself: The fulfillment of female sexuality.* New York: Doubleday.

Bo-Linn, G. W., Santa Ana, C., Morawski, S., & Fordtram, J. (1983). Purging and caloric absorption in bulimic patients and normal women. *Annals of Internal Medicine, 99,* 14–17.

Brownell, K. (1988, January). Yo-yo dieting. *Psychology Today,* pp. 20–23.

Burns, D. (1980, November). The perfectionist's script for self-defeat. *Psychology Today,* pp. 34–52.

Johnson, C. L., Lewis, C., Love, S., Lewis, L. D., & Stuckey, M. (1984). Incidence and correlates of bulimic behavior in a female high school population. *Journal of Youth and Adolescence, 13,* 15–26.

Katzman, M. A., & Wolchik, S. A. (1989). Bulimia and binge eating in college women: A comparison of personality and behavioral characteristics. *Journal of Consulting and Clinical Psychology, 52,* 423–428.

Levine, M. P. (1987). *How schools can help combat student eating disorders.* Washington, DC: National Education Association.

Morris, K. T., & Shelton, R. L. (1974). *A handbook of verbal group exercises.* Springfield, IL: Thomas.

Smith, M. (1975). *When I say no, I feel guilty.* New York: Dial Press.

Weiss, L., Katzman, M. K., & Wolchik, S. A. (1985). *Treating bulimia: A psychoeducational approach.* New York: Pergamon Press.

Weiss, L., Katzman, M. K., & Wolchik, S. A. (1986). *You can't have your cake and eat it too: A program for controlling bulimia.* Saratoga, CA: R&E Publishers.

Weiss, L., & Katzman, M. K. (1984). Group treatment for bulimic women. *Arizona Medicine, 41,* 100–104.

Wolchik, S. A., Weiss, L., & Katzman, M. A. (1986). An empirically validated, short-term psychoeducational group treatment program for bulimia. *International Journal of Eating Disorders, 5*(1), 21–34.

10
Developmental Facilitation Groups for Children of Divorce: The Elementary School Model

Neil Kalter
Shelly Schreier

Introduction and Overview

The dramatic rise in the rate of divorce in the United States, Canada, and other Western countries has been well documented. Between 1960 and 1980 the percentage of children who experienced parental divorce tripled. Prior to 1960, approximately 10 percent of youngsters under the age of 18 saw their parents divorce. By 1980 that figure had reached 30 percent (Furstenberg, Nord, Peterson, & Zill, 1983; Glick, 1979; National Center for Health Statistics, 1990). Though the rate of divorce, and the number of children affected by it, declined slightly through the early and middle 1980s, over one million children per year in the United States had their family life disrupted by divorce between 1978 and 1987 (National Center for Health Statistics, 1990). That these youngsters were all under the age of 18 and presumably still living at home suggests that a large number of minors must confront and attempt to cope directly with the upheavals in their lives so often associated with parental divorce.

Most social scientists and clinicians now agree that parental divorce constitutes an immediate and major disequilibrium in the lives of youngsters. Key domains of child development frequently are disrupted. Researchers and clinicians have noted interferences in academic achievement, cognitive development, peer relationships, relations with adults in positions of authority, the ability to modulate aggressive and sexual impulses, and feelings of self-esteem and self-worth (see Guidubaldi & Perry, 1984; Hetherington, Cox, & Cox, 1979; Kalter, 1977; Wallerstein & Kelly, 1980). The specific manifestations of these difficulties are played out through somewhat different behaviors depending on the age and developmental stage of the youngster.

Though it is clear that youngsters are vulnerable to divorce-related stresses, and many develop problems in the short run (usually defined as the first two years after parents separate), of even greater concern is the possible long-term effects of divorce on the trajectory of child development. Several studies, employing diverse research methodologies and rooted in differing conceptual frameworks, indicate that a substantial minority of youngsters suffer from divorce-related troubles even years after their parents' separation (see Glenn & Kramer, 1987; Guidubaldi, Perry, & Nastasi, 1987a, 1987b; Hetherington, Cox, & Cox, 1985; Hetherington, 1989; Kalter, 1987; Wallerstein, 1985, 1987, 1991). Areas of development affected adversely by divorce in the long run include academic achievement, peer relationships, impulse control, sense of emotional well-being, and stability of intimate relationships in late adolescence and early adult years.

To explain the short- and long-term effects of divorce on the youngsters involved, Kalter (1987, 1990) has suggested a "developmental vulnerability model." This model draws on the stress-and-coping paradigm and views parental divorce as an act that sets in motion a host of subsequent life changes that unfold or persist for years after parents separate and divorce. Each of these changes may constitute a significant, ongoing source of stress in a youngster's life. In order of importance, beginning with the most significant, these stressors are: *hostilities between parents* which sadden and anger children of all ages, and which stir loyalty conflicts in them; the *presence of a distraught custodial parent,* which creates anxiety in youngsters and often results in children inappropriately being put in adult roles such as "man of the house," "coparent," or "parent" to the distressed mother or father; *loss (partial or complete) of the relationship with the nonresident parent,* which children often self-blamingly attribute to some shortcoming in themselves, and which therefore can lead to low self-esteem and depression; *parent dating,* which frequently engenders competitive feelings toward the parent's partner, fears over loss of the parent's affections and, for older children and adolescents, raises concerns as well as forbidden curiosities about their parent's sexuality; *remarriage* with the plethora of complex adaptations it requires, including sharing the parents with the stepparent and accepting the intimacy of the parent's marriage, forming a reasonable relationship with the stepparent, coping with conflicted feelings of loyalty toward the stepparent and parent of the same gender as the stepparent, coming to terms with the stepparent's role as a parentlike authority in the family, and adjusting to having step- and/or half-siblings; *downward economic mobility,* which brings with it the emotional stresses associated with poverty or severely reduced economic resources; and *changes in residence* with the concomitant loss of established peer relationships and loss of a familiar school environment and/or loss of consistent and familiar caregivers. Separately and collectively, these stressors can exert ongoing, negative effects in the lives of children.

Our focus in this intervention is on helping elementary school-age children whose parents have parted cope more adaptively with the feelings and concerns aroused by the divorce process and the life changes it engenders. For some youngsters who are struggling with painful feelings, behavioral problems, and/or difficult life circumstances, this intervention can be enormously helpful. In fact, a controlled, four-year follow-up study indicates that children who participated in our support groups were doing significantly better than their peers whose parents had divorced but who did not take part in this intervention (Rubin, 1990). For elementary school-aged children who are already coping well with the divorce and its aftermath, these groups can serve to confirm and lend support to their positive direction. However, there will be a small minority of youngsters, suffering from long-term emotional and behavioral disorders, for whom this intervention will not be helpful in major ways. This program is not intended as a substitute for individual or family treatment of enduring emotional or behavioral disorders. Nor can it fully offset a palpably painful, highly conflictual, current family environment.

Rationale for Developmental Facilitation Groups

An earlier view of preventive intervention for children of divorce rested on a *crisis intervention model*. The premise was that there were pronounced divorce-engendered conflicts and disruptions in social, emotional, and academic functioning that were best ameliorated by the earliest possible intervention, one timed as close to the initial parental separation as possible. Implicit in this perspective is the notion that such interventions can serve to "inoculate" children against developing divorce-related difficulties in the future. Such a view leads to the conclusion that the children who are most likely to profit from a prevention effort are the ones whose parents have recently been separated. In fact, many programs screened out youngsters whose parents had been divorced for over a year or two, providing no special support services for those who were attempting to cope with the long-term stresses associated with parental divorce.

Though we agree that early intervention holds the promise of reducing immediate levels of distress and may serve to help youngsters regain their developmental equilibrium more quickly, we are impressed by the *long-term, ongoing nature of the psychological tasks confronting the child whose parents divorce*. The stresses noted above continue, or first appear, well beyond the initial period of marital disruption. In conducting our groups, and when interviewing research subjects (see Garvin, Leber, & Kalter, 1991; Kalter, Kloner, Schreier, & Okla, 1989; Kalter, Pickar, & Lesowitz, 1984; Kalter & Plunkett, 1984) many children clearly give the message that these *postseparation stresses* require as many or more coping efforts than the parental separation, per se. For this reason we choose not to restrict entry into the program to only those youngsters whose parents have recently parted. Instead, we include all children who have experienced a parental divorce at some time in their lives regardless of when the divorce occurred. We find that our groups afford youngsters grappling with postdivorce issues a chance to focus on and develop better ways of coping with stressful life situations and the conflicts, feelings, and questions that they stimulate. It also gives these children an opportunity to reexamine and rework old concerns about the marital disruption that were never fully dealt with. At the same time children whose parents have only recently separated can see in their peers who are years postdivorce that there is indeed "life after divorce." And they can learn from the more "veteran" of our group members ways to cope with the initial separation and the painful feelings and worries associated with it.

We chose a *group format* for several reasons. First, it creates an opportunity for *peer support* which we find invaluable in helping youngsters deal with divorce and postdivorce stresses. What peers think and believe is extremely important to elementary school–aged youngsters. Second, the groups provide a sense of *"safety through numbers"* which individual approaches cannot achieve. Within a group, children are more likely to feel comfortable expressing ideas, questions, worries, and personal experiences than when seen by an adult in a one-to-one intervention or as part of a family therapy. Finally, it is simply *more efficient* to see between four and eight youngsters at one time than to see each individually or with his or her family. But even if it were not more efficient, a time-limited, group preventive intervention still has the other advantages over individual or family-focused sessions. Children are simply more able, in a relatively short time, to become comfortable expressing inner concerns, to learn new coping strategies, and to come to understand the normality of being a child of divorce when a peer group format is used.

The *themes* covered in the group sessions were chosen on the basis of our collective clinical experience, a careful examination of the research literature, and the nature of children's concerns as they emerged spontaneously in the first 60 groups we conducted. The issues which we focus on include: (1) predivorce parental fighting and arguing; (2) hearing from the parents that they will in fact be separating and getting a divorce; (3) the transition from a two-parent family to a single-parent family, and the changes that transition brings to the lives of children; (4) visiting with the nonresident (or nonprimary) parent; (5) continuing hostilities between parents; (6) parent dating; and (7) remarriage and "blended" family life. These themes unfold in roughly the order given so as to mirror the sequence of experiences that children of divorce often have. We find that this temporally based organization to our intervention lends a pronounced sense of *coherence* to it for our participants.

We have five major *aims* in conducting this intervention. They are: (1) to *normalize* the sense and experience of being a youngster whose parents have divorced; (2) to *clarify* divorce-related concerns and questions that can be upsetting and confusing; (3) to provide a safe place for youngsters to *experience and rework* emotionally painful aspects of parental divorce and postdivorce life; (4) to help children *develop coping skills* for particularly troubling feelings and family interactions; and (5) to *communicate to parents* the nature of the concerns, conflicts, and questions youngsters of this age may have when their parents have divorced.

Composition and Format of the Groups

Our groups can be held in a variety of settings, including public or private schools, community mental health centers, church/synagogue–based settings, or in outpatient mental health clinics. An advantage of school-based groups is the easy access for children, the presence of a ready-made peer group, and the increased regularity in attendance by group members due to the fact that parents need not transport them to sessions. However, our groups have been conducted in all of these settings with good results.

Several specific guidelines have governed the formation of these developmental facilitation groups. The centrally important parameters are listed below.

1. Children in a group should not be more than one (the early elementary school model) or two (the later elementary school model) grades apart. This reduces cognitive, social, and emotional developmental differences, thus facilitating the use of peer support and enhancing the development of a sense of group cohesion.
2. There should be roughly an equal number of boys and girls in a group. This reduces the feelings of isolation that arise if a child is the only boy or the only girl in a group, and increases peer support, which tends to come from same-sexed peers.
3. There should be between four and seven (the early elementary school model) or five and eight (the later elementary school model) youngsters in a group. This number permits participants to have a feeling that there is "safety in numbers" while still affording everyone enough "air time" for them to voice their concerns and comments.
4. Groups are not constructed according to current living arrangements, family type, or time since divorce. In fact, heterogeneity along these dimensions appears to be a great strength of the intervention, as members can model, inform, and remind each other about the various phases and circumstances of postdivorce life.
5. Sessions typically last 50 minutes.

6. The groups use a coleader model, ideally utilizing a male and female leader. This allows for a same-sex role model for all group members, facilitates role playing in this intervention, and models a positive working relationship between a man and a woman. However, we have also conducted our groups using a single leader with good results.
7. The intervention consists of 10 weekly sessions (the early elementary school model) or 8 weekly sessions (the later elementary school model).
8. The groups are semistructured by design so that leaders can provide for the particular needs of group members. The relative emphases of various themes can be tailored to the specific life circumstances of members in a particular group.

These guidelines constitute the structural components of the developmental facilitation groups.

Techniques for Conducting the Groups

What we have discussed to this point are the rationale for and the structural features of the groups. We now turn to the substantive aspects of our intervention. The heart of this program is the twin use of *displacement activities* in order to facilitate youngsters' expression of thoughts and feelings and *universalizing statements* by group leaders to communicate to children in ways that they can hear the messages.

Displacement activities are well known to many child therapists. Puppet play, drawing, the use of dolls and action figures, and talking about imaginary youngsters and families are facets of traditional play therapy. The use of displacement permits youngsters to talk about, observe, and gain further understanding about their private feelings and ideas. It avoids direct questioning and discussion about a particular child's inner life. Direct confrontation with the majority of children most typically is met with defensive shrugs, "I don't know," or silence. Occasionally, a particularly verbal youngster will substitute adult-approved, "party-line" types of statements for these more common defenses. Responses to displacements stand in sharp contrast to these defensive reactions. Group members usually can be engaged easily when their conflicts, feelings, fears, worries, and wishes are presented "one-step-removed" in a displacement activity.

Universalizing statements are used to communicate important issues to group members. Such statements are essentially general comments such as, "It seems like most kids whose parents have split up have worries about what will happen after the divorce" and "A lot of kids have angry feelings toward their parents about the divorce." These statements serve two major purposes: first, they allow leaders to reflect back to the youngsters key issues that help to normalize children's concerns without singling out individual group members (which would make them uncomfortable); and second, such statements, because they are cast in a general form, can be heard by all group members as being potentially relevant to them.

We now turn to the implementation of each of the two elementary school–age models: one for children in later elementary school (grades 4–6) and the other for youngsters in early elementary school (grades 1–3). We will present an outline of the sessions for each of these models in turn. It is important for readers to know that what follows is a distillation of two leaders' manuals, totaling 280 pages (Kalter & Associates, 1985, 1988). As such, the details regarding what leaders say, how youngsters react, and which responses leaders can then make are often summarized rather than displayed fully. The interested leader may wish to obtain the full versions of these manuals from the senior author. Further, a middle/junior high school program is also available (Kalter & Associates, 1993).

The Later Elementary School Model

Since this model was developed first, we will begin by presenting it. We will then present the early elementary school model, noting the changes that we made as we moved to the younger age group.

Session 1—Introduction to the Group

The aims of this session are to introduce the coleaders and children to one another, to communicate a sense of the general goals of the group, to obtain a brief "divorce history" from each child, and to begin to build a sense of group cohesion among the members. As a way to assure a sense of safety and the smooth running of the group, leaders introduce rules during this session. The four rules include: (1) listening—children are told that they have important things to say, and to ensure that they all have their turn, it is important that only one person talk at a time; (2) right to pass—youngsters are told that we will be talking about many different ideas and feelings, and in this group if they do not wish to participate they have the right to pass; (3) no put-downs—leaders tell the children that it is important for everyone to feel comfortable about sharing their ideas and feelings so that there will be a rule that there is to be no teasing of one another; and (4) confidentiality—leaders emphasize that issues discussed in the group are personal and private, so that they may not tell anyone what people other than themselves or the group leaders say. In most of our groups, these rules are accepted easily. Occasionally, the confidentiality rule requires some elaboration. Leaders may refer to it as the "top secret" rule, and underscore the fact that each youngster is permitted to tell what he or she said in the group as well as what the leaders have said in the group, but are not free to reveal what other group members have said.

Following the introduction and explanation of the rules, youngsters are then told about the construction of a group story about an *imaginary family* which is "headed for a divorce." One of the leaders tapes a piece of newsprint to a wall, while the other leader helps direct the children's participation in deciding on a name for the family and who is in it. Leaders then encourage the group to include at least two children in the family, as well as the two parents. One child is about the same age as the group members, and one is a few years younger. The latter serves as a displacement figure through whom many youngsters feel comfortable expressing somewhat regressive feelings and fears. Pets too are often included, although leaders may need to limit them once suggestions have moved down the phylogenetic scale from dogs and cats to gerbils, goldfish, and beyond. The leaders begin the story by saying, "One night Mr. and Mrs. Green were having an argument." The leader then asks the next child in the circle (going either to the left or right) what sentence she or he would like to add. Youngsters usually begin right away, and may say something like, "Mr. Green got really mad that Mrs. Green didn't have a clean house." Leaders are careful to allow the children the opportunity to add whatever they wish to the story. Although the content of the stories can be quite violent or very sad, it is important to provide the children the sense that all their ideas are welcome. Leaders should only intervene if the behavior of the group members becomes giddy or silly as the story develops. After children have several turns, at times punctuated by a leader providing an additional stem such as "While Mr. and Mrs. Green were fighting, Billy and Susie were upstairs in their bedrooms feeling . . . ," the children are told that it is time to think of an appropriate ending. Some groups come to a consensual ending, while others may allow each youngster a turn to provide his or her own individual ending.

After the creation of the story, the leaders read it, commenting on the concerns and feelings that have been expressed. For example, a story may include the fact that "Mrs. Green got hit over the head with a frying pan." A leader may say, "It seems that kids get worried that when parents start to fight, things may get out of control and somebody might get hurt." Another example is, "Susie went downstairs, stood right between her parents, and told them to stop fighting right now." Leaders may comment upon this by saying, "Kids must really feel like they want to get right into the middle of a fight to make their parents stop. It can be tough knowing that you can't make them stop when so many kids wish they were able to do that." Similarly, the endings of the stories often vary, with some concluding that the couple make up and live happily ever after. Leaders ask the group what kinds of stories end like that, eliciting the answer "fairy tales." It is then suggested, "It seems like kids wish the divorce story could end kind of like a fairy tale, but that isn't usually how it works, is it?" After the story has been read and the leaders have commented upon it in these ways, leaders note that the session is coming to a close and remind the children that the group will meet the following week at the same time and in the same place.

Following the session, leaders may wish to take time to review the story, for it is often a diagnostic sign of the concerns and dynamics of the specific group with which they are working. Some stories are predominantly sad and suggest that a depressive tone will likely pervade subsequent sessions for that group. Other stories are characterized by much more overt hostility, lack of control, and rage surrounding the divorce. Still others reflect worries about children being cared for and increased dependency needs are in evidence.

Session 2—Predivorce Fighting between Parents

The aims of this session are to permit thoughts, feelings, and worries about parental hostilities to emerge, to correct self-blaming perceptions of the causes of interparental friction and divorce, to normalize feelings about parental fighting which children may feel guilty or ashamed about, and to provide concrete suggestions for coping with parental warfare.

The session often begins with a reintroduction of the leaders and members, and a recapitulation of the rules. Children are also often asked, "Who remembers the story from last week?" This serves as a bridge between sessions and lends a sense of continuity from one meeting to the next. The youngsters are then told that they are going to do some skits about parents who are heading for a divorce. The leaders begin the first role-play scenario which involves the female leader playing the mother and the male leader playing the father. (In groups conducted by one leader, this role play can take place by having the leader use hand puppets to enact the skit.) The group then selects a new name for this family (in contrast to the name assigned to the family for the group storytelling activity in the previous session). Again, there are two children in this imaginary family. One youngster is a boy, and one is a girl, one of them is about the age of the group members, while the other is several years younger. After this is done the leaders stand up, move a few feet apart from the group, and begin the role play.

Mrs. Blue: (Walking around irritated and looking at her watch) "Where is he? He was supposed to be home an hour ago."

Mr. Blue: (Enters the room) "What's for dinner?"

Mrs. Blue: "What's for dinner? Where have you been? The kids ate half an hour ago. I get home from work, make dinner, and there isn't even a phone call from you saying you're going to be late."

Mr. Blue: "Oh fine, start in right away again. I don't even know why I bother trying to come home on time at all. After all, you're always *so* much fun to spend time with."

(And so on.)

The leaders continue for a few moments, then stop the skit and return to the group members and ask, "What is going on here for the Blue family?" The members usually say something about the fact that Mr. and Mrs. Blue are in another fight. Leaders then inquire about what types of things parents fight about, how fights usually go, and what the group members think will happen next with Mr. and Mrs. Blue. Often members say, "Oh, that's nothing. That isn't even a fight yet, no one is throwing anything" or "Wait until she smells the beer on his breath—he was probably at the bar" or "It's just that all she does is yell at him for not making enough money." Leaders then incorporate the children's ideas into a continuation of the skit by saying, "Those are really great ideas. Let's use some of them and see what happens with Mr. and Mrs. Blue." The fight then continues with the children's suggestions woven into the dialogue as the argument escalates. It concludes with the father storming out of the house.

After a while, leaders stop the skit again, and ask where the children are during this fight. Answers elicited include anywhere from outside the house to listening at the door. Leaders can suggest that children often wish they were not around when parents fight, or that they worry that if they don't hear what's happening, they may be in for some big surprises.

After further discussion, the leaders then suggest a skit where they will play the two Blue children upstairs overhearing the fight. The skit can look like this.

Billy: "I hate it when they fight—it makes me so scared."
Susan: "I know, it's always the same thing. I wish Dad wasn't always so late."
Billy: "It's not Dad's fault! All Mom does is yell."
Susan: "That's not true. You're just like him! Plus, it's partly your fault. Mom is in a bad mood because you didn't set the table like you were supposed to."
(And so on.)

The leaders then stop the skit and ask what is going on with the two children. They identify how the children are taking sides and suggest that sometimes when parents fight, children can start to fight too. They ask if Susan is right about it being Billy's fault, and use this as an opportunity to correct the common misperception that fighting is the fault of the children. Leaders may say, "Even if the parents fight about something the kids have done, it's because the grown-ups just can't get along and not because the kid did something wrong like not setting the table. When parents stop being able to get along, a lot of times they will fight about anything." Leaders then try to emphasize coping strategies around parental fighting, asking youngsters in the group what kinds of things they can do when parents fight. Wishes that children can break up the fights themselves are countered with suggestions for finding appropriate ways to weather the storm. Communicational strategies with parents are also encouraged (see the full version of this manual, Kalter and Associates, 1985, for an elaboration of coping strategies).

Session 3—Telling Children about the Divorce

The aims of this session are to permit feelings of loss, vulnerability, self-blame, and confusion about the very early stages of divorce to emerge. We also seek to encourage coping skills for communicating these concerns to a parent. The session typically begins with a brief review of the previous session. Children actively remind the leaders that the parents had "been fighting and that the dad had left." Leaders ask the children where they think the father may have gone. Some youngsters say he has gone to their grandparents' house, while others say that he is at a hotel. Leaders may comment on children's worries about the parent who is not there and whether he or she is all right. The leaders then introduce the first skit in which the father returns home, and the parents have a resigned discussion about the fact that no matter what efforts they make, they still end up always fighting and feeling angry. One reason to reemphasize the process of continued fights is to dispel the "one-event" theory of divorce many young children appear to hold. That is, many youngsters have the idea that a *single* fight or *one* argument can lead to divorce. It is helpful to identify this issue for the youngsters, so that those whose parents have remarried need not worry at the first sign of friction between the parent and stepparent that this marriage too will end in divorce. Further, it reduces a youngster's sense that any one act that *they* may have engaged in was the "single thing" that led to the divorce. It is our experience that group members wish to discuss this issue, and it is helpful for leaders to address the various concerns that arise in that discussion.

The skit ends with the two parents deciding that a divorce would be the most adaptive decision for the family, and they discuss the need to tell the children. Leaders then ask the group members, "How do kids usually find out about divorce?" Group members share a variety of ways in which they have been told, or report that they were never directly informed and had to figure out for themselves what was happening. One youngster, in a very poignant manner, described how he had heard his mother and father fighting, and then his mother left the house. His father took him and his sister into their "storybook chair" and told them that he and their mother were going to get a divorce. He reassured them that he and their mother would both still love them. This example was striking, because as the child remembered this painful time, which had been dealt with in such a comforting and supportive manner, the other group members seemed to receive some reassurance and support as well.

Leaders then ask the children what hearing the word "divorce" makes them think about, and what kinds of questions children may have when they are told their parents are going to separate. A list of questions may be generated on a newsprint taped to a wall for all to see by going around the group circle asking for each child's ideas.

Two role plays then ensue: in one skit the male group leader plays a boy and the female group leader plays his mother; and in the second skit the male leader plays the father and the female leader plays his daughter. The ways in which these role plays unfold are highly variable across groups. Typically, in the first role play, the mother begins by reiterating for the children that they know that she and their father have been fighting for a long time, and have not been able to get along. She tells the children that they are planning to get a divorce and invites them to ask any questions. Group members tend to ask questions that focus on whose fault the divorce is, how the father (the nonresident-to-be parent) will fare; whether there will be enough money, whether they will have to leave their home, and perhaps most centrally, with which parent they will live. The female leader, in the role of mother, takes the stance of being both reassuring as well as direct about the fact that there may be many changes. Some of these questions do not have immediate or pat answers. Youngsters are told that for now they will stay in their house, but it may be necessary to move. She empathizes with how difficult divorce is for children. Following this skit, a role play is enacted with the father talking to his children. Similar questions and concerns arise in the context of this skit. (For those interested in a more complete elaboration of how these skits tend to unfold, and the variety of ways that leaders can address the specific issues raised by the children, see Kalter and Associates, 1985.)

Session 4—Custody Issues

The aims of this session are to permit feelings and questions regarding the determination of custody to emerge, to address the conflicted loyalty often associated with custody decisions, to clarify the realities of how custody is decided and under what conditions it can be reconsidered, and to normalize feelings of loss and sadness about having to give up one parent in order to live with the other. The session begins with a general discussion about what a custody decision involves, and identifying the people who play key roles in making custody decisions. Children are then invited to participate in a courtroom scenario about a custody dispute. This role play is quite familiar to many children, from personal experience as well as those who report watching "Divorce Court" on television. One of the leaders plays the judge and the children play the parts of parents, the children, attorneys, and the bailiff. The other coleader facilitates the complex role playing that this skit demands by acting as a "floating coach" to the youngsters.

After dividing up the parts, the leaders help the different "attorneys" prepare with their respective "clients." Legal pads are often provided and questions are mapped out. The trial begins with the bailiff calling the court into session, where all the members rise as Judge X (often dressed in a black robe) enters the room to hold court. The witnesses are sworn in and the attorneys begin the examination and cross-examination of the parents. Allegations surrounding the best interests of the children are often independently brought up by the group members, and the lawyers try to discredit the opposing party. (This scene is a particularly complex one, with children raising many issues. Among the most common are those of divided loyalty regarding which parents to side with, a fear of hurting or angering a parent that they do not side with, and feeling both saddened and enraged by the antagonism between parents that is portrayed in this scene and which so often accompanies custody disputes. Group leaders can both empathize with and normalize each of these issues using universalized statements such as, "Kids can be real angry and sad at the same time to see their parents arguing and bad-mouthing each other like we just saw" (in the role play). Another sort of comment that leaders can make is, "It's very hard for most kids to be asked questions about which parent they want to live with. After all, the *parents* are the ones getting a divorce; the kids aren't getting a divorce from either parent. And besides, most kids love *both* parents."

After the courtroom scene the group members are told that they will enact another skit in which the children are interviewed by the judge in his or her chambers. Leaders point out that this is a more private discussion than the proceedings in an open courtroom, and is, in fact, the more likely way for a judge to proceed in custody disputes. Youngsters are told that their opinions can be taken into account by a judge, but that there are many other factors that judges have to consider when trying to reach a decision about custody. The aim here is to relieve participants of the burden of believing that they are primarily, or solely, responsible for the final decision. We have found it helpful to dispel the "12-year-old" myth which emphasizes that children have nearly full control over where they will live once they reach that age. Following all of the testimony, the judge announces that he or she will take a recess to review all of the materials, and will render a verdict in the following week's session. Children are told, "Sometimes you have to wait a long time before you hear how things will turn out when a divorce is happening."

We have found this session to be particularly engaging in our later elementary school groups. Children readily take to this scene, and make use of the dramatic license that this role play permits. The multitude of themes that emerge in this session often have important implications for children's understanding of the custody decision process as well as the development of their feelings of self-worth (as opposed to self-blame) regarding the custody arrangements.

Session 5—Visiting Issues

The aims of this session are to permit feelings and thoughts about visits with the nonresident parent, or the lack thereof, to emerge. The child's feelings about parental competition for his or her affection, anger over continued interparental hostility, and sadness about minimal or no contact with the nonresident parent are also discussed. Leaders seek to normalize these feelings, to clarify possible reasons that a nonresident parent would have little or no contact with a child, and to develop coping strategies for dealing with these feelings and family interactions.

The session begins with a brief recap of last week's meeting, followed by the judge's verdict. Typically, youngsters respond briefly to the judge's decision, and the leaders move on quickly to the topic of visitation. The discussion may begin with a review of each group member's particular visitation arrangement. This is done by the leaders saying, "Today we're going to be talking about visiting the parent you don't live with most of the time. Let's go around the circle and see what different kinds of schedules we have in our group." The leaders then introduce the idea of a skit where children are waiting to be picked up for a visit with their father. Group members volunteer to participate in the skit and play the children who are waiting for their father to arrive. The female group leader plays the mother who is waiting with the children, and the male leader plays one of her sons. In this scenario the children are anxiously awaiting their father, who is not on time. As the children get more and more upset, their mother begins to get angry. She berates the father for being late. After a few minutes the skit is stopped, and the leaders ask the group what is happening. The discussion that follows often includes youngsters' frustration that the divorce was supposed to make things "work better" but "they still fight like they did when they were married." Leaders suggest that one reason that the mother may be angry is because she knows that her children are feeling worried and disappointed that their father is not there on time. Using the universalized statement format, leaders can say, "Maybe the reason that the mom is bad-mouthing the dad is because she's trying to help her kids feel better about their disappointment." This usually leads to fairly extensive discussions within the group about how children wish to feel important to their nonresident parent. Leaders may then talk about the fact that after parents divorce, they "Sometimes have big grown-up problems. Sometimes it's hard for parents to act in ways that kids would want them to, but that doesn't mean that parents don't care about their kids. And it doesn't mean that there's anything wrong with the kids." This helps reduce children's feelings that they are not worthy of their parent's attention and affection, without derogating the nonresident parent.

The second scene of this skit involves a visit with father during which they go to McDonald's for lunch. Several of the group members can participate in this skit as the children and the male leader plays the father. In this scene the children tend to order a great deal of food: it is not at all unusual to hear *each* child order two or three Big Macs, a large order of french fries, a milkshake, and a piece of pie. After several large orders are placed by the children, leaders may say, "Boy these kids sure seem hungry. What do you think is going on?" Leaders can suggest that because the youngsters do not get to see their father as much as they would like, they want to "fill up as much as they can on good things such as food, presents, and other fun, good stuff when they are with him." At times participants spontaneously express anger about their nonresident parent trying to "buy them off." This affords leaders an opportunity to make the connection between "hurt, sad feelings and how kids sometimes use angry feelings to sweep the hurt away." Again, the focus is on children's feelings of self-worth as well as their anger.

This skit ends with either an announcement that it is time to return to their mother's home, or a plan to stop at a video store to pick up a tape because that night the father has a date and the children are going to be left with a babysitter. In the latter case, angry and resentful responses flare up about father having plans that do not include the children, and the intrusion of someone new (the dating partner) into their special time with their father.

The final scene in this skit involves the return home, when the children are "grilled" about the visit by their mother. Competitive feelings between the parents for the children's attention and affection are discussed, and the ways in which this leaves youngsters feelings are interpreted. Group participants respond to this skit in a variety of ways. For example, one girl, upon the return home, said to the mother, "Dad has a new girlfriend, but she wasn't as pretty as you, Mom." Another youngster said, "Dad said he would buy me new jeans next week. He said I could pick whatever pair I wanted." Leaders can address comments of this sort by noting, "Kids can sure worry that a mom might feel bad when she hears about the dad's new dating partner. Sometimes kids even think that they sort of have to protect their mom from feeling bad." Leaders can also comment on the competitive feelings that parents sometimes have with each other in which parents attempt to become a youngster's "favorite parent." Leaders can empathize with the feeling of being put in the middle between two competitive parents.

Finally, depending on the composition of the group, and the particular life circumstances represented in the group, leaders can raise the issue of what it is like for children who do not get to see the parent they do not live with. Newsprint is taped to the wall, and group members are invited to help construct a "Letter to a Missing Parent." One of the leaders can begin the letter with, "Dear Missing Parent." Then, going around the circle, group members take turns adding a line to the letter. Letters have included comments such as, "I love you still and hope to see you soon" and "I hope you don't answer this letter back. We are doing fine without you!" Leaders can then discuss the mixed feelings youngsters have when a parent does not seem to have a place for them in his or her life. Leaders can also empathize with underlying feelings of sadness and rejection that lead to anger. We have found it helpful to tell our participants, "Because grown-ups can have some big problems, it's sometimes very hard for them to be the kind of parent that a kid wishes they could have. That's not because of anything bad that the kid did. And it's not because the parent is bad." In this way feelings of diminished self-worth, which are so often connected with egocentric interpretations on the part of youngsters about why a parent does not visit frequently, or at all, can be constructively addressed.

Session 6—Remarriage and Stepparenting Issues

The aims of this session are to permit feelings such as competition with the stepparent, loyalty conflicts regarding the stepparent and parent of the same sex, and resentment over the stepparent's attempt to discipline the child to emerge. It is also important to normalize these feelings and to emphasize coping strategies that will serve to maximize the possibility of constructing a positive relationship with a stepparent. Typically, the first scene of the role play in this session involves the female leader playing the mother, the male leader playing her dating partner, and the children participating as the youngsters in the family. The scene is set at a family dinner. The mother begins by saying, "You know that Bob and I have been dating for a while now. We've decided that we're going to get married." Responses to this introduction vary considerably from one group to another. Spontaneously, some children say things such as, "That's great," or "It'll be nice to have Bob around more," while other group members have said, "You're what? You can't be serious, What about us? Don't we have anything to say about it?", or "Not Bob! He's such a jerk!" Leaders can address the reactions by making comments such as, "It sure sounds like the mom's kids like the idea," "It sounds like the kids feel left out of this big decision," or "I think a lot of kids have some angry feelings and upset feelings when they hear that their mom is going to get married again." These comments serve to articulate, empathize with, and normalize the reactions that the children express.

In some groups what is emphasized in this session is discipline by mother's dating partner. This issue tends to generate discussion regarding loyalty conflicts in youngster's feelings toward the dating partner or stepparent and the parent of the same gender, the legitimacy of a stepparent's or dating partner's authority over the children, and the reason that mother is permitting her partner to have so much authority. A short skit may be used in which Bob, the dating partner, takes a parental role. The role play may begin with Bob saying, "Susan, you can't be excused from the table before you clear your dishes away." The youngster may respond with various expressions of reluctance to comply with this chore. Ultimately, she may say, "You aren't my dad and I don't have to be excused by you at all!" Susan then looks to the leader playing the mother in hopes of gaining confirmation for that position. The leader, as mother, stumbles around in a manner in which it appears that she is attempting to appease both her dating partner and daughter, simultaneously. Leaders can stop the skit at that point and ask the group what they see happening in the role play. This usually leads to reactions that the group members have to the dating partner assuming a parental role. In one group a participant asked to go back to the skit, and then independently got up from the "table" and placed a phone call to his father to complain about the dating partner's behavior. Leaders were able to use this opportunity to discuss the loyalty concerns children have in this situation: to comply with a dating partner's or stepparent's parentlike authority feels akin to being disloyal to their father.

Finally, leaders and group members discuss the benefits of stepparents, and the ways in which youngsters can come to an understanding about the new roles, expectations, and rules in a remarried family. To facilitate this understanding, youngsters may be encouraged to role-play explaining to Bob that they just don't feel comfortable calling him "Dad" because they already have a father, or engage in a skit where they tell their mother that they are worried that they will no longer have special time with her. The twin issues that are most common in our groups concerning the issue of stepparents are the unwanted parentlike authority of the stepparent and the feelings of competition with him (her) for the parent's time and affection. It is helpful for leaders to empathize with these feelings, normalize them, and suggest ways of communicating their concerns to parents and possibly stepparents. (For a more complete discussion of coping strategies, the reader is referred to the full, original manual, Kalter and Associates, 1985.)

Session 7—The Divorce Newspaper

The aims of this session are to summarize and integrate issues that have been discussed in the course of the group meetings, to give children a concrete remembrance of the group, and to provide a potential vehicle for parent–child communication. Between this session and the next one, leaders use materials gathered to construct a divorce newspaper. The group leaders begin the session by introducing the idea of developing a newspaper and naming it (for example, *Divorce Gazette, Divorce Post*). Next, leaders ask the group what kinds of things go into a newspaper. A brief discussion then follows during which ideas about interviews, articles, an advice column, and polls/surveys surface. Typically, we use sheets of newsprint taped to a wall as well as tape recorders during the session. The tape recorders are not only an excellent prop, but also provide a record of what has been said in this session for the leaders to refer back to when constructing the newspaper.

We usually begin with one of the leaders acting as a reporter for the newspaper who is interviewing a youngster about his or her ideas about divorce. The leader may say, "This is your ace reporter from the *Divorce Ga-*

zette. I'm at _____ school to interview kids about their ideas and feelings about divorce. I see a girl coming toward me now. Hi, I'm Ms. _____ from the *Divorce Gazette.* I'd like to ask you some questions about divorce. First, tell me your name, and then let's tell our readers what it's like for kids when their parents split up." A brief interview is then conducted, after which group discussion takes place. Then leaders suggest that one of the group members take the role of a reporter, and conduct an interview with another group member or a group leader. These interviews are excellent vehicles for summarizing and discussing key themes that emerged over the course of the group sessions.

After several youngsters have had a turn at interviewing (and/or being interviewed), we introduce the idea of a survey or poll. This concept is explained to the group, and a topic for this activity is suggested. Some topics have included the Five Best (Worst) Things about Divorce, What Parents Need to Know about How Kids Feel about Divorce, Things Kids Can Do When They Feel Upset, and so forth. Leaders (or participants) introduce a particular focus for a survey or poll, and then leaders go around the circle asking youngsters to respond to that survey. This activity too leads to active discussion of important issues that have been covered in the group.

Finally, an advice column is constructed. Youngsters, with the help of group leaders, make up letters to an expert. Children have picked names for this column such as Dear Divorce Expert, Dear Mr. Divorce, and, of course, Dear Abby. Using the format of going around the circle to construct a group story, the group contributes collectively to two or three such brief letters. As is the case with such advice columns, the "person" writing the letter (actually it is the entire group) signs the letter in ways such as "Puzzled in Pittsburgh," "From a Kid Who Likes His Stepfather," "Angry in Alabama," and the like. After each letter is written and recorded by a group leader on the newsprint taped to a wall, the group discusses how the advice columnist can respond. Because of time constraints, a full response is not constructed verbatim. Instead, discussion about what would go into a response takes place, and the group leaders then write the response when they put together the newspaper in between this session and the next one. Examples of completed newspapers can be found in the original manual (Kalter & Associates, 1985).

This session rapidly flows through nearly all of the centrally important themes that have emerged in the course of previous sessions. It is usually regarded by group members as one of their favorite sessions. As the session is ending, leaders remind the group members that the next meeting is the last one, and there is then a brief discussion of the group-ending party. Leaders tell the group that they will be providing food and drinks, and will be distributing the group newspaper. In nearly all of the groups youngsters opt for pizza and soda pop. Finally, a member of the school's staff comes into the group room in order to take a picture of the entire group, including the leaders. This is done with an instant-developing camera. It is a good idea to take several pictures, so that there is a good chance of having one that will photocopy easily. The picture of the group appears on the front page of the divorce newspaper.

Following this session, the leaders meet and use the material that has come up in order to construct a three-to-five-page newspaper for the final meeting. The newspaper will contain a combination of brief articles, reports of surveys and polls, and an advice column. The front page of the newspaper has the group picture photocopied on it and a list of the "staff reporters" (the group leaders' and group members' names).

Session 8—The Group Party

The aims of this session are to summarize issues covered during group sessions, to encourage parent–child communication about divorce feelings and ideas, and to reduce our participants' sense of loss as the group comes to an end. Leaders provide pizza and soda pop, and youngsters often bring other snacks and/or desserts to the meeting. The leaders distribute three copies of the group newspaper to each youngster for them to take home. Members take turns reading the paper aloud (usually with great pleasure) and this is then used as a springboard to both review important issues and to reminisce together.

After reading and discussing the group newspaper (which takes approximately 10–15 minutes), leaders remind the group that they will be meeting with their parents. Leaders emphasize that they will not reveal individual confidences, and go on to elicit suggestions from the group about what they "want parents to know about divorce and how it affects kids." Ideas that usually surface include wanting parents to know how bad it feels when parents fight, argue, and bad-mouth each other; how much youngsters resent being disciplined by a parent's dating partner or by a stepparent; that children worry about each parent feeling bad after divorce; and so on.

With approximately 25 minutes remaining in the session, the food is brought in. Leaders usually arrange to have the pizza delivered at a particular time, or the school cafeteria keeps pizzas delivered earlier warm. Paper plates, napkins, and paper cups are distributed and the party begins. During this time group members are often very relaxed, joke with one another and the leaders, and generally seem to enjoy a sense of closeness with one another. Leaders from time to time make comments such as, "Sometimes it's kind of hard to say good-bye after people have been together talking about important things" and "Kids sometime have sad, missing feelings when a group is going to end, almost like it felt when the divorce happened and their family changed and sort of ended and stopped being the family they were used to." Surfacing these feelings of sadness and loss is important, and children will sometimes express a wish to have more sessions and/or to know more about the leaders' personal lives. The final few minutes are spent cleaning up and saying good-bye in an informal way. Leaders note, "We've enjoyed meeting with you and getting to know you. We're going to miss you, but we're glad we had a chance to work together because we think that you'll be able to make things go even better for yourselves now that we've had a chance to talk about all of these importance divorce things." The ending of the group is a poignant moment; both leaders and youngsters have a mix of good feelings of accomplishment and closeness as well as sad feelings about saying good-bye.

The Early Elementary School Model

Adaptations for Children in Early Elementary School

Following the successful implementation of this model for later elementary school–aged children, we developed a revised program for early elementary school–aged youngsters in grades 1 through 3. Because of the different developmental abilities and needs of this population, we modified the original model in several ways.

First, due to their age and relatively limited level of cognitive ability to understand complex issues, we increased our focus on providing basic information about divorce and divorce-related issues. This included attention to defining terms such as "stepparent," "stepbrother/sister," "half-brother/sister," "custody," "child support," and so forth. Second, although the use of displacement activities and universalized statements remained the centrally important techniques for conducting the groups, it was necessary to further sharpen the distinction between the displacement activities and the real relationships within the group. We found, for example, that when group leaders enacted a role-play scenario about parents fighting, our young group members in grades 1 through 3 became quite frightened at times. It was hard for them to make the emotional distinction between the leaders as helping adults and the leaders in their role as angry parents. To facilitate the experiential distinction between the leaders in role-play actions versus their being concerned and caring adults, we introduced the use of hand puppets for the skits. Thus, as leaders played their roles, they did so by each manipulating a hand puppet. As leaders shifted between being in a particular role and making comments from the perspective of a group leader, the puppets could be either put forth in front of them (as a role was being enacted) or simply put behind their back when they talked directly to the group as leaders. Third, given the difficulty that young children have in sustaining their role as a member of a group confronting conflictual and emotionally charged issues, and their need for increased activity to discharge emotional tension, it became necessary to incorporate an activity that permitted youngsters to productively *disengage* from the group process from time to time. Thus, we introduced the idea of a weekly drawing exercise. The focus of the drawings included "What You Can Do When Parents Fight," "A Visit with the Parent You Don't Live With," "Meeting a Parent's Dating Partner," and the like. These drawing activities take place in the last 10 minutes or so of a session, and permit leaders to circulate in the group and provide individual attention to members. It also permits youngsters a chance to settle down (if they have been upset by the material of the session), as they quietly address divorce-specific issues individually through the medium of drawing. Thus it serves as an excellent session-ending activity. The pictures are also used, frequently, to provide a sense of continuity across sessions. Leaders can begin a subsequent session with a review and sharing of pictures completed at the end of the previous session.

These changes led to several alterations in the way in which the program is implemented. These were noted briefly in our general description of the intervention. They include having 10 sessions rather than 8, having slightly smaller groups, and having group members be not more than one grade apart.

Session 1—Introduction to the Group

The aims of this session are to introduce the children and leaders to one another and to identify the rules and focus of the group. In addition, the process of normalizing the experience of being a child from a divorced family and building a sense of group cohesion begins. The session starts with leaders introducing themselves to the children and noting that the focus of the group will be on "divorce and how kids feel and think about it." The leaders also note that the group will meet for 50 minutes each week and that they will have a total of 10 meetings. Leaders then suggest an activity called "The Name Game" which youngsters of this age enjoy. This activity begins with a group leader asking for a volunteer to say his or her name. After a youngster has stated his or her name, the next youngster in the group circle (going to the left or right) says his or her name as well as the name of the child who spoke first. This activity passes around the circle with each member saying his or her name and the names of all other children who have preceded them in the circle.

Next, leaders note the importance of "having some rules so that a group can go better." They then introduce the four *group rules*. These rules are the same ones that were used in the Later Elementary School model: (1) no interruptions, (2) no put-downs, (3) one can pass, and (4) confidentiality.

Leaders then tape a large sheet of newsprint to the wall, and tell the group that they are going to draw a picture of a "Family before Divorce." One of the leaders facilitates the discussion of what this might look like, while the other draws the various family members and pets that the children describe. Usually youngsters come up with the idea of the family having a mother, father, two or three children, a baby, and various pets. The leader who is recording this on the sheet of newsprint draws small figures in the house that is on the large sheet of newsprint, and records the identity of each. One of the leaders facilitates group discussion while the other draws the various family members and pets that the participants describe. This is done on the left-hand half of the large sheet of newsprint taped to the wall. Then leaders say, "Now we're going to draw a picture of what this family might look like after a divorce." The youngsters provide various family configurations which are drawn on the right-hand half of the newsprint. The drawing on the lefthand is labeled the "Family before Divorce" and the one on the righthand is labeled the "Family after Divorce." Usually, the righthand, "Family after Divorce" picture consists of the original house with the mother and children in it as well as a smaller house (or apartment building) in which the father lives. Initially, it is common for groups to describe the postdivorce family configurations as consisting of the mother, girls, baby, and cat while the other postdivorce household has a father, the boys, and the dog in it. When leaders ask the group if this is really what it's like after divorce, most groups come up with the first configuration described above.

Finally, participants are each given their own piece of paper with a line drawn down the middle vertically and crayons or markers. Leaders tell the group that they are going to draw a picture of their own family before and after divorce. The leaders then circulate around the room and assist the children with the project. One common occurrence across groups has been that the youngster's emphasis on the "Before" picture leads to difficulty in moving on to drawing the "After" picture. Leaders make universalized comments to the group such as, "It seems like kids try and remember what it was like before the divorce and have a hard time drawing what things are like after a divorce. Sometimes it feels good to remember what it was like before divorce and kids like to think more about that than what it's like after the divorce." As the session draws to a close, the pictures are collected and placed in individual folders. The group is told that the folders will be used throughout the group and then it will be theirs to take home when the group ends. The children are reminded when the group meets again, and good-byes are said.

Session 2—The Group Story

The session begins with a review of the "Name Game" as a way of reminding everyone who is who. Leaders then show each child's picture from the previous week's session. This is a way to review as well as to help illustrate the similarities and differences in postdivorce families. This time is used to normalize the children's shared experiences and to try to clarify any remaining cognitive confusions. For example, it is not uncommon for at least one youngster to be uncertain about who regularly lives in his or her house or what the visiting schedule is with the parent who does not live with them. It is important that leaders note all of the different kinds of changes that youngsters go through when their parents divorce and articulate for the group that "All these changes can make kids feel sad and confused."

Following this brief review, the leaders introduce the main activity for the day. Youngsters are told that the group will be making up a story about a family that is "headed for divorce." The development of the story remains much the same as it did for the later elementary school–aged group, with group members first identifying who is in this imaginary family and then going around in the circle with each youngster adding a line to the story. After each youngster has given his or her end to the story, leaders read the story that has been written on the newsprint taped to the wall for everyone to see. Major themes that emerge in this activity include concerns about receiving basic child care and anxieties, as well as sadness over being separated from one or both parents. Fantasies of reconciliation are also quite common and are discussed as a wish that "lots of kids have." The leaders remind children, however, that "this is sort of like a fairy tale, but like fairy tales it's something that doesn't happen." Leaders empathize with and normalize the concerns that children express in this displacement activity using universalized statements.

Session 3—Parent Fighting

In this session the idea of interparental hostility is the central focus. Leaders begin the process of helping children understand and identify the reasons why some parents divorce. This is the first session that incorporates the use of puppets as the primary vehicle for the role play. The children become very emotionally involved in the skits that leaders put on using the hand puppets. Leaders can sit side by side facing the group or may sit behind a table when performing the puppet skits. It is important to emphasize that when using the hand puppets leaders should put the hand holding the puppet behind their back when making comments from the perspective of a group leader. This helps to sharpen the distinction between the leaders as helping adults and the leaders in their roles as angry parents. Since the skits are enacted by the group leaders, it is helpful to use a "stop-action" format in which the role play is stopped frequently. Discussion can then follow about what is going on in the skit and how the group members understand and feel about what they are observing.

The first skit involves a father arriving home late for dinner. Although similar to the skit introduced for the older children, the initial level of aggression between parents is modulated for these younger children. It has been our experience that youngsters in early elementary school are quite reactive to the hostilities between parents that are portrayed in this displacement activity and their concerns are easily stimulated. Following this skit, the leaders ask the group about the argument and elicit suggestions about what should follow. The second skit involves an escalation of the fight between the parents. In the third skit two "children puppets," who are upstairs overhearing the parents fighting, are introduced. The leaders play these children and ask the group for suggestions about what the imaginary youngsters can do when they overhear their parents fighting. These ideas are incorporated into the role play. The leaders then enact a final scene in which the father decides to leave the house for the night.

Leaders then introduce the idea of how youngsters can cope when their parents fight. It is important to note that in this discussion with younger children leaders need to be mindful of the fact that coping options are often limited by what age-appropriate responses are. For example, although a child may wish to leave the house while the parents are yelling at each other, it is not the most reasonable choice since most children of this age need a parent's permission before they leave the house, especially in the evening. Leaders may say, "It sure would be nice to be able to get out of there when all that fighting is going on, but going out without asking permission, or interrupting a fight between parents in order to ask permission, is really not the best idea." A leader may follow up by asking, "But, what could kids do *inside* the house to feel safe and keep their mind off the fight?" Youngsters usually come up with ideas such as going to their room and closing the door, going to the basement and turning on the TV which is down there, or playing with some favorite toys in their room or in the basement. These coping strategies, which rest on the idea of removing oneself from the field of battle, are reinforced by leaders as being smart and helpful ways of coping with hostilities between parents. Leaders also note, "Divorce is grown-up business. Even though kids feel like they should do something to help out or stop parents from fighting, that's really not the best thing to try." Following this discussion, children are told that they are going to draw a picture about one of their ideas of what to do when parents fight. The remaining 5 to 10 minutes of the session is spent in this activity, with group leaders circulating among the youngsters, helping them articulate their ideas and translate them into drawings. Pictures often have represented children watching television, hiding under their beds, calling friends on the telephone, playing with toys in their room, or even coloring or drawing a picture.

Session 4—Parents Tell the Children about Their Separation

The session begins with a recap of the previous one, using a review of the children's pictures as the main way to accomplish this. The puppets are reintroduced to the group, and the parent puppets briefly meet and decide that they are going to pursue a divorce. The mother puppet then says that she will need to find a way to tell the children. The leaders stop the skit and ask the group how children hear about divorce, and the kinds of questions that children have when their parents tell them that they are going to split up. Leaders tape a piece of newsprint to the wall and create a list of questions that kids may want to ask their mom when she tells them that she and dad are going to get a divorce. Group discussion results in several common questions: (1) Whose fault is the divorce? (2) Where will we live? (3) Will we get to see Dad (Mom)? (4) Will we have to move? (5) Will we have enough money to buy food to eat?, and the like.

Leaders then tell the children that they will have a chance to participate in the puppet play this week. In some groups each youngster is given a puppet to use, while in other groups we have passed the "boy puppet" among the boys in the group and the "girl puppet" among the girls in the group. The youngster holding a puppet at any given time is "in the skit" and has an opportunity to ask his or her question. Youngsters eagerly participate in this skit, asking the sorts of questions noted above. The female leader, in the role as mother in this skit, reassures the children as best as possible about their concerns and makes comments such as, "Divorce is about a man and woman deciding not to be a husband and wife, but it is *not* about them deciding not to be a mommy or a daddy. They will always be your mom and your dad." Using universalized statements, leaders also emphasize how much children of this age worry when they hear their parents are getting a divorce. Sometimes, in order to facilitate the flow of this skit, the male leader will take one of the child puppets and ask questions to further the discussion. He might ask, "Is it my fault that you're getting a divorce?" The discussion of this skit also includes ideas about what can help children feel better when they feel sad, mad, or worried. The leaders then introduce the idea of a picture about "How kids feel when their parents are getting a divorce." The children then leave the circle that the group usually sits in and go to the desks or tables to draw their pictures. The leaders circulate among the youngsters talking quietly with each child and helping them think about and draw their pictures.

Session 5—Meeting with Father Following the Marital Separation

This session allows the children the opportunity to describe and experience the feeling of loss surrounding the initial marital separation with the concomitant loss of the nonresident parent. It also gives the group a chance to clarify and concretize the changes that divorce so often brings to the lives of children. The session begins with the sharing of last week's drawings. Leaders attempt to normalize the feelings surrounding the children learning about their parents' plans to divorce by making universalized statements such as, "It seems like most kids feel sad when they find out that their mom and dad are going to get divorced." It is not uncommon for young elementary school children to be quite open about their sadness once they have been given permission to do so.

After this discussion, leaders introduce the idea of a skit that involves children asking their father questions when he comes to see them. The group is told that they will do a skit about "A dad who has just started living in a different place coming back to the house to talk to the children about divorce." The leaders tape a piece of newsprint to the wall, and invite the group to think of questions that kids might want to ask their dad when he comes to see them. The questions that come up are similar to the ones raised in the previous session that were directed to mother. However, in addition to those questions, children raise several new ones for the father: Will he feel sad living all by himself? Will he be able to provide for himself living all alone? Will he remember and think about his children? The children take turns asking the male leader, in his role as father, these sorts of questions. It is also common for group members to ask the "father" when they will see him again. Leaders articulate and normalize the concerns that emerge in the course of this puppet play and in the discussions that take place as the action is stopped and started during it.

With about 5 to 10 minutes remaining in the session, the leaders introduce the drawing activity for the week. They suggest to the group that they draw something that "Kids can do to help make themselves feel better when they're feeling sad, mad, or bad." Again, as is usually the case, leaders circulate among group members addressing each youngster's concerns quietly.

Session 6—Visiting the Nonresident Parent

The aims of this session are to allow the children to deal with issues of continued parental hostility, the loyalty conflicts that often emerge in the context of visiting the nonresident parent, and—more specific to this age group—the separation concerns that often accompany visiting away from home. The session begins with a review of the week before, using the drawings from the previous session as a way of building in a sense of continuity between sessions. The key issues are highlighted by group leaders as they emerge in the context of reviewing the drawings, and leaders empathize with and normalize the concerns that arise in this discussion.

After approximately 5 to 10 minutes, leaders introduce the idea of an overnight visit with the nonresident parent. Group members are asked to describe what their visiting schedule is with the parent with whom they do not live regularly. It is helpful for the leaders to have some knowledge (from the parents) about what the visiting arrangements are to assist the youngster who says, "I don't remember" or "I don't know." Leaders can then remind a youngster who makes comments of this sort what the facts of the visiting schedule are. Leaders then introduce the first skit, a telephone call from the nonresident parent to discuss an upcoming visit. Each child gets a turn at part of the telephone conversation, using a toy telephone that is passed around the circle among the group members. The group member in possession of the telephone is the one who participates in the role play at that point. This telephone discussion with the nonresident parent usually includes conversation about how the child is doing and making plans for the upcoming visit. This skit elicits various reactions and responses from children including not wanting to talk to the parent, wanting to talk quietly to the parent on the telephone without the other parent being in the room, and asking if they can do something very special during the upcoming visit, such as to go to Disney World for that weekend. The leaders stop the skits for discussion and note that "sometimes kids think they need to do something special with the parent they don't live with as a way to make sure that *they* are special, but even if they can't go somewhere like Disney World, that doesn't mean that they aren't really important to that parent." This universalized statement addresses a common concern of young elementary school children: they are worried that they are no longer important, or even thought about, by the nonresident parent.

Depending upon a particular group's visitation arrangements and concerns, leaders can choose which skits to focus on in the remainder of this session. A detailed accounting of those skits, including what youngsters usually say in them and how group leaders might most helpfully respond, is given in the original manual (Kalter & Associates, 1988). For the youngest children, a skit focused on packing a suitcase in preparation for a visit with the nonresident parent provides the opportunity to discuss the concerns and even anxieties that many young children feel about being separated from their primary custodial parent for overnight visits. Other skits employed are similar to those done with the older elementary school children. These include role playing a trip to McDonald's in which the children all place huge orders, and a telephone call from the children when they are with the nonresident parent to their primary custodial parent. At the end of this session the picture for the week is introduced and children are encouraged to select from one of two choices: "What a kid likes to do on a visit with the parent they don't live with" or "What a kid would like to say or do with a parent on a visit." Themes that we have observed in drawings about these topics include going to special places like amusement parks or sporting events, going to dinner at a restaurant of their choice, playing a game with the parent, and the like. Leaders talk to group members individually in order to help them select the topic for their drawing and work on it.

Session 7—Parent Dating

The aims of this session are to identify the issues that continue to arise around visitation and to introduce the idea of parent dating. Children's con-

tinued difficulty with loyalty issues, feelings of competition for parental attention and affection, and the wish to hold on to reconciliation fantasies are
all explored.

Following the review of the previous week's drawings, leaders introduce
a skit that includes a parent's girlfriend (or boyfriend) joining the parent and
the children during a visit. Group members have little difficulty expressing
their anxiety, anger, and discontent about the idea of parent dating when
this is introduced through the puppet play. Usually this is done by enacting
with the puppets the role play that appears in Session 5 in the later elementary school model. Leaders can comment on children's feelings about wanting time alone with the parent they do not live with, and how difficult it is
to share him (her) with someone new who is special to that parent. Leaders
also identify youngsters' worries about telling the other parent, upon return
home, about this new development. In fact, this is usually accomplished
through a skit in which the children, upon returning to their primary residence, tell their mother (father) about the other parent's new dating partner.
Leaders use this opportunity to discuss with the group the mixed feelings
children have about a parent's dating partner. Because young elementary
school children are particularly receptive to affection and attention from
adults, this can lead to conflicted feelings in their loyalty toward the parent
who is of the same gender as the other parent's dating partner. In fact, we
have observed that youngsters often attempt to protect a parent's feelings by
noting that the other parent's dating partner is not as pretty, as smart, or as
nice as that other parent.

In the group picture for the week, youngsters are offered a choice between drawing about "What kids think or feel when they see their dad's
girlfriend or their mom's boyfriend" or "How kids feel when the visit is over
and they come back home." Group members often express feelings of curiosity about the parent's dating partner, sadness and/or anger about having
to share the parent with his (her) dating partner, and concerns about the
other parent feeling hurt and/or angry about the children spending time with
a parent's dating partner. Leaders articulate and normalize these feelings as
they quietly circulate among group members during the drawing activity.

Session 8—Remarriage and Stepfamilies

This session aims to provide a forum for discussing remarriage and the idea
of a blended family. Leaders attempt to help children define the different
roles that people take when there is a remarriage, providing terms and labels
such as "stepbrother," "half-sister," "stepgrandmother," and the like. For
these young elementary school–age children, it is particularly important to
clarify cognitively the different roles and relationships that arise in the context of remarriage.

In addition to attempting to reduce cognitive confusion about remarriage and stepfamily life, leaders also address the myriad emotions that tend to emerge when parents remarry. Loyalty concerns, discipline issues, worries about one's place in a new family and in the heart of the parent who is remarried, and feelings about having to begin to give up reconciliation wishes are all addressed. Skits include a discussion of a parent's decision to marry as well as a stepfather's efforts to hand out chores and discipline his (her) stepchildren. Group leaders play the role of parents and stepparents in these skits while the youngsters take turns playing the stepchildren. The organization and structure is achieved by passing the "boy puppet" and the "girl puppet" around the group circle so that at any point in time there is one boy and one girl group member who is "in the skit," the ones in possession of the child puppets. In addition, because it appeared to be such a prevalent issue for many of the youngsters in groups we have done with children in this age group, there are several options for skits that deal with telling the children that there will be a new baby in the family. This clearly evokes concerns with being displaced and often provides for provocative and helpful discussion.

The picture choices for this session are "How kids feel about a parent getting remarried" and "The kinds of things kids and stepparents can do together." We have found that children in early elementary school are usually more receptive to the idea of a blended family, and of having a good relationship with a stepparent, than are older elementary school children. Group leaders reinforce the value of having a good relationship with a stepparent, while at the same time normalizing the loyalty conflicts that children tend to have as they begin to have positive feelings for a stepparent, or the idea of a stepparent.

Session 9—The Group Newspaper

The aims of this session are to review the materials from previous weeks and to develop a group newspaper. The latter provides a new vehicle for enhancing parent–child communication and also serves as a concrete reminder of the group meetings. This session is modeled after the one in the later elementary school program, and includes children and leaders interviewing one another as "roving reporters for the *Divorce Post*," taking polls about key divorce issues, and writing letters to an advice column expert as well as discussing replies to those letters. As was the case for the older children, tape recorders are used for the interviews, both as props and as ways to record information, and large pieces of newsprint taped to a wall are used by the leaders to write down the results of the polls and the letters to the advice column. As issues arise in the context of these activities, leaders remind the group of the nature of previous discussions around these issues, emphasizing and underscoring how common they are.

With approximately 15 minutes left in the session, the children are reminded that the next session will be the last, and plans for the group-ending party are discussed. As is the case for the older elementary school groups, early elementary school children almost invariably choose pizza and soda pop as the food for the party. The leaders then call the group's attention to the pictures that children have drawn during the groups. Each child is given his or her folder of drawings, and told that if they wish, they can select one of their drawings to be included in the newspaper. This activity serves both to generate discussion about key topics covered during the course of the group and to permit children and the leaders to reminisce together about what they have shared. This review of the drawings takes the place of actually making a picture at the end of this session.

Session 10—The Group Party and Saying Good-bye

The session begins with a review of the group's sessions and what the children remember as their "favorite" and "not-so-favorite" parts. The children reminisce about things that they liked as well as things that were hard, and the leaders take this opportunity to empathize with and normalize feelings that arise. Next, the newspaper is distributed, and the participants take turns reading articles aloud. Each youngster reads just a sentence or two since reading skills usually aren't very well developed at this age. The reading of the group newspaper is usually accompanied by much pleasure and laughter, as members recognize comments that they have made and/or pictures they have drawn that appear in the newspaper.

The food and drinks are then passed out, and children enjoy their pizza and soda pop while one leader reads the children a story. We have found that reading a story at this time both alleviates some of the anxiety about the group ending as well as providing an opportunity to further recap the central issues of divorce. Our review of the children's literature led us to select Janet Sinberg's book, *Divorce Is a Grown-Up Problem,* although several other age-appropriate divorce-related books would work as well. Children of this age are used to having parents and teachers read to them; it feels natural and comforting.

Following the reading of the story, members are reminded that the leaders will be meeting with their parents and telling them about what children think and feel about divorce. They are assured that confidentiality will be maintained, and are asked what kinds of things they think parents should be told about "What's on kids' minds when their parents get a divorce." Comments from the children often include that parents should be told that "Divorce is hard for kids," "Kids need to ask a lot of questions and need good answers," "Kids want time with both parents," and "Kids hate it when parents fight or say bad things about each other." The leaders compliment the children on their good ideas, and promise to let their parents know that these are important issues for children.

With five minutes remaining in the session, leaders tell the children, "We've really enjoyed being able to meet with you for all these weeks. We have some sad feelings, ourselves, about saying good-bye. We like you kids and we think that we've done a lot of good work together. Even grown-ups like us can have some sad, good-bye feelings." At that point the leaders note that it is the end of the group, and it is time to clean up. During the clean-up time leaders and children have a few more moments to say individual and informal good-byes. The children leave with three copies of the newspaper and their picture folders.

Parent Meetings

An important component of this intervention is the opportunity for group leaders and parents to interact with one another. There are two sessions in which parents and leaders come together; one just prior to the beginning of the children's sessions and the other shortly after the group has ended. Each meeting lasts for about an hour, and is conducted at the children's school.

The first parent–leader meeting has two primary purposes: to enable leaders to introduce themselves and the program to parents, and to enable parents to share their perspectives and/or concerns about their youngster with each other and the leaders. Group leaders begin by introducing themselves to the parents, noting their credentials and experience, and answering directly any questions from parents about who they are ("Where did you go to college?," "How long have you worked with children?," "Are you married?," and the like). Next, parents are asked to share some background information about their family such as who currently lives in their household, the ages of their children, how long they have been separated/divorced, and whether they or their ex-spouses have remarried. This gives group leaders a context within which to place each child in the group. For the Early Elementary School Module, this is especially important because young children so often are confused about the timing and occurrence of important events.

These mutual introductions usually take about 20 minutes. In the remaining time, group leaders describe divorce as a process that consists of many different potential changes in the life of a family. These changes (for example, open warfare between parents, seeing the nonresident parent infrequently or not at all, residential moves, parent dating, and parent remarriage) can be stressful to children and often stimulate questions, feelings, and worries. Leaders emphasize that this is not intended to be a group for troubled youngsters, but rather a way to help prevent difficulties by giving children a chance to learn to understand what is going on around them as well as their internal feelings and to cope effectively with these divorce-related reactions.

Leaders briefly describe the nature of the groups, focusing on the temporal unfolding of common divorce themes and especially underscoring the use of *imaginary* figures/families through the use of role play, group storytelling, puppet play, and drawings. Parents are told that leaders rarely if ever ask direct questions of children with respect to their divorce experiences. Instead, the imaginary children and families used in the displacement activities serve as vehicles for discussion of important divorce-related themes as well as triggers for children discussing their own situation. The value of group discussion and of the intervention, generally, is explained in terms of normalizing children's sense of being a youngster whose parents have divorced, clarifying questions children may have, helping children work through difficult feelings, and teaching group members coping skills. Leaders tell parents about the confidentiality rule, but also assure parents that if particularly troublesome issues arise for youngsters, that parents will be contacted after leaders have had a chance to discuss that issue with the child involved. Parents are invited to call the leaders at any time during the course of the program if they have questions about the interventions or concerns about their children.

After all of the children's group sessions have been conducted, parents and leaders meet again. The major aims of this meeting are to communicate to parents (and stepparents, if they wish to attend) the nature of the children's concerns and questions, to provide parents with suggestions about how they might cope with these issues, and to elicit feedback from parents and stepparents about how the children seem to have responded to the group.

Leaders begin by presenting the questions, ideas, and feelings that children in that particular group had. Care is taken to remind parents of the promise of confidentiality, so that statements are cast in such forms as, "Many of the kids in our group had questions about . . . ," "Nearly all of the group members had feelings about . . . ," and "Just as we found in our other groups, most of the kids in this group had worries about. . . . " Leaders usually tell parents, "We've enjoyed working with your children. They came up with a lot of issues and we were able to discuss them in constructive ways. We'd like to share the group's questions and concerns with you, but this isn't a formal lecture, so please feel free to say what's on your mind as we proceed. Let's start with a feeling that's very common for kids to have; upset feelings they have when they see their parents arguing or hear one parent put the other one down." Themes are introduced in this format, and parents are often eager to discuss them.

In the context of this second and final parent–leader meeting, leaders introduce suggestions for how to help children cope effectively with divorce-related issues. These include giving youngsters clear permission to love the other parent and enjoy being with him or her without necessarily painting an unrealistically positive picture of that parent, restricting as best one can on-going arguments between parents to times when children are not present, avoiding speaking ill of the other parents within earshot of the child, resisting the temptation to quiz the child about what happened when he or she was with the other parent, how to introduce a new dating partner to one's child, and so forth. We also introduce the idea of displacement activities and universalizing statements, and instruct parents and stepparents on how the use of such communicational styles can be helpful to children. Although parents initially express skepticism about the usefulness of such simple and transparent (to them at least) methods, they quickly and eagerly take to them when examples are given.

Finally, parents are asked what they have observed about their children over the course of the program, and what suggestions they may have for future groups. Parents are nearly unanimous in noting positive changes, especially reduction in their child's tension, anger, and/or sadness, and a greater willingness of the child to discuss divorce-related concerns with parents, and at times stepparents. Suggestions for future groups usually include having more sessions and conducting the groups each year so that children can repeat this experience. Parents rarely make other suggestions.

Value of Divorce Support Groups

Our Developmental Facilitation model has been used in over 1,500 sites representing 35 states and 2 Canadian provinces. We have conducted systematic, quantitative research on this intervention using standardized instruments to measure group members' social and emotional adjustment, self-esteem, and perception of parents. We have found that immediately after the groups, six months later, and one year later children improve significantly in many areas (Kalter, 1986, 1989; Garvin, Leber, & Kalter, 1991). Although the patterns of results using several research instruments are complex, overall there is evidence for statistically significant positive changes among children who have participated in our groups.

In addition to these relatively short-term assessments, we have conducted a four-year follow-up study of children who participated in our groups while in elementary school. Rubin (1990) compared children four years after having participated in our groups with a matched control group of youngster whose parents had divorced but who had not been in a divorce group. He found that there were statistically significant differences favoring the good adjustment of graduates of our groups, when compared to controls, on 15 of 37 standardized measures and a trend toward statistical significance on an additional 7 variables. Further, children who had never participated in our groups were referred for counseling services substantially more frequently than those who had participated in our support group (54 versus 14 percent, respectively), and the group graduates were significantly better adjusted.

In addition to these formal, quantitative assessments of the efficacy of this program, informal feedback from parents, teachers, children, and group leaders has been notably positive. Parents and teachers report that over the course of this intervention group members became less anxious, sad, and/or angry, and are much more willing than ever before to ask questions and voice concerns about their parents' divorce. Group members say that it was helpful to see that they were not "alone" and that other children have the same ideas and feelings that they had, that it was good to have a place to "get feelings out," and that they felt better able to handle worries and upsets (Kalter, Pickar, & Lesowitz, 1984). Group leaders also frequently reported having observed such changes in children, and most report that they find the intervention easy and comfortable to implement.

Systematic research and informal feedback indicate that carefully developed, conceptually guided divorce support groups can be helpful to many children. However, since neither the divorce process nor child development are static phenomena, it would be enormously useful to assess whether serial, brief interventions might add to the long-term efficacy of such support groups. We have had numerous youngsters participate in our groups several times over a period of years. Does this enhance the effects beyond what is achieved in the first intervention? Much as rereading a good book imparts new meaning and perspectives as we grow and mature, perhaps several experiences in support groups would provide incremental help for children of divorce at various phases of their adjustment to postdivorce family life. Now that we have interventions for children in early elementary school, later elementary school, and middle/junior high school, perhaps it would be useful to have children participate in a divorce support group at each of these nodal developmental points. Such a series of interventions may well help children address newly arising, or ongoing, divorce-related stresses from new developmental vantage points.

References

Furstenberg, F. F., Nord, C. W., Peterson, J. L., & Zill, N. (1983). The life course of children of divorce. *American Sociological Review, 48,*656–658.

Garvin, V., Leber, D., & Kalter, N. (1991). Children of divorce: Predictors of change following preventive intervention. *American Journal of Orthopsychiatry, 61,*438–447.

Glenn, N. D., & Kramer, K. B. (1987). The marriages and divorces of the children of divorce. *Journal of Marriage and the Family, 49,*811–825.

Glick, P. C. (1979). Children of divorced parents in demographic perspective. *Journal of Social Issues, 35,*170–182.

Guidubaldi, J., & Perry, J. D. (1984). Divorce, socioeconomic status, and children's cognitive-social competence at school entry. *American Journal of Orthopsychiatry, 54,* 459–468.

Guildubaldi, J., Perry, J. D., & Nastasi, B. K. (1987a). Assessment and intervention for children of divorce. In J. P. Vincent (Ed.), *Advances in family intervention assessment and theory* (Vol. 4, pp. 33–69). Greenwich, CT: JAI Press.

Guildubaldi, J., Perry, J. D., & Nastasi, B. K. (1987b). Growing up in a divorced family. In S. Oskamp (Ed.), *Annual review of applied social psychology* (pp. 202–237). Beverly Hills, CA: Sage.

Hetherington, E. M. (1989). Coping with family transitions. *Child Development, 60,* 1–14.

Hetherington, E. M., Cox, M., & Cox, R. (1979). Play and social interactions in children following divorce. *Journal of Social Issues, 35,* 26–49.

Hetherington, E. M., Cox, M., & Cox, R. (1985). Long-term effects of divorce and remarriage on the adjustment of children. *Journal of the American Academy of Child Psychiatry, 24,* 518–530.

Kalter, N. (1977). Children of divorce in an outpatient psychiatric population. *American Journal of Orthopsychiatry, 47,* 40–51.

Kalter, N., & Associates (1985). *Time-limited developmental facilitation groups for children of divorce: The later elementary school manual.* Technical report, Michigan Department of Mental Health.

Kalter, N. (1986). *Evaluation of later elementary school divorce support groups.* Unpublished manuscript.

Kalter, N. (1987). Long-term effects of divorce on children: A developmental vulnerability model. *American Journal of Orthopsychiatry, 57,* 587–600.

Kalter, N. (1989). *Evaluation of early elementary school divorce support groups.* Unpublished manuscript.

Kalter, N. (1990). *Growing up with divorce.* New York: Free Press.

Kalter, N., & Associates (1988). *Time-limited developmental facilitation groups for children of divorce: The early elementary school manual.* Technical report, Michigan Department of Mental Health.

Kalter, N., & Associates (1993). Time-limited developmental facilitation groups for children of divorce: The middle/junior high school manual. Technical report, Michigan Department of Mental Health.

Kalter, N., Kloner, A., Schreier, S., & Okla, K. (1989). Predictors of children's postdivorce adjustment. *American Journal of Orthopsychiatry, 59,* 605–618.

Kalter, N., Pickar, J., & Lesowitz, M. (1984). Developmental facilitation groups for children of divorce: A preventive intervention. *American Journal of Orthopsychiatry, 54,* 613–623.

Kalter, N., & Plunkett, J. (1984). Children's perceptions of the causes and consequence of divorce. *Journal of the American Academy of Child Psychiatry, 23,* 326–334.

National Center for Health Statistics (1990). Advance report of final divorce statistics, 1987. *Monthly Vital Statistics Report,* (Vol. 38, no. 12, supp. 2). Hyattsville, MD: U.S. Public Health Service.

Rubin, S. (1990). *School-based groups for children of divorce: A 4-year follow-up evaluation.* Unpublished dissertation, University of Michigan at Ann Arbor.

Wallerstein, J. S. (1985). Children of divorce: Preliminary report of a ten-year follow-up of older children and adolescents. *Journal of the American Academy of Child Psychiatry, 24,* 545–553.

Wallerstein, J. S. (1987). Children of divorce: Report of a ten-year follow-up of early latency-age children. *American Journal of Orthopsychiatry, 57,* 199–211.

Wallerstein, J. S. (1991). The long-term effects of divorce on children: A review. *Journal of the American Academy of Child & Adolescent Psychiatry, 30,* 349–360.

Wallerstein, J. S., & Kelly, J. B. (1980). *Surviving the break-up.* New York: Basic Books.

11
The Treatment of Depressed Children: A Skills Training Approach to Working with Children and Families

Kevin D. Stark
Linda Raffaelle
Anne Reysa

Introduction and Overview

The successful treatment of depressed youths is a complex process that requires an understanding of depressive disorders during childhood and of the treatment procedures used in this manual. Information related to both of these areas can be found in Stark (1990). This manual cannot simply be picked up and applied with maximum efficacy without an understanding of childhood depression and cognitive behavioral treatment procedures. It also is important to have an understanding of family therapy and systems models of childhood disorders.

This treatment manual is designed to be used with children between the ages of 9 to 13 years who have a unipolar depressive disorder. Alterations to the program would need to be made for younger and older children, and for children with coexisting disorders. The basic treatment model and procedures are appropriate for younger and older youths. However, the method of delivery would have to be developmentally appropriate. For example, the concepts would have to be presented in a more concrete fashion and in a more engaging and playlike manner for younger children. The presentation would have to be altered to be less "cute" and more interactive for adolescents. If the youngsters are experiencing a co-occurring disorder, the core procedures would remain the same, but additional treatment components would have to be added and the family therapy component would have to be altered to handle the acting out of the depressed and conduct-disordered or Attention Deficit Hyperactivity Disordered (ADHD) youth. The program could be implemented with minimal alterations for depressed and anxious youths. We do not believe that the treatment program is appropriate for the outpatient treatment of a depressed and seriously suicidal youth; a more protective environment and more intense individual and family therapy program would be required for such youths.

The treatment program as written is designed to be delivered using a group format. The group size can range from four to eight children. Our experience has been that too much time is spent managing the children's behavior and not enough time is spent teaching skills when the number of group members exceeds eight. With a larger group, we recommend using a pair of cotherapists. One therapist can be leading the group while the other is reviewing the children's written homework assignments and developing ways to integrate the content of the homework into the session. With a minimum of change in the delivery format, the intervention program is appropriate for use with individual youths. In fact, in many ways an individual delivery format is more effective than the group format. This is especially true during the sessions that emphasize the acquisition of cognitive restructuring techniques.

The average length of the sessions is one hour. However, they range in length from 50 minutes to 90 minutes. The length is in part dependent on how successful the therapist is at getting the youngsters to add their own personal issues to the agenda and to discuss the therapeutic issues. Length is also dependent on how much presession planning the therapist does and how familiar he or she is with the goals for each session. Given the emphasis on skills training in this program, the group time has to be spent very efficiently, so as the skills being taught can be combined with the children's input about their own lives. The length of the sessions is also dependent on the age of the children in the groups. For younger children, we reduce the length of the sessions; for high school students, we lengthen them. When conducting the program in a school setting during the school day, we try to make the sessions one class period long. This may mean that a number of the sessions described in this manual actually require two meetings rather than one.

The group treatment program has been conducted in the schools during school hours, a procedure that seems to have some advantages and some disadvantages. A major advantage is that the children like missing class to attend the group meetings. We rotate the meeting time so that no single class is missed more than any other. In general, this procedure has worked very well for two reasons. First, we always obtain the full support of the superintendent of the school district and then the support of individual school principals. We ask the principals to send memos to the relevant teachers informing them that it was their philosophy that a child couldn't learn if his or her emotional problems were not attended to and that the teachers would be expected to work with the child to ensure that he or she didn't get behind in class. Second, we do a great deal of consultation with the teachers to help them understand the potential value of treatment for the children and to inform them about what skills are being taught to the children. Inevitably this sharing of information leads to the teachers volunteering to support these efforts in their classrooms. They want to know what they can do to help the youngsters acquire the skills.

Another advantage of conducting the program in the schools is that the children attend school on a daily basis. It seems as though this helps minimize absenteeism from the group sessions since there is no problem with parental transportation or conflicts with family schedules. In addition, the school is typically located within the family's community, thus making the school a convenient place to conduct the family meetings. Typically, they are conducted in the evening after other student functions have been completed.

The children in the groups are at least acquainted with one another. This is both an advantage and a disadvantage. In one instance, we had a couple of children who refused to be in the same group with a socially rejected child. They didn't want other children to see them associating with this youngster. In other instances, since the children saw each other on a daily basis outside of group meetings, it seemed as though the group was the catalyst for the development of some good and lasting friendships. In fact, when visiting the first school where I conducted the program in Texas with a small group of boys, the youngsters were now about to graduate from high school and three of them that had developed a close friendship had maintained it over the last six years. A disadvantage to the situation is that some children are reluctant to reveal information out of fear that everyone in school will find out about it. As the reader will see, we have taken steps to reduce this concern within the first session of the treatment program.

The program includes 27 sessions with the children and eleven with the family. We typically begin the family meetings after the fourth meeting with the children. The meetings with the children are conducted twice a week for the first four weeks and then once a week until completion. We meet more frequently in the beginning so that the children can experience some symptom relief as soon as possible. However, the teachers begin to feel uneasy with the twice weekly meetings typically by the fourth week which makes the continuation of this schedule a bit tenuous. In addition, parents begin to state some concern about their children missing so much class time. Toward the end of treatment as the children are working on self-improvement, it is useful to fade the meetings to every other week as the children need the additional time to create meaningful change. The sessions should be implemented in the order that they are presented in this manual. They have been placed in their current order on purpose and naturally build on one another. Thus, mastering of skills that are taught later in treatment is dependent on the successful acquisition of the skills that are taught earlier.

One of the keys to the successful implementation of the treatment program is that the therapist makes the treatment "real" for the children by eliciting and integrating the children's concerns into the treatment protocol. In other words, the therapist is able to apply the therapeutic procedures to the children's real-life problems. In addition, it is important to note that the goal of treatment is to help the children learn how to independently apply the skills to cope with their depressive symptoms. An overarching goal is to teach the children to take a problem-solving approach to life. This is an attitude that faces the truth that problems and emotional upset are inevitable, and recognizes that they should be treated as problems to be solved. The goal of the cognitive restructuring procedures is to produce a deep, seemingly philosophical, change in the way the children perceive themselves, the world, and the future. Another key to the successful implementation of treatment is to get the children to think about therapy between sessions and to practice the coping skills through homework assignments. To help motivate the children to complete the homework assignments, we involve the parents in the establishment of a reward system. A final key to success is changing the interactions and communications that occur in the family that support the children's depressive symptoms and depressive cognitions.

Child Component

Session 1

Objective 1: Introduce Therapist and Participants. Introduce yourself and your role in the group. Help participants introduce themselves by asking them to provide the following information: name, school and grade, who you live with, what you enjoy doing, favorite subject, one thing that you are good at. Encourage other group members to ask any questions they would like to ask. But also point out that the speaker has the right to decline to answer any question if he or she chooses.

Objective 2: Predict Participants' Thoughts and Feelings about Participation in Group and Help Shape Accurate Expectations. Discuss their expectations about group. Possible probe questions include the following: Who has participated in a group before? What did you do in that group? How do you think you feel talking about personal things in front of others? What do you think we will do in our meetings? Possible answers include the following: Talk about what we are thinking about and feeling. You will learn skills to better enable you to handle stress, solve problems, and cope with uncomfortable feelings. You will learn ways to enjoy life more. We will do some fun activities. It will involve work at times, but it is work that you will be doing for yourself—to help yourself.

Discuss their perceptions about why they are in the group. Ask the group members why they think they are in the group. Possible answers include: to help them learn how to feel happier, cope with things going on in their lives, have more fun, get along better with others.

Predict unfavorable reactions and utilize them for change.

Example. "Some people feel uncomfortable at first when our group starts meeting. Over time as they get to know each other they feel more comfortable talking and learn that it is helpful to talk about things in group. Some people are afraid of what the other people might think about them, so they keep things that are bothering them to themselves. Most people learn that group is a place to talk about those things and that it helps to talk about them because you learn that you are not the only one with those feelings and that we can often help you to come up with solutions to those problems. Some people worry about why they were chosen to be in the group while other kids weren't. We think that you are very in touch with your feelings and that you, like all other kids, could benefit from learning how to cope with your feelings."

Discuss how the children feel about being in group; ask "How are you feeling right now about being here?"

Objective 3: Set Rules for Group. Discuss confidentiality.

Example. "Who knows what the word *confidential* means? If we have a rule that everything that is said in group is confidential, what would that mean? It means that everything we talk about in group stays in the group. You don't tell anyone else what someone in group said. It's OK to say to your parents or friends general statements like "We talked about things that are fun to do." But it is not alright to tell anyone what a specific person said. Does everyone understand this?"

Discuss the therapist's limits of confidentiality.

Example. "Everything will remain confidential—I won't tell your parents or teachers or the principal. There are only three extreme exceptions: if you state that you are going to hurt yourself, if you state that you are going to hurt someone else, and if you tell us that someone is hurting you. Then, since I care about your well-being, I would have to tell the appropriate people so that you wouldn't get hurt. I have to do this by law—there are no exceptions."

Hand out the Confidentiality Contract (see figure 11–1) and ask all participants to read it and sign it: "OK, then we are all going to sign this agreement that we will keep everything that we talk about in group confidential."

Ask the group members to develop a set of rules for running the meet-

---

Confidentiality Contract

I recognize that it is important for me to respect the other group members'
confidentiality. I will not tell anyone else what any other group member said
during our meetings. What is said in group will stay in the group.

_____   _____
Name   Date

Figure 11–1.

ings. Be sure that the following rules are on the list: treat other members
with respect, one person talks at a time, no one can make threatening or
hurtful statements, everyone will support fellow group members.

Objective 4: Assess Current Severity of Depressive Symptoms. Ask children
to complete the Symptom Checklist (see table 11–1). Subsequently talk as a
group about their experience of each symptom.

Objective 5: Set Therapist's Expectations for Participants. The therapist
wants participants to think about what was discussed or learned between
meetings. The therapist expects participants to complete practice assignments—this is extremely important. The therapist expects them to raise their
own concerns each time they meet.

Objective 6: End on a Light Note. Ask participants to draw a picture of
themselves doing their favorite activity. Very briefly discuss the pictures and
then save them for later use.

Review and Summarize

Session 2

Review: Group rules, confidentiality, importance of talking about things.

**Objective 1: Set the Expectation that Group Members Will Contribute to the
Agenda Each Meeting.** To break the ice, say something like, "I'm writing

Table 11–1
Symptom Checklist

Read each statement carefully. If the statement is true about how you felt over the last week, circle that statement. If the statement is not true about how you felt over the last week, then go on to the next one.

1. I felt sad, or down, or unhappy, or like crying.
2. I was angry.
3. I felt guilty.
4. I felt like no one loved me.
5. I didn't like myself.
6. I felt like life was harder on me than on other people.
7. I had aches and pains.
8. I worried about my health.
9. I was tired.
10. I had trouble concentrating.
11. I couldn't sit still.
12. I felt like I was moving in slow motion.
13. I wanted to be by myself.
14. Nothing seemed fun.
15. I had trouble sleeping.
16. I slept longer than usual.
17. I didn't feel like eating.
18. I ate more than usual.
19. I tried to hurt myself.
20. I thought about hurting myself.

down the things that I would like us to cover today. What would you all like to add to this list?" Typically the participants have trouble coming up with additional agenda items. Help them by asking them if anyone had anything happen recently that he or she was really proud of, that made him or her really happy, or that made him or her really sad or mad. What about anything that was just of concern or confusing? Encourage as many answers as possible. Write down suggestions as they are contributed.

Set therapist's agenda. State each item verbally and write it down on the chalkboard along with the participants' items.

Objective 2: Build Group Cohesion and Establish Labels for Emotions. Introduce the Emotion Vocabulary. Prior to group meeting, on 3 × 5 cards write the name of each of the following emotions (the list should vary in number and sophistication dependent on the age of the children):

Happy	Frustrated
Sad	Surprised
Down	Embarrassed
Lonely	Excited
Scared	Wild
Proud	Bored

Angry	Hyper
Super happy	Sleepy
Mad	Disappointed
Nervous	Anxious

Tell the group, "Today we are going to play a game. I have a stack of cards here. On each card is the name of an emotion. We are going to go around in a circle taking turns drawing a card from the deck. When you pick a card, you should read aloud the name of the emotion and then describe how you would feel if you were having that emotion now. Then you should describe what was happening the last time you felt that way. So after you pick a card you will do three things (Write them down on the chalkboard): first, you will read the name aloud; second, you'll describe that emotion; and third, you'll describe a time when you felt that emotion."

Go around the group a number of times until everyone has had an equal number of chances and it seems as though everyone understands the feeling associated with each of the emotion labels.

Try to involve all group members in the discussion. For example, ask the other members if they have had similar experiences. How do they think they would have felt if they had experienced the same situation? Point out consistencies in the things that seem to cause upset or lead to positive emotions. Watch for anyone to mention the relationship between feelings and thinking. If an example arises, do your best Columbo (investigative questioning) and try to get the person and the group to convince each other that their thoughts and feelings are related and then reinforce their conclusion. Be alert for any patterns and any evidence of dysfunctional thinking. If it is evident, make a note for yourself to use it in the future.

Objective 3: Give the Participants a Basis for Setting Their Own Goals for Treatment. As a group discuss what a goal is and then generate a common definition. Next, discuss what would be appropriate and reasonable goals for participants in the group.

Review and Summarize.

Homework: "Between now and next meeting I would like each of you to write down your own goals for this group. I realize it may be hard since you don't know that much about the group yet, but I would like you to do your best. Actually spend some time thinking this through and write down your goals. Then turn them in to me at the beginning of the next group. To help you to remember to do this, I have written down this note to remind you (pass out the Reminder Note [see table 11–2]).Can any of you think of a reason why you wouldn't be able to complete this assignment?" Problem solve as examples arise.

Table 11–2
Reminder Note

Remember to write down your goals for our meetings.

1. _____

2. _____

3. _____

4. _____

5. _____

Session 3

Review: Ask the children, "What do you remember about our last meeting?" Get the children to describe the major points of the previous meeting. Fill in where necessary.

Set Agenda: Solicit the participants' input and work out how you are going to integrate their agenda into yours. Praise the contributors for their contributions and encourage the other group members to come up with items.

Review Homework: Collect homework and use problem solving to deal with those children who did not complete their homework. While you are waiting for all of the participants to arrive, review each child's goals and look for anything that might be difficult to state out loud in the group.

Objective 1: Discuss the Participants' Concerns. Try to work their concerns into the rest of the agenda.

Objective 2: Continue to Foster Group Cohesion and Build an Understanding of the Relationship Between Thinking, Feeling, and Behaving. Use the emotion cards from Session 2. Once again, place the deck of cards in the middle of the group and ask the children to take turns drawing a card from the deck. However, this time, after picking a card and reading it aloud, describing how the emotion feels, and what was going on the last time he or she felt that emotion, the child is also to describe what a person who is feeling that emotion might be thinking and how that person might be behaving. If the child can describe what he or she was thinking and how he or she was behaving the last time he or she felt that way, all the better. Often, they are unaware of their thoughts at this point in the treatment process. The objective is to help the children see that their feelings don't arise from thin air, rather, they are associated with what they are thinking. Take turns playing the game until the children have a clear understanding of the relationship between thinking and feeling. They should all be able to give realistic examples of thoughts that could accompany specific emotions. Point out themes in thinking that are related to certain emotions. Once again, watch for examples of distorted thinking and processing errors. Note any of these for future use.

Objective 3: Introduce the Group to Problem Solving. Write down the steps one follows when solving problems: (1) What's the problem? (2) What are all the plans? (3) Which is the best plan? (4) Choose and do it. (5) How did it work? (6) I did a good job! or I'll try another plan. Discuss what each step means and the important characteristics of each step:

1. "A problem can be a feeling that you don't like. A bad situation, a serious situation, a complicated situation. Something that bothers you. The actions another person takes when around you." Solicit examples from the group.
2. "Think of at least five plans or possible solutions to the problem. Brainstorm and be creative. Don't think about what will happen, the consequences. You can always add to your own ideas the ideas/plans of other people you trust. Let yourself go and think freely." Solicit examples from the group for one of the problems; emphasize the brainstorming process.
3. "After you have identified all the plans, at least five of them, think of the potential consequences of each one." Demonstrate this process with the example that has been used above.
4. "Look at each of the plans and its consequences and choose the one that looks like it will work out best for you. Then, do it! Sometimes this is hard, but you have to push yourself to follow through and make things better for yourself. You are worth it!"
5. "As you are doing your plan, check to see how it is turning out. Are you following your plan? Is it working as planned, or is there a need to change the plan? Often, we have to make some changes because something unexpected happens. That is alright. In fact, it's great to be flexible enough to change. Remember to go with the flow. Did the plan work?"
6. "When your plan is completed, if it has worked, give yourself a pat on the back—you deserve it. Say to yourself, I did a good job! If it didn't go well, say to yourself, OK, I tried it, I'll just have to try something else."

Note that the group is going to be using problem solving a lot. Talk about times when group members have used it in the past. Give examples of how other kids in previous groups have used it. Try to tie it into the concerns the children raised during the meeting. As a group, try to use problem solving to develop plans for dealing with their concerns.

Review and Summarize.

Homework: Instruct the children to catch what is happening and what they are thinking when they experience a strong emotion. They should write down at least one example to share with the group at our next meeting. Hand out the Practice Reminder sheet (see table 11–3).

Session 4

Review: Use a socratic approach and rely primarily on the recollections of the children. Supplement where necessary.

Set Agenda: Encourage participant input and merge it with your agenda.

Review Homework: Ask for examples of problems they came across.

Objective 1: Extend Participants' Understanding of the Mood-Thought-Behavior Relationship. Discuss the children's homework assignments. Emphasize the thought-feeling-behavior relationship.

Teach the children how to play Emotion Charades. Use the deck of cards that was used in the previous sessions. Once again the players take turns drawing cards from the deck, only this time they don't read them out loud. Instead they read the card to themselves and think about what a person who is feeling that emotion might look like. Then, the child acts out the expression of the emotion while the other players try to guess its name. Once an emotion is correctly identified, the identifier states what the actor did that clued him or her into the name of the emotion, what was happening the last time he or she felt that way, and what he or she was thinking at that time. Again, note any themes in the participants' thinking and feeling. Discuss these. Note for future use any distortions in thinking, and probe to see if the kids can think of other healthier ways to think.

Objective 2: Begin to Link Mood and Engagement in Pleasant Events. As a group generate an extensive list of: (1) fun things to do, (2) great thoughts to have, and (3) good things that happen. Keep probing until the members have run out of ideas. When generating the list, encourage them to include activities that range from mildly fun to extremely fun. The tendency of children is to include only the extremely fun things. However, these activities typically are not available to the children on a daily basis.

Table 11–3
Practice Reminder

Remember to complete this whenever you have a strong feeling and to bring your booklet with you to group.

I felt _____

What was happening:

What I was doing:

What I was thinking:

I felt _____

What was happening:

What I was doing:

What I was thinking:

I felt _____

What was happening:

What I was doing:

What I was thinking:

Objective 3: Create Individualized Pleasant Events Scales. On a sheet of self-duplicating paper, have each child create his or her own list of pleasant activities by writing down those activities that he or she finds fun. Emphasize that this is a very individualized thing. Everyone has their own preference—their own likes and dislikes—and this is OK. Before the next session type up each child's list and include a 10-point Likert-type scale on the bottom of the form. Add a space for the date in the upper right corner. Type the child's first name on each sheet. Add spaces for other fun things not on the list (see table 11–4).

Objective 4: Extend Participants' Understanding of Problem Solving. Review each of the six steps. Play a game that presents the children with multiple choices at each move. First, describe the game and the rules. Once the children understand the rules of the game, model how you can use problem solving to be more successful. Overtly verbalize your thoughts and each of the six problem-solving statements as you take your turn. Coach the children in the overt use of the problem-solving statements and encourage them to think out loud. Look for any misuse of the steps, watch for signs of misunderstanding, and be sure that the steps are followed in the correct order. Be alert for signs of pessimism and negatively evaluating the plans during Step 2 when they should be brainstorming. Children find it difficult to verbalize the steps. Be sure to instruct them to do this and model where necessary.

Homework. "Take your list of pleasant events home and try to do as many of them as you can. Place a star next to the ones that you are able to do. Note any problems you face over the interim. Write them down on the back of the Pleasant Events schedule."

Session 5

Review

Set Agenda

Review Homework. Through your questions and the participants' examples, help the kids recognize that "you feel good when you do fun things."

Objective 1: Extend Mood-Behavior-Thought Relationship. Teach the children how to play Emotion Password. The game is played in a similar fashion to the TV game show. The same deck of 3 × 5 cards that was used in the previous games is used once again. This time, the group is divided into two teams. On each team one child is designated to be the clue giver and another

Table 11–4
Sarah's Pleasant Events

Date _____

As often as possible, check-off the *things that happen, that you do and think* each day. Try your best to remember to carry these diary sheets to school and back home again. If you do something fun, or, if you think about or have something good happen that is not on your list, check-off "Other" and write it down. At the end of the day, compare the right side of your list with your Mom and Dad's list, and then rate how you felt in general over the entire day.

_____ Help out at school
_____ Play cards
_____ Play with friends
_____ Go to a concert
_____ Go to a play
_____ Ride bikes
_____ Play with Kristin
_____ Play with friends
_____ Play board games
_____ Help Mom cook
_____ Latch hook
_____ Draw
_____ Roller skating
_____ Go to a party
_____ Practice Pips
_____ Going to the mall
_____ Going grocery shopping
_____ Going to bookstore
_____ Going to the library
_____ Doing something with Dad
_____ Go to pet store
_____ Play catch with Ronnie
_____ Make bracelets
_____ Build forts
_____ Hobby kit
_____ Jump rope
_____ Run track
_____ Other
_____ Other
_____ Other

Worst Ever					OK				On Top of the World	
0	1	2	3	4	5	6	7	8	9	10

child is designated to be the guesser. The therapist picks an emotion card from the deck and shows it to each of the clue givers. Other group members are not shown the card. The clue givers are allowed a few minutes to think of verbal, visual, or auditory clues that they can give to help the guessers to figure out the name of the emotion. The game begins with one child giving a clue. His or her teammate then tries to guess the name of the emotion. Subsequently, the teams take turns giving clues and guessing until the emotion is correctly identified. Once the emotion is correctly identified, the child is asked to: (1) state the clue that helped him or her figure it out; (2) describe the last time he or she felt that emotion; and (3) describe what he or she was thinking.

Objective 2: Extend Pleasant Events Schedule. Ask the children as a group to expand their list of positive activities. Try to get the children to brainstorm additional items. Once again use self-duplicating paper and have the kids write down their additional items to be added to the list. Also, have them generate positive self-evaluative thoughts—at least four per child—and add their thoughts to their Pleasant Events Lists.

Objective 3: Teach the Children How to Self-Monitor Pleasant Events. Prior to this session, take a deck of index cards and write down all of the children's pleasant events items one by one, and add additional fun things not on their lists. Also prior to this session, make enough copies of each child's Pleasant Events List so that they can be used for practice within the session, and as homework over the next few days. Place the lists in a three-ring binder for each child. Distribute the binders to the children. After the children have looked through the folders, explain that you are going to be asking them to use these sheets to keep track of how many pleasant things they do each week. You would like them to:

1. Complete one sheet per day.
2. To put a checkmark or X in front of the things that they do or think on that day.
3. If they do it more than once, just mark it one time.
4. Identify with the kids at least three times a day when they can check off items, preferably at least at lunch, dinner, and at bedtime.
5. Work out how they are going to remember to take their folders home and bring them back to school.
6. Before going to bed each night, they are to rate their mood for the whole day. Explain the rating scale and elicit examples.

Place the deck of cards in the middle of the group. The game is played by taking turns drawing a card from the deck. Instruct the children to read the item and check it off on their list if it is there; if not, and if they think it would be fun, they write it in under the "other" slot. If they don't think it would be fun, they just skip it. After all of the cards have been collected and the children have checked off the items, they take turns reading aloud what they have hypothetically done and how they would rate their mood if they had done all of those things. Discuss the mood ratings and how they were made.

Objective 4: Extend Participants' Understanding of How to Use Problem Solving. Play another game, once again practicing the overt use of problem solving. Again model verbalizing the self-instructions. Monitor the children's verbalizations of the problem-solving steps. Be sure that they are demonstrating the correct understanding of each step, and watch for pessimism and signs of the process getting short-circuited due to hopelessness.

Objective 5: Use Problem Solving as a Group to Help Each Child Better Handle/Cope with the Problems He or She Has Been Facing.

Review and Summarize.

Homework: Explain what is in each child's binder. Instruct the children to complete a self-monitoring diary everyday. They should check-off the fun activities that they enact each day. They should check off the items as soon after they do them as possible—at least three times a day, at lunch, after dinner, and before going to bed. Before going to bed, they should make an overall mood rating. Also, they should write down any problems they face.

Session 6

Review.

Set Agenda.

Review Homework. Reinforce their efforts. Discuss any impediments they came across and use group problem solving to create a plan to ensure future success. Use participants' experiences to illustrate the relationship between mood and engagement in fun activities. Collect completed Diary Sheets.

Objective 1: Extend Mood-Behavior-Thought Relationship and Group Cohesion. Play the game of Emotion Statues. Once again the deck of emotion cards is used. This time, the group members take turns being the sculptor and the clay to be molded. The sculptor draws an emotion card from the deck and then works with the child who is the clay to shape his or her physical appearance to illustrate the emotion. Actions are allowed. In addition, since one of the objectives of the exercise is to have fun and experience success, the child-sculptor is encouraged to seek the assistance of other group members to shape the statue. Once another group member identifies the emotion, he or she states: (1) what the clues were that enabled him or her to make an accurate guess, (2) what was happening the last time he or she felt that way, and (3) what he or she was thinking at that time.

Objective 2: Personalize and Clarify the Tie Between Events, Thoughts, and Feelings. Prior to the meeting, type in the changes to the children's Pleasant Events Diaries. Also, using the children's Diary Sheets, begin graphing their mood ratings and frequency of enactment of pleasant events. Now give each child a copy of his or her Mood Graph. Talk about any patterns that the group notices. There should be a strong relationship between frequency of enactment of pleasant events and mood.

Objective 3: Increase Engagement in Pleasant Events. Instruct the kids to add up the number of pleasant events they engaged in on each day. Based on their average, they should set a goal to increase the number of pleasant events that they enact each day. Discuss this goal as a group and point out the need to be reasonable and realistic. Have the group discuss what would be a reasonable increase. Have each child sign a Pleasant Events Contract (see Figure 11–2) stating the number of pleasant events that he or she will try to enact each day. Use problem solving as a group to help the children overcome impediments to increasing engagement in pleasant events. Also, use it as a means of developing plans to enact certain events.

Pleasant Events Contract

I _____ recognize that increasing the number of

fun things I do each day is very important and I will do my best to increase the

number of fun things I do each day by_____ fun things.

_____
Name   Date

Figure 11–2.

Objective 4: Use Problem Solving as a Group to Help the Children Cope with the Problems That are of Concern to Them. Solicit examples of independent use of problem solving.

Review and Summarize.

Homework. Continue to monitor enactment of pleasant events and try to increase the number of events engaged in each day so as to achieve your goal.

Session 7

Review.

Set Agenda.

Review Homework and Collect Forms.

Objective 1: Extend Mood-Behavior-Event-Thought Relationship. Teach the game of Emotion Expression. Once again, use the deck of emotion cards. Before playing the game, pull the cards with more difficult to identify emotions out of the deck. This time, the group members take turns drawing cards from the deck. Each child keeps the name of the emotion he or she draws a secret from the rest of the group. Without using any words, the child makes noises to express the emotion. The other children try to guess what emotion it is. The child that identifies the emotion correctly states what clues he or she used, what was going on the last time he or she felt that way, what he or she was thinking, and what he or she did to get over it if it was an unpleasant feeling.

Objective 2: Increase Engagement in Pleasant Events. Once again, use problem solving to increase the number of fun events engaged in on a daily basis where appropriate to do so. Once again, contract for an increase. Be sure reasonable and realistic goals are set.

Objective 3: Improve Problem-Solving Skills. Prior to the session, write down a hypothetical problem on a 3 × 5 card. Create a deck of problem cards based on the problems the children have raised during the previous meetings. Now have each child take a turn drawing a card from the deck. He or she then verbalizes the use of the problem-solving steps. Encourage the children to seek help from other group members. Begin by modeling how it is done and then coach the children through the correct use of problem solving. Discuss the possibility of trying out some of the plans for real. Identify any interfering thoughts.

Objective 4: Extend Activity Scheduling to Mastery Tasks. Talk about the fact that we all have some tasks that need to be completed, like daily chores and school projects as well as homework assignments.

Example. "Sometimes we have projects to complete that are fun to do, like building a model or coloring in a drawing or painting a picture. While some of these tasks are fun, others are not so much fun, but we usually get a good feeling out of having successfully completed the task. We often experience a sense of accomplishment. How do people feel when they don't finish an assignment and get a zero or a poor grade? How do people feel when they know they have something to do but they keep putting it off? What do your parents do when you delay completion of a chore or other task? How do they act when you finish it on time or without them having to nag you? Completion of these activities can also make you feel good, by relieving stress and hassles." Discuss things that they have not been doing or have been delaying, and problem solve plans for doing them. Contract for completion of some of these tasks. Again, set reasonable expectations.

Objective 5: Fill in Mood Graphs Detailing Mood and Event. Help the children fill in their own graphs.

Review and Summarize.

Homework. Continue to monitor engagement in pleasant events and complete Mastery Activity Contract (figure 11–3) and try to use problem solving. Keep track of attempts to use problem solving.

Session 8

Review.

Set Agenda.

Review Homework and Collect Forms.

Objective 1: Identify Additional Problems the Children Have Faced That Have Led Them to Experience a Negative Feeling. As a group, have the children talk about things that have happened to them that led to a negative feeling state. Ask the kids what they were thinking at the time. Use problem solving to help them develop plans for coping. Make note of their negative thoughts for later use and tie this back to discoveries made during the emotion games about the relationship that exists between thinking and feeling.

Mastery Activity Contract

I _____ recognize that it is very important to try

to complete mastery activities. I will do my best to try to complete the

following tasks:

1.

2.

3.

_____

Name   Date

Figure 11–3.

Objective 2: Extend Problem Solving to Interpersonal Situations. Prior to the meeting, make a deck of cards in which each card has an interpersonal problem on it. Now ask one child to draw a card. He or she is the designated problem solver. The child to his or her immediate left serves as the other actor in this role play. The pair of children discuss the role play and then act it out. The child who drew the card then overtly verbalizes the problem-solving process, and with the help of other group members proceeds to reenact the situation using the better plan. Make this a fun, humorous, and successful experience.

Objective 3: Check on Children's Progress Toward Completion of Mastery Activities. Use problem solving to develop plans for completion of these activities. Discuss the importance of rewarding themselves through engagement in a very enjoyable activity.

Objective 4: Fill in Mood and Activity Graphs.

Review and Summarize.

Homework. Continue to monitor pleasant events and complete Problem-Solving Diaries. Whenever they face a problem, they should use the Diary Form (see table 11–5) as a guide to solving it and they should fill in the

Table 11–5
Problem-Solving Diary Form

What's the problem?

What are *all* of the possibilities?   What would happen if each were chosen?

1.

2.

3.

4.

5.

My choice is:

How did it go? *I did a good job!*

blanks to show how they did it. This can be done for very small problems as well as big ones.

Session 9

Review.

Set Agenda.

Review Homework and Collect Forms.

Objective 1: Extend Problem-Solving Skills. Develop and enact additional role plays of interpersonal problems. This time the hypothetical problems should involve an adult. Once again, one child role-plays one character and another child role-plays the other character. The group uses problem solving to create a solution to each situation and then the actors reenact the situation using the new plan. Where possible, use these role plays as an opportunity to point out effective social skills and to identify adaptive as well as maladaptive thoughts.

Objective 2: Check on Progress Toward Goal Attainment and Mastery Activities and Engagement in Pleasant Events. Once again use problem solving as necessary.

Objective 3: Complete Mood and Activity Graphs.

Review and Summarize.

Homework. Same as previous session. Ask the children to sign the More Problem-Solving Sheets Contract in which they promise to do more problem solving.

Session 10

Review.

Set Agenda.

Review and Collect Homework.

Objective 1: Review Success with Problem-Solving, Mastery Activities, and Pleasant Events.

Objective 2: Introduce Relaxation Training. "There is a skill that adults use to help themselves handle stress and feel better. It is called relaxation. What

---

More Problem-Solving Sheets Contract

I _____ recognize that it is very important for

me to learn how to do problem solving. I will try to complete ____ problem

solving diary sheets this week.

_____

Name   Date

Figure 11–4.

do you think relaxation is? How do people relax? You can learn to do it too."

Example. "First, you have to learn to notice the difference between when you are tense versus when you are relaxed. What would be the difference in your body and thoughts? We're going to work on teaching you to first notice the difference between when you are tense, and then how to get relaxed. To start, let's review the names of the major muscles in your body that get tense." Now point to each of the major muscle groups used in the script and have the kids touch that muscle on their own bodies. Then, quickly review it. Arrange things so that the children can get as comfortable as possible. Invite them to take restroom breaks if needed. Let them know that it might feel a little strange to do this, but they should just relax, block everything else out of their minds and listen to the instructions. If they follow along, they will learn how to gain greater control over their bodies and feelings. Note that you want them to tense their muscles but not to the point that it would hurt. Also, note that it works best if they lay back and close their eyes, but they don't have to if they don't want to. Lead them through a 20-minute exercise. Discuss their experience with it.

Objective 3: Complete Mood and Activity Graphs.

Review and Summarize.

Homework. Same as previous session.

Session 11

Review.

Set Agenda.

Review Homework and Collect Forms.

Objective 1: Extend Relaxation Skill. Complete the relaxation exercise in a similar fashion to last week.

Objective 2: Complete Mood and Activity Graphs.
Homework: Same as last session.

Session 12

Review.

Set Agenda.

Review Homework and Collect Forms.

Objective 1: Improve Relaxation Skill. Follow same procedure as previous week. Between sessions make a cassette recording of the relaxation exercise for each group member. Now pass out the tapes and explain how to use them. Identify those kids who need to borrow a tape player. Pass out the tape players. Explain how to use the relaxation tapes:

1. Before going to sleep
2. Identify a quiet time
3. Identify a quiet place
4. Ask family members not to disturb you
5. Get comfortable
6. Clear your mind
7. Concentrate on the instructions
8. Let go and enjoy.

Objective 2: Complete Mood and Activity Graphs.

Homework: Same as last week plus listen to the relaxation tape each day and complete the Relaxation Rating Diary (see table 11–6) each day.

Table 11–6
Relaxation Rating Diary

Monday

Super Tense									In a Dream	
0	1	2	3	4	5	6	7	8	9	10

Super Tense									In a Dream	
0	1	2	3	4	5	6	7	8	9	10

Tuesday

Super Tense									In a Dream	
0	1	2	3	4	5	6	7	8	9	10

Super Tense									In a Dream	
0	1	2	3	4	5	6	7	8	9	10

Wednesday

Super Tense									In a Dream	
0	1	2	3	4	5	6	7	8	9	10

Super Tense									In a Dream	
0	1	2	3	4	5	6	7	8	9	10

Thursday

Super Tense									In a Dream	
0	1	2	3	4	5	6	7	8	9	10

Super Tense									In a Dream	
0	1	2	3	4	5	6	7	8	9	10

Friday

Super Tense									In a Dream	
0	1	2	3	4	5	6	7	8	9	10

Super Tense									In a Dream	
0	1	2	3	4	5	6	7	8	9	10

Saturday

Super Tense									In a Dream	
0	1	2	3	4	5	6	7	8	9	10

Super Tense									In a Dream	
0	1	2	3	4	5	6	7	8	9	10

Sunday

Super Tense									In a Dream	
0	1	2	3	4	5	6	7	8	9	10

Super Tense									In a Dream	
0	1	2	3	4	5	6	7	8	9	10

Session 13

Review.

Set Agenda.

Review Homework and Collect Forms.

Objective 1: Extend Relaxation and Problem Solving. Complete an abbreviated relaxation exercise. Once the children are relaxed, have them complete an imagery exercise. Follow this outline: "Keep your eyes closed and now get your mind completely clear so that you can completely concentrate. Your mind is free of worry and powerful. You are going to be a great problem solver. Take a minute to think of a problem that you are facing. It can be any problem—either little or big, simple or complicated. (Allow some time for subjects to come up with a problem.) Now that you have the problem in mind, check to be sure that you are completely relaxed. Identify any tight muscles and now relax the tightness away. Get completely relaxed. With your mind clear and your body relaxed, think of a plan for your problem. It can be any plan. . . . Now, think of a second plan. . . . Once again, let your mind loose and think of another plan. . . . Be creative and come up with a fourth plan. . . . Feel the power of a clear, positive mind and come up with a fifth and this time funny or silly plan. . . . Take a minute to recall all five plans, and think of the potential consequence for each one. What would happen if you tried the first one? Think hard and imagine what would happen. Now, think of what would happen if you tried your second plan. Imagine it in as much detail as possible. Is it a good plan? Check your body to be sure that you are completely relaxed. Loosen up any tension. Concentrate on getting more and more relaxed. Now, think of what would be the consequence of choosing the third plan. . . . What about the fourth plan. . . . Now, the fifth funny plan. Choose the best plan for your problem, and imagine that you are following through on this plan. You can see yourself doing it and it is working. Your plan is working and you feel very good as your problem is brought to an end. It is over. It no longer exists. Let yourself relax and feel good. Now that you are completely relaxed, I am going to ask you to remember the steps to solving a problem. I want you to think about the energy it will take to slowly open your eyes and go on with our meeting. You will be more relaxed and alert. (Slowly count backward from 10 to 0.) Open your eyes!"

Objective 2: Extend Spontaneous Use of Problem Solving. Use Simon Says as the medium for (1) practicing the identification of tension and relaxing it away (for example, "Karen, Simon says tense your right shoulder, now relax it away—Simon says relax the tension away."), and (2) problem solving (for example, "Steve, Simon says you are angry, Simon says tell me five possible plans for feeling better. Tell me the consequences for the third plan—Simon says tell me the consequence for the third plan.").

Objective 3: Complete Mood and Activity Graphs.

Homework. Same as last week.

Session 14

Review.

Set Agenda.

Review Homework and Collect Forms.

Objective 1: Comment on Relaxation and Problem Solving. Play another round of Simon Says. This time include lots of examples of dealing with problematic situations (for example, "Simon says give one plan for your best friend who is mad at you.").

Objective 2: Introduce Cognitive Restructuring. Review what was learned about the relationship between thinking and feeling in previous meetings. Remind the children that we are constantly thinking and that most of the time we are unaware of it because it is habit. Our mind is constantly filled with thoughts that either take the form of words or pictures—images like when you dream. Ask the children to think about the dreams they've had over the last few days. "Who can tell us about the ones they remember? (Only elicit a couple examples.) Did you notice how your feelings were related to the pictures you created in your mind? Today we want to help you get better at catching the thoughts and images you have that lead you to feel something that you don't like."

Objective 3: Help the Children to Learn How to Tune Into Their Thoughts. Ask, "What would be a negative thought? What would be a positive thought. Are there neutral thoughts? (Yes—task-related instructions.) Today we are going to spend some time putting together puzzles. While you are doing this, I want you to catch your negative thoughts and write them down. Each time you catch one, write it down. What do you think are some examples of negative thoughts that might occur while building these puzzles?" Proceed to building the puzzles. Then discuss the thoughts the kids have caught.

Homework. Same, plus self-monitor negative thoughts and when they occur. Have the kids write their thoughts on a piece of notebook paper, and keep it in their three-ring binders.

Session 15

Review.

Set Agenda.

Review Homework and Collect Forms.

Objective 1: Practice Catching Thoughts. Help the children identify positive and negative thoughts. Put the emphasis on self-evaluative thoughts. The activity the children complete while doing self-monitoring is a series of increasingly difficult mazes. The most difficult maze should exceed the children's frustration level. Once again, the children jot down their self-evaluative thoughts, both positive and negative.

Objective 2: Introduce Cognitive Restructuring. Discuss why it is in the children's best interest to change their thinking: changed thought = changed mood. Introduce the notion of being a thought detective.

Example. "A thought detective is a detective who looks for clues about whether a thought is true or not true. A detective hunts for evidence that his or her thoughts and beliefs are true or not true. You are going to learn to check the evidence that tells you whether your negative thoughts are true or untrue. What would you do if you found that a negative thought was true and you didn't like it? You would use problem solving to try to change it. Does anyone remember a time when I asked you 'What's the evidence?' when you told us a negative thought? When I did that I was helping you to be a thought detective."

Use the children's lists of negative thoughts generated during the puzzle-building and maze-completion activities as the source of negative thoughts to apply "What's the evidence?" to. Instruct the kids to take a few minutes to go through their lists to identify a negative thought that probably is not true. Help each child to identify blatantly false thoughts. Help each child to identify at least one of these. Then, have each child present the thought to the group and the evidence that indicates that it is false.

Homework. Continue to monitor engagement in pleasant events and write down negative thoughts and what is occurring at that time.

Session 16

Review.

Set Agenda.

Review Homework and Collect Forms.

Objective 1: Improve Understanding of How to Use Cognition Restructuring. Review the notion of being a thought detective. Give the children hypothetical examples involving other youths, including a fairly detailed description of each child. Imbedded within your descriptions is the data that can be used to determine the validity of the thoughts the hypothetical youngsters have. Following the description of a child, give examples of positive and negative thoughts that are clearly true and untrue. Have the children act as detectives who determine the validity of the hypothetical thoughts.

Objective 2: Improve the Children's Ability to Catch Their Own Thoughts. Identify common clues that can be used to identify thoughts that likely are untrue (for example, statements that include extreme words such as "always," "never," "everyone," "everybody," and "everything").

Objective 3: Personalize the Cognitive Restructuring Procedure. Use examples of thoughts from the children's homework that clearly are untrue or true and have the children, first as individuals and then as a group, act as detectives. Introduce the Cognitive Restructuring Diary (see table 11–7) as a means to facilitate cognitive restructuring.

Objective 4: Help the Children Use Problem Solving to Deal With Negative Self-Evaluations That Are True. Facilitate the children's use of problem solving as a means of developing plans for self-improvement where it is possible and desirable to do so.

Homework. Continue to self-monitor pleasant events and mastery activities. Complete the Cognitive Restructuring Diary forms.

Session 17

Review.

Set Agenda.

Review Homework and Collect Forms.

Table 11–7
Cognitive Restructuring Diary One

I was feeling:

What was happening:

My thoughts were:

What's the evidence for and against the thoughts?

For	Against
1.	
2.	
3.	
4.	
5.	
6.	
7.	
8.	

Objective 1: Introduce Alternative Interpretation. Help the children see that there are multiple ways to interpret things. You could use optical illusions, or you could show them some drawings that are open to different interpretations. Have the children independently write down their interpretations and then compare them to repeatedly make the point that any single stimulus can be interpreted in many different ways.

Objective 2: Demonstrate How This Concept Can Be Employed With Thoughts. Write down a number of vaguely defined situations, each on a small square of paper. Place the squares in a paper bag. Have the children take turns reaching into the bag and pulling out a square. After drawing an example, the child generates multiple interpretations of the situation.

Objective 3: Tie This Concept to the Children's Own Thoughts About Various Situations. Have the children identify situations that they have interpreted negatively and then have them generate alternative interpretations for these situations.

Objective 4: Introduce the Revised Cognitive Restructuring Diary (See table 11–8) **Which Includes a Place to List Alternate Ways of Thinking.** Distribute the revised forms and explain how to use them.

Homework. Complete the Revised Cognitive Restructuring Diary self-monitoring form.

Session 18

Review.

Set Agenda.

Review Homework and Collect Forms.

Objective 1: Illustrate the Notion of Negative Expectations and Have Fun. Prior to playing a game, ask the children to individually and confidentially write down their answers to the following questions:

1. Who is likely to win at this game?
2. How well will you do?
3. What will happen if you lose?
4. What does it mean about you if you lose?
5. How many/much (chips, points, play money) will you win?

After all of the children have written down their answers, collect their an-

Table 11–8
Cognitive Restructuring Diary Two

I was feeling:

What was happening:

My thoughts were:

What's the evidence for and against the thoughts?

	For	Against
1.		
2.		
3.		
4.		
5.		
6.		
7.		
8.		

Alternative ways of thinking:

1.

2.

3.

4.

5.

The thought I choose to believe:

swers and then play the game. Read through their answers while they are playing the game.

Objective 2: Introduce What If? = What Is Going to Happen? Tie this to the children's predictions and the actual outcome. Note how we can interpret things in many different ways. "We can predict that things will turn out positively or negatively. We have no way of knowing for sure how things are going to turn out ahead of time: they could turn out the way we think they will, or they could turn out very different from the way we think.

"Kids who are not happy tend to think that really bad or unwanted things are going to happen and that the consequences are going to be terrible. Most times everything turns out OK. "Besides feeling bad, what is likely to happen to a person who predicts that negative things are going to happen? Is this person setting themselves up for failure? People who predict that negative things are going to happen are more likely to have something negative happen.

"In addition to making negative predictions, people who don't feel happy exaggerate what will happen to them as a result of the unwanted event. To help yourself stop making negative predictions for the future, and to help yourself not to exaggerate what will happen if something bad happens, it is useful to ask yourself 'What if?' In other words, ask yourself, what will happen to me if this unwanted thing happens? Am I exaggerating what will happen to me. Will it really be as bad as I expect? For example, what did you think would happen to you if you lost the game? How did you expect to do in the game?"

Objective 3: Bring Together All Three Cognitive Restructuring Procedures Covered So Far. Review when the kids would use each of the procedures. Ask the group members to give examples of when they used each one in the past.

Objective 4: Introduce the Second Revised Cognitive Restructuring Diary (See table 11–9), **Which Now Includes the Question "What Will Happen to Me if It Is True."** Distribute the form and discuss how to use it.

Homework. Complete the new Cognitive Restructuring Diary form on a daily basis.

Session 19

Review.

Set Agenda.

Table 11–9
Cognitive Restructuring Diary Three

I was feeling:

What was happening:

My thoughts were:

What's the evidence for and against the thoughts?

	For		Against
1.			
2.			
3.			
4.			
5.			
6.			
7.			
8.			

Alternative ways of thinking:
1.

2.

3.

4.

5.

What will happen to me if it is true?

The thought I choose to believe:

Review Homework and Collect Forms.

Objective 1: Check on Engagement in Pleasant and Mastery Events. Check to see if the children are continuing to use engagement in pleasant events as a coping skill and as a means of keeping their activity level up. Problem solve when necessary to increase activity level.

Objective 2: Use Cognitive Restructuring Procedures as a Group Whenever a Negative Thought Is Identified.

Objective 3: Introduce Assertiveness. "Now that you are starting to gain greater control over your feelings by doing more fun things, we're going to start working on how you can get greater control of what's happening around you. I'm going to help you learn how to speak up for yourselves and how to ask people to stop doing the things you don't like them doing.

"There are three general ways to look at the way we behave around other people. We can be *aggressive, passive,* or *assertive.* How does a person who's being aggressive act? (Therapists role-play an aggressive interaction.) How do other people see the aggressive person? Aggressive kids are like little monsters. They're bossy, pushy, and bully other kids into doing what they want. They pick on other kids and put others down. They only care about one thing, getting what *they* want, when *they* want it. They usually don't care about others' feelings—they just care about themselves. They often get into fights and other trouble. They might know some other kids who sometimes hang around with them, but they have few friends because they're always taking advantage of and pushing others around.

"How does a passive person act? (Therapists role-play being passive.) The passive person lets other people walk all over him or her. The passive person doesn't ask for what he or she wants. A passive person just goes along with what others say, even if he or she doesn't want to. What would other people think of a passive person? They're kind of like a meek little mouse. They let other kids boss them around, tell them what to do, and usually don't stand up for their rights.

"They're usually just ignored by others. There is another way to behave that is between aggressive and passive—it's called acting assertively. An assertive person is fair and speaks up for himself or herself. Assertive people act like themselves. Assertive people are aware of their rights and speak up and let people know how they feel and think without offending them. They don't force themselves on others and they don't allow others to take advantage of them. (Therapists role-play an assertive person.)

"One way of being assertive is to ask people to do things with you that you would like to do. Rather than just sitting around waiting for someone to ask *you* to do something, you take the initiative to ask them. Let's start this by thinking about what you would like members of your family to do more often with you and for you. Sometimes your parents are real busy and it seems like they don't really care about doing things with you. At others times they may seem too tired or grumpy to care about you or do things with you. They still do care about you, probably more than you think, and if you asked them to do something with you, there's a good chance that they will. You just need to learn how to let them know how much it would mean to you to do something with them. Many times they're so busy, or just tired from work, that they don't think of asking you to do something. So you need to speak up and let them know that you would like them to do something with you. We're going to work on how to ask your parents and friends to do things with you."

Have each child identify someone that they want to do something with and what they want to do. Make them aware of the fact that they won't always get what they want, but they'll get more than they currently receive. Follow these steps while role-playing assertively asking someone to do something with each participant:

1. Utilize the child participant's presumed apprehension about asking that individual to do that activity.
2. The therapist role-plays the child participant and the child participant role-plays the target person. Add in how to state something assertively— What you would like them to do and how it would make you feel. While modeling, where appropriate, verbalize aloud the apprehension the child participants may feel about being assertive. Also, use a coping model.
3. Play this first role play out and allow or encourage the child participants to verbalize and act out their concerns and ideas about what will happen to them if they ask for what they want.
4. Switch roles and coach the child participants through his or her new part.
5. Give the child participant more feedback and coach him or her as to how he or she could further improve upon his or her request.
6. Role-play again if it seems as though it would be useful.
7. Schedule the day, time, and place that the child participant will make the request. Be sure to help the children identify good times to make the request: don't ask when dad is angry, mom is busy with the baby, and so on.

Complete this process with as many child participants as time permits. Keep a list of who is going to ask who and what. This will serve as a prompt for the next session.

Objective 4: Rehearse Positive Preparatory Self-Statements. Have each child generate a list of positive coping statements to be used before entering the actual assertive situation. These self-statements should be written down on a 3 × 5 card.

Homework. Follow through on assertiveness assignment and complete self-monitoring and cognitive restructuring form.

Session 20

Review.

Set Agenda.

Review Homework and Collect Forms.

Objective 1: Extend Assertiveness Skills to Giving Compliments.

Examples. "Today we are going to work on another way to gain greater control over what other people are doing that might affect you. _____, let's say that you opened the door for me when I was trying to carry the TV in here. If I said, 'Thanks _____, I really appreciate the help,' do you think you are more likely or less likely to open the door for me when I want to carry the TV back out after our meeting? What about if I had said nothing to you? Would you be as likely to open the door again if I just ignored you? What about if I had said something negative like 'You jerk'? Then you probably wouldn't want to help me at all. So, if you let the person know that you like what they did, they're more likely to do it for you again. It's almost like a reward when you tell someone that you liked what they did.

"There is another thing you can do that will encourage others to do more things that you like. It also will make them think more positively of you. You can give the other person a compliment. Let's try it out."

Ask each member of the group to think of two things that they like about themselves. Be prepared to offer suggestions to participants who are having a difficult time with this task. Then, beginning with yourself, ask each participant to tell the group what they like about themselves. Confirm their observations and discuss as appropriate.

Next ask each member of the group to think of three things that they like about each other group member. After allowing them a couple of minutes to think, designate one participant as the recipient of the compliments. You begin by giving the compliments. Then ask the children to give their compliments. Be prepared to help the participants come up with compliments. In turn, have each child receive group compliments. Ask the participants to describe how it felt to give and receive the compliments.

Objective 2: Role-Play Giving Compliments to Family and Friends. Begin by saying, "Something we often do is take our family and friends for granted. We forget to tell them what we like about them. I would like each of us to think about at least one thing we like about the other members of our families. Then we'll share these things with the group. (Begin with yourself and then work around the group facilitating further discussion wherever possible.) Now let's choose two people from our families that we are going to give compliments."

Proceed around the group. Have each person designate whom they are going to compliment. After everyone has shared with the group, role-play giving the compliments. Have one participant play the family member while the other gives the compliment. Encourage the other group members to help the person who is giving the compliments. Also, emphasize the idea that people like other people who give them compliments.

Objective 3: Generate Coping Statements. Once again, generate positive coping statements and write them down to be used later.

Homework: Same as last week.

Session 21

Review.

Set Agenda.

Review Homework and Collect Forms.

Objective 1: Assertiveness Training (Telling People That They Are Doing Something You Don't Like).
Example. "Sometimes people, even your family and friends, do things that you don't like. Much of the time, those people don't realize that they are doing something that you don't like. But unless you tell them that you don't like it, they will keep on doing it. When you tell them that it bothers you, they will stop doing it most of the time—not always, but much of the time. So, what you need to learn to do is to tell people that you don't like what they are doing when they are doing it. This isn't real easy to do, especially if the other person is an adult, like one of your parents, because you might worry that they are going to get upset with you. You might worry that a friend won't like you if you say something to them. It usually turns out that they don't mind and may even be glad that you told them.

"How your statement about what you don't like is received depends on what you say. If you snap, 'Stop that,' or 'You better stop that,' are people going to respond positively? What about if you shout, 'Cut it out, you creep'? With your parents or a teacher, you also have to be careful not to be disrespectful. You shouldn't raise your voice or command them to do something. However, you can ask them to do or not do something. It is your right to tell someone that he or she is doing something that is bothering you.

"We have found that the best way to tell someone that they are doing something that you don't like is to say the following three things: (1) what it is that they are doing that you don't like; (2) how it makes you feel; and (3) what you would like them to do instead.

"Let's work on an example. Let's say that every time I was talking, one of you would start goofing around and not listen. If you kept doing it, I would probably start to get pretty frustrated. I would think, "You don't care about helping yourselves," which would make me more frustrated. If I didn't say anything, and kept it inside, I would get angry. Instead of letting that happen, I'm going to try to stop it before I get too upset. I'm going to say something. Let's see, I'm going to tell you what you are doing that bothers me, how it makes me feel, and . . . , oh yeah,—what I would like you to do instead.

"What kinds of things do people do to you that you don't like?"

Discuss this topic for a while and address both family and peer issues. Help the participants to get a bit worked up about this. Following the discussion, role-play telling those individuals what they are doing that you don't like.

Homework. Follow through on assertiveness activity and complete self-monitoring and cognitive restructuring forms.

Session 22

Review.

Set Agenda.

Review Homework and Collect Forms.

Objective 1: Establish Standards in a Concrete Manner. Go through the directions of the My Standards Questionnaire (page 382) with the participants and then have everyone complete it. Once everyone has completed it, ask them to score it on the worksheet.

Objective 2: Introduce Self-Evaluation.

Example. "You're probably wondering what these scores mean. What we've all just done is created on paper the standards we set for ourselves. The first time you went through it, you circled the number that showed how well you have to be at these things—like sports—in order to feel really good

My Standards Questionnaire-R

Section 1: Please read the following 10 questions and answer them according to how you would really like to be. Tell how well you would need to do on each question to feel really good about yourself. If you could do very poorly, put an X over the zero. If you would only need to do average, put an X over the 5. And if you would have to do perfectly, put an X over the 10. If you would need to do better than average, put an X somewhere between 5 and 10. The closer to perfect you would have to be to feel really good about yourself, the closer to 10 you would place the X. If you feel satisfied with below-average performance, then you would put an X over a number between zero and 5.

Please read each question carefully. Take your time to really think about each question, and then tell how well you need to do to be absolutely satisfied with yourself.

1. How popular do you have to be to feel really good about (absolutely satisfied with) yourself?

I don't care if anyone likes me					Average				The most popular person in school	
0	1	2	3	4	5	6	7	8	9	10

2. How good do your grades have to be to feel really good about (absolutely satisfied with) yourself?

I can fail everything		30%	40%	50%	Average 60%	70%	75%	80%	85%	All A's 90%	90%
0	1	2	3	4	5	6	7	8	9	10	

3. How good-looking do you have to be to feel really good about (absolutely satisfied with) yourself?

Ugly					Average				Like a model	
0	1	2	3	4	5	6	7	8	9	10

4. How smart do you have to be to feel really good about (absolutely satisfied with) yourself?

Stupid					Average				Genius	
0	1	2	3	4	5	6	7	8	9	10

5. How well-behaved do you have to be to feel really good about (absolutely satisfied with) yourself?

I can do everything wrong					Average				Never do anything wrong	
0	1	2	3	4	5	6	7	8	9	10

6. How athletic (good at sports) do you have to be to feel really good about (absolutely satisfied with) yourself?

A complete klutz					Average				A superstar	
0	1	2	3	4	5	6	7	8	9	10

7. How fashionable do your clothes need to be for you to feel really good about (absolutely satisfied with) yourself?

Ragged and dirty clothes are OK					OK				Right out of a fashion magazine	
0	1	2	3	4	5	6	7	8	9	10

8. How funny do you have to be to feel really good about (absolutely satisfied with) yourself?

No sense of humor is OK					Average				A comedian	
0	1	2	3	4	5	6	7	8	9	10

9. How nice do you have to be to feel really good about (absolutely satisfied with) yourself?

Meanest person					Average				Nicest person	
0	1	2	3	4	5	6	7	8	9	10

10. How good must your possessions (things like money, jewelry, bicycle, toys, records, stereo) be in order to feel really good about (absolutely satisfied with) yourself?

The worst					Average				The best	
0	1	2	3	4	5	6	7	8	9	10

Section 2: Please read the next 10 questions and answer them according to how well your parents think you ought to do or be in each of the following areas. Show as you did in section 1—using the number scale—how well your parents think you should do or be on each question.

1. How popular do your parents think you ought to be?

Least Popular person in school					Average				Most Popular person in school	
0	1	2	3	4	5	6	7	8	9	10

2. What grades do your parents think you ought to make?

Can fail everything					Average All C's				All A's	
0	1	2	3	4	5	6	7	8	9	10

3. How good-looking do your parents think you ought to be?

Not at all					Average				Like a model	
0	1	2	3	4	5	6	7	8	9	10

4. How smart do your parents think you ought to be?

Stupid					Average				Genius	
0	1	2	3	4	5	6	7	8	9	10

5. How well-behaved do your parents think you ought to be?

Can do everything wrong					Average				Never do anything wrong	
0	1	2	3	4	5	6	7	8	9	10

6. How athletic do your parents think you ought to be?

Not athletic					Average				A superstar	
0	1	2	3	4	5	6	7	8	9	10

7. How fashionable do your parents think your clothes ought to be?

Unfashionable					Average				Very fashionable	
0	1	2	3	4	5	6	7	8	9	10

8. How funny do your parents think you ought to be?

Not funny					Average				A comedian	
0	1	2	3	4	5	6	7	8	9	10

9. How nice do your parents think you ought to be?

Mean					Average				Nicest always	
0	1	2	3	4	5	6	7	8	9	10

10. How valuable do your parents think your possessions ought to be?

The worst					Average				The best	
0	1	2	3	4	5	6	7	8	9	10

Section 3:. Please read the next 10 questions and answer them according to how you are feeling about yourself *right now*. Remember, this set of questions refers to how you feel right now.

Again, read each question carefully, take your time to really think about each question, and then place an X over the number that tells how you honestly feel you are like *now*.

1. How popular or unpopular are you?

No one likes me					Average				The most popular person	
0	1	2	3	4	5	6	7	8	9	10

2. How good are your grades?

I fail everything					Average				All A's	
0	1	2	3	4	5	6	7	8	9	10

3. How good-looking are you?

Ugly					Average				I look like a model	
0	1	2	3	4	5	6	7	8	9	10

4. How smart are you?

Stupid					Average				Genius	
0	1	2	3	4	5	6	7	8	9	10

5. How well-behaved are you?

I do everything wrong					OK				I never do anything wrong	
0	1	2	3	4	5	6	7	8	9	10

6. How athletic are you?

I'm a klutz					Average				I'm a superstar	
0	1	2	3	4	5	6	7	8	9	10

7. How good-looking are your clothes?

Ragged and dirty					OK				Right out of fashion magazines	
0	1	2	3	4	5	6	7	8	9	10

8. How funny are you?

Not at all funny					Average				I'm a comedian	
0	1	2	3	4	5	6	7	8	9	10

9. How nice are you?

The meanest person					Average				The nicest person	
0	1	2	3	4	5	6	7	8	9	10

10. How good are your possessions?

The worst					Average				The best	
0	1	2	3	4	5	6	7	8	9	10

Section 4: Please rank order the following 10 things according to how important each one is to you. For example, if having good looks is most important to you, you would put a 1 in the blank next to good looks. If nice possessions are least important to you, you would put a 10 in the blank next to nice possessions.

Again, please take your time to really think about each one of the 10 things before assigning a number to it.

_____ Popularity
_____ Good grades
_____ Good looks
_____ Intelligence
_____ Good behavior
_____ Athletic
_____ Good-looking and fashionable clothes
_____ Funny
_____ Nice
_____ Nice possessions (money, toys, records, and the like)

about yourselves. These are the standards you set for yourself. (Ask the kids to define a standard.) Standards are the rules you set for yourself about how well you have to do in each area to be happy with yourself. (Go through the ratings as a group with each member stating aloud what he or she marked down. Note any trends that you observe.)

"Does anyone have any ideas about what the second set of numbers means? They stand for how you think you are doing now. What we all naturally do is compare how we are doing now to how we think we have to do to feel good about ourselves. In other words, we evaluate ourselves by comparing how we are doing to how we think we should do. (Ask for examples of times when we evaluate ourselves or someone else evaluates us. Examples could include teachers on a test, ourselves while in a contest, ourselves after we make something and we look at it, judges in a contest, our parents when they see our report cards.)

(Note the relationship between self-evaluations and affect.) "If you aren't doing as well as you think you should do, how would you feel? How would you feel if you did the same as you thought you should do? What if you did better? What if you did a little worse?"

Proceed to go around the group and talk about how each participant rated themselves relative to how they felt they should do.

Objective 3: Explain the Relationship of Self-Evaluation to Ourselves.

Example. "Psychologists have found that kids who are sad tend to set standards for themselves that are too high. They think they have to be perfect or they are no good. (Work in examples from the group.) Is it possible to be perfect? Can anyone be perfect? Would someone who sets perfectionistic standards ever be satisfied with themselves? Not very often, would they? Is it OK to do well most of the time, but not all of the time? Could you feel good about that?

"How did we do as a group? Did we tend to set real high standards, medium standards, or low standards?"

Encourage a discussion about how they all did.

Objective 4: Identify an Area for Self-Improvement. Have the children read through the questions on the My Standards Questionnaire and circle the numbers of their three most important areas. Ask which things do they really care about doing well at? Give everyone some time to circle the numbers. Then, have each child look at those three and see if there is a difference between their standards and how they are doing now.

Go around the group and discuss the rationality of the standards they've set for themselves. Have they set standards that are unrealistically high? Tell them what would be more realistic.

Homework. Same as last week.

Session 23

Review.

Set Agenda.

Review Homework and Collect Forms.

Objective 1: Establish Goals. Compare new standards to how the children feel they are actually doing at this time in those areas. Have the children look at their questionnaires and put a star in front of the new standards that exceed their current level of performance. Turn the standards into goals. Ask for a volunteer who will allow you to use his or her standards as an example. Demonstrate how to turn his or her new standards into attainable goals that are in the child's control. Be sure that the goal is positive, something that could be increased in terms of frequency or duration—not getting rid of or decreasing something. "Attainable" means something that the child could actually expect to do or occur. "In the child's control" means that it is something that is within the child's own abilities and efforts, not something that depends on others. Work through this process out loud, thus modeling it. Be prepared to give concrete examples. After your example, ask the participants to do the same. Help the participants work out their goals on the practice sheets.

Objective 2: Break the Goals Into Subgoals.

Example. "Think of how you can break your goal down into small steps. Then you will be able to see how many small steps you have to complete before you finish. Let's say that your goal was to build a model of Columbus's ship for a history project. First, you would look through your model parts to see that they are all there. Then, you would put together the hull, then you would put on the masts, then you would put on the strings that hold the masts up. Finally, you would put on the sails. Let's try another example. Let's say you want to earn a black belt in karate. Is that something that you can do in a day, a couple of days, or even a couple of weeks? It takes a lot of time to do, doesn't it? What would be the steps?" After working through the example, help the participants break down their goals into subgoals.

Objective 3: Help the Participants to Start Working Toward Self-Improvement. Say something like, "Now that you have made some goals for yourselves, let's take some time to choose one that you would like to start working toward. Choose one and then fill in a reward you will give yourself for achieving it and the small rewards you will give yourself for completing the subgoals." Help the participants work this out.

Homework. Work toward completing the subgoals you have made for yourselves. When you complete the subgoal, reward yourself for it. Also complete your Diaries.

Session 24

Review.

Set Agenda.

Review Homework and Collect Forms.

Objective 1: Continue to Work Toward Self-Improvement. Check on the children's progress toward goal attainment. Help them set goals, subgoals, and rewards for successful progress toward goal attainment. Help them identify and administer rewards contingent on goal attainment. Help them identify areas in which they could benefit from improvement.

Objective 2: Use Problem Solving and Cognitive Restructuring to Facilitate Change. Facilitate the children as a group using problem solving and cognitive restructuring to deal with impediments to self-improvement.

Homework. Continue to work toward self-improvement and to monitor use of cognitive restructuring.

Sessions 25 to 27

Review.

Set Agenda.

Review Homework and Collect Forms.

Objectives: Content of These Sessions Is the Same as in Session 23.

Family Therapy Component

Session 1

Objective: Get Acquainted With the Family/Set a Goal for Therapy. Introduce yourself and have the head of the family introduce each family member to you.

Explain that this session is a "getting acquainted" session and ask each member of the family what they would like to see changed in their family. Begin the discussion by first approaching the parents about what they would like to see changed. Do not ask the depressed child to be the first one to describe what he or she would like to see changed. This can be too overwhelming for the child.

Help family members to clarify vague statements they may make about what they would like to see changed ("Our family needs to communicate better"). In such cases, ask for specific examples of the stated problem ("Can you give me some examples of how your family needs to communicate better?"). This will help you to provide a better focus for therapy.

Agree upon a goal for therapy. Try to make the goal as specific as possible. It may relate to the depressed child directly (for example, Tommy will not spend so much time alone in his room), but it would be preferable if the goal was broad enough to include other family members (for example, family members who are angry at each other will agree to sit down and talk about the problem rather than yelling at each other).

In this session, as much as possible, try to take the focus off of the depressed child. Remember that the goal of family therapy is to change specific patterns in family functioning that may be supporting or exacerbating the child's depression. Do not allow family members to dwell on the child's symptoms or to complain excessively about the child. It is important from the beginning to send the message that the point of this part of therapy is to work on family interactions.

End the session by explaining how therapy will proceed over the next 10 weeks. Explain that you will meet with the family once a week in the evenings and that it is very important that each family member be present for the sessions. Explain that you will be teaching the family some strategies for improving communication, dealing with conflict, and helping family members to enjoy each other more. Also, explain that there will be some homework that family members will be asked to do. Distribute the Forty Low-Cost/No-Cost Family Activities sheet (see table 11–10) to each family member and ask them to complete it and bring it back next week.

Following the session, write down any interaction patterns or communications that you observed that may be maintaining the depressed youngster's

Table 11–10
Forty Low-Cost/No-Cost Family Activities

___ 1.	Gardening	___21.	Listening to music
___ 2.	Playing card games	___22.	Dancing
___ 3.	Riding bikes	___23.	Playing sports (softball, catch, and the like)
___ 4.	Playing board games	___24.	Doing needlepoint or sewing
___ 5.	Going to the park	___25.	Arts and crafts
___ 6.	Swimming	___26.	Holiday decorations
___ 7.	Going to the library	___27.	Playing with pets
___ 8.	Visiting museums	___28.	Bowling
___ 9.	Playing basketball	___29.	Dollar movies
___10.	Doing home plays	___30.	Rent a movie and make popcorn
___11.	Fishing	___31.	Cooking/baking
___12.	Camping	___32.	Drawing
___13.	Hiking	___33.	Painting
___14.	Sledding	___34.	Visiting neighbors and relatives
___15.	Skating	___35.	Visiting historical buildings
___16.	Skiing	___36.	Walking
___17.	Collecting rocks/shells/leaves	___37.	Going out for frozen yogurt
___18.	Doing puzzles	___38.	Photography
___19.	Reading aloud	___39.	Picnics
___20.	Playing charades	___40.	Boating/canoeing

depressogenic schemata. In addition, note who seems to be aligned with whom (does Mom consistently try to protect the depressed child against Dad? How does this affect the parents' relationship?), who appears to be in control during the session (does Mom do all of the talking while Dad looks like he would rather be elsewhere?), and how the depressed child reacts to different family members (does the child sit close to the father? does he or she seem to withdraw—or become angry—when another child gets the parents' attention?). From such observations, begin to construct a picture of the patterns of communication that have developed in the family.

Remember that you will need to adapt the therapy to the particular issues that the family brings in each week. In other words, use the content the family provides to teach the skills that are outlined below. The family provides the content (what will be discussed), while you provide the structure (how the content will be approached and resolved).

Session 2

Objective: Test Hypotheses From Previous Week/Begin Family Activity Scheduling. Collect the Forty No-Cost/Low-Cost Family Activities sheet from each family member. Briefly discuss the responses and determine which activities family members might like to do together. This is done to begin to focus the family on enjoying each other's company more. The homework assignment for this week (to be given at the end of the session) will be for the family to choose one of these activities and do it together.

Test some of the hypotheses that you noted following the first session. You can do this by reflecting back to the family some of the things that you observed. For example, if you noticed that there was conflict between a child and the father, you might say something like, "I was thinking about your family this week and I realized in the last session that there was a lot of conflict between Dad and Johnny." You can then let the statement hang in the air and see who responds to it. Such hypothesis testing is designed to help you discover the specific maladaptive patterns that are occurring in the family.

In cases where there is a lot of negative talk about the child, you may need to do some reframing. For example, if the parents see the depressed child as lazy or unmotivated, you may need to introduce other alternatives (for example, the child is unchallenged, doing the best he or she can, or whatever).

Give the family the assignment of engaging in an activity from the Forty No-Cost/Low-Cost Family Activities sheet (or another activity of their choosing) this next week. Explain that the purpose of this activity is to help them (re)discover how to have fun together. This is an assignment that you may wish to give every week.

Session 3

Objective: Introduce Communication Training. Review homework from the week before. Process the outcome of the family outing. If the homework was not completed, explore what prevented the family from completing the assignment. Use problem solving to deal with any identified problems and to ensure that the family completes the assignment in the future.

Introduce communication training. The process we use is borrowed from Alexander and Parsons (1982). It is reasonable to expect to introduce and practice the first five points discussed below. The remaining four points should be introduced and practiced in the following session. The points are as follows:

1. *Brevity.* One family member states his or her need or reaction in 10 or fewer words.
2. *Source Responsibility.* Needs and reactions should be expressed in "I" statements. Rather than, "You are so inconsiderate for not helping me in the kitchen," the speaker states his or her point as, "When you don't help me in the kitchen, I feel angry and hurt."
3. *Directness.* Family members are taught to say exactly what they mean. Rather than "Nobody ever helps around here," the speaker would say, "I want you to help me in the kitchen on Wednesday and Friday nights."
4. *Concreteness and Behavioral Specificity.* Help family members learn how to be specific about what they want and need. A wife who tells her husband that she wants him to be more involved with the children is not being specific. She needs to let him know more precisely how she would like him to be more involved (for example, by picking the children up from school, taking the children to the park on the weekend, helping the children with their homework).
5. *Active Listening.* Family members need to be taught how to show that they are listening to each other. Such behaviors as nodding, saying "Um-hum," making eye contact, leaning toward, and restating the speaker's point or feelings all indicate to the speaker that the listener is interested and involved.
6. *Impact Statements.* These statements can be used to help family members to express how another family member's behavior has impacted them. They can be used to help the speaker make the distinction between feelings and behavior. For example, a mother who is annoyed with her daughter for not coming home on time might say, "When you are not home at the time we agreed, I feel worried" rather than "You are so irresponsible!" The former statement lets the daughter know what impact her behavior has had on her mother.

7. *Presentation of Alternatives.* The speaker is encouraged to move away from making nonnegotiable demands. Rather than "I want you to do your homework every night before dinner," the speaker would say, "You can either do your homework before dinner and play outside after dinner or do your homework after you help with the dishes rather than going outside to play after dinner."

8. *Feedback.* Family members need to be taught how to ask for clarification and feedback. Such processes help to ensure that family members are understanding one another.

9. *Congruence.* Family members are taught to send messages to other family members that are congruent at the verbal, nonverbal, and contextual levels. For example, a mother should tell her son that she loves him in a manner that communicates love and caring. Saying that you love someone in an exasperated or angry tone is sending an inconsistent message.

There are several methods that are used to teach the above skills to family members, including education, modeling, coaching, rehearsal, and corrective feedback. The way that we proceed is to introduce the first five skills (the next four are introduced in the next session) and explain them in such a way that all family members understand. Examples often help here. Next, family members are encouraged to discuss with each other a problem that they have been having and to apply the skills. Help the family members to do this by pointing out when they have successfully used one of the five skills and/or point out spots in which they might have used one of the skills but did not. Act as a coach in helping family members learn how to communicate better. This means interrupting the family when necessary.

Use the hypotheses you have developed about particular patterns that are maintaining the child's depressogenic schemata to help you come up with examples for teaching communication training. For example, if you have noticed that the child's mother is constantly nagging the child about cleaning up his or her room, teach the skill of brevity by using the example of how this mother might state her expectations for her child in a simple, straightforward manner.

End the session by giving the family a homework assignment to use the communication skills discussed in this week's session (that is, brevity, source responsibility, directness, concreteness and behavioral specificity, and active listening) this week and to record the outcomes. Each family member should keep his or her own record.

Session 4

Objective: Continue Communication Training. Review the homework from last week. Use the family's responses to the homework assignment as an opportunity to provide feedback to the family about any changes you have noticed. Continue to use reframing to change family member's perceptions of the depressed child as appropriate. Also, continue to block negative comments about the child.

Introduce the remaining four skills in communication training. As in last week's session, have family members practice using these skills while tackling a family problem. Have family members speak to each other as you coach them in using the skills. In some cases, it may be useful for family members to do some role-reversal if it is apparent that they are having difficulty understanding each other's point of view.

To end the session, give the family a homework assignment to practice the skills they learned in this session (that is, impact statements, presentation of alternatives, feedback, and congruence). Again, have them each keep a record of when they used the skills and how the situation turned out.

Session 5

Objective: Introduce Family Problem Solving. Review the homework from last week. Again, use the family's responses to the homework assignment as an opportunity to provide feedback about any changes you have noticed. Continue reframing and blocking negative statements about the child as needed. Encourage family members to use the communication skills they have learned in communicating with each other in the sessions. Let them know that this is an excellent time for them to practice the skills they have learned. Continue to coach family members in the use of these skills.

Introduce the five-step problem-solving sequence. Impress upon the family that difficulties are simply problems to be solved and that they can be dealt with most effectively through active effort. Braswell and Bloomquist (1992) outline the family problem-solving process as follows:

1. Stop! What is the problem we are having? In answering this question, family members should try to avoid blaming each other, focus on how each family member may be contributing to the problem, and state the problem specifically so that everyone is clear about what the problem is.
2. What are some plans we can use? In this second step, family members try to generate as many alternative plans as possible and avoid evaluating or criticizing anyone else's ideas.
3. What is the best plan we could use? In deciding upon the best plan, family members should think about the outcome of using each of the plans, how each plan would make each family member feel, and which plan is most likely to succeed. The family should then reach an agreement on a plan.
4. Do the plan. The family should implement the plan as best as possible

and avoid criticizing if the plan does not work as well as the family had hoped.

5. Did our plan work? In the final step, the family evaluates the plan, determines if everyone was satisfied with how the plan worked, and repeats the process again if the plan did not work.

Teach the family the problem-solving process in a didactic manner, using examples as needed to illustrate each of the steps. Again, education, modeling, coaching, rehearsal, and corrective feedback are used as needed. After the process has been explained, have the family use the process to tackle a problem that they have not been able to solve. As the family is attempting to use the process, act as a coach and keep them on track. Remind them to stay focused on the here-and-now while using the problem-solving process. Don't let them get sidetracked by bringing up old issues.

End the session by giving the family homework to implement the plan that they came up with in today's session. Let them know that you will evaluate how well the plan worked in next week's session.

Session 6

Objective: Continue Family Problem Solving. Review the homework from last week. Evaluate the effectiveness of the plan that the family generated in the last session and discuss family members' reactions to the plan.

Continue family problem solving by either having the family tackle a different family problem this week (if last week's plan was successful) or repeating the cycle using the problem from last week (if last week's plan was unsuccessful). If some family members have been hesitant to participate in the discussion, attempt to draw them out this week. Emphasize that it is important to get everyone's ideas because the more ideas that are generated, the more likely the family is to come up with a solution that works. Also, try to continue to get across the message that problems can be solved with a little collaborative effort.

End the session by giving the family homework to implement the plan that they came up with in today's session. Let them know that you will evaluate how well the plan worked in next week's session.

Session 7

Objective: Introduce Conflict Resolution. Review the homework from last week. Again, evaluate the effectiveness of the plan that the family generated in the last session and discuss family members' reactions to the plan. Impress upon the family that they should continue to practice the problem-solving process because it will take time before it becomes part of their normal routine.

Introduce conflict resolution. Again, we have borrowed a procedure from Alexander and Parsons (1982). It works as follows:

1. Two family members who are in conflict agree to discuss the issue and designate a time and place for the discussion to occur.
2. The initiator of the discussion states one issue clearly while the other family member uses his or her active listening skills (from communication training) and does not interject any new information.
3. The speaker gives two recent examples of the problem and the listener restates the examples.
4. The speaker states the personal impact of the examples and the listener restates the emotional impact of the examples on the speaker.
5. The two participants discuss the alternatives that would lead to a solution. A mutually agreed-upon solution is then chosen and enacted.

After explaining the process, have the family practice conflict resolution. Use education, modeling, coaching, rehearsal, and corrective feedback to help them learn the process. In this session, it is useful to have the family members apply the process to less emotionally laden and more easily resolved problems rather than the most controversial ones. Otherwise, family members may be too passionate in their opinions to allow the skill to be applied successfully.

End the session by giving the family homework to implement the solution that they came up with in today's session. Let them know that you will evaluate how well the solution worked in next week's session.

Session 8

Objective: Continue Conflict Resolution. Review the homework from last week. Evaluate the effectiveness of the solution that family members generated in the last session and discuss family members' reactions to the solution.

Have the family practice conflict resolution. It may be helpful to have a different family member bring up a problem for resolution this week. You should act as a coach and model while helping the participants to resolve the issue.

End the session by giving the family homework to implement the solution that they came up with in today's session. Let them know that you will evaluate how well the solution worked in next week's session.

Session 9

Objective: Teach Positive Communication. Review the homework from last week. Evaluate the effectiveness of the solution that family members generated in the last session and discuss family members' reactions to the solution.

Introduce positive communication. This skill is introduced later in therapy after the conflict and hard feelings have lessened, thus allowing family members to feel as though they can honestly say something positive about one another.

We teach positive communication through a game. Each family member takes five 3 × 5 cards and writes his or her name on each. The cards are collected, shuffled, and placed in the middle of the table. Subsequently, the therapist states one of the following directives and each family member draws a card and then responds to the directive with regard to the name of the person on the card:

1. Tell the person something that you like about him or her.
2. Tell the person something that he or she did over the past month that you liked.
3. Tell the person something he or she did over the past week that you liked.
4. Tell the person something he or she did tonight that you liked.
5. Tell the person something you would like him or her to do more often.

The first person responds by choosing a card and responding to directive 1. The second person then chooses a card and also responds to directive 1. If a person draws his or her own name, a statement is made about the self. After each family member has responded to the first directive, they repeat the process for directive 2, and so on.

The family is given a homework assignment to give positive feedback to each other during the week. In particular, it is useful for the parents to share with each child on a daily basis four things that they liked about the child or that the child did well. The children can then each make a list of four things that they either liked about themselves or did well. It is helpful for you to create a sheet for the children to take with them for this purpose. This is shared with you in the following session.

Prepare the family for termination in the following session by briefly reviewing the course of therapy. Ask the family to think over the next week about how they might spend the time they have spent for the past 10 weeks in therapy engaging in another family activity (for example, having a family meeting, going out to a restaurant, going to the park, and so on). It may be helpful to refer back to the Forty No-Cost/Low-Cost Family Activities sheet.

Session 10

Objective: Termination. Review with the family the progress they have made toward the goal they set in the first session. Ask each family member what he or she has learned in therapy and what (if anything) he or she still feels is unresolved.

It is helpful for you to state what you have learned about the family in the course of treatment and review for the family the changes that you have noticed.

End the session by asking the family to reflect on their thoughts with regard to how they might spend the time they have spent in therapy now that the therapy is coming to a close.

References

Alexander, J. & Parsons, B.V. (1982). *Functional Family Therapy.* Monterey, CA: Brooks/Cole.

Braswell, L. & Bloomquist, M.L. (1992). Cognitive-behavioral therapy with ADHD children: Child, family, and school interventions. *Contemporary psychology, 37*, 1173.

Stark, K.D. (1990). *Childhood depression: School-based intervention.* New York: Guilford Press.

Index

About the Contributors

Marquita Bedway, Ph.D. Children's Hospital of Michigan, School of Medicine, Wayne State University, Detroit, Michigan

Gary Buchik, M.C. Private Practice, Phoenix, Arizona

Raymond DiGiuseppe, Ph.D. St. John's University, Jamaica, New York, and Institute for Rational Emotive Therapy,

Eva L. Feindler, Ph.D. Psychological Services Center, C.W. Post Campus, Long Island University, Brookville, New York

Marcia Gilroy, Ph.D. Children's Hospital of Michigan, School of Medicine, Wayne State University, Detroit, Michigan

Brian A. Glaser, Ph.D. Department of Counseling & Human Development Services, College of Education, The University of Georgia, Athens, Georgia

Jennifer Guttman, M.A. Psy.D. Candidate, Psychological Services Center, C.W. Post Campus, Long Island University, Brookville, New York

Mindy Hohman, M.S.W. Ph.D. Candidate, School of Social Work, Arizona State University, Tempe, Arizona

Arthur M. Horne, Ph.D. Department of Counseling & Human Development Services, College of Education, The University of Georgia, Athens, Georgia

Neil Kalter, Ph.D. University of Michigan, Ann Arbor, Michigan

Melanie Katzman, Ph.D. Private Practice, Medical School Faculty, New York Hospital—Cornell Medical Center, New York

Ann Reysa, M.A. Ph.D. Candidate, Department of Educational Psychology University of Texas, Austin, Texas

Jean Linscott, M.A. Ph.D. Candidate, St. John's University, Jamaica, New York

Linda Raffaelle, M.A. Ph.D. Candidate, Department of Educational Psychology University of Texas, Austin, Texas

Arthur L. Robin, Ph.D. Children's Hospital of Michigan, School of

Medicine, Wayne State University, Detroit, Michigan

Shelly Schreier, Ph.D. University of Michigan, Ann Arbor, Michigan

Kevin D. Stark, Ph.D. Department of Educational Psychology, University of Texas, Austin, Texas

Joseph M. Strayhorn, Jr., M.D. Early Childhood Clinic, Medical College of Pennsylvania, Allegheny General Hospital, Pittsburgh, Pennsylvania

Lillie Weiss, Ph.D. Private Practice, Acting Director of the Clinical Psychology Center, Arizona State University, Tempe, Arizona

Sharlene Wolchik, Ph.D. Department of Psychology, Arizona State University, Tempe, Arizona

About the Editor

Craig Winston LeCroy is Associate Professor of Social work at Arizona State University. Dr. LeCroy teaches social work practice to graduate students and was the former director of the Ph.D. program. Dr. LeCroy's interest is in children's mental health, juvenile justice, the evaluation of practice, and prevention. He recently served as the principal investigator for a National Institute of Mental Health grant for training social workers in effective practice with emotionally disturbed children. Currently Dr. LeCroy is principal investigator for Youth Plus, a center for Substance Abuse Prevention grant, and for Healthy Families, a child abuse prevention project in Arizona. Dr. LeCroy is the author of *Social Skills Training with Children and Youth, Case Studies in Social Work Practice,* and is currently working on a book entitled *Human Behavior in the Social Environment: An Applied Perspective.*